Money in the Middle East and North Africa

Monetary policy in the Middle East and North African (MENA) countries remains an understudied area; this book fills an important gap by examining monetary policy frameworks and monetary policy strategies in the region. Building on the editors' earlier book, *Monetary Policy and Central Banking in the Middle East and North Africa*, which focused on central bank independence issues and on exchange rate regimes, this book emphasises monetary policy strategies.

Part I contains an overview of the financial markets and institutions which condition the choice of monetary policy strategy in the countries of the region, followed by single-country studies on aspects of the monetary policy frameworks of Lebanon, Egypt, Jordan, the Palestinian Territory and Turkey. Part II includes analyses of the prospects for inflation targeting in Egypt, Morocco and Tunisia, of the monetary transmission mechanism in the Gulf Cooperation Council countries, of the relative advantages of inflation targeting and exchange rate fixity with reference to Egypt, of the problem of fiscal dominance in Egypt and of the inflationary implications of exchange rate fixity for Saudi Arabia and Kuwait.

The contributors are experts from universities inside and outside the MENA region, from central banks in the region and from outside institutions such as the European Central Bank and the International Monetary Fund.

David Cobham is Professor of Economics at Heriot-Watt University, UK. His publications include (as co-editor with Ghassan Dibeh) *Monetary Policy and Central Banking in the Middle East and North Africa* (Routledge, 2009), which complements this book.

Ghassan Dibeh is Professor of Economics at the Lebanese American University in Byblos, Lebanon. He is the editor of the journal *Review of Middle East Economics and Finance*.

The Routledge Political Economy of the Middle East and North Africa Series

Series editor: Hassan Hakimian
Director, The London Middle East Institute, School of Oriental and African Studies (SOAS), University of London

Editorial Board:

David Cobham
Professor of Economics at Heriot Watt University, UK

Nu'man Kanafani
Associate Professor of Economics at the University of Copenhagen, Denmark.

Massoud Karshenas
Professor of Economics at the School of Oriental and African Studies (SOAS), University of London, UK

Jeffrey B. Nugent
Professor of Economics at the University of Southern California, Los Angeles, USA

Jennifer Olmsted
Associate Professor of Economics at Drew University, New Jersey, USA

Karen Pfeifer
Professor Emerita of Economics at Smith College, Northampton, Massachusetts, USA

Wassim Shahin
Professor of Economics and Dean of Business School at the Lebanese American University (LAU), Byblos, Lebanon

Subidey Togan
Professor of Economics and Director of the Centre for International Economics at Bilkent University, Ankara, Turkey

Jackline Wahba
Reader in Economics at the University of Southampton, UK

Tarik Yousef
Dean of the Dubai School of Government, UAE

 The aim of the London Middle East Institute (LMEI) is to promote, through education and research, knowledge of all aspects of the Middle East including its complexities, problems, achievements and assets, both among the general public and with those who have specialist interests in the region.

The LMEI is based in SOAS, which hosts the largest concentration of Middle Eastern expertise in any European university. The LMEI provides teaching, training, research, publication, consultancy, outreach and other services related to the Middle East. It serves as a neutral forum for the study of issues concerning the region and helps to link individuals and institutions with academic, commercial, diplomatic, media or other specialisations.

Money in the Middle East and North Africa

Monetary policy frameworks and strategies

**Edited by David Cobham
and Ghassan Dibeh**

LONDON AND NEW YORK

First published 2011
by Routledge
2 Park Square, Milton Park, Abingdon, Oxon, OX14 4RN

Simultaneously published in the USA and Canada
by Routledge
270 Madison Avenue, New York, NY 10016

Routledge is an imprint of the Taylor & Francis Group, an informa business

Typeset in Times New Roman by
HWA Text and Data Management, London
Printed and bound in Great Britain by
CPI Antony Rowe, Chippenham, Wiltshire

British Library Cataloguing in Publication Data
A catalogue record for this book is available from the British Library

Library of Congress Cataloging-in-Publication Data
Money in the Middle East and North Africa: monetary policy frameworks
and strategies / edited by David Cobham and Ghassan Dibeh.
    p. cm. – (The Routledge political economy of the Middle East
    and North Africa series; 9)
  Includes bibliographical references and index.
  1. Monetary policy–Middle East. 2. Monetary policy–Africa, North.
  I. Cobham, David P. II. Dibeh, Ghassan, 1963-
HG1206.M664 2011
339.5`30956–dc22   2010022667

ISBN 13: 978-0-415-58768-6 (hbk)
ISBN 13: 978-0-203-83653-8 (ebk)

Contents

Figures

Tables

Contributors

Rania A. Al-Mashat has been Assistant Sub-Governor and Head of Monetary Policy at the Central Bank of Egypt since October 2006. Prior to that, she was an Economist in the Asia and Pacific Department at the International Monetary Fund, covering a range of countries which included India and Vietnam. She received her doctoral degree in economics from the University of Maryland at College Park in 2001.

Hesham Alogeel obtained his PhD in Economics from the University of Colorado at Boulder in 2009. His main research interest is in evaluating dynamic stochastic general equilibrium models of the business cycle and studying the dynamics of different macroeconomic variables. Currently, he is working at the Saudi Arabian Monetary Agency in the Economic Research and Statistics Department.

Mohammad Atallah obtained an MSc in Economics from Yarmouk University, Jordan in 1989. He worked as an instructor in Yarmouk University and the Arab Community College in Jordan from 1989 to 1996. Since then he has been working in the Research and Monetary Policy Department of the Palestine Monetary Authority (PMA).

Berksoy Bilgin obtained his BA in Economics and Political Science and International Relations from Bogazici University in Turkey and his MSc in Economics from the University of York, UK. He has worked on the structural dynamics of fiscal, monetary and industrial policies in Turkey and real convergence of Central and Eastern European countries within the EU. Currently, he is working in the manufacturing sector in the area of global planning and pricing.

Thierry Bracke is Deputy Head of Division of the EU Neighbouring Regions Division of the European Central Bank. He holds an MA in Economics from Ghent University as well as from Aix-Marseille University. He has worked at the European Central Bank since 2000, with a main focus on international policy issues and international macroeconomic issues. He has previously worked at the National Bank of Belgium.

David Cobham is Professor of Economics at Heriot-Watt University, UK. His main research area is UK monetary policy, but he has also worked on European monetary integration, central bank independence, financial systems and the economies of the Middle East. He was a Senior Houblon-Norman Fellow at the Bank of England in 2001. He co-edited with Ghassan Dibeh *Monetary Policy and Central Banking in the Middle East and North Africa*, Routledge, 2009, and is Associate Editor of the *Review of Middle East Economics and Finance*.

Ghassan Dibeh holds a BA in Physics and a PhD in Economics from the University of Texas at Austin. He is Professor of Economics and Chairman of the Department of Economics at the Lebanese American University, Byblos, Lebanon. He is the editor of the journal *Review of Middle East Economics and Finance*. His research areas include macroeconomics, political economy, financial economics and econophysics. His research has appeared in journals such as *Physica A*, *Review of Political Economy*, *Energy Economics*, *Journal of International Development and Middle Eastern Studies*. His most recent co-edited book (with D. Cobham) was *Monetary Policy and Central Banking in the Middle East and North Africa*, Routledge, 2009.

Michal Franta obtained his MA in Mathematics at the Charles University, Prague and PhD in Economics at CERGE-EI, Prague. He currently works at the Monetary and Statistics Department of the Czech National Bank. Previously he worked at La Trobe University, the European Central Bank and the Economics Institute of the Academy of Sciences of the Czech Republic.

Maher Hasan is a Deputy Division Chief for the European, Central Asian and Middle Eastern Regions division in the Monetary & Capital Markets Department in the IMF. Mr Hasan has written several research papers on issues related to simulation-based estimation methods, GCC countries' monetary and financial systems, and the MENA region's financial sector. Before joining the IMF in 2005, he served as a Director for the Governor's Office and Assistant Director for the Banking Supervision Department in the Central Bank of Jordan. Mr Hasan obtained his PhD in Economics and MSc in Statistics from Washington State University.

Samar Maziad is an economist at the International Monetary Fund. She has researched and worked on a number of emerging and developing countries in Africa, Latin America and the Middle East. She holds a PhD from the University of St Andrews in Scotland.

Gülçin Özkan is Reader in the Department of Economics and Related Studies at the University of York, UK. Her main research interests are international macroeconomics, international finance and emerging markets. Her recent research has covered sudden stops and financial crises; external debt and exchange rate regime choice; investment and exchange rates; central bank independence and political instability and public investment decisions. She is an associate editor of the *Bulletin of Economic Research* and the *Central Bank*

Review. She is also the secretary of the Money, Macro and Finance Research Group.

Shaker A. Sarsour is a Research Fellow in the Research and Monetary Policy Department of the Palestine Monetary Authority. He has a BSc in Mathematics Applied to Economics (2001) and an MSc in Economic Science (2006, awarded with Distinction) from Birzeit University, Palestine, and is a PhD candidate in the Department of Economics, University of Siena, Italy.

Hoda Selim has been working for the World Bank's Cairo Office since 2006 in the Poverty Reduction and Economic Monitoring department. Prior to joining the bank, she held research-related positions at the Global Development Network and the Economic Research Forum for the Arab Countries, Iran and Turkey. She has participated in research on macroeconomic issues in Egypt including economic growth, monetary and exchange rate issues. She has a BA in economics from Cairo University and an MA in Corporate and International Finance from Sciences Po in Paris, where she is currently finalising her PhD thesis on inflation targeting and exchange rate regimes.

Wassim Shahin is the Dean of the School of Business and Professor of Business Economics at the Lebanese American University, Byblos, Lebanon. He has authored, co-authored and edited three books, several monographs, and over twenty academic articles dealing with monetary policy, banking, exchange rates, budgetary politics and the application of economic methodology to hostage-taking activities. He is the founding editor of the *Review of Middle East Economics and Finance* and serves on the editorial board of several academic journals.

Jan Stráský is an economist with the European Central Bank. He holds an MA in Economics from Charles University, Prague, and has recently submitted his PhD thesis to Oxford University. He has previously worked for the Czech National Bank, Magdalen College, Oxford, and Oxford Analytica.

Jihad K. Wazir has been the Governor and Chairman of the Board of the Palestine Monetary Authority (PMA) since January 2008. He is the chairperson of the Palestinian National Committee on Anti-Money Laundering, and was a deputy governor and member of the Board of the PMA from 2006 to 2008. Dr Wazir obtained his PhD in Business Administration from Loughborough University in the UK in 2001. He also holds a BSc in Electrical Engineering (1986), and an MSc in Engineering Management (1990) from Marquette University, USA.

Hoda Abdel Ghaffar Youssef holds a PhD in economics from Sciences Po Paris school in France. She currently works as an economic research analyst at the World Bank Cairo office. She has authored several publications on the Egyptian macro-economy, more particularly on monetary and fiscal policies. Her research interests include macroeconomics, inflation targeting, fiscal policy, poverty and political economy.

Preface

This book presents a selection of papers from the workshop on 'Monetary Policy and Financial Markets in the Middle East and North Africa: Frameworks, Institutions and Objectives', held at the 10th Mediterranean Research Meeting organised by the European University Institute's Robert Schuman Centre for Advanced Studies, on 25–28 March 2009 in Montecatini Terme, Italy. The workshop was designed to elicit papers on a number of issues in monetary policy and financial markets in the MENA region: the recent and ongoing development of monetary policy frameworks in MENA countries; the current status and development of the financial infrastructure (markets and institutions) in the region; and the choices of monetary policy strategy and exchange rate regime facing MENA countries. We would like to thank the Robert Schuman Centre, its director Professor Stefano Bartolini, and Imco Brouwer and Aleksandra Djajic Horvath, the scientific coordinators of the Mediterranean Research Meeting, for the opportunity to organise this workshop at the Meeting and for their hospitality. We are grateful to all the workshop participants who made the workshop so productive and agreeable. Finally, we are grateful to Hassan Hakimian, the series editor, for his advice and comments at different stages of the process, and to Peter Sowden, our editor at Routledge.

David Cobham and Ghassan Dibeh
May 2010

1   Introduction

David Cobham and Ghassan Dibeh

For many years the monetary policy frameworks in the Middle East and North Africa (MENA) region were largely both unchanging and unstudied. On the one hand, most MENA countries kept their currencies pegged to the US dollar, which restricted the scope for independent monetary or macro policy. On the other hand, most research was focused elsewhere. It is striking, for example, that none of the three main general treatments of economic development in the region – Richards and Waterbury (2008), Noland and Pack (2007) and Devlin (2010) – include chapters on countries' monetary policy frameworks or financial systems.

Over the last decade or so, however, major transformations have been under way in the financial systems of many (but not all) of these countries, and monetary policy strategies are now being accorded greater attention by policymakers and in public debate. Some of the research which is being undertaken is seeing the light of day through the revived *Review of Middle East Economics and Finance*, which has recently been joined by the *Middle East Development Journal* (which has, however, a wider economic focus). Other important references in this area include the Neaime and Colton (2005) volume and single-country studies such as Abdel-Khalek (2001) and Makdisi (2004).

There are still a number of gaps in our knowledge about both financial systems and monetary strategies, but more importantly there are significant policy issues raised by the developments that are occurring and are likely to continue. This book is intended to contribute to the rising demand for research and analysis in this area. It builds on and complements the volume which we have previously edited in this series (*Monetary Policy and Central Banking in the Middle East and North Africa*, eds Cobham and Dibeh, 2009). That volume had a strong emphasis on central bank independence and on exchange rate regimes, mainly through multi-country studies, and included single country studies on Lebanon (mainly pre-civil war), Algeria, Tunisia and Turkey (the central bank's reaction function).

This volume puts the emphasis more on monetary policy frameworks and monetary policy strategies. It starts in Part I with an overview of the financial markets and institutions which condition the choice of monetary policy strategy in the countries of the region, followed by single-country studies on the monetary policy frameworks of Lebanon (post-civil war), Egypt, Jordan, the Palestinian Territory and Turkey (the nature of the banking sector and its implications for macroeconomic performance). Part II starts with an analysis of the prospects for inflation targeting in Egypt, Morocco and Tunisia. This is followed by investigations of the monetary transmission mechanism in the Gulf Cooperation Council (GCC) countries, of the relative advantages of inflation targeting and exchange rate fixity with reference to Egypt, of the problem of fiscal dominance in Egypt, and of the inflationary implications of exchange rate fixity for Saudi Arabia and Kuwait.

In Part I, David Cobham provides an overview of the 'financial infrastructure', that is the financial institutions and markets which condition the choice of monetary policy strategy in the various MENA countries. He emphasises in particular the potential contribution of money markets – which enable the central bank's policy rate decisions to be passed through to the commercial banks' own lending and deposit interest rates – and bond markets – which allow budget deficits to be financed without monetary expansion. Cobham distinguishes between three 'polar types' of 'monetary architecture' which have different requirements in terms of infrastructure and make possible different types of monetary strategy. He argues that most MENA countries lack key elements of the infrastructure necessary for a 'modern' monetary policy strategy such as inflation targeting. But he also suggests that for some countries the costs of establishing and operating some of the infrastructure concerned might outweigh the benefits of a more modern monetary policy strategy, if we were able to measure these costs and benefits accurately.

Ghassan Dibeh examines the political economy of stabilisation in Lebanon. Lebanon has had an exchange rate-based stabilisation (ERBS) programme since 1993, a record duration for such programmes which have typically been abandoned much earlier than this amidst the strains of real exchange rate appreciation and/or fiscal indiscipline. Lebanon experienced real appreciation up to 2002, and a striking lack of fiscal adjustment before 2001. Dibeh locates the source of the support for the ERBS in the particular nexus of relationships between the commercial banks and the central bank, upheld by official and private capital inflows linked to the commitments to Lebanese reconstruction by foreign governments and the Lebanese diaspora, and by the distributional policies of post-war governments (in terms of sect and factor shares) within Lebanon's 'consociational' democratic system.

Hoda Selim surveys the evolution of Egyptian monetary policy since the late 1970s. She analyses the changes in the objectives, intermediate targets and instruments of monetary policy, examines the reasons for recurring high inflation and considers the prospects for further evolution of the monetary policy framework. Over the period studied the exchange rate has become more flexible, monetary policy operations have shifted towards indirect market instruments rather than direct credit controls and banking sector reforms have been introduced. At the same time, the central bank has acquired some independence and is undergoing significant modernisation. But the objectives of monetary policy have still not been adequately clarified, the central bank's independence is neither complete nor secure, and fiscal dominance remains a serious danger.

Samar Maziad analyses the evolution of the monetary policy framework in Jordan, heavily influenced by the currency crisis of 1989–90, which was associated with high levels of government borrowing from abroad. Policy now involves a very hard peg of the Jordanian dinar to the US dollar, together with increased instrument independence for the central bank, which since 2001 is not allowed to lend directly to the government. Over the 1990s the central bank also shifted its monetary policy operations towards indirect monetary instruments, based on the issue by auction of its own certificates of deposit and later the introduction of standing facilities for the commercial banks. Maziad also investigates the degree of Jordan's monetary policy independence: she finds that, despite the peg, the central bank has some limited ability to vary its policy rate in response to internal economic developments (inflation and the output gap), which presumably reflects the credibility it has acquired over the period.

Jihad K. Wazir, Mohammad Atallah and Shaker A. Sarsour analyse the development of the Palestine Monetary Authority (PMA), which is a kind of prototype central bank for the West Bank and Gaza. Its main current activity is banking supervision, since it does not issue or operate a separate currency, but it aspires to transform itself into a fully-fledged modern central bank. The authors show that the PMA's independence would be greatly increased by the adoption of the draft law on central banking, and then discuss a number of issues involved in the transformation of the PMA. They consider different methods of estimating the size of the money supply in Palestine (which is composed of a mix of Israeli shekels, US dollars and Jordanian dinars, where data are available on bank deposits but not on currency in circulation). They discuss the idea for the PMA to issue its own certificates of deposit as a way to provide a basic instrument for interbank operations and, ultimately, for the operation of monetary policy through market interest rates. And they discuss the question of dollarisation (replacement of the shekel and the dinar by the dollar), a question which has been posed sharply by the recurring difficulties over the recent period in ensuring an adequate supply of shekel currency in Gaza.

Berksoy Bilgin and Gülçin Özkan focus on the role of the banking sector in Turkey. Here, as in many other MENA countries, it is the banks which are the main holders of government debt. They present a formal model which highlights this role, in order to identify the determinants of the cost of government borrowing, and then compare movements in that cost graphically with changes in the various determinants: the degree of competition in the banking sector, the depth of the deposit market, the cost to banks of illiquidity, reserve requirements, and the authorities' time preference. They then explore the bank lending channel of the monetary transmission mechanism in Turkey, using data for individual banks from 2002 to 2008. These results provide clear evidence that bank lending in aggregate responds to changes in the policy interest rate and to other variables in broadly expected ways. However, they show that the response to the policy rate is lower for larger and for well-capitalised banks.

In Part II, Thierry Bracke, Michal Franta and Jan Stráský examine the changes taking place and in prospect in three southern Mediterranean countries which have shown interest in adopting formal inflation targeting: Egypt, Morocco and Tunisia. They examine the 'preconditions' for inflation targeting in each country: 'economic', e.g. exchange rate flexibility, financial market depth; 'institutional', e.g. central bank independence; and 'technical', e.g. the forecasting and modelling capacity of the central bank. They then present Bayesian estimates of a small macro model for each country along the lines of Berg *et al.* (2006), and compare these results with similar findings in the literature for other emerging economies. Their conclusions are that, although in each of these countries some progress has been made on the preconditions, more is required before they could move to fully fledged inflation targeting; and that the price formation and monetary transmission processes in the three countries are not incompatible with an inflation targeting strategy. They also emphasise that any move to IT needs to be supported by the whole spectrum of policymakers if it is to be successful.

Wassim Shahin uses an analysis of the monetary transmission mechanism in the GCC countries to derive implications for the type of monetary policy appropriate for them. He starts by reviewing the array of different transmission mechanisms in the literature, with an emphasis on the environment in terms of the financial markets and institutions of different kinds required for these mechanisms to function. He then examines the environment which actually exists in developing and transition countries in general and the GCC countries in particular, arguing that for the latter the effective transmission mechanisms are through liquidity effects (via interest rates), the credit channel and the exchange rate. He reviews recent macro performance and the current monetary framework in the GCC countries, and recommends that they should move away from the hard exchange rate pegs which dominate the current framework towards greater exchange rate flexibility, with the interest rate as an implicit policy anchor and a credit aggregate as a possible intermediate target.

Rania A.Al-Mashat examines the role of the exchange rate under inflation targeting, in the light of the emphasis often placed on exchange rate variability and the pass-through from the exchange rate to the domestic economy for open and emerging economies. She sets up a New Keynesian macro model in which uncovered interest parity (UIP) is modified so that the exchange rate is a weighted average of an exchange rate target and the standard UIP equilibrium level, while the central bank's reaction function is modified so that the interest rate is a weighted average of a rate set by the central bank along Taylor-rule lines and the rate determined by foreign rates through the UIP condition. This model is then calibrated for Egypt, and simulated under alternative values of the two sets of weights. This generates predictions of inflation and output variability and the central bank's loss under different assumptions about exchange rate flexibility and inflation targeting. The key result is that inflation and output variability and the welfare loss are higher under a pure fixed exchange rate regime, but lowest at a point close to (but not quite at) pure inflation targeting plus full exchange rate flexibility.

Hoda Abdel Ghaffar Youssef investigates the extent of fiscal dominance in Egypt. After exploring the existing analytical and empirical literature on fiscal dominance, and the structure of government expenditure and revenues in Egypt, she uses cointegration tests and an error correction model to assess the short run and long run impact of claims on the government (i.e. government borrowing) on the price level in Egypt. She finds clear evidence of long run effects of government borrowing (together with broad money and real GDP) on the price level, but no significant evidence of short run effects. Granger causality tests suggest claims on the government 'cause' prices, and not vice versa, while a range of tests indicate there is no structural break in the relationship, for example around recent announcements of changes in the monetary policy framework. She concludes that changes to the fiscal policy framework, so that fiscal policy no longer dominates monetary policy, are an essential precondition for any move to inflation targeting.

Maher Hasan and Hesham Alogeel set out to identify the nature of the inflationary process in Saudi Arabia and Kuwait, as representative GCC countries, in the light of the recent rise in inflation in those countries and the debate it has provoked. They estimate an error correction model in which the change in prices is related to foreign prices, the nominal effective exchange rate and the oil price, together with a domestic excess demand variable and domestic money supply shocks. For both countries they find that external factors play a dominant role in inflation, with a strong relationship in the long run between domestic prices and trading partners' prices, and a less strong relationship with the exchange rate (but no significant role for the oil price). In the short run, domestic prices respond also to excess money supply and, in the Kuwaiti case, excess demand. They suggest that prices respond more strongly to trading partners' inflation than to exchange rate movements because the former are typically permanent but the latter are often reversed. They also note that the similarity between the two countries bodes well for the planned GCC monetary union.

References

Abdel-Khalek, G. (2001), *Stabilisation and Adjustment in Egypt: Reform or De-Industrialisation*. Cheltenham: Edward Elgar.

Berg, A., Karam, P., and Laxton, D. (2006), 'A practical model-based approach to monetary policy analysis – Overview', IMF working paper no. 06/80.

Cobham, D., and Dibeh, G. (eds) (2009), *Monetary Policy and Central Banking in the Middle East and North Africa*, London: Routledge.

Devlin, J. (2010), *Challenges of Economic Development in the Middle East and North Africa Region*, Singapore: World Scientific.

Makdisi, S. (2004), *The Lessons of Lebanon: The Economics of War and Development*. London: I.B. Tauris.

Neaime, S., and Colton, N. (2005), *Money and Finance in the Middle East: Missed Opportunities or Future Prospects*, volume 6 of *Research in Middle East Economics*.

Noland, M., and Pack, H. (2007), *The Arab Economies in a Changing World*, Washington, DC: Peterson Institute for International Economics.

Richards, A., and Waterbury, J. (2008), *Political Economy of the Middle East*, Boulder, CO: Westview, 3rd edition.

Part I

Monetary policy frameworks

2 Monetary policy architecture, financial institutions and financial markets in the Middle East and North Africa

An overview

David Cobham

1 Introduction

This chapter is designed to provide an overview of the financial infrastructure in terms of financial institutions and markets which conditions the choice of monetary policy strategy for the MENA countries. Section 2 identifies three polar types of monetary architecture together with the institutional and market infrastructure required for each type and the kinds of monetary policy feasible in each case. These polar types represent specific, easily definable points on a continuous spectrum, but individual countries may be situated anywhere along that spectrum. Section 3 introduces a range of qualitative and quantitative information designed to locate countries on the spectrum, and uses it to comment on the MENA countries as a whole. Section 4 uses that information to consider where each of the MENA countries currently fits in this typology. Section 5 summarises the findings and comments upon them.

2 Three polar types of monetary architecture

Three polar types of monetary architecture can be identified, in terms of the financial environment in which central banks operate and hence what they can (and cannot) do.

First, at one end of the spectrum a *basic monetary architecture* can be defined, in which there is only a minimal financial system with few or no banks and no organised financial markets, but where a monetary authority or central bank operates a hard exchange rate peg (or currency board) as a substitute for a monetary policy. Such a central bank needs substantial foreign exchange reserves and/or a control of the flow of foreign exchange; the latter could take the form of a country's exports being dominated by one or a few commodities produced and marketed under the control of the government, so that the bulk of export revenues accrues to the government and the central bank then operates as the counterparty to the majority of transactions in foreign exchange. However, the central bank does not need to be independent, it does not need to make discretionary monetary policy decisions on an ongoing basis, and it does not need to produce forecasts of the development of the economy. In addition, since the operation of the exchange rate fixing arrangements automatically adjusts money supply to money demand, via balance of payments disequilibria, this type of monetary arrangement can handle non-extreme fiscal deficits automatically. It therefore economises on expertise and decision-making resources. It also does not require any significant development of other financial institutions or markets.

The typical case of a basic architecture is that of a colonised country with its own separate currency controlled via a currency board on the metropolitan currency, as was common for British, French, Belgian and Portuguese colonies. Many of these countries continued to operate a currency board for a few years at least after formal decolonisation. A number of other countries which were not formal colonies also operated similar arrangements in the 1950s and 1960s.

It is obvious that this type of monetary arrangement is sub-optimal: it means the country concerned has no significant monetary independence, ties its price level over the medium term to that in the anchor country and is exposed to cyclical fluctuations and shocks from the anchor country. However, the resources required to operate such a monetary policy are much less than those for the more sophisticated arrangements considered below. And, if the anchor is appropriate, it should ensure a reasonable degree of price stability despite the lack of central bank independence (CBI). Cukierman, Webb and Neyaptı remarked in their study of central bank independence that 'Austria, The Bahamas, Belgium, Luxembourg, Netherlands and Panama have lower inflation in the 1980s than their central bank independence would indicate, because their monetary policy is dominated by a policy rule fixing their exchange rate to a relatively stable currency' (1992: 382), and it is easy to provide some harder evidence in support of this.

Table 2.1(a) shows the results of simple regressions of inflation on CBI (measured on a 0–1 scale) for the Cukierman, Webb and Neyaptı (1992) sample of developing countries. In column [1] inflation is regressed on CBI plus dummies for the different time periods (the sample includes 1950–59, 1960–71, 1972–79 and 1980–89, the latter being the decade with the highest average inflation for developing countries). The coefficient on CBI is positive and insignificant. When a dummy for hard exchange rate pegs is included in column [2] that dummy is significantly negative but nothing else changes much. When a dummy for soft exchange rate pegs is included in column [3] the two exchange rate dummies are each a little larger and more significant.[1] And this result is broadly maintained when the central bank governor turnover rate TOR, favoured by Cukierman *et al.* as a better indicator of real central bank independence for developing countries, is included in column [4].

Table 2.1(b) repeats this sort of analysis for the limited sample of countries in Fry, Julius, Mahadeva, Roger and Sterne (2000) with their more up-to-date measure of CBI (on a 0–100 scale). When the entire sample (78 countries including 16 developed[2] and 22 transition) is used in a simple regression of inflation on CBI, the coefficient on CBI is insignificant (but negative). When a dummy for hard

Table 2.1(a) Inflation, CBI and fixed exchange rates

	1	2	3	4
Constant	25.97 (1.41)	28.05 (1.54)	27.79 (1.55)	17.92 (0.99)
CBI	55.27 (1.16)	59.28 (1.25)	70.62 (1.51)	47.52 (1.01)
DFIXHARD		−23.57 (−1.97)	−32.88 (−2.62)	−27.19 (−2.17)
DFIXSOFT			−30.79 (−2.14)	−30.87 (−2.19)
TOR				56.93 (2.33)
D50	−32.95 (−1.80)	−23.54 (−1.26)	−16.46 (−0.88)	−9.94 (−0.54)
D60	−34.65 (−2.54)	−25.85 (−1.82)	−18.49 (−1.28)	−20.59 (−1.46)
D70	−25.28 (−2.05)	−24.16 (−1.99)	−18.34 (−1.50)	−14.32 (−1.18)
R^2	0.08	0.07	0.10	0.14
observations	113	113	113	113

Data: CBI and TOR taken from Cukierman, Webb and Neyaptı (1992); average inflation for each 'decade' from International Financial Statistics; DFIXHARD and DFIXSOFT constructed from Reinhart and Rogoff (2004). (T-statistics in parentheses).

Table 2.1(b) Inflation, CBI and fixed exchange rates

	5	6	7	8
Constant	8.62 (1.73)	11.35 (2.14)	4.40 (0.78)	10.97 (1.85)
CBI	−0.005 (−0.08)	−0.03 (−0.46)	0.06 (0.73)	−0.01 (−0.11)
DUMER		−3.92 (−1.41)		−7.76 (−2.48)
R^2	−0.013	−0.000	−0.011	0.102
observations	78	78	43	43

Data: CBI from Fry *et al.* (2000); average inflation 1996–2005 from International Financial Statistics; DUMER constructed from calculations on 1999–2004 alignments in Cobham (2008), plus Namibia (hard peg to South Africa) and Eastern Caribbean (currency board on dollar). (T-statistics in parentheses).

exchange rates, based on the evidence in Cobham (2008),[3] is included that dummy is negative but not significant. However, when the sample is restricted to the 43 developing countries, the inclusion of the fixed exchange rate dummy raises the explanatory power of the regression and the coefficient is significantly negative.

The second polar type of monetary architecture is what we shall call *intermediate*. Here, there is substantially more financial development (institutions and markets), and the central bank has both some ability to formulate policy and strategy and some tools with which to control monetary and/or credit growth. There are banks which keep reserves at the central bank, so that the latter can use reserve requirements as a policy instrument, together with the discount rate, credit controls and/or moral suasion. In addition, there must be enough fiscal discipline and/or scope for selling bonds to the non-bank private sector for monetary and/or credit growth to be insulated from (non-extreme) fiscal deficits.

In this intermediate type of monetary arrangement, the monetary authority has the expertise and the technical capacity to pursue one (or possibly more) of a range of objectives. It could target the exchange rate, it could target monetary or credit growth, or it could pursue some more discretionary mix of inflation, unemployment and growth objectives, together, perhaps, with an external objective in the form of balance of payments equilibrium and/or exchange rate competitiveness.

Several developed countries were close to this polar type of monetary architecture under the Bretton Woods system and well into the 1970s or 1980s, while most emerging market economies have moved towards this type in the last two decades (and some beyond it).

Many of the most important debates in monetary policy since the 1960s have been implicitly located in the context of an intermediate monetary architecture. In particular, the time inconsistency problem is relevant because the central bank is not fully independent but financial markets are sufficiently liberalised that they can react adversely if the central bank is seen or imagined to respond to expansionary temptations. Moreover, given that monetary control is not precise enough to guarantee that monetary or other intermediate targets will be attained, the combination of incomplete central bank independence, imperfect monetary control and significant financial liberalisation means that where exchange rates are fixed they are vulnerable to speculative crises. It is clear, therefore, that there might be advantages to moving on from the intermediate monetary architecture to something which offered more stability.

The third polar type is what we shall call a *modern monetary architecture*. This involves a substantial development of both the banking system and the financial markets, and a central bank which has both the technical capacity to make decent economic forecasts in order to compare the effects of different policy decisions and the independence to make decisions on purely economic grounds. There is a well-developed money market in which the central bank intervenes and which is a fundamental source of liquidity for the commercial banks, so that the central bank's operations in the money markets to influence interest rates are transmitted through to the banks' deposit and lending rates. In addition, there is a deep and active bond market in which non-bank private sector agents are major players, so that even large fiscal deficits can be covered by borrowing from the private sector rather than the banking system.

In this modern type of monetary arrangement, the central bank is able to operate largely through interest rates, which it controls by its interventions in the money markets, and can therefore operate policy on a much more discretionary basis, responding to the development of domestic and other economic indicators on a continuing basis (rather than setting a monetary target for the year ahead and just trying to keep to it). It can therefore pursue an inflation target of some kind, explicit or informal (discretionary), strict or flexible. But it could also choose to pursue an exchange rate target, using interest rates as well as foreign exchange market interventions.

Monetary arrangements close to this polar type can be found in the US, the UK, the Euro area and other west European countries. They have been widely considered to be the most efficient arrangements possible in terms of their ability to deliver price stability and growth, with the time-inconsistency problem solved by the delegation of decision-making to central banks that are perceived to be both non-political and technically competent, and highly developed financial markets providing flexibility, efficiency and a rapid pass-through from policy to the rates that influence behaviour. The financial crisis and recession of the last few years have, of course, cast some doubt on both the competence of these central banks (notably in their failure to take account of asset prices) and the efficiency (in the wider sense) of the private sector institutions and markets. But it is also important to emphasise that monetary arrangements of this type are socially costly, in the sense that large numbers of skilled professionals and large amounts of capital are tied up in the operation of the institutions and markets concerned. Such costs need to be weighed against a range of benefits, which might include more efficient allocation of scarce financial resources, but as yet no serious studies of the costs and benefits have been undertaken.

3 Methodology and the MENA countries as a whole

This section explains the qualitative and quantitative data used to locate the various MENA countries in terms of these three polar types of monetary architecture. A wide range of quantitative and qualitative data are used for this purpose; some crucial qualitative data are taken from the very useful database on financial sector development in MENA countries compiled by Creane, Goyal, Mobarak and Sab (2004) (hereinafter CGMS).[4] In addition, statistical evidence on one crucial monetary relationship is presented: the extent to which changes in central bank policy interest rates are transmitted to commercial banks' lending and deposit rates. In this section the data are presented and discussed in general terms, with comments on the MENA countries as a whole. It should be noted that the information from CGMS mostly relates to end-2002. In some countries there have been some significant changes since then, but there is no fully up-to-date source comparable to CGMS. Some known changes are mentioned in the following section.

Table 2.2 presents data on countries' banking systems. It provides information first on the average ratio for 2002–6 of bank assets to GDP, together with the ratios of money and money + quasi-money (IMF definitions) to GDP, as basic measures of financial development. Then it reports (from CGMS, as of end-2002) the number and type of banks, the ease of entry into the banking system, the degree of concentration and the weight of the public sector in the banking system. The purpose is to investigate for each country, first, whether its banking system is sufficiently substantial and sophisticated to allow an 'intermediate' as opposed

Table 2.2 Banking systems

	1 Total bank assets (% GDP)	2 Money (% GDP)	3 Money + quasi-money (% GDP)	4 Number/type of banks	5 Entry (date of last entry)	6 Concentration	7 Public sector weight
Algeria	55.8	28.3	56.4	19 comm (6 state-owned)	Easy but limited	n.a.	Dominant
Bahrain	125.5	21.7	72.4	21 comm, 2 spec, 79 other, plus foreign bank offices	Easy	Very high	Very small
Egypt	123.3	19.7	95.1	28 comm, 21 spec, 32 other	Not easy	High	Large
Iran	60.1	16.2	37.6	9 comm, 4 spec (10 state-owned)	Difficult	Very high	Dominant
Jordan	205.1	39.7	128.4	9 comm, 5 spec, 12 other	Easy (1997)	Very high	None
Kuwait	96.0	16.5	66.5	7 comm, 2 spec (no foreign)	Not easy	Very high	Large state shares in most banks
Lebanon	297.6	9.2	220.5	68 various	Difficult	High	Very small
Libya	46.0	26.7	34.0	6 comm, 3 spec, 18 other	Easy (1996)	Very high	Dominant
Morocco	86.2	66.5	85.9	19 (6 state-owned)	Easy	High	Significant
Oman	49.8	10.6	33.1	15 comm, 3 spec	Easy (1998)	High	Significant state shares
Qatar	83.5	14.1	43.0	15 comm (8 domestic, 7 foreign)	Not easy	High	Large
Saudi Arabia	88.2	26.4	50.6	11 comm, 5 spec	Easy (2002)	Moderate	Very large
Sudan	15.2	11.1	18.5	26 comm, several spec	Not easy	Moderate	Very large
Syria	92.2	46.0	77.0	1 comm, 4 spec	Not easy	n.a.	All banks state-owned
Tunisia	77.5	23.4	58.3	14 comm, 14 other	Not easy	High	Very large
UAE	118.9	20.3	65.7	47 comm, various other	Not easy	Moderate	Significant
Yemen	23.4	13.5	32.7	14 comm, 2 spec	Easy (2002)	High	Large

Sources: Columns 1–3 are averages for 2002–6 (or a shorter period in some cases where data for the last year or two were not available) from *International Financial Statistics*; columns 4–8 have been extracted by the author from Tables 1A, 1B and 3B in CGMS (2004).

Note: comm = commercial; spec = specialist

to a 'basic' type of monetary policy, and, second, the extent to which its banking system is capable of functioning as the backbone of a 'modern' monetary system operated through central bank intervention in the money market. The table makes clear that the size of banking systems varies quite widely, from around 20 per cent of GDP in Sudan and Yemen and around 50–60 per cent in Libya and Iran, to well over 200 per cent for Lebanon.[5] All of these countries (except – at this date – Syria) have a number of different types of banks. But in many the public sector banks are dominant and in others there are very high levels of concentration, while in many there are significant barriers to entry. Concentration and barriers to entry are important for the efficiency of the interbank market and its capacity to transmit policy rate changes from the central bank. A recent IMF study has emphasised these factors rather than the number of banks as the key to efficiency.[6]

Table 2.3 presents information about countries' payments systems taken from the World Bank's 2008 Global Payment Systems Survey. Payments systems are important because if monetary policy is to operate through money market interventions and interest rates it is essential that the payments system operates rapidly and smoothly.[7] Column 1 lists the number of ATMs per million inhabitants, as a basic measure of the efficiency and modernity of retail payments systems: it shows how far countries such as Algeria, Sudan and Yemen lag behind the leaders in the GCC countries (which are well behind the USA, as shown in the memorandum items). Columns 2 and 3 indicate the existence and importance of real time gross settlements (RTGS) systems – the most efficient and modern mechanism for large value funds transfers: most MENA countries now operate, or are about to introduce (Egypt), an RTGS system, but cheque clearing houses are still important and the volume of payments passing through RTGS systems is in many cases quite limited. Column 4 identifies the degree of development of security market settlement; in most countries where securities markets themselves are reasonably established the settlement infrastructure has been modernised, with most securities dematerialised and the existence of one or more central securities depositories.[8]

Table 2.4 brings together information from CGMS (2004) on countries' financial markets (as of late 2002). The first column covers the degree of activity in the interbank market, which is fundamental to the operation of a modern as opposed to an intermediate monetary policy. The other columns cover the nature of government securities issued, the extent to which they can be traded in a secondary market and the degree to which they are held by the non-bank private sector, in order to get at the question of whether the bond market provides a mechanism to insulate monetary growth from fiscal deficits. In general, most of these countries still have limited interbank markets, which is consistent with the lack of competition in the banking systems seen in Table 2.2. And although they nearly all have some government securities issued, secondary trading is typically limited and only in Bahrain and Oman is a significant share of government securities held in the non-financial private sector.

Table 2.5 presents information on central bank governance. The first column gives the assessment of central bank independence (CBI) by Gisolo (2009)

Table 2.3 Payment and settlement infrastructure

	1 *ATMs per million inhabitants*	2 *Main system for large-value funds transfers*[a]	3 *RTGS turnover/GDP*	4 *Securities market/ settlement development*[b]
Algeria	11	RTGS	20.2	Securities market nascent
Bahrain	n.a.	n.a.	n.a.	n.a.
Egypt	27	Other[c]	–	Settlement post-nascent
Iran	98	RTGS	n.a.	Securities market nascent
Jordan	n.a.	RTGS, CCH	18.4	Settlement post-nascent
Kuwait	275	RTGS, CCH	4.8	Settlement post-nascent
Lebanon	248	CCH, other[d]	–	Securities market nascent
Libya[e]	n.a.	n.a.	n.a.	n.a.
Morocco	91	RTGS	5.5	Settlement post-nascent
Oman	205	RTGS	4.4	Securities market nascent
Qatar	522	RTGS, CCH	n.a.	Securities market nascent
Saudi Arabia	257	RTGS	10.7	Settlement post-nascent
Sudan	3	CCH[d]	–	Securities market nascent
Syria	n.a.	n.a.	n.a.	n.a.
Tunisia	n.a.	n.a.	n.a.	n.a.
UAE	346	RTGS, CCH	5.7	Settlement post-nascent
Yemen	8	CCH	–	Pre-nascent
Memorandum items				
India	18	RTGS, CCH	4.2	Settlement post-nascent
Turkey	226	RTGS	23.6	Settlement post-nascent
USA	1317	RTGS	43.4	Settlement post-nascent

Source: extracted from Tables II.1, II.3/a, III.1/a and V I.1 of World Bank (2008)

Notes

a This is the answer to a question about the main system used, to which central banks could tick one or more of 'RTGS', 'cheque clearing house' (CCH) or 'other' (undefined).

b This is compiled from a table covering the state of the securities market itself, and then the nature of the settlement infrastructure within it: 'nascent' means the securities market itself is nascent, 'post-nascent' means the security market is established together with at least some of the settlement infrastructure required, 'pre-nascent' means there is no securities market.

c Egypt is in the process of introducing an RTGS system.

d Lebanon and Sudan are working on the introduction of RTGS systems.

e According to its central bank website, Libya is working on the introduction of an RTGS system.

Table 2.4 Financial markets

	1 Interbank markets	2 Government securities	3 Secondary market in government securities: activity	4 Non-bank private sector (NBPS) holdings of government securities
Algeria	Inactive	Yes, up to 10 years	Limited	…
Bahrain	Yes	Yes	Yes	64% Held by non-financial sector (2001)
Egypt	Yes	Yes	Limited	…
Iran	Inactive	Yes, administered, 2- and 7-year bonds	No	…
Jordan	Yes	Yes, central bank CDs, TBs, up to 12 months	Limited	…
Kuwait	Limited	Yes, up to 5 years	Limited	Most held by banks
Lebanon	Limited	Yes, TBs, up to 24 months	Limited	Non-financial sector holdings very small
Libya	Inactive	Yes, administered, up to 5 years	No	…
Morocco	Inactive	Yes, TBs, up to 5 years	Limited	Most held by financial institutions
Oman	Yes	Yes, TBs, bonds, up to 7 years	Limited	Over 50% held by nbps
Qatar	Inactive	Yes, up to 5 years	Limited	…
Saudi Arabia	Inactive	Yes, TBs, bonds, FRNs, up to 7 years	Limited	Most held by autonomous govt agencies
Sudan	Inactive	Yes	Limited	…
Syria	Inactive	No	No	…
Tunisia	Inactive	Yes, TBs, up to 10 years	Limited	Limited
UAE	Yes	No (but central bank issues CDs for liquidity purposes)	…	…
Yemen	No	Yes, TBs, up to 1 year	Limited	Less than half held by non-banks (pension funds)

Source: extracted by the author from Tables 2 and 4B in CGMS (2004)

Note: CDs = certificates of deposit; TBs = Treasury bills; FRNs = floating rate notes

Table 2.5 Central bank independence

	1	2	3	4	5	6
	Independence (Gisolo)	Economic independence (LAS)	Political independence (LAS)	Transparency (LAS)	Accountability (LAS)	Overall governance (LAS)
Algeria	4.0	0.63	1.00	0.40	0.47	0.56
Bahrain	n.a.	0.63	0.25	0.47	0.45	0.45
Egypt	1.25	0.63	0.13	0.37	0.37	0.37
Iran	0.6	0.75	0.00	0.23	0.27	0.29
Jordan	-0.7	0.50	0.25	0.53	0.48	0.46
Kuwait	n.a.	0.50	0.13	n.a.	n.a.	n.a.
Lebanon	1.5	0.75	0.25	0.17	0.33	0.34
Libya	0.75	0.63	0.25	n.a.	n.a.	n.a.
Morocco	-2.15	0.75	0.25	0.44	0.37	0.43
Oman	n.a.	0.50	0.13	n.a.	n.a.	n.a.
Qatar	n.a.	0.25	0.13	n.a.	n.a.	n.a.
Saudi Arabia	n.a.	0.75	0.25	0.26	0.23	0.33
Sudan	n.a.	0.63	0.00	n.a.	n.a.	n.a.
Syria	-0.1	0.50	0.38	0.23	0.27	0.31
Tunisia	3.25	0.75	0.63	0.47	0.52	0.56
UAE	2.1	0.50	0.38	0.47	0.43	0.45
Yemen	n.a.	0.50	0.38	n.a.	n.a.	n.a.
Memorandum items						
Advanced countries (average of 25)		0.81	0.70	0.70	0.69	0.72
Emerging (average of 31)		0.75	0.56	0.67	0.66	0.66
Developing (average of 42)		0.71	0.45	0.46	0.58	0.54
MENA average		0.60	0.28	0.37	0.38	0.41

Source: Column 1 from Gisolo (2009) (weighted index of CBI); columns 2–6 from Laurens et al. (2009)

for the countries he covers, in an analysis which follows the Gutiérrez (2003) methodology, where the theoretical maximum for weighted CBI is 15.8 (the highest in the sample is Algeria with 4.0). Columns 2 and 3 give the more recent assessment (on a 0–1 scale) of economic and political CBI from Laurens, Arnone and Segalotto (2009) (hereinafter LAS), which draws on the methodologies of Grilli, Masciandaro and Tabellini (1991) and Cukierman, Webb and Neyaptı (1992). Columns 4 and 5 give the LAS assessment of central bank transparency and accountability, while column 6 gives their assessment of overall governance.[9] The memorandum items show the averages for those advanced, emerging and developing countries for which transparency and accountability scores are available, as well as the average for the MENA countries. In general, it is clear that MENA central banks rank relatively low on all aspects of governance; nearly all are below the averages for developing as well as emerging countries, with particularly large gaps on political independence and accountability.

Table 2.6 uses the information available on central banks' websites to provide an assessment of their technical expertise.[10] Columns 1 and 2 indicate the amount and timeliness of the statistical information available on central bank websites. Columns 3 and 4 provide data on the amount of information about monetary policy decision-making made available through monthly bulletins or reports regularly published by the central banks and through speeches and statements by central bank governors and/or monetary policy committees. The last two columns show whether the central banks publish research papers and forecasts of growth and/or inflation. In general, these central banks provide some (mostly not fully up to date) data on their websites but most of them offer little in terms of explanation of monetary policy decisions and show little evidence of technical expertise. The memorandum item provides a striking contrast: the emerging market central bank of India (which has a rather different tradition) provides much more useful information than most MENA country central banks.

Table 2.7 brings together two sets of information on the monetary policy instruments used in each country. The first five columns, extracted from CGMS (2004) and referring to end-2002, report the extent to which interest rates have been liberalised and credit controls removed, then the use of reserve requirements, of the rediscount window and of open market operations. Credit controls and reserve requirements can be thought of as 'intermediate' types of monetary policy instrument, whereas a 'modern' monetary policy relies mainly on open market operations. Interest rates have been liberalised in most countries but not in all, and credit controls are still in use in a number of them. Most countries do not use reserve requirement changes actively, none use the rediscount window regularly and most also do not use open market operations (OMOs) actively; a number of countries do not use any of these three actively or use OMOs only in a limited way. The final column offers a rather different perspective from Schnabl and Schobert (2009). Their focus is on the techniques by which debtor central banks – which all of these are – absorb liquidity. This shows that – even though reserve requirements may not be changed frequently – in most MENA countries required reserves vary substantially and provide the main instrument for liquidity

Table 2.6 Central bank expertise

	1 Website monetary data	2 Website economic data	3 Monetary policy bulletins/reports	4 Monetary policy statements	5 Research papers	6 Forecasts published
Algeria	Yes	No	Limited	Yes	No	No
Bahrain	Timely	Timely	No	Yes	No	No
Egypt	Timely	Yes	No[1]	Yes	No	No[a]
Iran	Yes	Yes	No	Limited	Limited	No
Jordan	Timely	Timely	No	Yes	No	No
Kuwait	Yes	Yes	No	No	No	No
Lebanon	Timely	Yes	No	No	No	No
Libya	Yes	Yes	No	No	No	No
Morocco	Timely	Timely	Yes	Yes	No	Yes
Oman	Timely	No	No	No	Limited	No
Qatar	Yes	Limited	No	No	No	No
Saudi Arabia	Timely	No	Yes	No	No	No
Sudan	Yes	No	No	No	No	No
Syria	Yes	No	No	No	No	No
Tunisia	Timely	Timely	No	No	No	No
UAE	Yes	No	No	Limited	No	No
Yemen	Timely	No	No	No	No	No
Memorandum item						
India	Timely	Timely	Yes	Yes	Yes	Yes

Sources: Constructed by the author from central bank websites; column 1: 'timely' requires that monetary data available in early January 2010 covered part of 2009 Q4; column 2: 'timely' requires that real economy data available in early January 2010 covered 2009Q3; column 3: 'yes' requires regular and up-to-date bulletins discussing policy choices; column 4: 'yes' requires significant recent statements or speeches about monetary policy decisions by the Governor or the monetary policy committee.

Note
a The CBE is about to publish a regular Inflation Report which will include an inflation forecast

Table 2.7 Monetary policy instruments

| | Monetary policy instruments from CGMS (2004) | | | | | Liquidity-absorption from Schnabl and Schobert (2009) |
| | 1 | 2 | 3 | 4 | 5 | 6 |
	Interest rates liberalised?	Credit controls removed?	Active reserve requirement changes?	Active rediscount window?	Active open market operations?	Main liquidity-absorbing operations (2000–2006)
Algeria	Yes, de jure	Yes, de jure	Yes	No	No	Required reserves [+ government forex deposits]
Bahrain	Yes	Yes	No	No	Yes	n.a.
Egypt	Yes, de jure	Yes	No	No	Limited	Required reserves and other bank deposits in CB, plus rising importance of open market operations (OMOs)
Iran	No	No	No	No	Limited	Required reserves [+ government forex deposits]
Jordan	Yes	Largely	No	No	Yes	OMOs, plus required reserves and other bank deposits
Kuwait	Partially	Yes	No	No	Yes	Required reserves and OMOs [+ some government forex deposits]
Lebanon	Yes	Yes	No	No	Limited	Required reserves and other bank deposits (+ sales of CDs)
Libya	No	No	No	No	No	n.a.
Morocco	Yes	Yes	Yes	No	Limited	Required reserves, some OMOs
Oman	Partially	No	No	No	Limited	n.a.
Qatar	Yes	Yes	Yes	No	No	n.a.
Saudi Arabia	Yes	Yes	No	No	Yes	Required reserves and other bank deposits in CB [+ government forex deposits]
Sudan	Yes	Partially	Yes	No	Yes	n.a.
Syria	No	No	No	No	No	Required reserves [+ government deposits]
Tunisia	Partially	Yes, de jure	No	No	Limited	Limited sterilisation, mainly through government deposits and forex deposits of banks
UAE	Yes	Yes	No	No	No	n.a.
Yemen	Partially	Yes	Yes	No	Limited	n.a.

Sources: Columns 1–5 extracted by the author from Table 4A in CGMS (2004), column 6 from figures and text in Schnabl and Schobert (2009)

absorption. And in some countries OMOs have become increasingly important in recent years.

Table 2.8 provides three perspectives on countries' external relationships. The first column shows the exchange rate regime operated in 2003 in terms of the Reinhart and Rogoff 'natural classification' (as updated to 2003 by Adam and Cobham, 2009). The second shows the extent to which the currencies were in fact aligned with the dollar or the euro between 1999 and mid-2007, using data from Cobham (2008). These two columns make clear the prevalence in the region of hard pegs to and managed floats on the dollar, with only one country (Sudan) floating freely and only the Maghreb countries having any relationship with the euro. The third column gives countries' average scores on the Chinn and Ito (2008) financial openness index, which attempts to measure the intensity of capital controls of different types. Here, there is a wide range from the relatively open smaller GCC countries, Egypt, Jordan and Yemen which are at, or close to, the maximum level of 2.54 prevalent in the US and most west European countries, to the relatively closed economies of Syria (which is at the lowest possible level of –1.81 found in post-Soviet countries at the beginning of transition), Libya and the Maghreb countries, followed by Iran and Sudan, with Kuwait, Lebanon and Saudi Arabia in the middle.

Finally, Table 2.9 reports some simple tests of the pass-through from policy rates to deposit and lending rates for the MENA countries; it shows the regression coefficients on the policy rate when the deposit and lending rates are regressed on the policy rate (plus the same for a regression of the lending rate on the deposit rate). In some cases results are reported for the pass-through from a domestic money market rate or (in the Saudi case, where there is a hard peg and no domestic rate is published) from the US Federal funds rate. The MENA results can usefully be contrasted with those shown for the US at the bottom of the table, where the regression coefficients are all very close to unity.[11] In general the MENA results indicate a wide variety in the pass-through, from relatively high pass-throughs in Bahrain, Egypt and Kuwait, for example, to much lower pass-throughs in Lebanon, Libya and Oman.

4 Individual MENA countries

In this section, the Gulf Cooperation Council countries (Bahrain, Kuwait, Oman, Qatar, Saudi Arabia and the UAE) are considered one by one and then as a group, and then the other countries are taken one by one in alphabetical order. The features of each country's monetary architecture in which we are interested are:

a.   the basic contours of the banking system: how far do they go beyond the basic polar type?

b.   the interbank market and payments system: are they adequate to support an interest-rate based monetary policy?

c.   the government securities market: does it provide a mechanism for insulating monetary growth from fiscal deficits?

Table 2.8 External relationships

Country	*1* *Reinhart–Rogoff 'natural' classification of exchange rate regime for 2003*	*2* *Currency alignment 1999–2007*	*3* *Financial openness index*
Algeria	Managed float on euro	Relatively more aligned with dollar	–1.13
Bahrain	Peg to dollar	Very narrowly aligned with dollar	2.54
Egypt	Managed float on dollar	Unaligned	2.29
Iran	Managed float	Unaligned	0.14
Jordan	Peg to dollar	Very narrowly aligned with dollar	2.54
Kuwait	Managed float on dollar	Relatively more aligned with dollar	1.18
Lebanon	Peg to dollar	Very narrowly aligned with dollar	1.18
Libya	Managed float on dollar	Unaligned	–1.13
Morocco	Managed float on euro	Relatively more aligned with euro	–1.13
Oman	Peg to dollar	Very narrowly aligned with dollar	2.54
Qatar	Peg to dollar	Very narrowly aligned with dollar	2.54
Saudi	Peg to dollar	Very narrowly aligned with dollar	1.18
Sudan	Free float	Unaligned	–0.11
Syria	Managed float on dollar	n.a.	–1.81
Tunisia	Managed float on euro	Unaligned	–1.13
UAE	Peg to dollar	Very narrowly aligned with dollar	2.54
Yemen	Managed float	Relatively more aligned with dollar	2.54

Sources: Column 1 from Adam and Cobham (2009)'s extension of the Reinhart and Rogoff (2004) classification (which only went up to 2001); column 2 classification of alignment with dollar or euro from Cobham (2008); column 3 average for 1999–2007 of the financial openness index of Chinn and Ito (2008), as updated in 2009 to cover 2007, available at http://www.ssc.wisc.edu/~mchinn/research.html

Table 2.9 Relationships between interest rates

	1 Period	2 'Policy' rate	3 Deposit rate on policy rate	4 Lending rate on policy rate	5 Lending rate on deposit rate
Algeria	1994Q1–2009Q2	Discount rate	1.06 (19.32); 0.86	0.87 (20.20); 0.87	0.78 (24.08); 0.90
Bahrain	1994Q1–2008Q2	Treasury bill rate	0.89 (28.51); 0.93	0.75 (7.93); 0.52	0.80 (7.45); 0.49
Egypt	1994Q1–2009Q1	Discount rate	0.91 (18.86); 0.86	0.62 (10.86); 0.67	0.63 (10.54); 0.65
Iran	Policy rate not available except 2003Q4–2004Q3				
Jordan	1994Q1–2009Q2	Discount rate	0.94 (13.63); 0.75	0.47 (5.34); 0.31	0.66 (13.08); 0.74
Jordan	2004Q4–2009Q2[a]	Money market rate	0.70 (3.86); 0.44	0.18 (1.44); 0.06	0.48 (8.76); 0.81
Kuwait	1994Q1–2009Q2	Discount rate	0.88 (21.32); 0.88	0.75 (20.04); 0.87	0.78 (16.78); 0.82
Lebanon	1994Q1–2009Q2	Discount rate	0.26 (5.70); 0.34	0.48 (5.84); 0.36	1.78 (44.82); 0.97
Libya	1998Q2–2009Q2	Discount rate	0.32 (1.46); 0.03	0.50 (4.55); 0.31	0.36 (5.16); 0.37
Morocco	1998Q1–2009Q2[b]	Discount rate	1.17 (27.76); 0.94	0.60 (7.20); 0.63	0.48 (6.97); 0.62
Oman	1994Q1–2009Q1	Discount rate	0.40 (4.97); 0.28	0.34 (10.09); 0.63	0.46 (10.51); 0.65
Qatar	2004Q3–2009Q2	Discount rate	0.95 (2.69); 0.25	0.58 (2.67); 0.24	0.42 (4.04); 0.45
Saudi Arabia	1997Q1–2008Q2	Federal funds rate	0.99 (24.85); 0.93	Lending rate n.a.	
Sudan	No rates available				
Syria	Policy and other rates constant to 2003Q1, then policy rate not available				
Tunisia	No deposit or lending rates available				
UAE	No rates available				
Yemen	1996Q1–2009Q2	Treasury bill rate	0.85 (18.95); 0.87	0.98 (10.80); 0.69	1.13 (12.96); 0.76
Memorandum item					
US	1994Q1–2009Q2	Federal funds rate	0.95 (38.91); 0.96	0.99 (184.78); 0.998	1.01 (44.90); 0.97

Notes
The numbers reported are the regression coefficients on the second rate when the first is regressed on a constant and the second rate, with the t-stat in parentheses, followed by the adjusted R-squared
a This period excludes an erratic movement of the money market rate in late 1999 and early 2000
b Lending rate available only up to 2005Q3

d.   the central bank: does it have the independence and the technical expertise to operate an intermediate type of monetary policy, or a modern type?

e.   monetary policy instruments: are the main instruments in use those common in intermediate or modern types of monetary policy?

Bahrain

Bahrain has a large banking system (assets over 100 per cent of GDP), with easy entry, no state ownership but a very high level of concentration (two banks accounting for 57 per cent of bank assets, see CGMS, Table 1B). It has a good payments system according to CGMS (Table 3B; no data available in World Bank, 2008), and an active interbank market. The pass-through from the discount rate to the deposit and lending rates is relatively strong. It has an active government securities market, with 64 per cent of securities held by the nonfinancial sector. Its central bank has reasonable economic but low political independence, according to LAS (2009), and overall governance at 0.45 below the developing countries average of 0.54. The central bank publishes timely monetary and economic data and some speeches by the governor (mostly on banking rather than monetary policy issues). However, it publishes no monetary policy or inflation report or bulletin, no research papers and no forecasts, which suggests that its technical expertise is limited. Its interest rates are liberalised and not subject to credit controls (and it has high financial openness). Its main monetary policy instrument appears to be open market operations;[12] its currency is very closely aligned with the dollar. What this amounts to is a monetary architecture which has gone well beyond the intermediate polar type on many dimensions, notably in terms of the interbank market, government securities and monetary policy instruments, but has a central bank which is no more developed or independent than the intermediate polar type.

Kuwait

Kuwait also has a relatively large banking system, but entry is not easy, there are large state shares in most banks and it is highly concentrated (two banks account for 52 per cent of assets, see CGMS, 2004, Table 1B). The payments system is modern (though the RTGS volume is low), but activity in the interbank market is limited; however, there seems to be a strong pass-through from the discount rate to the deposit and lending rates. Trading in the secondary market for government securities is limited, and most securities are held by the banks. The central bank is assessed by LAS as having some economic but very low political independence. It publishes monetary and economic data on its website but no recent governor's speeches or monetary policy report or research papers or forecasts. Interest rates are only partially liberalised, but open market operations seem to be a key instrument of monetary policy (despite the lack of secondary trading in interbank or government securities markets) and reserve requirements are also important according to Schnabl and Schobert (2009). The exchange rate is a managed float, rather than a hard peg, on the dollar, while financial openness has declined somewhat since the early 1990s. Kuwait's monetary architecture is therefore in most respects close to the intermediate polar type and above it on monetary policy instruments, but monetary growth is not well insulated from fiscal deficits and the central bank is below the intermediate polar type in terms of independence and expertise.

Oman

Oman has a much smaller banking sector than Bahrain or Kuwait, with easy entry but significant state shares and a high degree of concentration. Its payments system is modern (but the RTGS volume is low), and the interbank market is active. The pass-through from the policy rate to the deposit and lending rates is weak.[13] In the government securities market secondary trading is limited but more than half of the stock is held by the non-bank private sector. The central bank is rated by LAS as having some economic but very low political independence. Its website publishes timely monetary data, but no economic data, monetary policy bulletin, governor's speeches or forecasts. However, it lists a small number of occasional research papers. As for monetary policy instruments, interest rates are only partially liberalised, credit controls are still used and there is only limited use of open market operations, though reserve requirements may also be important. The exchange rate is pegged hard to the dollar, and financial openness is high. Overall, the Omani monetary architecture is around or below the intermediate polar type; it is clearly closer to the basic polar type than that of Kuwait.

Qatar

The Qatari banking system is of medium size, with easy entry but high concentration and a large public sector element. The payments system is relatively modern, but the interbank market is inactive. Table 2.9 indicates a good pass-through from the discount rate to the deposit rate, but a much weaker pass-through to the lending rate. In the government securities market secondary trading is limited and there is no information on the holdings of the non-bank private sector. The central bank is assessed by LAS as having low economic and very low political independence. Its website publishes timely monetary data but not much else. Interest rates are liberalised and there are no credit controls. CGMS (2004) identified reserve requirement changes as the main monetary policy instrument, but the emphasis is now more on managing short-term interbank interest rates.[14] The currency is very narrowly aligned with the dollar, and financial openness is at the maximum. Overall, therefore, the Qatari monetary architecture is below the intermediate polar types on many, but not all, dimensions; on balance, it is comparable to that of Oman.

Saudi Arabia

The Saudi banking system is medium-sized, there is a very large public sector element but concentration is moderate and entry easy. The payments system is efficient but the interbank market is inactive. Most government securities are held by autonomous government agencies and secondary activity is limited. The central bank is rated by LAS as having high economic but low political independence, and an overall governance score which is well below the developing country average. It publishes timely monetary data, but this does not include any policy rate or any lending rate; it publishes an inflation report but no governor's speeches or research papers or forecasts. Interest rates are liberalised and the main monetary policy instrument is identified by CGMS (2004) as open market operations (despite the lack of secondary trading in financial markets), while Schnabl and Schobert (2009) emphasise the importance of required reserves. The currency is very narrowly aligned with the dollar, and financial openness has declined since the early 1990s. Overall, the Saudi monetary architecture is around the intermediate polar type on most dimensions.

The UAE

The UAE's banking system is intermediate in size (relative to GDP) between those of Bahrain and Kuwait, and considerably larger than those of Qatar and Saudi Arabia. There is a significant public sector element and entry is not easy, but concentration is moderate. The payments system is modern (though the RTGS volume is low) and the interbank market is active. On the other hand there is no government securities market (though the central bank issues its own CDs for liquidity purposes). The central bank is scored at 2.1 by Gisolo; according to LAS it has some economic and a bit less political independence, is around the developing country average on transparency but below it on accountability, and is below the average (but well above the Saudi central bank) on overall governance. It publishes monetary data, which do not include policy or lending rates, and some limited statements by the governor, but no monetary policy reports, research papers or forecasts. As regards monetary policy instruments, interest rates are liberalised but according to CGMS (2004) no active use is made of reserve requirements or the rediscount window or open market operations. However, the central bank's website emphasises the passive (demand-led) issue of CDs, on the one hand, and dollar/dirham swaps and central bank loans to banks on the other. The currency is pegged hard to the dollar and financial openness is at the maximum. Overall, the UAE has a monetary architecture which is around the intermediate polar type on most dimensions, above it on the interbank market, but below it in terms of fiscal-monetary linkages and monetary instruments.

The GCC countries as a whole

The GCC countries all have hard pegs to the dollar, with the minor exception of Kuwait which recently switched its peg to an (unspecified) basket in which the dollar is probably still the largest component. Fifty to sixty years ago they were all close to the 'basic' polar type: they had minimal banking systems and no organised financial markets, but elementary central banks which controlled the bulk of the foreign exchange inflow and were able to fix their exchange rates with zero margins of fluctuation.[15] They have now experienced considerable financial development, particularly in terms of their banking systems. They are also relatively open (though Kuwait and Saudi Arabia are less open now than they used to be). However, with the exception of Bahrain they remain around or below the intermediate polar type on most criteria. Four of these countries are committed to the creation of a monetary union with a single currency, as reaffirmed in their summit in December 2008. Oman had already announced in 2005 that it was unprepared and would not aim to join the union with the others, while the UAE withdrew in May 2009 (following the decision to locate the union central bank in Saudi Arabia). The evidence discussed here suggests that Oman is indeed behind most of the other countries in some important respects, but that is also true of Qatar. However, two further points may also be made. First, if the intention is to operate a new currency which would not necessarily be fixed in the same way to an external anchor, these countries need to establish a union central bank which has a significantly higher technical capacity than any of the existing national central banks (and goes beyond the level of the intermediate polar type). Second, some elements of financial development which would be essential for moving beyond the intermediate type of monetary architecture might be considerably easier to implement at the level of the union. For example, the creation of a monetary union should effectively increase the degree of competition in the banking sector, and it might also make interbank and government securities markets more efficient because of the economies of scale that would be within reach.[16]

Algeria

Algeria has a banking sector which is small and completely dominated by the public sector element. Its payments system is weak on retail ATMs but good on RTGS turnover, while its interbank markets are not very active. There is limited secondary trading in government securities (and no information on the share held by the non-bank private sector). The central bank's independence is contested. Gisolo and LAS both score it highly, particularly in terms of political independence. However, Zouache and Ilmane (2009) have argued that its de facto independence has diverged significantly at times from its de jure independence, but that it is (as of 2007–8) relatively independent in practice. It publishes monetary but not economic data, a half-yearly report on the conjuncture which includes significant monetary policy material, and some governor's speeches, but no research papers or forecasts. CGMS report that interest rates have been liberalised and credit controls removed de jure; it appears that the main monetary policy instrument is changes in reserve requirements.[17] Financial openness is very low. The exchange rate regime looks like a managed float on the euro in terms of the natural classification, but in practice the currency has been relatively more aligned with the dollar. What this all amounts to is a monetary architecture which is well below the intermediate polar type on all dimensions except, perhaps, central bank independence.

Egypt

The banking sector in Egypt is large relative to GDP which, given the size of the economy, should tend to make it naturally quite competitive. However, as of 2002 at least, it was difficult to enter and highly concentrated and had a large public sector element. The payments system is weak but the interbank market is active, and the pass-through from the policy rate is relatively strong to the deposit rate but weaker to the lending rate. There is limited secondary trading in government securities, and no information on the share held by the non-bank private sector. The central bank is rated by Gisolo at 1.25, well below the average of his Mediterranean sample, and scored by LAS as having considerable economic but very low political independence and low accountability and transparency, with overall governance well below the developing country average. Its website includes monetary and economic data and some monetary policy statements (by the new Monetary Policy Committee), but no research papers. However, Egypt is one of the countries in this sample which have been undergoing the most change (including some bank privatisation) in the recent period, and the central bank is expected shortly to start publishing an Inflation Report which will include an inflation forecast. Interest rates have been liberalised de jure, and credit controls removed, but reserve requirements are not actively changed and it seems that open market operations are being used to an increasing extent as the key monetary instrument. Externally the country is open (with the Chinn–Ito index at its maximum since 2004), while the currency now seems to be unaligned with the dollar (or the euro). Overall, on the information available here, the monetary architecture of Egypt has to be considered as at or above the intermediate polar type on some dimensions, but below it on government securities.

Iran

Iran's banking sector is small, very highly concentrated and dominated by public sector banks. The interbank market is inactive, and the payments system includes an RTGS system (but there are no data on its volume). There is a government securities market, but it has no secondary trading activity, and there is no information on holdings of securities. The independence of the central bank is rated as low by Gisolo, while LAS give it good economic but zero political independence, together with low transparency and accountability; its overall governance is the lowest in the sample. The central bank publishes monetary and economic data (which do not, however, include a policy interest rate) and occasional monetary policy statements and research papers, but no monetary policy bulletins or forecasts. Interest rates have not been liberalised nor credit controls removed, open market operations are used but only to a limited extent, and reserve requirements are important. Financial openness is limited, but less so than it was in the 1990s. The exchange rate regime is a managed float, with no alignment on the dollar or the euro. Overall, this monetary architecture is below or well below the intermediate polar type, on all dimensions.

Jordan

The banking sector in Jordan is significantly larger than those in nearly all other MENA countries and almost entirely private-sector, but it is very concentrated. There is an active interbank market and an efficient payments system, and the simple regressions in Table 2.9 indicate that the pass-through from the policy rate is relatively strong to the deposit rate but weaker to the lending rate.[18] There are some Treasury bills but the more important security is CDs issued by the central bank itself; CGMS have no information on non-bank holdings of government securities. The central bank's independence is rated below the MENA average by Gisolo and also by LAS, but it does rather better on transparency and accountability. It publishes timely monetary and economic data and some monetary policy statements, but no monetary policy report, research papers or forecasts. Interest rates have been liberalised and credit controls largely removed, and the active monetary policy instrument is open market operations. The currency is very narrowly aligned with the dollar, with maximum financial openness. Overall, the monetary architecture is around or above the intermediate polar type on all dimensions.

Lebanon

Lebanon has the largest banking sector relative to GDP of the MENA countries; the public sector element is very small, but entry is difficult and concentration high. The payments system does not yet include an RTGS system, and interbank activity is limited. Table 2.9 indicates a poor pass-through from the discount rate to deposit and lending rates (but more than one for one pass-through from the deposit rate to the lending rate). There is a large stock of Treasury bills but there is little secondary trading and most bills are held by the banks. Gisolo puts the central bank's independence at the relatively low level of 1.5, while LAS give it considerable economic but low political independence and overall governance well below the developing country average. However, other observers (notably Dibeh, 2009) have suggested a rather higher degree of de facto independence. The bank provides timely monetary and economic data, but little else: there is no evidence of serious technical expertise. Interest rates are fully liberalised, but there is only limited use of open market operations and required reserves are still important. Financial openness remains well below its historical levels (it was at the maximum of 2.54 between 1970 and 1996, but went as low as 0.14 in 2001), while the currency is very narrowly aligned with the dollar. Overall, Lebanon's monetary architecture is around or below the intermediate polar type, except with respect to its banking sector.

Libya

Libya's banking sector is small, dominated by state-owned banks and very highly concentrated. Its payments system is very weak and its interbank market is inactive. Government securities exist but they are not traded in a secondary market and there is no information on non-bank holdings. The central bank has some economic but low political independence; it provides monetary and economic data but there is no evidence of technical expertise. Table 2.7 seems to imply that monetary policy is operated primarily through direct controls on banks, and Table 2.9 suggests only a limited pass-through from the discount rate to the lending rate. Financial openness is very low, and the currency is managed but not in recent years aligned with the dollar (or the euro). Overall, this is a case where the monetary architecture is well below the intermediate polar type on every dimension.

Morocco

Morocco has a medium-sized banking sector with easy entry but high concentration and a significant public sector share. Its payments system is modern (though the RTGS volume is low). As of end-2002 its interbank market was inactive and there was limited secondary trading in government securities, most of which were held by financial institutions. The central bank's independence is scored very low by Gisolo, but LAS give it high economic but low political independence and overall governance below the developing country average. However, it publishes timely monetary and economic data, a regular monetary policy report which includes a fan-chart inflation forecast, and significant monetary policy statements by the governor (but no research papers). Interest rates are fully liberalised, but open market operations are limited and reserve requirements remain important. Financial openness is very low, while the exchange rate is managed with reference to the euro. Overall, while Morocco's monetary architecture is clearly evolving rapidly and the information used here may not be completely up to date, on that evidence it is around or below the intermediate polar type on most dimensions but above it on the technical expertise of the central bank.

Sudan

Sudan's banking sector is small, with a significant public sector element but only moderate concentration. The payments system is weak, and the interbank market is inactive. There is a government securities market, but limited secondary activity and no information on non-bank holdings. The central bank has some economic but zero political independence according to LAS; it publishes monetary data but little else. Monetary policy instruments include both reserve requirement changes and open market operations (no regressions are reported on interest rates because no policy rate is available). Financial openness is low, while the currency floats freely. Overall, this monetary architecture is below or well below the intermediate polar type on all dimensions.

Syria

The banking sector in Syria is medium-sized, but entirely state-owned. No information is available on the payments system. The interbank market is inactive, and there is no market for government securities. The central bank is clearly non-independent, with LAS scoring its overall governance at the second lowest (after Iran) in the sample; it publishes monetary data but little else. Credit controls have not been removed and Table 2.7 reports no other actively used monetary policy instruments.[19] Financial openness is at the minimum level. On the natural classification the exchange rate regime is a managed float on the dollar. Overall, Syria's monetary architecture must be considered well below the intermediate polar type on nearly all dimensions.

Tunisia

Tunisia has a medium-sized banking sector which (as of end-2002) was difficult to enter, highly concentrated and with a very large public sector component. Its payments system is considered efficient by CGMS (2004, Table 3B), but its interbank market was inactive. There was limited secondary market activity in government securities and limited holdings by non-banks. The central bank scores relatively well on Gisolo's index of independence; LAS give it good economic and considerable political independence, with overall governance above the developing country average. It publishes timely monetary and economic data, but no significant monetary policy report, governor's speeches, research papers or forecasts. Interest rates as of end-2002 had been partially liberalised and credit controls removed 'de jure', and there was limited use of open market operations. Financial openness was low. The currency regime was a managed float but not in practice aligned on the euro. Overall, Tunisia's monetary architecture is shown here as below, but not well below, the intermediate polar type on all dimensions other than central banking.

Yemen

Yemen has a small banking sector with a large public sector component and high concentration. The payments system is weak and the interbank market inactive. In government securities there is limited secondary trading and less than half the stock is held by non-banks. The central bank has some economic but less political independence according to LAS, and it publishes timely monetary data but little else. Interest rates have been partially liberalised, reserve requirement changes are actively used and there are limited open market operations, but there is evidence of a relatively strong pass-through from the discount rate to deposit and lending rates. Financial openness is at the maximum. The currency regime seems to be a managed float on the dollar. Overall, this is a monetary architecture which is well below the intermediate polar type on all dimensions.

5 Conclusions

The individual country assessments can be summarised by grouping the countries into three categories. First, Iran, Libya, Syria, Sudan and Yemen have the least developed monetary architecture (they also have the least developed financial systems on CGMS's index). In particular, these countries have small banking sectors, little or no financial market activity, and non-independent, low-expertise central banks. At the other end of the spectrum, the most 'advanced' monetary architecture can be found in Bahrain (which also tops CGMS's financial development index) and Jordan. These are followed by Egypt, which is now above the intermediate polar type on most dimensions and is modernising fast, particularly insofar as concerns the central bank. Of the remaining countries some, like Lebanon, the UAE, Kuwait and Saudi Arabia, have larger banking systems but weak financial markets and central banks. Morocco now seems to have a more advanced central bank, but lacks development in other areas. Both Oman and Qatar lag behind their partners in the GCC. Tunisia is between the basic and intermediate poles on all dimensions except central banking. Algeria's relative position relies heavily on its more independent central bank; without that it would be closer to Sudan.

Three more general observations are warranted. First, given their different historical trajectories the MENA countries are less differentiated in their monetary architecture than might have been expected: it seems almost certain that if the same exercise was undertaken for, say, 1970 the differences would look much larger. Now, however, although countries continue to differ along specific dimensions there are signs of convergence. Second, none of these countries are anywhere near the type of monetary architecture which would be necessary for a 'modern' monetary policy of the inflation-targeting type. And third, it should be recognised that while there are benefits to be obtained from a move towards the modern polar type there are also costs in terms of the employment of scarce capital, intellectual and physical resources. Research is needed to estimate those costs and compare them with the likely benefits. It should also be recognised that, on the basis of a proper cost-benefit analysis, the strategic monetary choice made so far by some of the MENA countries, to fix the exchange rate, may turn out not to be inappropriate.

Notes

1 The data for these pegs were constructed from the Reinhart and Rogoff (2004) 'natural' classification of exchange rate regimes, on the basis of the dominant regime over the period. Hard pegs refers to Reinhart and Rogoff's fine codes 1–4 (coarse code 1); soft pegs refer to fine codes 5–9 (coarse code 2) or to a combination of a hard peg for most years and a softer regime for the rest of the period.

2   The members of the Euro area are dropped because the inflation data cover pre- and post-1999.

3   Table 3 of Cobham (2008) lists countries which had hard pegs (coded +/– 2 or +/– 3) to the US dollar or the euro; in addition the East Caribbean currency union (which has a currency board on the dollar) and Namibia (currency union with South Africa) are included as hard pegs.

4   The MENA countries are taken here to include all the Arab countries and Iran. The Palestinian Territory is excluded because there is at present no national currency or monetary policy. Djibouti, Mauritania and Pakistan are included by CGMS but not included here.

5   The corresponding ratios for money (given the effects of dollarisation in some cases) confirm the story told by banking sector assets.

6   See Laurens *et al.* (2005, pp. 17–18): "While there is no firm evidence, the experience gathered in the case studies suggests that interbank markets with as few as four or five participants can be efficient, provided none of them dominates the market … Indeed, more than the number of participants, what most promotes competition is that participants are discouraged from setting prices above the prevailing rates. The reason is that, in perfectly competitive markets, if they did not adhere to prevailing rates, other participants could enter the market quickly and find it profitable. In this context, measures to increase the effectiveness of the interbank market involve removing barriers to entry. Privatizing state-owned banks can also help eliminate market segmentation, and opening access to foreign banks can help upgrade banking skills." See also Ferhani *et al.* (2009, ch. IV).

7   For example, an important component in the establishment of European Monetary Union was the creation of the TARGET system which linked the real time gross settlement systems of Euro area member countries, and thereby ensured that interest rates were harmonised throughout the area.

8   It is, however, not possible to distinguish in the survey between the settlement arrangements for bonds, money market instruments and company shares.

9   This is the average of the scores for CBI (itself the average of economic and political independence), transparency and accountability.

10 The approach draws in part on that in CGMS (2004).

11 If the sample is restricted to exclude the last few quarters (which cover the financial crisis), the coefficients are all indistinguishable from unity.

12 Bank deposits at the central bank have grown rapidly, so if the Schnabl–Schobert approach was applied to Bahrain it is likely that required reserves would show up as a major means of liquidity absorption.

13 Monetary policy seems to have changed radically in 2004–5 (before that the discount rate was hardly ever changed), but data from 2005 show an even weaker pass-through.

14 See the Qatar Central Bank website, http://www.qcb.gov.qa/English/PolicyFrameWork/MonetaryPolicy/Pages/MonetaryPolicyGoals.aspx.

15 Commercial banks were (and are) allowed to operate a small spread on exchange transactions.

16 The quote from Laurens *et al.* (2005) cited in note 6 above continues, "In the case of small countries with shared economic interests, participation in a currency union can help reach the critical size needed for markets to emerge" (2005, p. 18). See also Ferhani *et al.* (2009, ch. VI).

17 The strong pass-through shown in Table 2.9 from the discount rate to the deposit and lending rates apparently reflects responses by the central bank to the (concerted) actions of the banking system rather than a pass-through from the policy rate to the banks' rates (Ilmane, 2007).

18 Poddar, Sab and Khachatryan (2006) measured the pass-through from 1995M12, given the changes made in mid-1995, but altering the start date made very little difference to the results in Table 2.9.

19 No interest rate regressions are possible. IFS gives a discount rate for Syria only up to early 2003; between 1990 and 2003Q1 the policy rate, the lending rate and the deposit rate were all unchanged, and after 2003Q1 no data on the policy rate are given.

References

Adam, C., and Cobham, D. (2009), 'Alternative exchange rate regimes for MENA countries: gravity model estimates of the trade effects', in D. Cobham and G. Dibeh (eds), *Monetary Policy and Central Banking in the Middle East and North Africa*, London: Routledge.

Chinn, M., and Ito, H. (2008), 'A new measure of financial openness', *Journal of Comparative Policy Analysis,* 10: 309–322 [data set updated to 2007, available at http://www.ssc.wisc.edu/~mchinn/research.html or http://web.pdx.edu/~ito/].

Cobham, D. (2008), 'Changing currency alignments: euro versus dollar', mimeo, July 2008, available at http://www.sml.hw.ac.uk/dc34/€\$alignment.pdf.

Creane, S., Goyal, R., Mobarak, A.M., and Sab, R. (2004), 'Financial sector development in the Middle East and North Africa', IMF working paper 04/201.

Cukierman, A., Webb, S., and Neyaptı, B. (1992), 'Measuring the independence of central banks and its effect on policy outcomes', *World Bank Economic Review*, 6: 353–98.

Dibeh, G. (2009), 'The political economy of central banking in the MENA region with special reference to Lebanon', in D. Cobham and G. Dibeh (eds), *Monetary Policy and Central Banking in the Middle East and North Africa*, London: Routledge.

Ferhani, H., Stone, M., Nordstrom, A., and Shimizu, S. (2009), *Developing Essential Financial Markets in Smaller Economies: Stylized Facts and Policy Options*, Washington DC: IMF.

Fry, M., Julius, D., Mahadeva, L., Roger, S., and Sterne, G. (2000), 'Key issues in the choice of monetary policy framework', in L. Mahadeva and G. Sterne (eds), *Monetary Policy Frameworks in a Global Context*, London: Routledge.

Gisolo, E. (2009), 'The degree of legal central bank independence in MENA countries: international comparison and macroeconomic implications', in D. Cobham and G. Dibeh (eds), *Monetary Policy and Central Banking in the Middle East and North Africa*, London: Routledge.

Grilli, V., Masciandaro, D., and Tabellini, G. (1991), 'Political and monetary institutions and public financial policies in the industrial countries', *Economic Policy*, 13: 341–92.

Gutiérrez, E. (2003), 'Inflation, performance and constitutional central bank independence: evidence from Latin American and the Caribbean', IMF working paper 03/53.

Ilmane, M. (2007), 'Efficacité de la politique monétaire en Algérie 1990–2006: Une appréciation critique', unpublished.

Laurens, B. and staff team (2005), *Monetary Policy Implementation at Different Stages of Market Development*, Occasional Paper 244, Washington DC: IMF.

Laurens, B., Arnone, M., and Segalotto, J.-F. (2009), *Central Bank Independence, Accountability and Transparency: A Global Perspective*, Basingstoke and New York: Palgrave Macmillan.

Poddar, T., Sab, R., and Khachatryan, H. (2006), 'The monetary transmission mechanism in Jordan', IMF working paper 06/48.

Reinhart, C., and Rogoff, K. (2004), 'The modern history of exchange rate arrangements: a reinterpretation', *Quarterly Journal of Economics*, 119: 1–48.

Schnabl, G., and Schobert, F. (2009), 'Monetary policy operations of debtor central banks in MENA countries', in D. Cobham and G. Dibeh (eds), *Monetary Policy and Central Banking in the Middle East and North Africa*, London: Routledge.

World Bank (2008), *Payment Systems Worldwide: A Snapshot: Outcomes of the Global Payment Systems Survey 2008*, Washington DC: World Bank.

Zouache, A., and Ilmane, M.-Ch. (2009), 'Central bank independence in a MENA transition economy: the experience of Algeria', in D. Cobham and G. Dibeh (eds), *Monetary Policy and Central Banking in the Middle East and North Africa*, London: Routledge.

3 The political economy of stabilisation in post-war Lebanon

Ghassan Dibeh

1 Introduction

In 1993 Lebanon started a stabilisation programme that ended the inflationary period of the 1980s and early 1990s. The programme was one of the main economic policy pillars of the post-war reconstruction programme which formally started in 1992 in the aftermath of the 15 year long civil war that lasted from 1975 to 1990. Disinflation was achieved through the stabilisation of the Lebanese currency, using the exchange rate as a nominal anchor in a typical exchange rate-based stabilisation programme (ERBS). Now, 17 years after the start of the programme, Lebanon is still maintaining the stabilisation of the Lebanese pound, an exceptional feat in the record of ERBS programmes around the world which have had much lower survival rates. The interesting aspect of this long-term success is not that Lebanon was doing the right things, which other countries did not, to avoid the unwinding of its ERBS programme. Other countries that have abandoned these programmes early on or even at much later stages, such as Argentina and Uruguay, did so as a result of unsustainable real currency appreciation and/or fiscal indiscipline. These are considered by most observers to be the Achilles' heels of ERBS programmes which eventually lead to their collapse. Compared with other countries that implemented such programmes in the aftermath of high inflation, Lebanon fared no better in terms of real appreciation between 1993 and 2002, or in terms of fiscal indiscipline throughout the period except for 2007–2009. In addition, the ERBS programme had adverse effects on economic growth in the post-war period. The ERBS combined with fiscal expansion during the early period of the reconstruction process formed a monetary-fiscal policy mix that led to a real interest rate shock which caused a recession in 1998 that effectively ended the early post-war reconstruction boom (Dibeh, 2008).

In this respect, Roubini and Setser (2004: 70) have written that 'Lebanon remains a crisis waiting to happen.' Roubini and Setser attributed their prognostication to the inability of Lebanese governments to generate successive and sustainable primary surpluses to arrest the growing debt-to-GDP ratio. Six years have passed since this prediction and the debt-to-GDP ratio in Lebanon stands at around 150 per cent (as of 2009), one of the highest levels in the world. Why has Lebanon been 'successful'? And why has Lebanon been able to maintain the stabilisation programme despite persistently large deficits and public debt growth?

The political economy of the stabilisation programme explains the ability of the Lebanese economy and successive governments since 1993 to withstand pressures to devalue at various stages of the programme, especially during the period 1998–2002 which witnessed increased financial fragility of the economy and a skyrocketing debt-to-GDP ratio. The political economy of stabilisation in Lebanon shows that the main support for the ERBS across all its stages had four pillars: first, the congruence of interests between the state and commercial banks which was the main pillar of support for the programme; second, the central bank's unwavering commitment to the currency peg; third, sustained capital inflows generated by foreign countries' commitment to Lebanon's financial stability and private capital inflows skewed by a 'home-bias' effect; and fourth, the distributional policies of the post-war governments at both sectarian and factor levels, and a consociational democratic system that subdued any potential political opposition to stabilisation.[1]

The chapter is structured as follows. Section 2 presents the nominal anchor policy of Lebanese governments from 1993 and an analysis of the fiscal deficits and debt growth in the early period of the programme. Section 3 presents and discusses the results of the ERBS for output and the increased financial fragility of the Lebanese economy. Section 4 presents a political-economic explanation for the maintenance of the ERBS programme. Section 5 concludes.

2 The anchor, deficits and debt

The choice of the exchange rate as an anchor in post-war Lebanon came in the wake of a currency crisis in February 1992, the last severe episode in a series of episodes of high inflation and currency crises that had beset Lebanon since 1984, destroying the traditional sound finance and currency policies Lebanon had implemented since its independence in 1943 (Dibeh, 2002). The need for a nominal anchor for disinflation, given the traditionally high pass-through from the exchange rate to domestic inflation and the high dollarisation that resulted from the long period of inflationary and currency crises, made the exchange rate the most favourable choice for such a nominal anchor. Bhattacharya (2003) has argued that the uncertainty regarding money demand at the end of the civil war and the need for remonetisation of the economy also played a role in this choice.

The central bank's other possible alternative of disinflation through a money-based stabilisation (MBS) would have been impossible to implement because of the small open economy nature of the Lebanese economy, the instability of money demand and the non-availability of the traditional tools of monetary policy in Lebanon such as open market operations.[2] The ERBS was gradually implemented from 1992 by reducing the volatility of the exchange rate in the period 1993–1997, then moving to a hard peg in December 1997. That hard peg still exists today.

Figure 3.1 shows that the gradual stabilisation of the exchange rate from the end of 1992 to a hard peg in December 1997 came after a period of extreme

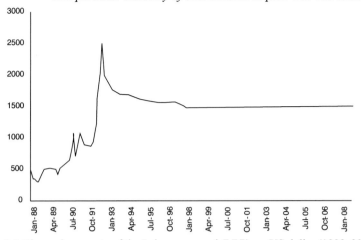

Figure 3.1 The exchange rate of the Lebanese pound (LBP) vs. US dollar (1988–2008)

instability in the exchange rate, which intensified in early 1992 with the exchange rate jumping by around 300 per cent between February and September 1992 after the central bank announced that it would stop intervening in the foreign exchange market. The currency crisis led to riots in May and to the coming to power of the first Hariri government which started the implementation of the disinflationary programme by the end of 1992.

The first stage of the ERBS from 1993 to 1997 reflected the typical macroeconomic dynamics of ERBS programmes, which have produced so-called stylised facts in the countries adopting such programmes. These include a characteristic evolution over time of inflation rates, GDP growth rates, consumption, the real exchange rate, the real wage, real interest rates, the degree of remonetisation of the economy, trade and current accounts and the fiscal deficit (Rebelo and Vegh, 1995; Kiguel and Liviatan, 1992). Elsewhere (Dibeh, 2008) I have shown that the time paths of these major variables during the early years of the ERBS programme in Lebanon correspond to the standard patterns of ERBS programmes except for the persistence of budget deficits.

The lack of fiscal adjustment in the Lebanese ERBS programme forms the main anomaly given that all the programmes that were even only temporarily successful implemented significant fiscal adjustments. Initially successful programmes, such as the Brazilian Real Plan, eventually collapsed under the weight of high real interest rates and public debt growth.[3] Figure 3.2 shows a comparison between the evolution of public debt in Brazil and Lebanon during the first six years of their respective ERBS programmes.

It is obvious that the rate of growth of the debt-to-GDP ratio is much higher in the Lebanese case than in the Brazilian case. Figure 3.3 shows comparative deficit-to-GDP ratios during the first five years of various ERBS programmes including Lebanon, while Figure 3.4 gives further detail for Lebanon. The

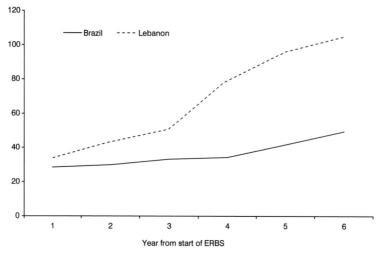

Figure 3.2 Debt-to-GDP ratios (%) during Brazil's and Lebanon's ERBS programmes

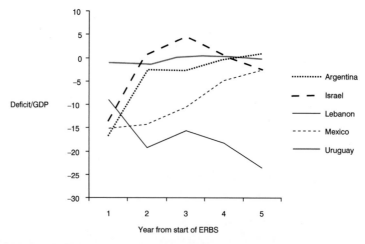

Figure 3.3 Fiscal adjustments during ERBS programmes (% GDP)

successful programmes show significant fiscal adjustment in the immediate years following the adoption of exchange rate stabilisation while Lebanon shows no such adjustment.

3 Adverse results of the ERBS programme

The ERBS programme passed through different stages with varying degrees of threat to the currency peg. The first stage, 1993–1997, coincided with the post-war reconstruction boom. The second stage, 1998–2002, coincided with economic

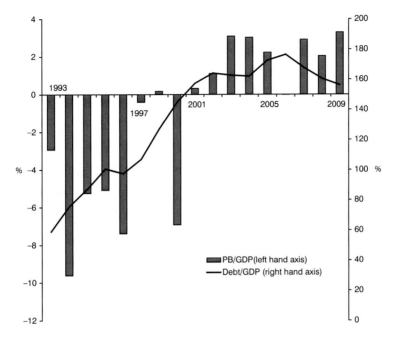

Figure 3.4 Evolution of primary budget surplus/deficit and public debt in Lebanon 1992–2009

recession and increased financial fragility which almost led to a debt crisis in 2002. The third stage, 2003–2005, coincided with the positive effects of the Paris II bailout, with economic growth, a real interest rate decrease and positive capital inflows. The last stage from 2005 started with the assassination of ex-prime minister Rafik Hariri and witnessed, for the first time since the start of the programme, a de facto fiscal adjustment and mixed economic performance.

ERBS programmes cause typical macroeconomic dynamics. In the early phase, economies experience a consumption boom and high GDP growth rates accompanied by exchange rate appreciation. The programme ends in a recession and eventual abandonment of the programme and currency devaluation. Reinhart and Vegh (1999: 2) said that 'most of the major exchange rate-based stabilisations in chronic inflation countries in the last 30 years have ended in spectacular financial and balance of payments crises'.

I have shown elsewhere (Dibeh, 2008) that Lebanon experienced a typical ERBS-induced boom–bust cycle in the period 1993–1998. The recession ended the first stage of the ERBS programme. Figure 3.5 shows the business cycle in this period. Moreover, the continued de facto fixed exchange rate regime after 1999 led to persistent stagnation in the Lebanese economy, interrupted by spurts of growth induced by the Paris II bailout in 2003 and 2004 and in the period following the Paris III conference in 2008 and 2009. The interest rate policy conducted in defence of the peg caused major shocks to the economy as a result

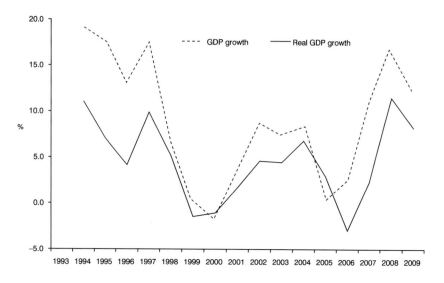

Figure 3.5 The business cycle in post-war Lebanon 1994–2009

of the high level of real interest rates generated. These protracted negative real effects of fixed exchange rates have been highlighted by Krugman (2000). Miles (2003) also showed that in emerging economies macroeconomic shocks in the presence of fixed exchange rates lead to large output costs. In this respect, the main shocks that have hit the Lebanese economy traditionally have been demand and supply shocks rather than monetary shocks (Bhattacharya, 2003). Hence, the adoption of the fixed exchange rate made Lebanon more susceptible to these shocks in terms of output loss. Berthélemy *et al.* (2007) claimed that Lebanon entered a slow growth trap after 1996 partly because of the real appreciation that harmed Lebanese competitiveness and the real exchange rate appreciation that led to a switch to the production of non-tradables where productivity gains are lower than in the tradable sector.

As discussed, the main variables that led to the negative effect on output were the real exchange rate appreciation and the real interest rate.[4] Table 3.1 shows the comparison between Lebanon and other ERBS programmes in terms of real exchange rate appreciation. It demonstrates that Lebanon experienced high real exchange rate appreciation relative to other countries in the period up to the end of 1997. This real exchange rate appreciation continued until 2002. Afterwards the appreciation of the euro versus the US dollar caused a de facto real depreciation of the Lebanese pound which mitigated the effects of the currency peg.

Interest rates were set by the Banque du Liban (BdL) to achieve the goal of exchange rate stability. According to Poddar *et al.* (2006), the BdL used two operational targets, the spread between interest rates on local deposits in foreign currency and the international markets in order to attract foreign capital, and the spread between interest rates on local Lebanese pound deposits and deposits in

US dollars, to encourage deposits in the Lebanese pound. Figure 3.6 shows the resulting evolution of real interest rates.

The need for capital inflows to maintain the exchange rate in the presence of high levels of public debt and lack of fiscal adjustment led to higher interest rates because of the higher premium required by international and local investors to mitigate the risks associated with the high level of the public debt and 'the risk of forced exit from the exchange rate peg', in the words of Poddar *et al.* (2006: 5). These authors showed that sovereign risk fluctuated between 2 per cent and 5 per cent in the 1995–1999 period. The increased financial fragility in the post-2000 period led the spread to increase sharply from mid-2001 to reach 10.9 per cent in September 2002, an increase which was triggered by negative inflows and a drop in gross reserves at the BdL. In addition, the exchange rate risk increased in the post-2000 period reflecting 'fiscal dominance' and the probability of devaluation expectations. These were the symptoms of the 'near-debt crisis' in 2002 (Finger

Table 3.1 Real appreciation in ERBS programmes

Country	Real exchange rate appreciation
Argentina	15.0%
Chile	25.0%
Lebanon*	72.5%
Uruguay	78.8%

Sources: For Uruguay, Chile and Argentina: Calvo and Vegh (1995); for Lebanon, until end 1997: Eken and Helbling (1999).

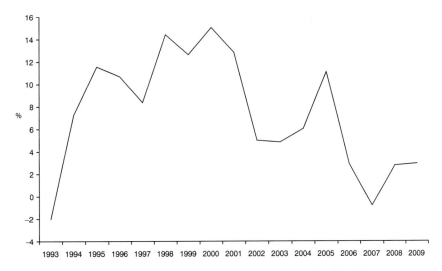

Figure 3.6 Real interest rates in Lebanon (1993–2009) (% growth of GDP)

and Hesse, 2009: 4). This together with disinflation led to a rise in real interest rates under the fixed exchange rate regime.

On a more general note, Finger and Hesse consider that the dependence of the financing of public debt on the growth in commercial banks' deposits led to the rise of what they called a 'macrofinancial system' (2009: 4) that is dependent on continued growth of bank deposits partly fuelled by interest rate spreads.

Capital inflows reinforced the central bank's policy of financial and currency stability and helped in the creation of a non-productive rentier economy. Rentier income, foreign aid, immigrant remittances and foreign capital inflows became a deadweight on production as high real interest rates and real exchange rate appreciation suffocated the industrial sector. By 1997, it was obvious that high interest rates and real exchange rate appreciation were causing a loss of competitiveness and a drop in tradable sector activity (Bolbol, 1999). The process of deindustrialisation in the post-war period was significant, indicating a sort of Dutch disease phenomenon that shifted the economy towards commerce and the production of non-tradables. The average annual rate of growth of industry in the post-war period from 1993 to 2003 was –0.4 per cent while for manufacturing it registered –1.8 per cent annually (World Bank Database).[5] The productive capacity of the economy suffered anaemic growth in this period. Berthélemy *et al.* (2007) report the stagnation of imports of machinery equipment, which had annual growth of –2.1 per cent in the period 1993–2005. Moreover, 67 per cent of investment expenditures between 1997 and 2002 were in buildings.

In addition, the increasing need for foreign inflows to sustain the ERBS, starting in 1997, led to the diversion of 'scarce' foreign capital away from the financing of reconstruction that was the dominant form of foreign aid from 1992 to 1998 towards the financing of the government and the propping up of BdL reserves. The latter took the form of direct deposits with the BdL and the foreign aid generated by the Paris II conference in 2002. Foreign aid geared towards reconstruction dwindled in the post-1997 period at a time when the reconstruction plans were still largely unfulfilled. The qualitative shift in foreign aid from reconstruction to stabilisation, together with the recession of 1998, ended the reconstruction phase of the post-war economic model. By the end of 2004, the total amount of foreign financing for reconstruction was around US$5.8 billion with around 70 per cent allocated during 1992–1997 compared to only 30 per cent during 1998–2004. Post-war reconstruction plans were delayed, and during 1992–1997 only around 60 per cent of the planned projects were realised or were in the process of being completed. The original reconstruction objectives for various sectors for 1992–97 went largely unfulfilled with some achieving their objectives only with delays extending up to 2004, such as the physical and productive sectors. In contrast, only 50 per cent of the original expenditures in the social sector for the period 1992–1997 were achieved by the end of 2004 (Dibeh, 2010).

4 The persistence of the ERBS: political economy considerations

The adverse effects of the ERBS programme on output and economic activity generated by high real interest rates and currency appreciation were 'overcome' by successive Lebanese governments. This overcoming occurred despite the rise of public debt to one of the highest levels in the world according to the debt-to-GDP ratio measure, which imparted a financial fragility that continuously threatened the sustainability of the ERBS. According to di Giovanni and Gardner (2008), Lebanon has passed the empirical thresholds identified by Reinhart *et al.* (2003) and Manasse and Roubini (2005), after which, countries face a debt crisis. They added, 'By such measures, however, Lebanon should have faced a crisis long ago' (di Giovanni and Gardner, 2008: 3). Moreover, Finger and Hesse (2009) said that Lebanon's debt-to-GDP ratio of 160 per cent in 2008 was well beyond conventional debt sustainability thresholds. These adverse output effects and the public debt explosion would in other experiences of ERBS programmes have been triggers for the abandonment of the ERBS. Theoretically, in the absence of fiscal adjustment and the rise of potential fiscal dominance and debt evolution, the ERBS programme would have been impossible to maintain in a credible fashion. As Alfaro (2002: 133) has noted, 'Programs where fiscal adjustment has been either partial or absent have failed. Indeed, the elimination of large public sector deficits has proven to be a necessary condition for their success.' From country experiences, all ERBS programmes ended in currency crises except Brazil in the 1960s which had periodic devaluations. The longest 'successful' stabilisation programmes were in Argentina and Uruguay. However, these programmes collapsed in 2002. The Uruguay stabilisation was successful because in addition to the 'nominal anchor' it had a 'real' anchor of deficit reduction (Licandro, 2001). The Argentinian programme was successful because of convertibility. However, the Uruguayan programme collapsed because it became unsustainable in the wake of the collapse of the Argentinian programme (Roubini and Setser, 2004). Why then did Lebanon not abandon its ERBS? The success of the programme (measured by its survival up to now) is perplexing for both theoretical and country experience reasons.

Notwithstanding the different country experiences and their specificities, Reinhart and Vegh (1999) have said that in the final stages of ERBS programmes, a 'dark side' emerges and countries are faced by the inevitable dilemma: devaluation or deflation. In most countries, the choice was devaluation. In Lebanon, it was deflation. Lebanon's political-economic interests that were intertwined with the stabilisation programme led to the persistence of the programme and to the choice of deflation rather than devaluation. The political economy and political determinants of monetary and exchange rate policies have been discussed and analysed by various economists and political economists of different stripes (Alfaro, 2002; Drazen, 2000; Epstein, 1992; Maxfield, 1998; Posen, 1993, 1995; Froyen and Waud, 2002; Eichengreen and Leblang, 2003).[6] Eichengreen and Leblang (2003) discuss with relevance to the topic at hand the political-economic considerations of exchange rate choice and the hierarchy of monetary policy autonomy versus fixed exchange rate policy. In this respect, committing to a fixed exchange rate can lessen the pressure for redistributive policies emanating from interest groups in society. For example, the extension of democratic suffrage in Europe in the 1920s and 1930s reduced the ability of governments to defend the currency values at all costs. Alfaro (2002) focuses, on the other hand, on the distributional impact of exchange rate appreciation in temporary stabilisation programmes and shows that, under certain plausible conditions, the owners of non-tradables gain from real exchange rate appreciation experienced under temporary stabilisation programmes. Blomberg *et al.* (2005) have shown using the experience of Latin American countries with exchange rate regimes that social interests and electoral pressures play a role in the political economy of such arrangements. Finally, the return to the gold standard in the interwar period at the pre-war parity in Great Britain was driven by political considerations, the power of the rentier and the doctrine of sound finance. Keynes was vehemently against this policy, given its effect on output, wages and employment (Keynes, 1963).

The political economy of stabilisation in Lebanon shows that the main support for the ERBS across all its stages was built on four pillars: first, the congruence of interests between the state and commercial banks; second, the central bank's unwavering commitment to the currency peg; third, sustained capital inflows generated by foreign countries' commitment to Lebanon's financial stability and private capital inflows skewed by a 'home-bias' effect; and fourth, the vertical and horizontal distributional policies of the post-war governments, and a consociational democratic system that subdued any potential political opposition to stabilisation.[7]

The commercial banks became the main source of finance for government deficits throughout the ERBS period.[8] The share of the commercial banks in government bonds was very high in the early period when it constituted more than 80 per cent of subscriptions. Later on, subscriptions by the BdL and by foreign institutions after Paris II in 2002 reduced this share. The shares of commercial banks in holdings of Treasury bills (T-bills) and eurobonds in 2009 stood at 60 per cent and 65 per cent respectively. In the first stage of the ERBS in the period 1993–1997, subscriptions to government bonds were extremely profitable for the commercial banks. The probability of default, the opportunity cost of capital and the expected depreciation rate were all very low.[9] It allowed commercial banks to transform the huge growth in deposits that they witnessed after the end of the war into lucrative, stable and relatively safe investments in Lebanese T-bills. Starting in 1998 and as the spectre of currency collapse loomed, commercial banks pressured the government to issue foreign currency denominated eurobonds. The optimal decision for the banks was to continue to finance the state but in foreign denominations. This allowed commercial banks to adjust their accounts as balance sheets were becoming too vulnerable to a currency depreciation which would have caused a twin currency–banking crisis. The increase in the eurobond issue coincided with the start of the second stage in the ERBS, in which the commercial banks played a political-economic role in the prevention of the currency crisis. This is not the first time that the banks played a political-economic role. During the civil war, by rolling over debt during times when the probability of repayment was very low and currency depreciation wiped out asset values, the commercial banks held the political elite together (Henry, 1987).

This special relationship between the banks and the state mediated by the central bank was instrumental in the prevention of state default or currency crisis in the period 1998–2002. The banks and the state became locked in a game whose sustainability meant the survival of both and its collapse the demise of both. At the start of this period, the strong commercial bank–state collusion made Lebanon immune to the emerging markets crisis in 1998. The spreads on the eurobonds held steady. This was caused by the fact that the commercial banks of Lebanon were the largest holders of eurobonds issued by the government. The Lebanese pound withstood severe pressures and predictions of an impending currency crisis in 1998–2002. In an IMF study on debt-generated financial vulnerabilities in emerging markets, IMF (2004: 45) concluded that 'Lebanon has defied pessimistic predictions, including those of the Fund, and a debt crisis has been avoided. While investor confidence plays a role in any emerging market economy, … .in Lebanon it has become the lynchpin of a unique symbiosis between the public-sector and the banking-sector balance sheets and how the authorities used this to overcome the near roll-over crisis of 2001–2002.' In this respect, di Giovanni and Gardner (2008: 3) attributed the ability of the Lebanese economy to have 'unusually high debt tolerance' to the willingness of commercial banks to finance the debt issues by using their vast pool of foreign exchange deposits.[10]

The commercial banks' interest in the maintenance of the currency peg was manifold. First, the exchange rate anchor and liability dollarisation intensified the currency mismatches in the Lebanese economy and put constraints on any potential softening of the peg by the BdL and on the corresponding commercial banks' interests in any such softening. This can be explained partly by what Calvo and Reinhart (2002) called a 'fear of floating' that resulted from the increased liability dollarisation in the post-war period, which reached a staggering average of 86 per cent between 1992 and 2008 in the private sector, and due to the substitution of dollar-denominated eurobonds for Lebanese pound-denominated treasury bills in the public sector liability structure. Devaluation under such conditions would have led to the collapse of the banking system.

Second, the subscriptions in the government bonds provided the main source of commercial banks' profits. In a study of profitability of the banking sector in Lebanon from 1993 to 2000, Peters, Raad and Sinkey (2004) showed that, in addition to GDP growth and interest margins, the commercial banks' holdings of T-bills were the major determinant of banks' profits. An interesting result in their paper is that compared with a control group of banks from five Middle Eastern countries Lebanon's banks have a lower profit rate. These results show that the profitability of the banking sector was highly dependent on its financing of government deficits in this post-war period. State financing led to higher returns on equity (ROE) in commercial banks in the period 1995–2000 compared with ROEs in the Middle East and in emerging markets (AUDI, 2004).

Third, high interest rates led to a rise in the share of rentier income in the economy.[11] Lower interest rates or a currency crisis would have threatened this source of income to the rentier.[12] It is the dependence of banks' profits on deficit finance and the high rentier income share that formed the broad political-economic support for the ERBS programme. Figure 3.7 shows the interest share of GDP as calculated from the national income accounts in Lebanon. The data, which is available only from 1997, shows an upward trend in the share of rentier income from around 5.3 per cent in 1997 to around 10 per cent in 2007. It is clear that in the early period of the ERBS programme (1993–2000) rentier income grew rapidly as stabilisation took hold together with high budget deficits. This extraordinary growth in the share of interest in the GDP is the most significant indicator of the effect of the stabilisation programme on factor shares in Lebanon.

In addition to the commercial bank–state nexus, the BdL played a major role in the sustainability of the ERBS, with commitment to the currency peg and its contribution to building the capital base of the commercial banks. The central bank, as an institution that historically was subservient to the interests of the banking sector, was instrumental in mediating between the interests of the state and the interests of the commercial banks. In contrast to the experience of many central banks in civil wars (Addison *et al.*, 2001), Lebanon's central bank maintained its status and functions throughout the civil war period. In this context, the unscathed central bank took a leading role in the post-war reconstruction period, becoming an important part of the public institutional nexus and the political economy of that period. The central bank conducted an industrial policy of reviving and developing the banking sector. The banking sector emerged from the war largely intact despite the bank failures of the 1980s that mainly hit small banks speculating heavily in foreign exchange

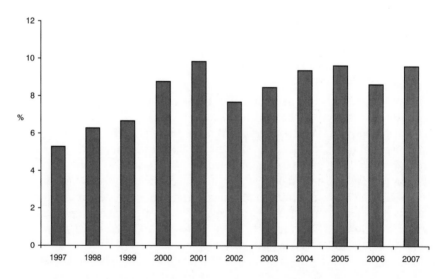

Figure 3.7 Evolution of the interest-to-GDP ratio in Lebanon (1997–2007)

markets. The banking system, however, had very poor capital adequacy ratios. The central bank's policy of high interest rates and its conduct of the Lebanese Treasury bills auction market effectively created a monopolistic debt market which allowed banks to make high profits in the period 1993–1997 when the cumulative premium on Lebanese T-bills over foreign denominated eurobonds reached around 54 per cent, which was seen by many as the central bank's policy of propping up commercial banks with low adequacy ratios in an overcrowded banking sector (Hakim and Andary, 1997).[13] The capitalisation of banks and the high deposit growth rates attracted by high interest rate differentials led to a spectacular growth of the banking sector in the post-war period. The asset-to-GDP ratio reached 332 per cent in 2003 compared with 101 per cent for the Middle East and 123 per cent for emerging markets. The ratio continued to rise, reaching around 360 per cent of GDP in 2009.

The BdL's commitment to the currency peg was tested throughout the ERBS period. Table 3.2 shows major episodes of intervention by the central bank in the defence of the currency during the post-war period, often aided by foreign capital inflows earmarked for the defence of the currency.

The resolve of the commercial banks and the BdL would have been insufficient to maintain the peg without the international support Lebanon received for its stabilisation. Realised and promised foreign aid have played such a role throughout the post-war period. The Hariri governments always trumpeted the willingness of donors in the Arab world and elsewhere to provide Lebanon with financial assistance. Moreover, such foreign aid (and in many instances just promises of aid) had a significant impact on the fiscal stance of the government.[14] This provided incentives for the postponing of reforms needed to avert the developing fiscal crisis of the state. In addition, capital inflows of various kinds (foreign capital flows, remittances and overseas development assistance – ODA) further contributed to the sustainability of the ERBS programme. These capital inflows were mediated by the commercial banks to finance successive governments (di Giovanni and Gardner, 2008). After 1997, there was an increasing dependence of the post-war economic model on foreign capital, especially foreign aid generated by the two international conferences held in Paris in 2002 and 2007 and foreign deposits with the BdL (Dibeh, 2010). This caused a national reliance on the rest of the world to prevent economic crisis and currency collapse The international 'bailouts' of the Paris II and Paris III conferences also had significant impacts on the prevention of currency and financial crises that would have signalled the end of the stabilisation programme. Both came at crucial times, in 2002 and 2007 respectively, providing Lebanon with both a hard asset (capital inflows) and a soft asset (investor confidence) to withstand pressures to abandon the hard peg. The Paris II 'bailout' was instrumental in averting financial crisis and the collapse of the ERBS in 2001–02 which some observers have called a 'near-debt crisis'. The conference was attended by many countries and international institutions including the IMF and World Bank. The package received one year after the conference totalled $10.1 billion made up as follows: $2.4 billion of concessionary foreign loans, $4.1 billion from the BdL and $3.6 billion of subscriptions of commercial

Table 3.2 Central bank intervention and foreign deposits in support of ERBS

Period	Events	BdL Intervention/Foreign Deposits
July 2006	War with Israel	US$1 billion deposit by Saudi Arabia and US$500 million by Kuwait
February 2005	Assassination of Rafik Hariri	Market intervention
September 2004	Hariri resignation	Market intervention ($2 billion) between October and November
2001	Near-debt crisis	BdL directly buys T-bills issued by government denominated in Lebanese pounds
	Increased dollarisation rate	Increased reserve requirements
	Long dollar speculative positions	Market intervention ($2 billion with $1 billion in February–April 2001)
	IMF 2001 report calls for devaluation of the Lebanese pound	Deposits solicited by Hariri from Arab governments totalling c.$1 billion) $1 billion loan of which $500 million went to boost BdL reserves.
1998	Government crisis	BdL sends strong signals of no intent of devaluation
1997	Speculative activity	BdL market intervention c.$1.5 billion
	First signs of uneasiness of markets given mounting deficit and debt	Saudi and Kuwaiti deposits of $700 million at the BdL
	Hariri plan to raise taxes rejected by government in September	
1995–6	Renewal for President Hrawi	T-bill rates drastically increased
End of 1994	Hariri threat to resign	BdL drastically increased interest rates

Source: compiled by author from various sources and news bulletins

banks in zero-interest T-bills. The total inflows to the Lebanese treasury amounted to more than 50 per cent of the GDP. Investor confidence in the readiness of countries to help Lebanon with such 'bailouts' has led some international traders to dub Lebanon a 'moral hazard' trade (Schimmelpfennig and Gardner, 2008) which further attracted foreign liquidity into investing in Lebanese assets.

In addition to the finance-biased development of the Lebanese economy which provided the main political-economic support for the ERBS programme, vertical and horizontal redistribution played a role in the political economy of the ERBS. The real appreciation of the Lebanese pound increased real wages in Lebanon initially which provided a broad support for the programme. This effect is seen across country experiences. Rudiger Dornbusch said that 'A real appreciation quickly raises real wages in terms of tradables and quickly reduces inflation ... No wonder that overvaluation is a very popular policy. It created a broad short-term political support in Chile for Pinochet, in Argentina ... for Martinez de Hoz, for the Thatcher government ... and for ... Reaganomics' (quoted in Alfaro, 2002: 135). However, early on the governments worked at imposing nominal wage caps to stem unit-labour cost real exchange rate appreciation and to avoid wage-price spirals that would have threatened the ERBS. The successive Hariri governments took an anti-labour stance during the period 1993–1997 aimed at defeating the labour movement through a deliberate strategy of political suppression and manipulation. Baroudi (1998: 549–50) said that 'At no time in Lebanon's history was there more conflict in state–labour relations than ... July 1993–April 1997 ... Hariri was determined to prevent the CGTL from forcing concessions from the government, or becoming an alternative forum, to that of his government, for launching policy initiatives'. In an unprecedented policy, the government in 1995 gave the army a continuous standing order to suppress trade union strikes and demonstrations. The trade unions' activity reached a peak in 1995–1996 with the unions declaring a general strike in 1996 in their attempt to raise minimum wages and halt the continuing rise in indirect taxes. However, the government responded with a heavy-handed approach, sending in the army to break up demonstrations and imposing a curfew in one instance which was another precedent in the history of labour unrest in Lebanon. The increases in nominal wages were seen as a threat to the stabilisation and reconstruction plans of the post-war period. The labour demands were coming in a period when it was obvious to the Hariri government that the financial and resource burdens of reconstruction were weighing heavily on government finances. Such anti-labour measures were also seen as a form of 'socialisation of parts of the reconstruction costs' (Perthes, 1997). In 1997, the government engineered a de facto split in the General Federation of Labour and since then the unions have been marginalised. This marginalisation paved the way for successive governments in the post-1997 period to freeze wages and increase indirect taxes. The minimum wage was frozen from 1996 to 2008 (Figure 3.8) and many indirect taxation measures with severe distributional effects were passed after 1997. The real wage, although increased at the beginning of the ERBS programme due to disinflation and wage adjustments in the years 1994, 1995 and 1996, decreased in the period 1996–2008. The wage share in the GDP was only 35 per cent in 1997 compared with 50–55 per cent before the war.

With respect to horizontal distribution, the sectarian redistribution of political power codified in the Taif accords was also instrumental in maintaining the ERBS. The accords, which ended the civil war in Lebanon, were signed in October 1989 and provided the political and constitutional basis for a new post-conflict consensus between the different sects of Lebanon. It signalled the birth of what came to be known as the 'Second Republic'. The necessities of political reconstruction and the redistributional content of the Taif accords added a political-economic dimension to the nexus of economic policies implemented in the post-war period and the ERBS. The fiscal crisis of the state intensified as a result of the military and security expenditures, demands by regions and sects for resources and the usage of public employment as an instrument of social welfare. The post-war political arrangement represented a way of tackling the problem of *horizontal inequality* that had been a major source of conflict since independence in 1943 and played a major role in the eruption of the civil war. It can also be seen as the 'social contract' that ended the war, which is considered a necessary pre-requisite for the success of reconstruction in post-conflict societies (Addison and Murshed, 2001). The reallocation of political power towards greater representation, especially for the previously marginalised Shiite population, was one of the major achievements of the Taif accords and the Second Republic.[15] Thus distributional conflict was played out in the *sectarian space*. Initially, the necessity of the construction of the state and the transition from the First Republic to the Second Republic in which power is diffused led to enormous expenditures on public employment, the security apparatus and the allocation of public funds to the various sects. This cooperative phase lasted until around 2001. During this period, the political-economic support for the ERBS programme was forged as the sects gained from the huge state expenditures and the ERBS was strongly supported by the main political parties which formed the post-Taif governments.

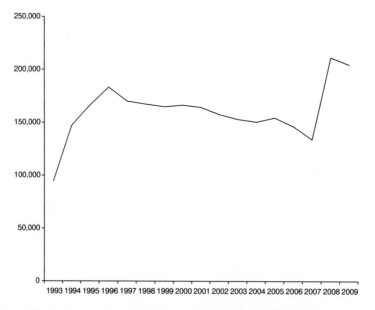

Figure 3.8 Real minimum wage in Lebanon (1993–2009) (LL, 1992 prices)

In effect, the Second Republic reinforced sectarian divisions by focusing reform on power sharing and redistribution rather than the formation of a secular democratic system (Rigby, 2000; Ofeish, 1999; Hudson, 1999). The political settlement of the post-war period not only reflected the outcome of the civil war where Syria and its allies gained the upper hand but also reflected the outcome of shifting demographics and even economic wealth distribution. The influx of capital from the Gulf mainly through Sunni channels was already shifting the sectarian distribution of commercial bank ownership in the 1980s. Henry (1987) provides evidence that shows that in 1974 Christians controlled 62 per cent of the total capital of the top 15 banks while Muslims controlled 18 per cent, but by 1982 the ownership structure had changed to 32 per cent Christian versus 33 per cent for Muslims. Although there is no evidence on ownership shares by the end of the civil war and during the reconstruction period, it is highly probable that such a trend continued. Moreover, the incursion of Muslims into wealth spaces traditionally held by Christians was also extended to the commercial and service sector. The sectarian distribution of state funds that took outright and open channels included the Shiite-dominated Council of the South, the Druze-dominated Fund for the Displaced and the Sunni-dominated Greater Beirut Public Works Council which was later disbanded under the Lahoud regime with its functions relegated to the Council for Development and Reconstruction (CDR).[16]. The amounts disbursed in the period 1993 to 2004 reached around $850 million for the Council of the South and around $1.2 billion for the Displaced Fund.

In effect, the consociational democracy in Lebanon broke the possible relation between the exchange rate policy and popular pressure and electoral politics. Blomberg *et al.* (2005) have shown, using the experience of Latin American countries with exchange rate regimes, that social interests and electoral pressures play a role in the political economy of such arrangements. They found that governments are more likely to abandon the fixed exchange rate after elections, when the currency peg is misaligned due to appreciation and when the manufacturing sector is strong. In contrast, the currency peg in Lebanon has become a 'constitutionalist' institution that is immune from day-to-day political pressures as a result of a political process where the banking sector is the 'median voter' that decides on the composition of debt and interest rates.[17] This median voter influence was demonstrated by the push by the commercial banks towards a more equal composition of debt in Lebanon between US dollar- and Lebanese pound-denominated debt from the process of conversion in 1998, as the probability of collapse of the ERBS increased in the period post-2000. Moreover, the 'median voter' status of the commercial banks in the consociational democratic system of Lebanon allowed the rentier share of the GDP to rise, as was shown earlier, from 5.1 per cent to around 10 per cent in a very short time period, without any political and social fallout. In contrast, a study on the implications of stock price growth in the 1990s by Fair (2000) showed that a continued boom in stock prices for an additional 10 years would mean a growth of earnings that would cause the after-tax corporate profits to GDP ratio to grow from 5.7 per cent to 11.9 per cent which he said 'seems highly unlikely it would occur. Constraints on reaching this ratio would arise from social, political and economic forces. In short, the macroeconomic implication of the earnings growth rate implicit in the current level of stock prices seems unrealistic' (2000: 9).

5 Conclusion

The failure of ERBS programmes around the world has raised many doubts concerning the viability and optimality of such programmes. The experience of Lebanon suggests that a convergence of political-economic interests can maintain such programmes despite their dire record in terms of lost output, loss of competitiveness, and negative distributional and welfare costs. This chapter has shown that the commercial banks' and the state's overlapping interests formed the main source of stability of the currency. High profits of the banking sector and the high rentier income share formed the material basis for this broad political-economic support for the policies conducted by the central bank, which created in the long run a finance-biased post-war economy. The commercial banks remained resilient in this political-economic nexus throughout the different stages of the ERBS.

In addition, a significant role was played at later stages of the ERBS time-line by international donors that held the Paris II and Paris III international conferences in support of Lebanon's finances in 2002 and 2007 respectively. These bailout plans came at crucial times to support Lebanon's ERBS programme: Paris II after the increased threat of currency crisis in the period after 2001 and Paris III after the July 2006 war with Israel. The anti-labour stance of successive Lebanese governments and the marginalisation of the labour movement that enhanced the ability of the state to impose a nominal wage freeze in Lebanon, which lasted from 1996 to 2008, was instrumental in the success of the programme and the stemming of a potential wage–price dynamic that would have put the stabilisation programme in jeopardy. The consociational democratic system in Lebanon also played a role in forming a wedge between potential political pressures for a change in policy and the choice of the exchange rate regime, making the commercial banks the median voter in such a system.

The programme's resilience is up against serious tests in the near future: the global financial and economic crisis threatening the inflow of funds into Lebanon promised in Paris III, the return to explosive debt dynamics and widening budget deficits, exchange rate appreciation and real shocks. Most importantly, the viability of the 'macrofinancial system' is dependent on the continuous growth in commercial banks' deposits that are needed to finance the government's deficits and the continuous rolling over of public debt. All these factors may lead to a brittle commercial banks–state nexus that will threaten the sustainability of the currency peg.

Notes

1　In addition, the predominance of the service sector and the import trade sector (which benefited from currency appreciation and the ensuing consumption boom) formed a supporting element to the political-economy nexus of the state–banks relationship.

2　Calvo and Mishkin (2003) have argued that the choice of an optimal exchange rate regime for emerging countries is a mirage. There is no guarantee that any type of arrangement whether fixed, floating or soft peg would produce optimal results at all times. The eventual outcome of policy choices depends on institutional arrangements guaranteeing fiscal, financial and monetary stability. However, they also show that under certain circumstances the choice of the exchange rate matters. For example, in countries with high liability dollarisation, policymakers cannot allow the exchange rate to depreciate because this leads to a generalised financial collapse as borrowers default on their foreign currency liabilities.

3　The Asian and Russian crises in 1997–8 had ripple effects through the world economy, especially in emerging markets, as portfolio investment in these economies dried up and countries were forced to tighten monetary policy in order to defend their exchange rates. Brazil experienced serious capital flight and depletion of international reserves which led to interest rate hikes in defence of the currency, with detrimental effects on public debt evolution, and to the subsequent abandonment of the Real Plan, an ERBS programme in effect since 1994 (Amman and Baer, 2003).

4　See Dibeh (2008) for model and details.

5　Addison and Murshed (2001) have considered various possible outcomes for post-war economies in terms of the relative output of agriculture and services sectors. A relative price shift in favour of services can cause the economy to be service-biased and hence growth will be less likely to be poverty reducing.

6　I have argued elsewhere (Dibeh, 2002) that the Lebanese political-economic structure has passed through three regimes since the inception of the BdL in 1964. The first regime (1964–1971) was dominated by financial interests and hence monetary policy was anti-inflationary. The second regime (1971–1979) witnessed an industrial-financial interest convergence that supported a moderately loose monetary policy. However, this political-economic structure finally collapsed in the 1980s under the pressure of inflationary state finance, under-utilisation of capacity in industry, and the relative rigidity of wages. This old structure gave way to a new political economic regime that still prevails today. In the post-1984 period, monetary policy became more in favour of currency depreciation and inflation with the purpose of lowering the value of real wages and increasing seigniorage. This policy was both the cause and the result of a new political economic structure characterised by a burgeoning export-oriented industry; speculative and dollarised finance; and a fiscal and political crisis of the state. Moreover, the BdL lost its traditional relative independence from the political authorities to become more accommodating of state finances in the 1980s. This political-economic structure remained dominant until 1992.

7　In the post-2005 period after the assassination of ex-prime minister Hariri, two developments supported the ERBS programme in addition to this political-economic nexus. First, the political deadlock in the country led to a de facto fiscal adjustment as no budgets were passed for 5 years. This led the GDP-to-debt ratio to decline from its peak in 2006 of 180 per cent due to successive primary surpluses up until 2009. Second, the appreciation of the euro vis-à-vis the US dollar led to the arrest of the real appreciation of the Lebanese pound which was pegged to the US dollar.

8　The banking sector in this respect initially played a positive role in the post-war period as it provided the main source of capital to the economy, given the low level of national savings (Gressani and Page, 1999).

9　In Henry's iterated prisoner dilemma model, commercial banks would roll over debt if $p > \dfrac{r}{(1+i)(1-d)}$

where p = probability of repayment, r = discount rate (or opportunity cost of capital), i = interest rate on debt and d = expected depreciation rate. In the post-war period, p was high, r was low, i was high and d was low, all factors that ensure the above inequality.

10 The commercial banks' ability to continue financing the government since 1993 has been supported by the interest rate spread that attracted depositors and the existence of what Poddar *et al.* (2006: 4) called an 'ostensibly committed Diaspora.'Finger and Hesse (2009) stated that there is anecdotal evidence on the wealth deposits by the Lebanese Diaspora in the commercial banking system. They actually show some correlation between deposit growth and real GDP growth in GCC countries, the main region where Lebanese emigrants are. Poddar *et al.* (2006) showed that this 'home-bias' effect led to a less than one for one pass-through from foreign interest rates to local interest rates.

11 Central banks can increase rentier income in the economy by raising real interest rates and lowering inflation (Epstein, 2001) and in the 1980s and 1990s there was a secular rise in the GDP share of rentier income in many industrialised countries (Epstein and Power, 2003).

12 Epstein and Power (2003) have shown that in many semi-industrialised countries such as Mexico and Turkey, financial crisis caused rentier income to decrease.

13 One reason Hakim and Andary (1997) give for high interest rates during this period is the auction mechanism adopted by the central bank. The auction shielded the market from competition by foreign investors by committing to fulfil all foreign demand for T-bills regardless of size or interest rate even if such a demand exceeded the financing needs of the government.

14 Such fiscal behaviour is in accordance with the role of foreign aid in affecting the fiscal stance of governments in the developing world and in post-conflict societies as identified by McGillivray and Morissey (2004).

15 The question of horizontal inequality among different groups in culturally diverse societies has been largely neglected in the development literature. Stewart (2000) considers that horizontal inequality should be as important as vertical inequality in the design of development policies because such multidimensional inequality that encompasses economic, political and social differentiation can have severe consequences on individual and social welfare.

16 Even the CDR was seen by many as dominated by Sunnis (Hudson, 1999). The CDR was, until the Hoss government came to power in 1998, a haven for Hariri loyalists.

17 The argument that an independent monetary policy that is free from daily political pressures is a form of 'constitutionalism' is advanced by Drazen (2002), who argues that it is as compatible with democracy as other forms of constitutionalist measures. See also Drazen (1996) for the political economy of debt composition.

References

Addison, T., and Murshed, S.M. (2001), 'From conflict to reconstruction: reviving the social contract'. WIDER Discussion Paper 2001/48.

Addison, T., Geda, A., Le Billon, P., and Murshed, S.M. (2001), 'Financial reconstruction in conflict and 'post-conflict' economies,' WIDER Discussion Paper 2001/90.

Alfaro, L. (2002), 'On the political economy of temporary stabilisation programmes.' *Economics and Politics*, 14(2): 133–161.

Amman, E., and Baer, W. (2003), 'Anchors away; the cost and benefits of Brazil's devaluation,' *World Development*, 31 (6): 1033–1046.

AUDI (2004), *AUDI Bank Country and Market Update 2004.* www.audi.com.lb.

Baroudi, S. (1998), 'Economic conflict in postwar Lebanon: state–labour relations between 1992 and 1997', *Middle East Journal*, 52(4): 531–550.

Berthélemy, J.C., Dessus, S., and Nahas, C. (2007), 'Exploring Lebanon's growth prospects,' World Bank Policy Research working paper 4332.

Bhattacharya, R. (2003), 'Exchange rate regime considerations for Jordan and Lebanon,' IMF working paper 03/137.

Blomberg, S., Frieden, J., and Stein, E. (2005), 'Sustaining fixed rates: the political economy of currency pegs in Latin America', *Journal of Applied Economics*, 8(2): 203–225.

Bolbol, A. (1999), 'Seigniorage, dollarisation and public debt: the Lebanese civil war and recovery experience, 1982–1997'. *World Development*, 27(10): 1861–1873.

Calvo, G., and Mishkin, F. (2003), 'The mirage of exchange rate regimes for emerging market countries', *Journal of Economic Perspectives*, 17(4): 99–118.

Calvo, G. and Reinhart, C. (2002), 'Fear of floating', *Quarterly Journal of Economics*, 117(2): 379–408.

Calvo, G., and Vegh, C. (1995), 'Fighting inflation with high interest rates: the small open economy case under flexible prices', *Journal of Money, Credit and Banking*, 27(1): 49–66.

di Giovanni, J., and Gardner, E. (2008), 'A simple stochastic approach to debt sustainability applied to Lebanon', IMF working paper 08/97.

Dibeh, G. (2002), 'The political economy of inflation and currency depreciation in Lebanon: 1984–1992', *Middle Eastern Studies*, 38(1): 33–52.

——(2008), 'The business cycle in postwar Lebanon', *Journal of International Development* 20(2): 145–160.

——(2010), 'Foreign aid and economic development in post-war Lebanon', in *Foreign Aid for Development: Issues, Challenges, and the New Agenda*, G. Mavrotas (ed.), Oxford University Press.

Drazen, A. (1996), 'Towards a political-economic theory of domestic debt', Paper prepared for the IEA-Deutsche Bundesbank conference, 'The Debt Burden and Its Consequences for Monetary Policy,' Frankfurt, March 20–23, 1996.

——(2000), *Political Economy in Macroeconomics*. NJ: Princeton University Press.

——(2002), 'Central bank independence, democracy and dollarisation,' *Journal of Applied Econometrics*, 5(1): 1–17.

Eichengreen, B., and Leblang, E. (2003), 'Exchange rates and cohesion: historical perspectives and political economy considerations', *Journal of Common Market Studies* 41(5): 797–822.

Eken, S., and Helbling, T. (eds) (1999), 'Back to the future: postwar reconstruction and stabilisation in Lebanon', IMF Occasional Paper 176.

Epstein, G. (1992), 'Political economy and competitive central banking'. *Review of Radical Political Economics*, 24(1): 1–30.

——(2001) 'Financialization, rentier interests, and central bank policy,' paper presented at Political Economy Research Institute (PERI) Conference on 'Financialization of the World Economy', December 7–8, 2001, University of Massachusetts.

Epstein, G., and Power, D. (2003), 'Rentier incomes and financial crises: an empirical examination of trends and cycles in some OECD countries', Political Economy Research Institute (PERI) working paper No. 57.

Fair, R. (2000), 'Fed policy and the effects of a stock market crash on the economy,' *Business Economics*, April: 7–14.

Finger, H., and Hesse, H. (2009), 'Lebanon – determinants of commercial bank deposits in a regional financial center,' IMF working paper 09/195.

Froyen, R. and Waud, R. (2002), 'The Determinants of Federal Reserve Policy Action: A Re-examination', *Journal of Macroeconomics*, 24: 413–428.

Gressani, D., and Page, J. (1999), 'Reconstruction in Lebanon: challenges for macro-economic management', *MENA Working Paper Series* 16, World Bank: Washington DC.

Hakim, S., and Andary, S. (1997), 'The Lebanese Central bank and the treasury bills market', *Middle East Journal*, 51: 230–248.

Henry C. M. (1987), 'Prisoners' financial dilemma: a consociational future for Lebanon?,' *American Political Science Review*, 81 (1): 201–218.

Hudson, M. (1999), 'Lebanon after Ta'if: another reform opportunity lost', *Arab Studies Quarterly*, 21(1): 27–40.

IMF (2004), 'Debt-related vulnerabilities and financial crises – an application of the balance sheet approach to emerging market countries', *Policy Development and Review Department Paper*, available at http://www.imf.org/external/np/pdr/bal/2004/eng/070104.pdf.

Keynes, J. (1963), *Essays in Persuasion*. New York: Norton.

Kiguel, M., and Liviatan, N. (1992), 'The business cycle associated with exchange rate-based stabilisation,' *World Bank Economic Review*, 6(2): 279–305.

Krugman, P. (2000), 'Crises: the price of globalisation?', in Federal Reserve Bank of Kansas City, *Global Economic Integration: Opportunities and Challenges*.

Licandro, J.A. (2001), 'The scope for inflation targeting in Uruguay,' paper presented at LACEA Winter Camp, July 15–18, 2001, Santiago de Chile.

Manasse, P., and Roubini, N. (2005), '"Rules of thumb" for sovereign debt crises,' IMF working paper 05/42.

Maxfield, S. (1998), *Gatekeepers of Growth: The International Political Economy of Central Banking in Developing Countries*. Princeton: Princeton University Press.

McGillivray, M., and Morissey, O. (2004), 'Fiscal effects of aid,' in T. Addison and A. Roe (eds), *Fiscal Policy for Development: Poverty, Reconstruction and Growth*. New York: Palgrave Macmillan for UNU-WIDER.

Miles, W. (2003), 'Fixed exchange rates and sticky prices in emerging markets', *Journal of International Development*, 15: 575–586.

Ofeish, S. (1999), 'Lebanon's Second Republic: secular talk, sectarian application', *Arab Studies Quarterly*, 21(1): 97–116.

Perthes, V. (1997), 'Myths and money. Four years of Hariri', *Middle East Report*, 27(2): 19.

Peters, D., Raad, E., and Sinkey, J. (2004), 'The performance of banks in post-war Lebanon', *International Journal of Business*, 9(3): 259–286.

Poddar, T., Goswami, M., Sole, J., and Icaza, V. (2006), 'Interest rate determination in Lebanon', IMF working paper 06/94.

Posen, A. (1993), 'Why central bank independence does not cause low inflation: there is no institutional fix for politics,' in R O'Brien (ed.), *Finance and the International Economy*. Oxford: OUP.

——(1995), 'Declarations are not enough: financial sector sources of central bank independence,' *NBER Macroeconomics Annual 1995*, (eds.) B. Bernanke and J. Rotemberg, pp. 253–274.

Rebelo, S., and Vegh, C. (1995), 'Real effects of exchange-rate based stabilisation,' *NBER Macroeconomics Annual 1995*, (eds.) B. Bernanke and J. Rotemberg, pp. 125–174.

Reinhart, C., and Vegh, C. (1999), 'Do exchange rate-based stabilisations carry the seeds of their own destruction?', MPRA Paper no. 8592.

Reinhart, C., Rogoff, K., and Savastano, M. (2003), 'Debt intolerance,' *Brookings Papers on Economic Activity*, 1: 1–62.

Rigby, A. (2000), 'Lebanon: patterns of confessional politics', *Parliamentary Affairs*, 53(1): 169–180.

Roubini, N., and Setser, B. (2004), *Bailouts or Bail-ins? Responding to Financial Crises in Emerging Economies.* Peterson Institute of International Economics.

Schimmelpfennig, A., and Gardner, E. (2008), 'Lebanon – weathering the perfect storms,' IMF working paper 08/17.

Stewart, F. (2000), *Horizontal Inequalities: A Neglected Dimension of Development.* WIDER Annual Lectures 5. Helsinki UNU/WIDER Publications.

4 The evolution of the monetary policy framework in Egypt and the elusive goal of price stability

Hoda Selim

1 Introduction

The reorientation of monetary policy in Egypt towards price stability came with the adoption of the Economic Reform and Structural Adjustment Programme (ERSAP) in 1991. Key elements of the reform included a large fiscal adjustment, an exchange rate anchor supported by a tight monetary policy and structural reforms including some price liberalisation. Yet, in pursuit of this goal, monetary policy was overburdened with inconsistent objectives including the short-term stimulation of output, exchange rate stability, financing the fiscal deficit and preserving the solvency of the banking system. Naturally, monetary policy was not always successful in maintaining low inflation, particularly since the announcement of the float in mid-FY03.[1] Since then, double-digit inflation has spiked three times, peaking in July 2008 at a 20-year high of 22 per cent.

These recent developments have brought to the forefront the issue of price stability. They have also triggered changes in the management of monetary policy. For instance, the Central Bank of Egypt (CBE)'s decision in 2005 to adopt inflation targeting (IT) in the medium-term placed a more formal emphasis on price stability as a medium-term objective of monetary policy and also entailed modifications in intermediate targets and policy instruments.

This chapter explains the role of the Egyptian monetary policy framework in preserving price stability. It is divided into three main sections. The next section analytically reviews the evolution of its long-term objectives, intermediate goals and policy instruments since the 1970s.[2] Section 3 presents various explanations for the rise in inflation in Egypt. Section 4 discusses the prospects for the future evolution of the framework. Section 5 concludes.

2 The monetary policy framework

The macroeconomic background

Throughout the 1960s and early 1970s, the Egyptian economy relied on central planning and had an inward-looking trade regime geared towards import-substitution. It was marked by heavy government interventions in the investment and pricing system, which allowed Egypt to enjoy a moderate inflation rate of 3.9 per cent on average (El-Sakka and Ghali, 2005). With the open-door policy in 1974, the economy became more open to investment inflows and migrants' remittances. And while this stimulated short-term growth, it was associated with deepening inflationary pressures, which were compounded by a rise in international oil prices. Moreover, the public sector dominated the key productive sectors and a wide array of administered prices (subsidies increased from LE (Egyptian pounds) 9 million in the early 1960s to around LE 2 billion in FY82)[3] served as instruments of price control. These subsidies allowed an artificial curbing of inflation, but they also distorted markets, undermined the efficient allocation of investment and overburdened the government budget.

In the latter half of the 1980s, the decline in oil prices, a main source of foreign exchange, was followed by a sharp decline in investment, a slowdown in growth, an increase in unemployment, a widening of the balance of payments deficit and massive foreign debt accumulation. In addition, monetisation of the fiscal deficit resulted in inflation.

A first effort at macroeconomic reform came with the adoption of the ERSAP in 1991. The first phase of reforms helped to shift the economy partly from central planning towards market-based mechanisms, more trade openness and a more leading role for the private sector. At the heart of the stabilisation package was a large fiscal adjustment that brought the fiscal deficit down from 17.5 per cent to 3.6 per cent of GDP between FY91 and FY00. This phase also involved partial price liberalisation (including agricultural prices),[4] the introduction of a competitive exchange rate, the liberalisation of interest rates and the removal of limits on lending to the private and public sectors (Subramanian, 1997). The second phase witnessed the privatisation of some public enterprises but not the financial sector, which could have contributed to a more efficient mobilisation of savings and allocation of credit (Al-Mashat and Grigorian, 1998).

As a result, GDP grew at an average rate of almost 5 per cent between FY94 and FY00, with a peak of 6.1 per cent in FY00 (from 2.8 per cent in FY91–FY93). Yet, this robust economic performance was interrupted as a result of sluggish reform efforts and the combined effect of a series of external shocks since 1997: the East Asian crisis, the sharp decline in oil prices, falling tourism revenues (a main source of foreign currency), the September 11 attacks, the slowdown of world trade in 2001 and regional conflict. Moreover, the slowdown was prolonged by a shortage of foreign currency, which was not accompanied by appropriate and timely economic policies. As a result, economic growth fell to around 2.4 per cent in FY03.

The advent of a more reformist government in FY05 embarked Egypt on a second wave of reforms involving stabilising the exchange rate, rationalising the tariff structure, drastic cuts in income tax rates and a streamlining of tax administration – yielding a smaller budget deficit – and efforts to promote the private sector. These supportive macroeconomic policies coupled with an improved external environment have contributed to higher broad-based growth (between 6 and 7 per cent between FY05 and FY08 from an average of 3 per cent in FY01–FY03). Large FDI inflows (8.1 per cent of GDP in FY08) were accompanied by a rapid credit expansion, leading to an investment boom. The privatisation programme gained momentum and was extended to the banking sector. However, the rise in inflation (to 23 per cent in August 2008) has been the government's biggest challenge.

The following section aims to provide a comprehensive analysis of the management of monetary policy in Egypt. It also takes stock of recent reforms that have not been analysed yet, and reviews the role of the exchange rate which is an important component of monetary policy as well as the inflation performance. Previous work on monetary policy management is outdated (Dailami and Dinh, 1991; Dinh and Giugale, 1991; Abou El-Eyoun, 2003), focused on specific issues related to monetary policy such as the liquidity issue (El-Refaie, 2000) or the transmission mechanism (Al-Mashat and Billmeier, 2008), or provided only brief reviews about the conduct of monetary policy (Moursi, El Mossallamy, and Zakareya, 2007; Noureldin 2005a).

Objectives, intermediate targets and instruments

Monetary policy management went through three phases. During the first phase (1974–1990), direct credit control measures such as the administrative setting of interest rates and credit ceilings were used to provide seigniorage revenues for the government and subsidised debt to public enterprises (Dailami and Dinh, 1991). The second phase (1991–2003) witnessed the first attempt to address the inconsistencies in the monetary policy framework, within the adoption of the ERSAP in 1991. The last phase (2003–) began with the announcement of the float of the Egyptian pound and has witnessed the implementation of several reforms that helped stabilise the exchange rate. The CBE also announced in June 2005 its intention to put in place a formal inflation targeting framework 'once the fundamental prerequisites are met' (CBE, 2005).[5]

Objectives

Before 2003, monetary policy lacked specific objectives that were clearly defined, either through legislation or otherwise. A central banking law already existed in 1975, but identified general objectives such as the regulation of money and credit policies to achieve broader economic development goals (Abou El-Eyoun, 2003). The adoption of the ERSAP in 1991 entailed the (implicit) redefinition of monetary policy objectives towards disinflation, even though the law remained unchanged. It is only with the issue of the Banking Law in 2003 that monetary policy became formally geared towards achieving price stability. The Law stipulates that the 'Central Bank shall work on realising price stability and banking soundness, within the context of the general economic policy of the State'. This objective is also stressed in all CBE annual reports. However, there is no mention of a numerical objective for inflation. And while the Law refrained from citing real objectives (output and employment), CBE reports mention that low inflation should 'maintain high rates of investment and economic growth' (CBE, 2004/2005).

The absence of a clear set of objectives between 1974 and 2003 may explain the poor inflation performance. In the absence of an effective credit policy between 1974 and 1990, monetary policy had lost much of its traditional role; it was used to provide seigniorage revenues to the government and to maintain low interest rates so as to provide cheap borrowing to both 'state-owned' banks (a main source of financing of the deficit) and public enterprises. Instead, the fiscal deficit (which averaged around 21.8 per cent of GDP)[6] was an important tool of economic management.

Between FY93 and FY97, monetary policy often hesitated between low inflation (requiring a contractionary policy) and the short-term stimulation of output (requiring a reduction of the interest rate on the Egyptian pound) (Moursi *et al.* 2007). It was also encumbered with maintaining the solvency of a poorly regulated banking system. In the 1980s, the banks were indebted to the large and inefficient public sector enterprises and in the 1990s they were indebted to uncreditworthy large businessmen, who were unable to repay their loans.

Exchange rate policy was also often at odds with the aim of low inflation. An 'impossible trinity' occurred following increased capital inflows in the late 1970s (Kamar, 2005) and during the liquidity crunch of the late 1990s (Noureldin, 2005a). During this latter period, monetary policy seemed to confuse exchange rate stability, an intermediate target, with the longer-term objective of price stability. Pressure on the nominal exchange rate arose from three different sources from 2000 including (i) the external shocks of the late 1990s which provoked significant capital flight (Abou El-Eyoun, 2003), (ii) a foreign currency liquidity shortage in the banking sector, and (iii) the implementation of major infrastructure projects resulting in a growing fiscal deficit which in turn contributed to the drying up of liquidity.[7] Instead of relaxing the exchange rate regime, monetary policy started to defend a rate that was moving further and further away from its market value. In the end, it achieved neither exchange rate stability nor low inflation (Figure 4.1). More recently, CBE concern over pressures for the appreciation of the exchange rate in a context of rising inflation since FY07 placed the two objectives in conflict. Higher interest rates, which were necessary to control inflation, continued to attract foreign inflows and exacerbated the upward pressure on the exchange rate.

Obviously, the 2003 law did not prevent monetary policy from pursuing other objectives at the expense of price stability.

Intermediate targets

Except for the period FY91–FY03, Egyptian monetary policy lacked an explicit intermediate target. This was not surprising given that it did not have well-defined objectives before then. Because Egypt had had a fixed peg to the US dollar since the 1960s, it can be argued that maintaining the peg has been an *implicit* objective throughout the 1980s. However, the exchange rate is unlikely to have served as

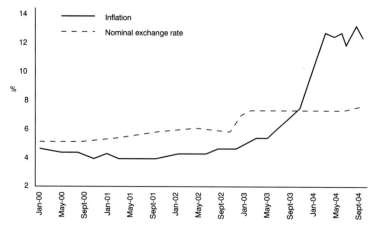

Figure 4.1 CPI inflation and the exchange rate, 2000–2004

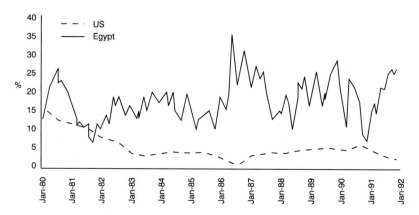

Figure 4.2 CPI inflation in Egypt and the US, 1980–1992

an anchor for inflation expectations, given that it was a multiple exchange rate system including a sizable black market (Figure 4.2).[8]

With the adoption of the ERSAP, Egypt adopted a 'conventional fixed peg arrangement', which was maintained between 1991 and 2000. And while there was no scope for an independent domestic monetary policy, the peg provided a credible and explicit nominal anchor that facilitated the reduction of both inflation and inflation expectations (Figure 4.3). The peg was supported by a tight monetary stance between the mid-1990s and 2000, to dampen the expansionary impact of capital inflows (ERF and IM, 2004). While the peg officially remained until 2003, it started to experience serious problems in the late 1990s. Moderate depreciations were introduced between May and December 2000. But as the pressures did not subside, the peg went through a series of step devaluations between 2000 and 2002 that ended with the announcement of the float in January 2003.

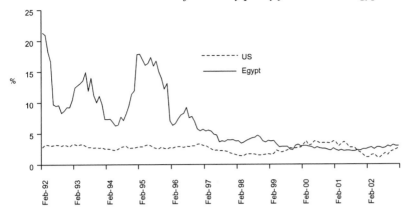

Figure 4.3 CPI inflation in Egypt and the US, 1992–2002

Since then, there has been no explicit nominal anchor for monetary policy. It is thus difficult to determine what intermediate target the CBE is using to anchor private inflation expectations. However, the CBE has fluctuated between the implicit targeting of several variables including monetary growth, the exchange rate and inflation. Up to the early 2000s, CBE reports mentioned ex-post annual targets for money growth (in the 10–11 per cent range). However, as increasing FDI inflows from FY05 significantly fuelled high money growth, it became difficult to stick to the targeted rates. More recently, and despite the *de jure* float, the exchange rate remained surprisingly stable despite strong capital inflows, between mid-FY05 and FY08. Meanwhile, it has also been claimed that monetary policy had an implicit inflation target of around 6–8 per cent (IMF, 2007). However, the multiple shocks witnessed recently again pushed inflation beyond this range into the double-digit level.

If the CBE adopted an IT framework as announced, it would have to relinquish control of both money growth and the exchange rate to give priority to achieving its inflation target.

Instruments

As in many emerging market economies (EMEs), the transition from a centrally planned to a more market-based economy in Egypt shifted monetary policy instruments from direct to indirect measures. Between 1975 and 1990, the CBE set nominal interest rates at low levels, which often generated negative real interest rates (Dailami and Dinh, 1991). Naturally, this interest rate structure did not have a significant impact on the growth of credit (Abou El-Eyoun, 2003; Noureldin, 2005a) (Figure 4.4). This situation was essential to maintain both the fiscal position and the solvency of the banking sector (Dailami and Dinh, 1991).

In addition, the negative real interest rates in the late 1980s had created a greater incentive to borrow than to hold deposits, resulting in strong excess demand in the credit market, which prompted the CBE to resort to a rigid system of credit rationing (Dailami and Dinh, 1991). A fixed loan-to-deposit ratio (around 60–65

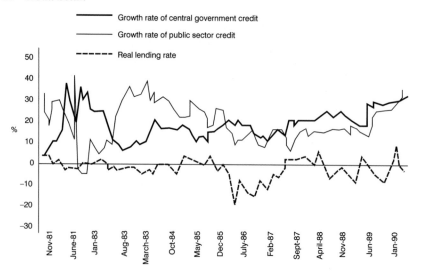

Figure 4.4 Growth of credit, 1981–1990

per cent in the late 1980s) was applied to each bank and supplemented by sub-ceilings for loans and advances. Reserve requirements (set at 25 per cent since 1979)[9] served only to provide a basis for the inflation tax used to finance the government deficit.

With the introduction of the ERSAP, reserve requirements on local currency deposits were lowered from 25 to 15 per cent in 1991 and further to 14 per cent in 2001, but they remain higher than the 10 per cent of the Basel agreement (Kamar, 2005). El-Refaie (2002: 316) argues that this was not 'an active monetary instrument in affecting domestic liquidity because liquidity growth was too fast for a reserve requirement adjustment to accommodate'. Reserve requirements on deposits in foreign currency (around 14 per cent) also existed.

The most remarkable changes in the 1990s were the liberalisation of interest rates, the abolition of credit ceilings and the introduction of indirect measures to manage liquidity (open market operations, OMOs). The latter became a major indirect instrument after 1997. They involved the sale of 3-month Treasury Bills to absorb excess liquidity resulting from foreign exchange sales designed to offset capital inflows and to support the exchange rate. But most importantly they provided a non-inflationary means of financing the budget deficit. The government set the T-bills rate high and positive in real terms at the beginning of the reform programme, gradually reduced it over the following years but raised it again in 2002 (Kamar, 2005).

Between FY98 and FY01, the CBE made increasing use of an alternative instrument, repurchase operations on Treasury Bills (repos), to provide liquidity and to stimulate economic growth. In FY04 reverse repos of Treasury Bills and certificates of deposit, with maturities spanning up to one year, were introduced and in August 2005 CBE notes with maturities of over one to two years. Since

FY04, the CBE has permitted outright sales of Treasury Bills (and also of other instruments) to banks through the market mechanism (Moursi *et al.*, 2007).

In addition, the discount rate was the key policy rate up to 2005. In an attempt to reduce its rigidity, it was set at two percentage points above the three-month T-bills rate, which was determined through an auction (Abdel Khalek, 2001). At first, the two rates moved together but from 1995, the discount rate ceased to respond to changes in the T-bills rate (Abou El-Eyoun, 2003) (Figure 4.5).

An overnight domestic currency interbank market was created in 2001 but it was thin and shallow, which rendered the interbank rate volatile. Moreover, between 1996 and 2005, the CBE also used banks' excess reserves as a daily operational target which was very volatile (Al-Mashat and Billmeier, 2008).[10]

Despite the liberalisation of interest rates, their use and effectiveness were limited before 2005. This is because none of the existing policy rates could be relied upon to identify the monetary policy stance, especially because their changes were not passed through into commercial banks' rates. Thus the weak banking sector and the lack of transparency about interest rate decisions prevented policy decisions from being transmitted to the real economy.

With the second wave of monetary reforms, the CBE shifted from the use of quantitative instruments to price instruments with the introduction in June 2005 of interest rates on two CBE standing facilities, the overnight deposit and lending policy rates. In addition, a Monetary Policy Committee (MPC) – affiliated to the CBE Board of Directors – was established to revise the rates every six weeks. By setting these rates, the CBE determines the corridor within which the overnight rate can fluctuate. The overnight deposit and lending rates were set at 9.5 and 12.5 per cent respectively in June 2005. Following the easing of inflationary pressures in the beginning of FY06 (by around 4 per cent), a more relaxed stance was adopted as they were reduced several times. In September and October 2005, the overnight deposit and lending rates were reduced by 50 and 150 basis points (bps) respectively. They underwent further reductions (each

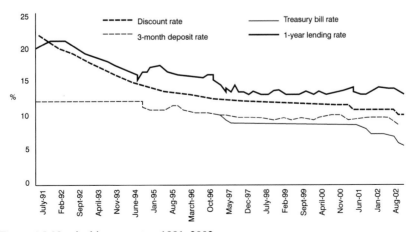

Figure 4.5 Nominal interest rates, 1991–2002

by 25 bps) in December 2005, February 2006 and April 2006, to reach 8 and 10 per cent respectively. Despite the acceleration of inflation since March 2006 (to 12 per cent in October of the same year following some partial liberalisation of administered prices), monetary policy remained inactive and was tightened only in November 2006 (by 50 bps) and December 2006 (by 25 bps). However, the stance of monetary policy was accommodating since real interest rates were negative and declining (Figure 4.6). With inflationary pressures fading after March 2007, the policy rates remained at 8.75 and 10.75 per cent, respectively. But as inflation surged again from January 2008, following the increase in international food prices, the CBE tightened monetary policy six consecutive times (by a cumulative 275 bps) between February and September 2008, so that the policy rates reached 13.5 and 11.5 per cent, respectively. But the CBE was still maintaining an expansionary stance since real overnight deposit rates remained negative and declined from –1.75 per cent in January 2008 to –9.6 per cent in September 2008. Following the global slowdown in 2009, the CBE embarked on a loosening cycle to accommodate domestic growth concerns. Overnight deposit and lending rates were reduced 6 times (by 325 and 375 bps to reach 8.25 and 9.75 per cent respectively) between February and September 2009. As inflation remains high, real rates remain negative.

Even after the introduction of these policy rates, policy tightening often occurred too late in the aftermath of shocks and was not sufficient in the face of mounting inflation. Also, decisions about short-term interest rates were not transmitted to longer-term rates (which are more relevant for investment decisions) because of excess liquidity in the banking system, illiquid secondary debt markets, and so on.

Exchange rate management

Egypt kept its currency pegged to the US dollar (US$) for over 40 years, from the 1960s until FY03. It is thus only natural for the exchange rate to remain an important component of monetary policy as well as the focus of the expectations

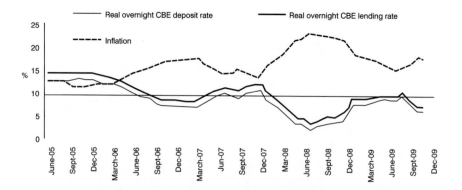

Figure 4.6 Real policy interest rates and inflation, 2005–2009

of the public. As long as Egypt was a closed economy, it was easy to maintain the peg. With greater trade openness and global financial integration, it became more difficult to do so. And with each increase in openness, Egypt had to introduce more flexibility in its exchange rate system.

From the 1960s, Egypt had a 'fixed but adjustable peg' to the US dollar, combined with foreign exchange controls. Efforts to streamline the exchange rate prior to the ERSAP were unsuccessful in unifying the exchange rate system (Abdel Khalek, 2001). By the end of the 1980s, the over-valued exchange rate had led to the emergence of an active black market. With the adoption of the ERSAP, the multiple exchange rate system was replaced by two exchange markets (a primary restricted market and a secondary free market) which were later unified (ERF and IM, 2004), following which the exchange rate was stabilised and maintained within an implicit band at around US$ 1 = LE 3.33. Sterilised intervention was successful and the nominal exchange rate remained stable between 1991 and 2000.

In spite of the pressures on the exchange rate resulting from the adverse external shocks and the domestic liquidity crunch, the initial CBE response was slow and limited, with insufficient release of foreign reserves. Hoping that the pressures on the current account were only temporary, the authorities introduced in 1998, through a 'gentlemen's agreement' with the banks, tighter import requirements (100 per cent local currency cash cover for import credits). But these measures were ineffective in eliminating the shortages of foreign currency, which continued to occur periodically. This caused a credibility problem and public expectations of a devaluation encouraged dollarisation, both within the Egyptian banking system and abroad. To defend a non-equilibrium peg, the CBE started to draw heavily and continuously on its reserves. This led to a significant loss of around US$ 6.2 billion in 3 years, with reserves falling to US$ 13.8 billion in January 2001 from US$ 20 billion in November 1998.

After some nine months of depreciation, a first devaluation occurred in January 2001. But the pressure on the nominal exchange rate did not subside, for several reasons. The first is that the devaluation – even though badly needed – happened too late. The public had already lost credibility in the monetary authorities, which led to a worsening of private expectations about the exchange rate. The second is that the devaluation still did not reflect the real value of the Egyptian pound, as evidenced by the re-emergence of a black foreign exchange market from January 2001. As a result, the exchange rate depreciated several times up to June 2002, with the cumulative devaluations amounting to 33 per cent by January 2003 (Figure 4.7).[11]

As a final attempt to resolve these policy inconsistencies, the government announced the abandonment of the exchange rate peg in January 2003. Because the exchange rate was still far from its market-clearing equilibrium, expectations resulted in an immediate fall in the Egyptian pound's value. It then continued to creep further downwards until October 2004 (to produce a cumulative depreciation of 83 per cent). Moreover, the parallel market persisted with the gap between it and the official rate reaching 2.6 per cent in January

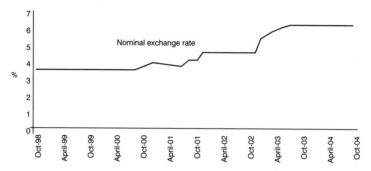

Figure 4.7 The official exchange rate (LE/US$), 1998–2004

2005. Realising that there was a 'leakage' of foreign currency out of the official market, the government decided to freeze government imports for three months except for basic food items and essential products, and to introduce foreign exchange surrender requirements, under which all exporters had to sell 75 per cent of their foreign earnings to domestic banks at the official rate, and to keep the remaining 25 per cent in the banking system. Other restrictive measures included the prohibition of foreign exchange dealers from quoting their own rates (ERF and IM, 2004).

However, the new government also adopted several measures to stabilise the exchange rate. The establishment of a foreign exchange interbank market in December 2004 eliminated the parallel foreign exchange market and stabilised the nominal exchange rate as from December 2005. Surrender requirements on foreign exchange earnings were also abolished. Following these measures, the nominal exchange rate started to appreciate in December 2004 and stabilised around LE/US$ 5.7 from December 2005 to October 2006. Strong capital inflows helped further boost the pound against the US dollar after that. The appreciation trend was mild at first but strengthened somewhat, reflecting increased capital inflows. Consequently, the IMF has reclassified Egypt's exchange rate regime as a 'managed float'.

Inflation performance

Unlike the situation in many other countries, inflation is not a major characteristic of the Egyptian economy. But since the late 1970s it has been witnessing cycles of high inflation (Figure 4.8). Inflation first increased with the open-door policy in the 1970s. High budget deficits were monetised, pushing inflation to its peak in the second half of the 1980s. Aided by a strong nominal anchor (the US dollar), fiscal adjustment and tight monetary policy, inflation then started to fall in the early 1990s to fairly low rates, until FY03. This task was facilitated by a benign external environment and a partial administration of prices.

Since the announcement of the float in FY03, the Egyptian economy has been subject to three successive rounds of double-digit inflation (Figure 4.9). The first period followed the nominal devaluation of the Egyptian pound, reflecting lagged

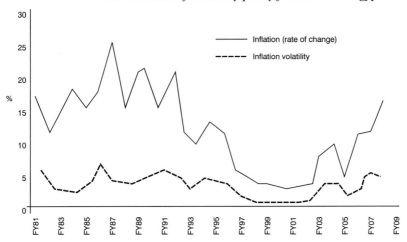

Figure 4.8 Inflation performance, 1981–2009

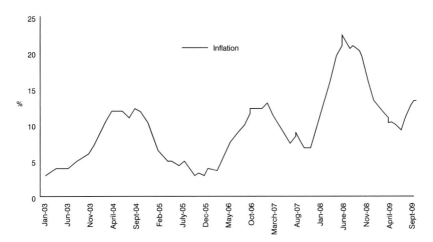

Figure 4.9 Inflation after the announcement of the float, 2003–2008

exchange rate pass-through pressures. CPI inflation, which had remained largely stable despite the step devaluations (because of the large number of goods with administered prices), shot up from 3.2 per cent in FY03 to 12.6 per cent in October 2004. Inflation then fell back in FY06 (to 4.2 per cent), following the stabilisation of the exchange rate, before surging again to low double digits in FY07 with the consumer price index (CPI) peaking at 12.8 per cent in March 2007. Despite some moderation in early FY08 (to 7 per cent), inflation soared again to double-digit figures after January 2008, peaking at 23 per cent in July and August 2008. This acceleration reflected rising food prices (which have the largest weight in the CPI basket), which climbed from 6.9 per cent in December 2007 to a 30 per cent peak in July 2008, as a result of soaring international commodity prices. In addition, the government increased basic wages of public employees by 30 per cent in May 2008 and introduced a new round of deregulation of energy prices and other administered prices. After the first-round effects of the price shocks took place, their second-round effects spilled over and persisted in other sectors.

To sum up, this section has shown that monetary policy has not been very successful in maintaining price stability, particularly since FY03. This happened despite the enactment of legislation which formally focused monetary policy on this goal. Over the period from the late 1970s, monetary policy was able to achieve this goal only within the context of a peg to the US dollar between 1991 and 2000. During this period, the implementation of consistent macroeconomic policies (restrictive fiscal policy and tight monetary policy to maintain a competitive exchange rate) was conducive to price stability. Once the exchange rate became subject to pressures, the government resisted the devaluation for political reasons. In addition, the expansionary fiscal policy adopted to fund national projects was inconsistent with the tight monetary stance required to support the peg. This situation ended with a strong devaluation, a large fiscal deficit and high inflation. In this context, the mere issue of new legislation establishing price stability as a formal goal for monetary policy was not enough to achieve this goal. Moreover, the absence of a transparent intermediate target and effective policy instruments is weakening the CBE's control of inflation.

3 Why do cycles of high inflation keep occurring?

This section reviews previous empirical evidence on the sources of inflation in Egypt. Following the high inflation of the late 1980s, various explanations have been put forward to identify its possible sources. Cost-push factors considered have included productivity lagging with respect to high wage growth and rising international prices in the context of a fixed exchange rate. Demand-pull factors made growth lag behind increasing demand and a large fiscal deficit was financed through monetisation. Other structural factors include the presence of a parallel pricing system, which may cause relative prices to change as the structure of the economy changes, and this may yield inflationary pressures (Kheir El-Din, 1992).

Today, 15 years later, Egypt still experiences periods of high inflation and their sources are not necessarily much different. The economy's productive capacity still lags behind the rise in aggregate demand, pushing inflation to rise beyond the price stability range. Demand pressures have resulted from strong domestic demand – stimulated by large cuts in income tax rates (in July 2005) and robust economic growth (between 6 and 7 per cent since FY06). Large capital inflows (around 8.5 per cent of GDP since FY07) have further resulted in a significant rise in M2 growth (up to 18 per cent in FY07 from an average of 14 per cent in the previous years), which has fuelled high inflation. Meanwhile, domestic supply shocks also helped to sustain these pressures. They were the result of the avian flu outbreak in February 2006, the surge in world commodity prices from 2006 and several rounds of price deregulation (partial elimination of fuel subsidies in July 2006, September 2006 and May 2008).

Empirical work indicates that money growth is the main driver of inflation in Egypt. Noureldin (2005b) finds that movements in the money gap explain 90 per cent of WPI inflation dynamics between 1999 and late 2005. Similar results are reached by Al-Mashat (2008). El-Sakka and Ghali (2005) find that money supply growth has a significant effect on inflation over the period 1969–2000. Metwally and Al-Sowaidi (2004) find evidence that inflation is due to changes in wages and costs of imports on the one hand and expansionary monetary and fiscal policies on the other. They also find evidence that the rate of price change is more sensitive to the latter.

Fanizza and Soderling (2006) show that during 1998 to 2005 the main reason Egypt did not succeed in curbing inflationary pressures was fiscal issues. These results are confirmed by Helmy (2008) who finds that over the period FY82–FY06 the fiscal deficit and its sources of financing are important drivers of inflation in Egypt. Furthermore, these variables also exhibit a two-way dynamic interaction (i.e. inflation has a feedback effect which pushes up the budget deficit). The author also finds that an increase in net government credit leads to inflation.

Meanwhile, Rabanal (2005) finds that the exchange rate pass-through to the CPI was slow and low (ranging between 6 and 27 per cent) because of the significant share of administered prices in the CPI. On the other hand, he found evidence of a quicker and higher (from 30 per cent to 60 per cent) pass-through to the WPI.

Only two papers have studied the impact of international prices on domestic inflation, with opposite findings. Bahmani-Oskooee and Malixi (1992) find no evidence that import prices affect inflation. These results are disputed by El-Sakka and Ghali (2005) who find that increases in international prices push up domestic inflation, though changes in domestic consumer prices do not seem to be highly sensitive to changes in import prices. They attribute this to the heavy subsidy scheme.

El-Sakka and Ghali (2005) also find that interest rate changes have a positive and significant impact on inflation. However, Al-Mashat and Billmeier (2008) find that the interest rate transmission channel is weak. Noureldin (2008) presents empirical evidence that relative price adjustments (due to the devaluation of the pound, the increases in the prices of energy-related products and the outbreak of the avian flu virus) are important factors in the dynamics of inflation. A recent paper by Hassan (2008) finds evidence of downward price rigidity in Egypt, particularly in the non-food sectors which are stickier than the food sector.

A study by Kheir El-Din and Abou Ali (2008) has found that higher and more volatile GDP growth is associated with higher inflation prior to FY91 while lower and less volatile growth is associated with significantly lower inflation afterwards. A study by Fares and Ibrahim (2008) finds that growth in private sector wages causes price inflation, but that wage growth in this sector is a function of lagged changes in prices rather than expected inflation rates.

This section has shown that while supply shocks or demand pressures may explain part of the story, other important factors could also be behind the inflation pressures. First, the Egyptian economy is still suffering from a structural fiscal deficit. Second, Egypt is still making its transition to a market economy, a process which is often accompanied by shocks to the price level. Finally, prices are rigid downwards, market institutions are weak and market concentration is still strong in some industries, while competition and ineffective consumer protection drive mark-ups and increase the tendency towards ad hoc pricing strategies by producers.

4 Prospects for future evolution

The main aim of this section is to highlight some of the deficiencies of the monetary policy framework which could be hampering its control of inflation. These elements could be seen as the pre-conditions for the implementation of an inflation targeting regime, since the government may move in this direction in the medium term. However, many of these elements are also preconditions for the success of any independent monetary policy framework.

Inflation trends

Inflation in Egypt (between 1980 and 2009) has averaged around 11.7 per cent with a volatility of around 7 per cent (Table 4.1). It was higher and more variable in the 1980s than it was afterwards. Between FY81 and FY92, inflation was 17.6 per cent on average, with a peak of 35 per cent in FY86, and was less volatile (5.3 per cent). After the implementation of the ERSAP, inflation became significantly lower (6.3 per cent) and less volatile (4.4 per cent). It fell to a minimum of 2.1 per cent in FY01 and FY02. However, from FY04 it was relatively higher on average (10 per cent), with a peak of 22 per cent in July 2008. And, although it has subsequently declined, inflation still remains high compared with the historical average and also compared with the threshold of 15 per cent, above which inflation has clearly negative effects on growth, as estimated empirically in the case of Egypt (Kheir El-Din and Abou Ali, 2008).

Table 4.1 Inflation in Egypt

	Average	Minimum	Maximum	Standard deviation
FY81–FY08	11.7	2.1	35.1	7.1
FY81–FY92	17.6	6.6	35.1	5.4
FY93–FY03	6.3	2.1	17.9	4.4
FY04–FY09	10.0	3.1	22.0	5.0

The existence of multiple nominal anchors

The Banking Law of 2003 declared price stability to be the overriding objective of monetary policy. A CBE monetary policy statement was also issued in June 2005 stating that price stability is the medium-term goal of monetary policy (CBE, 2005). Yet, as in any EME, the mere presence of legislation is not sufficient to ensure the commitment of the monetary authorities to price stability. What matters more is that this goal becomes a common priority for other policies, particularly fiscal policies.

Since the exchange rate ceased to be the explicit intermediate target for monetary policy in January 2003, no other nominal anchor has been officially announced. While the CBE declared its intention to adopt IT and despite the creation of a Coordinating Council in 2005 that is supposed to determine the policy target to be consistent with 'price stability and banking system soundness', there has been no announcement of an explicit inflation target.[12] And although this council is supposed to convene quarterly, it is not clear to the public whether it does and if so what are the outcomes of the meetings.

The absence of a transparent target has led to poor management of expectations. This situation has been exacerbated by the public perception that monetary policy has an implicit target, which is the exchange rate. Like many EMEs, Egypt cannot afford to overlook significant fluctuations in its exchange rate because it is an important transmission channel and because it remains the focus of the public's expectations. The CBE has thus been fighting appreciation pressures on the exchange rate since early 2005, and there has been little change in the official rate (Figure 4.10). The annual sterilisation costs involved were estimated at close to 1 per cent of GDP in 2007 (IMF, 2007). Nevertheless, as sterilisation was inadequate, the excess liquidity may have partly sustained the inflationary pressures during this period and thus compromised the goal of price stability.[13] Moreover, Al-Mashat (this volume) provides evidence that a fixed exchange rate generates the highest output and inflation variability. The latter declines as greater exchange rate flexibility is allowed.

The CBE's instrument independence

The instrument independence of the central bank can be compromised by government interference designed to stimulate the economy in the short-run or by fiscal dominance.

The *de jure* independence of the CBE improved in 2002 when it was placed under the authority of the President of the Republic (rather than that of the Prime Minister), a move formalised in the Banking Law (Official Journal, 2003). Yet, this gave the president the authority, under the emergency law in effect since 1981, to overrule any CBE decisions under any circumstances. This has also further reinforced its authority in the absence of statutory rules governing his appointments of both the governor of the CBE and its board (Oxford Analytica, 2006).

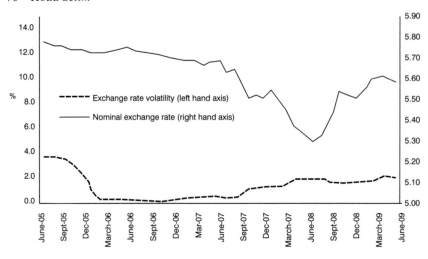

Figure 4.10 Exchange rate (LE/US$) behaviour, 2005–2009

In addition, the composition of the CBE board, its tenure and the remuneration of its members all raise questions about its autonomy vis-à-vis the government. First, the composition of the board does not allow for the inclusion of private sector representatives. Second, the appointments of the governor (by the President, based on a nomination by the Prime Minister) and government representatives (designated by the Prime Minister, based on nomination from respective ministries) last for four years, which is less than the five years in the previous legislation. The other members are designated by the President, without necessarily consulting with the governor. Third, the remuneration of the CBE Board members is determined by the Prime Minister, upon a proposal from the government (Youssef, 2007). In general, Gisolo's (2009) comparative study of central bank independence in 13 Mediterranean economies found that Egypt ranked very poorly (10th), above only Jordan, Libya and Morocco.

Meanwhile, there are concerns about fiscal dominance with Egypt's budget deficit standing at 6.8 per cent of GDP in FY08 and averaging around 8.4 per cent over the past 5 years (Figure 4.11).[14] Efforts to reduce it (from 9.8 per cent in FY02) reflect a rising nominal GDP and a cyclical revenue increase. The already high level of public expenditure (around 33.5 per cent in FY08) keeps the quality of fiscal performance low. But, more importantly, current expenditure on average represents close to 90 per cent of total expenditure between FY02 and FY08. It includes 'politically sensitive' items such as subsidies (8 per cent of GDP), interest payments (6 per cent of GDP) which reflect high public debt, and wages and salaries (6–8 per cent of GDP). The composition of public expenditure shows that there is not much flexibility in the short-term to reduce expenditure. Despite the announcement of a plan to reduce the budget deficit by 1 percentage point every year until FY11, the budget deficit increased in FY08 (from 5.7 in FY07).

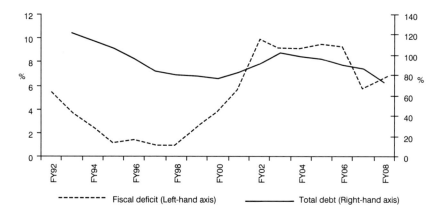

Figure 4.11 Fiscal deficit and public sector debt, 1992–2008 (% of GDP)

Furthermore, the government relies excessively on the CBE to finance the fiscal deficit (this does not exhibit any discernable trend but has averaged around 18 per cent of total financing between FY02 and FY07). And the CBE's net claims on the government have increased from LE 37.5 billion in FY99 to LE 81.8 billion in FY08 (a rise of 23.5 per cent in real terms). Meanwhile, the share of net domestic credit to the government in total domestic credit has also grown from 22 per cent in the late 1990s to 30 per cent in FY08. Moreover, Helmy (2008) shows that between FY01 and FY07 the average ratio of net credit to the government to M2 (a proxy for the monetary base expansion due to fiscal imbalance) was 37 per cent. Using data from 1960–2007, Youssef (this volume) provides empirical evidence that Egypt suffers from fiscal dominance. On the other hand, indicators of domestic public debt registered significant improvement. The net domestic debt of the public sector went down from 72.5 per cent of GDP in end-FY05 to 53.4 per cent in end-FY07. Yet these ratios remain high and their decline may be due mainly to high nominal GDP growth. Also, the large stock of debt puts pressure on the deficit through interest payments (6 per cent of GDP).

Furthermore, there is no legislation to prohibit CBE financing of the deficit. On the contrary, the Banking Law explicitly allows the CBE to lend to the government as long as the borrowing does not exceed 10 per cent of the average annual budget revenue during the previous three years. Such loans must be for a period of three months, renewable on the condition that repayment is made within a maximum of twelve months from the date of extending the loans.

It is also important to assess the soundness of Egypt's financial sector to determine whether the central bank is maintaining low interest rates to preserve the sector's solvency or whether this is constraining the government's capacity to issue domestic debt to finance the budget deficit.

As in many EMEs, the financial sector is mainly bank-based (39 banks as of end 2008), accounting for around 80 per cent of total assets. Following poor regulation in the past, credit was given to inefficient state enterprises on government instructions. Consequently, non-performing loans (NPLs) exceeded 20 per cent, which is extremely high when compared with global averages of about 5 per cent. Likewise, asset quality is poor and provision levels are far below the global average level of about 95 per cent (Fitch, 2008).

This has pushed the CBE to adopt a major restructuring effort since FY05. A Banking Reform Unit has been set up and given the responsibility to implement a four-point programme comprising: i) the privatisation and consolidation of the banking sector; ii) the restructuring of state-owned banks; iii) the financial and managerial restructuring of state banks (clean-up of NPLs); and iv) the upgrade of CBE supervision. In accordance with these objectives, the introduction of the minimum capital requirement (LE 500 million) in 2004 reduced the number of banks in the system from 57 at June 2004 to 40 to January 2008. The weak capitalisation of the two largest state-owned banks, which together account for about 40 per cent of system assets, is being addressed as part of their restructuring programme. Further efforts are being made to increase banks' competitiveness and ensure compliance with Basel II regulations. Following the sale in 2006 of the fourth largest state-owned bank and the divestiture of the state's holdings in a number of joint venture banks, just over half of banking sector assets are now in private hands. In addition, privatisation proceeds are being used to settle state-owned banks' problem loans. The NPL unit has managed to settle 92 per cent of irregular debts (excluding the public business sector) (CBE, 2007/2008). The outstanding debt of the latter to state-owned banks amounts to LE 10 billion. Banking supervision has been upgraded and a business monitoring unit has been set up to assess the financial soundness of banks and watch for early signs of potential problems.

This reform programme has strengthened Egypt's banking sector. Currently, loan to deposit ratios (around 56 per cent) have been declining since 2002. This excess liquidity in the banking system is due to overly prudent policies by Egyptian banks, which drive them to place their excess funds in government T-bills. Capital adequacy ratios increased (from 11.1 in FY04 to 14.9 in FY08, see IMF, 2007), and asset quality in terms of loan provisioning improved. Commercial banks have also maintained a reserve ratio slightly above 14 per cent and the aggregate earnings of the banking sector have remained healthy. The banking sector now has a low vulnerability to exchange and interest movements (IMF, 2007).

Stock markets have benefited from higher regional liquidity related to the oil boom. However, little effort has been exerted to develop a money market. There has been a primary T-bills market since the late 1990s but the secondary market is inactive. A deep and liquid long-term bond market could help shift the deficit financing from the banking sector. It should also help to establish a meaningful benchmark yield curve which in turn could improve the effectiveness of transmission mechanisms, help the CBE to assess the term structure of interest rates and also provide some information about private sector expectations of future inflation and the future monetary policy stance.

Inflation forecasting capabilities

Egypt still lacks some of the basic data needed for forecasting purposes. In particular, quarterly GDP series are very short and other high-frequency real sector indicators are not available for a long time span. The CBE monetary policy unit has developed models to forecast inflation and carries out both 'near-term' (a quarter ahead) and longer-term forecasts which are not yet published (Al-Mashat, 2008). Also, a core inflation measure was disclosed in late 2009 and excludes fruits and vegetables as well as regulated goods from the CPI (these items have a total share of 28 per cent of the basket). It is crucial to publish these forecasts and the models used so that they can be independently verified.

The transmission channels between the interest rate and inflation

The CBE has announced that, during the transition towards IT, it will meet its implicit inflation target by steering short-term interest rates, 'keeping in view the developments in credit and money supply, as well as a host of other factors that may influence the inflation rate' (CBE, 2004/2005). However, the scope for inflation control through the interest rate channel is limited, due to the under-developed transmission mechanisms (Figures 4.12 and 4.13). Several factors can explain this. First, banks are liquid, which weakens the pass-through from policy rates to lending rates. The spread between deposit and lending rates is as high as 6 per centage points. Second, the public sector banks were the only ones to adjust their interest rates following the CBE's decisions. Third, the economy is going through a transition towards a market economy, which makes transmission mechanisms more uncertain. Recent empirical research points out that the interest rate channel remains weak in Egypt (Al-Mashat and Billmeier, 2008). This confirms previous evidence by Hassan (2003) who shows that the nominal interest rate does not have a significant impact on real domestic credit to the private sector. More generally, Moursi *et al.* (2007) report that the direct impact of monetary policy shocks on real

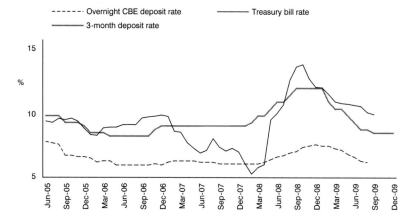

Figure 4.12 The transmission of policy deposit rate to other deposit rates

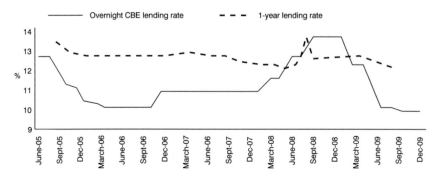

Figure 4.13 The transmission of policy lending rate to banks' lending rates

output is negligible. Meanwhile, Noureldin (2005a) provides empirical evidence that the impact of the credit channel on the real economy is quite significant. Nevertheless, the exchange rate seems to have a more potent and rapid effect than other channels (Al-Mashat and Billmeier, 2008). The transmission mechanism could improve with a new survey of inflation expectations that the CBE intends to conduct.

Accountability of the CBE and transparency of the monetary policy stance

According to Article 21 of the Banking Law, the CBE board has to submit annually to the president, the prime minister and the speaker of the parliament its audited financial statements and a report on its financial position and the outcomes of its activities including a survey of the economic conditions and the financial, monetary, banking and credit situations. Moreover, Article 28 of the Law commits the CBE governor to submit to the president a quarterly report on monetary, credit and banking developments, as well as foreign debt balances. Unlike the previous legislation, the current banking law does not explicitly prohibit the removal of any board member including the governor during his or her tenure. It only indicates that the president can accept board members' resignations. In any case, the presence of legislation is not enough to ensure the accountability of the CBE, especially in the absence of a target for which it is accountable.

The CBE has adopted a more transparent stance since 2005. In general, public statements have improved with the governor holding press conferences with the media. With the formation of the MPC, a first monetary policy statement was released in June 2005 setting out the objectives and instruments of monetary policy and the process of decision-making. Since then, a press release is issued regularly (posted every six weeks on the CBE's website) to communicate the MPC's decisions to the public. These statements usually signal changes in interest rates but give only limited explanation. And while an advance schedule of the MPC meetings is published on the CBE website, minutes of the meetings and details of voting are not given. There is also still no published inflation report but a monthly inflation note, published for the first time in late 2009, tracks inflation developments in both headline and core inflation measures. Also, the CBE website, which could be a main communication vehicle, does not contain sufficient information to shape the public's expectations. To conclude, efforts have been made to enhance the understanding of monetary policy implementation (the announcement of policy rates), but more transparency is still required with regards to the formulation of policy, i.e. justifications for policy changes, which cannot happen without the presence of an explicit intermediate target. This lack of transparency has resulted in poor management of expectations.

To sum up, despite some improvement in the monetary policy framework, the commitment to price stability needs to be complemented by reforms on three different fronts. First, to ensure complete *de facto* instrument independence, the CBE should not provide direct financing of the deficit. Other fiscal dominance concerns which require further consideration include the reduction of the fiscal deficit and the large debt stock. Banking sector reform, particularly that of public sector banks, should continue to ensure the complete clean-up of NPLs. The development of a long-term bond market is needed to diversify the deficit financing options. Second, the exchange rate needs to become more flexible. This would mean, not that the CBE will have to pay no attention to the exchange rate, but rather that it should give priority to price stability. All interventions to support the exchange rate must be transparent and justified in order not to confuse the public. Finally, a communication and dissemination strategy needs to be carefully designed. The CBE should make its medium-term goals and priority objectives known to the public, including the announcement of an inflation target to act as an anchor for public expectations. This would also help to enhance the monetary transmission mechanisms from policy rates to inflation (particularly the expectations channel).

5 Conclusions

Egypt has witnessed several cycles of high inflation since the 1970s. And while they are not typically very long, they are particularly harmful to the poor (around 20 per cent of the population), especially in the absence of an effective social protection system.[15] As in many EMEs, an exchange rate anchor has become unsuitable for an economy that is becoming globally integrated. But periods of high inflation have recurred, whether because of demand pressures, supply shocks or price deregulation, since the announcement of the float six years ago.

This chapter has tried to assess the role of monetary policy management in the inflation process. The second section analysed the objectives, intermediate targets and policy instruments since the late 1970s. It showed that price stability was not always the primary objective of monetary policy, even after the existence of a formal mandate through the 2003 legislation. In fact, monetary policy was not always able to deliver this goal, for several reasons. First, price stability is not integrated with other macroeconomic policies, particularly fiscal and exchange rate policies. Second, this task was made all the more difficult by supply shocks that hit the economy or by demand pressures. However, these do not fully explain the recurrence of inflation. As explained in the third section, a lagging productive capacity, weak public finances and an incomplete transition to a market economy are all factors that could be responsible for the persistence of inflationary pressures. Third, the announcement of the float should have provided domestic monetary policy with a more active role in controlling inflation. Monetary policy design was improved in the sense that price stability became the CBE's ultimate objective, policy tools were introduced to influence monetary conditions and the conduct of monetary policy was made somewhat more transparent. However, since the exchange rate framework was officially abandoned, the CBE has still not announced any underlying institutional framework, despite its declaration more than four years ago that it intends to adopt IT. This, together with a lack of transparency about the conduct of monetary policy has resulted in poor management of expectations, undermined credibility and weakened the central bank's control of both actual and future inflation.

The fourth section addressed the prospects for future evolution and suggested ways to make the transition towards a more coherent monetary policy framework. In order to build credibility and reduce inflation in Egypt, a range of reforms are required, some more important than others. Dealing with the fiscal dominance issue requires that the CBE ceases to finance the deficit, that the latter must be reduced, the banking sector must be cleaned-up of NPLs and a bond market should be developed. The exchange rate could be managed in the short-term but needs to become more flexible and more transparent over time, so as not to send conflicting signals to the public. Other complementary reforms such as the introduction of an effective communication strategy will help build credibility. The publication of an inflation forecast will help in making the CBE's objectives known to the public. More generally it will ensure that markets are better informed and market expectations better managed. Needless to say, these measures are in need of political support, given that any delay would only require harsher measures in due course.

Notes

1 In Egypt, most data are reported in fiscal years, which start in July and end in June. FY03 would start in July 2002 and end in June 2003.
2 Monetary policy targets are 'goals that are not objectives in and of themselves but, which if attained, will work directly towards the long-term objectives of monetary policy' (Khan, 2003: 3).
3 El-Sakka and Ghali (2005).
4 Abdel Khalek (2001).
5 Monetary Policy Statement, June 2005 (CBE, 2005).
6 Kamar (2005).
7 For a detailed discussion of the liquidity crisis in Egypt, please refer to El-Refaie (2000) and Handy (2001).
8 The system involved two official rates applying to different commodities (Abdel Khalek, 2001).
9 Kamar (2005).

10 Operational targets allow the central bank to better influence the intermediate targets in the short run (Khan, 2003).

11 A more complete discussion of the exchange rate movements during this period is available in ERF and IM (2004).

12 The council is made up of members of the CBE (including the governor and deputy), the government (including the minister of finance and the prime minister) and nine independent members (CBE 2004/2005). It apparently met only twice in 2006 (Oxford Analytica, 2006).

13 For a more detailed description of the causes and mechanisms of this intervention, see Schnabl and Schobert (2009).

14 The fiscal deficit excludes net financial acquisitions which may include privatisation proceeds.

15 World Bank (2007).

References

Abdel Khalek, G. (2001), *Stabilisation and Adjustment in Egypt: Reform or De-Industrialisation.* Cheltenham: Edward Elgar.

Abou El-Eyoun, M. (2003), 'Evolution of Monetary Policy in Egypt and Future Trends', Egyptian Centre for Economic Studies, Cairo, working paper 78.

Al-Mashat, R. (2008), 'Monetary Policy in Egypt: A Retrospective and Preparedness for Inflation Targeting', Egyptian Centre for Economic Studies, Cairo, working paper 134.

Al-Mashat, R., and Billmeier, A. (2008), 'The Monetary Transmission Mechanism in Egypt', *Review of Middle East Economics and Finance* 4(3):1–51.

Al-Mashat, R., and Grigorian, D. (1998), 'Economic Reforms in Egypt: Emerging Patterns and their Possible Implications', World Bank Policy Research working paper 1977.

Bahmani-Oskooee, M., and Malixi, M. (1992), 'Inflationary effects of changes in effective exchange rates: LDCs' experience'. *Applied Economics* 24(4): 465–471.

CBE (2004/2005), *Annual Report.* Cairo: Central Bank of Egypt.

——(2005), *Monetary Policy Statement.* Cairo: Central Bank of Egypt. Available at http://www.cbe.org.eg/public/Monetary-Policy/Framework.htm.

——(2007/2008), *Annual Report.* Cairo: Central Bank of Egypt.

Dailami, M., and Dinh, H. (1991), 'Interest Rate Policy in Egypt: Its Role in Stabilisation and Adjustment', World Bank Policy Research and External Affairs working paper 655.

Dinh, H., and Giugale, M. (1991). 'Inflation Tax and Deficit Financing in Egypt', World Bank Policy, Research and External Affairs working paper 668.

El-Refaie, F. (2000), 'The Liquidity Issue in Egypt: Reasons and Solutions', Egyptian Centre for Economic Studies, Cairo, working paper 41.

——(2002), 'The Coordination of Monetary Policy and Fiscal Policies in Egypt', In E. Cardoso and A. Galal (eds), *Monetary Policy and Exchange Rate Regimes: Options for the Middle East.* Cairo: Egyptian Centre for Economic Studies.

El-Sakka, M., and Ghali, K. (2005), 'The Sources of Inflation in Egypt: A Multivariate Co-integration Analysis', *Review of Middle East Economics and Finance* 3(3): 257–269.

ERF and IM (Economic Research Forum for the Arab Countries, Iran and Turkey and Institut de la Méditerranée; Femise Network) (2004), *Egypt Country Profile: The Road Ahead for Egypt.* Cairo, Economic Research Forum for the Arab Countries, Iran and Turkey.

Fanizza, D., and Soderling, L. (2006), 'Fiscal Determinants of Inflation: A Primer for the Middle East and North Africa', IMF working paper 216.

Fares, H., and Ibrahim, A. (2008), 'Wage–Price Causality in the Egyptian Economy (1990–2005)', Egyptian Centre for Economic Studies, Cairo, working paper 136.

Fitch (2008), *Egyptian Banking System and Prudential Regulations.* Country Report. London: Fitch Ratings.

Gisolo, E. (2009), 'The Degree of Legal Central Bank Independence in MENA Countries', in D. Cobham and G. Dibeh, eds., *Monetary Policy and Central Banking in the Middle East and North Africa.* London: Routledge.

Handy, H. (2001), 'Monetary Policy and Financial Sector Reform in Egypt: the Record and the Challenges Ahead', Egyptian Centre for Economic Studies, Cairo, working paper 51.

Hassan, M. (2003), 'Can Monetary Policy Play an Effective Role in Egypt?' Egyptian Centre for Economic Studies, Cairo, Working Paper Series 84.

——(2008), 'Inflation Dynamics in Egypt: Consumer Price Data at Elementary Product Level', Paper presented at the Egyptian Banking Institute Second Annual Conference, Cairo, June 2008.

Helmy, O. (2008), 'The Impact of Budget Deficit on Inflation', Egyptian Centre for Economic Studies, Cairo, working paper 141.

IMF (2007), *Article IV Consultation—Staff Report.* International Monetary Fund, Country Report 07/380.

Kamar, B. (2005), *Politiques de Change et Globalisation: Le Cas de L'Egypte.* Paris: L'Harmattan.

Khan, M. (2003), 'Current issues in the Design and Conduct of Monetary Policy'. IMF working paper 03/56.

Kheir El-Din, H., ed. (1992), *The Mechanisms of Inflation in Egypt.* Cairo: Centre for Economic and Financial Research, Faculty of Economics and Political Science, Cairo University.

Kheir El-Din, H., and Abou Ali, H. (2008), 'Inflation and Growth in Egypt: Is there a Threshold Effect?' Egyptian Centre for Economic Studies, Cairo, working paper 135.

Metwally, M., and Al-Sowaidi, S. (2004), 'The main determinants of inflation in Egypt'. *Middle East Business and Economics Review* 16(1): 31–40.

Moursi, T., El Mossallamy, M. and Zakareya, I. (2007), 'Effect of Some Recent Changes in Egyptian Monetary Policy: Measurement and Evaluation', Egyptian Centre for Economic Studies, Cairo, working paper 122.

Noureldin, D. (2005a), 'Understanding the Monetary Transmission Mechanism in the Case of Egypt: How Important is the Credit Channel?' Paper presented at EcoMod International Conference on Policy Modelling, Istanbul, June–July, 2005.

——(2005b), 'Alternative Approaches to Forecasting Inflation in the Case of Egypt', Paper presented at the Economic Research Forum's 12th Annual Conference, Cairo, December 2005.

——(2008), 'Relative Price Adjustment and Inflation Dynamics: The Case of Egypt', Egyptian Centre for Economic Studies, Cairo, working paper 133.

Official Journal (2003), *The Central Banking Law.* Issue No. 24 bis. Cairo.

Oxford Analytica (2006), *Egypt Monetary Transparency. Country Report 2006.* Oxford: Oxford Analytica.

Rabanal, P. (2005), 'Exchange Rate Pass-Through', In *Arab Republic of Egypt: Selected Issues.* IMF Country Report 05/179.

Schnabl, G., and Schobert, F. (2009), 'Monetary Policy Operations of Debtor Central Banks in MENA Countries', In D. Cobham and G. Dibeh (eds.), *Monetary Policy and Central Banking in the Middle East and North Africa.* London: Routledge.

Subramanian, A. (1997), 'The Egyptian Stabilisation Experience: An Analytical Retrospective', IMF working paper 97/105.

World Bank (2007), *Arab Republic of Egypt: Poverty Assessment Update 2007*. Washington, DC: World Bank.

Youssef, H. (2007), 'Towards Inflation Targeting in Egypt: Fiscal and Institutional Reforms to Support Disinflation Efforts', *European Economy Economic Papers* 288. Brussels: European Commission.

5 Monetary policy and the central bank in Jordan

Samar Maziad

1 Introduction

Jordan is a small open economy with a limited industrial base and relies heavily on foreign aid and workers' remittances for foreign currency resources. In the 1970s, Jordan witnessed high growth and large capital inflows due to the boom in oil prices, which contributed to increased foreign revenues through the large flow of aid and workers' remittances from the Gulf States. With the drop in oil prices in the early 1980s, the main sources of foreign exchange flows, aid and remittances, dried up, resulting in economic recession and stagnation throughout the decade. Jordan resorted to heavy external borrowing to compensate for the fall in foreign currency and public revenues more generally. The accumulation of foreign debt, coupled with expansionary fiscal policy and accommodating monetary policy, culminated in an exchange rate crisis in 1989–90 and a sharp devaluation of the fixed exchange rate. Jordan pursued macroeconomic stabilisation successfully in the aftermath of the crisis, has maintained prudent policies since and has restored exchange rate stability, supported by a marked development in the monetary policy framework, including improved monetary policy instruments and enhanced central bank independence.

This chapter will discuss the evolution of the monetary framework in Jordan, including the exchange rate regime, the conduct of monetary policy and the evolution of central bank independence, with reference to the impact of the currency crisis on the evolution of the monetary framework.[1]

It will also discuss the question of monetary policy independence in the context of Jordan's exchange rate peg to the US dollar (USD). Empirical research has shown that floating exchange rate regimes do not necessarily allow a country to operate an independent monetary policy given the strong influence of world interest rates. Similarly, countries operating a fixed exchange rate regime may have some flexibility in designing monetary policy, at least in the short run. The hypothesis of monetary policy independence will be tested in the case of Jordan using VAR/VECM analysis to study the influence of USD interest rates on monetary policy. The results show that, along with adjusting monetary policy in response to USD interest rate movements, the Central Bank of Jordan (C)BJ is also able to respond to domestic inflation and the output gap. There is some room for flexibility in operating monetary policy in the short run, where the CBJ has some autonomy in determining the spread between domestic and US interest rates. The results suggest that the response of the policy rate in Jordan to innovations in the US federal funds rate is less than one-for-one. In the short-run, the CBJ appears to conduct monetary policy in response to domestic inflation and a measure of the domestic output gap.

The chapter is organised as follows: section 2 describes the monetary framework prior to the currency crisis in 1989/90; section 3 discusses the evolution of central bank independence; section 4 describes monetary policy instruments and operations; section 5 presents the results of the empirical analysis on monetary policy autonomy; and section 6 concludes.

2 The monetary framework and the impact of the currency crisis

The CBJ was established in 1964 with little legal or statutory independence. Over time the degree of actual autonomy has increased substantially, mainly during the 1990s after the severe balance of payments crisis that saw the fixed exchange rate devalued by more than 100 per cent. The pre-crisis monetary framework relied on a fixed exchange rate with a parity that was pegged to the pound sterling as part of the colonial legacy but was officially abandoned with the devaluation of sterling in 1967, to be replaced by a peg directly to the USD. In 1975, the authorities abandoned the USD peg with the breakdown of the Bretton Woods system and pegged the Jordanian dinar (JD) to the SDR instead with a band of +/– 2.25 per cent, to avoid excessive fluctuations that might result from pegging to the USD alone (CBJ, 1989).

Until the early 1980s, Jordan enjoyed large inflows of capital in the form of aid and worker remittances, which supported the fixed exchange rate regime. Foreign grants amounted to 54 per cent of revenues in 1975 and until 1983 averaged 42 per cent of total government revenues, while remittances amounted to almost 47 per cent of GDP in 1979 and averaged 22 per cent of GDP annually until 1983. With the fall in world oil prices and the decline in production from Gulf States in the early 1980s, the flow of foreign capital almost came to a halt. Foreign grants were halved from their peak of JD 210 million in 1979 to JD 106 million in 1984, while remittances decreased sharply from JD 456 million (47 per cent of GDP) in 1979 to JD 310 million (16 per cent of GDP) in 1985.

To overcome this shortfall, the authorities resorted to heavy external borrowing. Foreign debt increased by an annual average of 17 per cent from 1983 to 1987, reaching a peak of 164 per cent of GDP in 1988. If domestic debt is also included, total government debt amounted to a staggering 203 per cent of GDP. With the large build-up of foreign debt, interest payments increased steadily from less than 2 per cent of GDP in 1983 to almost 11 per cent of GDP during 1990–91. This sharp increase also reflected the strong depreciation of the currency in 1988–89 (IMF, 1995: 28).

Jordan witnessed declining growth rates during the 1980s. Real GDP had been growing strongly from 1976 until 1982 at 13 per cent on average, before it declined to 1.5 per cent in 1988, with a sharp contraction (–10 per cent) in 1989 as a result of the crisis. The inflation rate was moderate and averaged 6 per cent during the 1980s (see summary Table 5.1 in the next section).

Monetary conditions were generally accommodating throughout the 1980s with broad money growth averaging 13 per cent and domestic credit growing at 20 per cent annually. Monetary policy from the mid-1970s into the late 1980s was largely passive and the CBJ had only a few instruments and limited ability to influence monetary conditions. Until 1990, the CBJ had only direct control instruments at its disposal to influence liquidity and credit conditions, including reserve requirements, liquidity ratios and interest rate ceilings. These instruments were adjusted frequently to support bank liquidity and encourage credit expansion, as monetary policy was geared towards supporting the overall government policy of stimulating the economy (IMF, 1995).

Jordan's dependence on foreign capital, expansionary fiscal policy, and the large build-up of foreign debt, led to the currency crisis that was inevitable by the end of the decade, as public debt reached unsustainable levels.

The first signs of the crisis appeared in mid-1986 when the exchange rate of the JD exceeded the official 2.25 per cent[2] fluctuation band around the SDR, and a parallel foreign exchange market appeared. The margin between the official and parallel market rates increased rapidly in 1988, with the parallel market premium rising to 20 piastres from 0.2 when the parallel market first appeared (interview with CBJ officials, 2004).[3]

The continued pressures on the currency resulted in a significant loss of reserves, as foreign reserves declined from almost JD 425 million in 1987 to JD 110 million in 1988, a decrease of almost 75 per cent; gold reserves declined by over 30 per cent over the course of the same year, and arrears in debt service started to appear by the end of 1988 (Kanakria, 2002). In April 1988, the CBJ suspended currency sales, but the pressures continued and forced a devaluation of 5 per cent by June of the same year. At the same time, the government introduced some measures to limit currency transfers abroad.[4]

The currency crisis resulted in the devaluation of the exchange rate (measured against the SDR) by 65 per cent in 1988 and an additional 33 per cent in 1989, after which the JD was re-pegged at JD 0.94/SDR in 1990, representing a devaluation of 140 per cent from its rate of JD 0.39/SDR before the crisis.

The Jordanian authorities have recognised that heavy government borrowing to finance current expenditure, and the associated debt service, led to the exchange rate crisis in 1988–89. The ministry of finance has also acknowledged that one of the main reasons behind the crisis was 'borrowing from the Central Bank' (Abu-Hammour, 2005: 5). In the post-crisis period, fiscal discipline and the enforcement of limitations on central bank financing of the budget deficit were critical reforms in the environment in which the CBJ operated, and contributed to an increase in its actual independence and its effectiveness in operating monetary policy. Similar views were also expressed by Kanakria (2002) and Abu-Hammour (2005). Thus the reform efforts that followed enjoyed the support of both the government and the CBJ. This facilitated the evolution of a more sophisticated monetary framework, including greater independence for the central bank, supported by increased fiscal discipline.

3 CBJ independence and monetary policy

Like many central banks in the MENA region and elsewhere, the CBJ was established with little autonomy, particularly in terms of political independence.[5] However, the CBJ's degree of independence, especially economic or instrument independence, increased noticeably from the early 1990s. This development both impacted on and was influenced by the increased sophistication of monetary policy instruments and the improved discipline of fiscal policy.

Given the highly centralised nature of government and decision making in Jordan (Carroll, 2003: 43), it is not surprising that the CBJ was established with little political independence. In this regard, the governor of the CBJ and his two deputies were, and still are, appointed by the Cabinet subject to the approval of the King for renewable five-year tenures. The remaining five members of the board of the CBJ are also appointed by the Cabinet for renewable three-year tenures. The law stipulates that board members should possess wide experience in economic and banking matters, with one member representing licensed banks and specialised credit institutions. Thus all eight board members are appointed by the government without requiring any formal consultation with or approval by the governor; this grants the CBJ very little political independence.[6] The CBJ is also formally accountable to the government and is required to submit a report of its operations along with its balance sheet to the minister of finance within three months of the end of the fiscal year.

The 1971 law states that the statutory objectives of the CBJ are to maintain monetary stability, ensure the convertibility of the JD and promote sustained economic growth according to the general economic policy of the government. The explicit mention of monetary stability grants the CBJ a degree of political independence in implementing monetary policy vis-à-vis the government; yet the same law states that the par value of the JD against gold or foreign currency is determined by the Council of Ministers. Given the fixed exchange rate regime pursued by Jordan, the CBJ has little target or goal independence. The law, however, grants the CBJ a higher degree of instrument independence, as it is free to set its discount rate and upper and lower limits for bank borrowing and lending rates and, in the absence of such limits, to make rules and directives to influence interest rate setting and credit expansion.

The earlier CBJ law of 1966 had limited temporary lending to the government to cover budget deficits of up to 10 per cent of the average government revenues for the previous three years and allowed the CBJ to charge interest on such loans. The 1971 law was more lenient and allowed the CBJ to provide interest-free loans of up to 20 per cent of government revenues as projected in the budget law for the year in which the advance was granted. In practice, the CBJ's lending to the government has systematically exceeded the 20 per cent limit since 1980 according to CBJ data. From 1983 to 1990, average annual CBJ lending to the government was 52 per cent of revenues with a peak of 95 per cent in 1989.[7]

As mentioned earlier, monetary policy was generally passive, and accommodated an expansionary fiscal policy in the 1980s; however, the balance of payments crisis and the sharp depreciation of the currency triggered a significant shift in both monetary and fiscal policies. In response to the crisis, monetary policy was tightened from late 1988 by raising interest rates and reserve ratios. The CBJ raised its discount rate from 5.75 per cent to 7 per cent in September 1988 and again to 8.5 per cent in August 1989. To tighten monetary conditions further, the CBJ raised the required reserve ratios on time and savings deposits from 6 to 9 per cent and the reserve ratio on demand deposits from 9 to 11 per cent in late 1989. The ceiling on bank deposit rates was removed and the ceiling on lending rates charged by commercial banks was increased. As part of the initial stabilisation and reform phase, the interest rate structure was liberalised in February 1990 and as a result the lending rate reached 12 per cent by September 1990, up from 10.3 per cent earlier in the year. However, inflation was still high, at 16 per cent in 1990, which meant that real interest rates were negative.

Monetary policy was tightened further from 1992 to 1994 as reserve requirements were raised several times (IMF, 1995: 44–6). Both credit to the government and overall domestic credit shrank in 1991 and 1992, while money supply grew by only 3 per cent. As a result of its having tightened monetary conditions and raised interest rates on local currency, the CBJ started to accumulate foreign reserves again and its stock of foreign exchange reserves almost doubled between 1990 and 1993.

The tight monetary policy continued into the late 1990s. Banking sector credit to the government continued to show negative rates of growth with overall domestic credit growing by an average of 5 per cent from 1990 to 1997, and money supply growing by 6 per cent on average over the same period. The CBJ discount rate stood at 9 per cent by 1998, and commercial banks' lending rates were in the range of 12.5–14 per cent as inflation continued to drop to 3 per cent, implying real interest rates of about 10 per cent (CBJ data).

Fiscal policy improved during the 1990s. CBJ data shows that in 1992, the fiscal balance registered a surplus of 1.2 per cent of GDP excluding grants. By 1999, there was a small fiscal deficit at 2.4 per cent of GDP including grants and 5.8 per cent without them, which is a significant improvement from the pre-crisis averages of 7 per cent and 15 per cent respectively in the 1980s. Total government debt was halved from over 200 per cent of GDP in 1989 to 100 per cent of GDP by 1999, while the stock of foreign debt was almost halved. Together the tightening of monetary policy and the efforts to control the fiscal deficit enabled Jordan to maintain the credibility and durability of its fixed exchange rate and achieve stable low inflation and sustainable growth. Table 5.1 summarises key macroeconomic outcomes.

The change in policy stance was supported by the introduction of indirect control instruments to influence monetary conditions, which increased the ability of the CBJ to conduct monetary policy (see details below). The increased sophistication of the monetary framework and the improved design and implementation of monetary policy both affected and reflected the enhanced status and independence of the CBJ.

In the post-crisis environment, the actual independence of the CBJ was enhanced as it had been advising against the risks of chronic fiscal deficits and

Table 5.1 Macroeconomic developments

Period average	1981–1985	1986–1990	1991–1995	1996–2000	2001–2005	2006–2008
Inflation	5.4	9.7	4.3	2.8	2.4	8.9
Real GDP growth	4.7	–0.3	6.3	3.1	6.6	6.7

Source: IFS.

excessive monetisation of the deficit. As the crisis erupted, the authorities felt that heeding the advice of the CBJ would perhaps have reduced the likelihood and/or cost of the crisis.

Although the central bank law itself did not change to reflect the increased actual independence of the CBJ, the legal framework governing its operations was improved significantly with the introduction of the new public debt law in 2001, which instituted ceilings on public debt and tightened the limits on government borrowing from the central bank, thus enhancing its actual independence (see details in the next section). In addition, Article 25 of the central bank law was amended to stipulate that the central bank must be consulted when the cabinet determines the par value of the currency, which had not been required in the previous laws. Those two amendments to the legal framework improved both the target and the instrument independence of the CBJ relative to earlier legislation.

In addition, the new law established a committee to manage the public debt, in which the CBJ was granted a larger role in the process of debt management. The committee is formed of three members, including the governor of the CBJ, the minister of planning and the minister of finance as chair. The law authorised the minister of finance to borrow on behalf of the government only after the approval of the Committee. Also, Article 11 of the new law states clearly that the minister of finance shall decide on the annual plan for issues of public debt and determine the terms of issue *upon consultation with the Governor*.

Some insight into the degree of independence of the CBJ during the 1990s can be found in a number of surveys on monetary frameworks such as Fry *et al.* (2000), Arnone *et al.* (2007), and Gisolo (2009). Fry *et al.* (2000) surveyed key aspects of the monetary framework in a sample of 94 countries around the world, using survey results obtained directly from individual central banks. The survey included questions in several categories, including the statutory objectives of monetary policy; the ability to use monetary policy instruments; the legal framework governing the appointment of the governor and the board; and operational aspects of monetary policy setting. An aggregated score for overall independence was then derived from the individual categories. The overall assessment of central bank independence thus incorporated elements of both legal and actual independence. On overall instrument and target independence indicators, the CBJ attained the full score of 100, reflecting a high degree of actual independence despite the low scores (50 out of 100) awarded to the individual indicators pertaining to the statutory objective of price stability and budget deficit finance. However, this particular aspect of budget deficit finance improved significantly in 2001 with the adoption of the new public debt law. The composite index score, reflecting the overall independence of the CBJ, was 75 out of 100, which compares well with other MENA countries included in the survey and is above the developing and emerging market countries' average (Table 5.2).

Arnone *et al.* (2007) provided an update of the widely cited CBI index by Grilli, Masciandaro and Tabellini (1991) (GMT) for the OECD countries to assess the improvement in CBI over time. They also expanded the index to assess CBI in a sample of 163 countries and they distinguished between advanced, emerging markets and low-income countries. In order to compare the evolution of CBI in emerging and low-income countries, the authors used the information available in Cukierman (1992) to calculate a streamlined version of the GMT index. Thus, the paper was able to compare CBI for a subset of 68 countries in their sample at two points in time: 1992 and 2003. Their results showed a significant improvement in the degree of CBI in developing countries over the decade, as some central banks have reached levels of autonomy comparable to those in OECD countries. In the group of emerging markets, overall autonomy has more than doubled over time and surpassed the level typical in the advanced countries in the late 1980s. The authors explained that this was achieved through strong political will for reform and generally took place in three stages. The first stage was laying the foundation for CBI through the adoption of appropriate legislation, the second stage was the development of the autonomous operational capacity at the central banks, and the final stage involved increased political independence in terms of policy formulation and the appointment of senior management. The paper also provided detailed classification and scores for CBI in all 163 countries. According to that classification, Jordan scored 0.25 on political independence and 0.5 on economic independence, resulting in a total score of 0.38 (out of a maximum score of 1).

A more recent study by Gisolo (2009) analysed central bank independence in a number of MENA and Southern Mediterranean countries, including Jordan.[8] The study adopts a methodology focused on quantifying central bank independence in terms of legal independence as specified in the various central bank laws, rather than measures of actual independence. The research assessed legal independence

Table 5.2 CBI indices – Jordan and select MENA countries

	Bank of England CBI Index	Arnone et al.	Gisolo[a]
	Score (max. 100)	Score (max. 1)	Score (max. 4.25)
Egypt	53	0.38	1.25
Jordan	74	0.38	−0.25
Lebanon	68	0.50	2.50
Turkey	70	0.81	2.25
Emerging Market Average	65	0.65	1.92[b]

Notes
a   Unweighted scores.
b   MENA average.

on various dimensions, including policy objectives and the emphasis on price stability, policy formulation, political independence, economic independence and accountability. Each central bank in the sample was assigned a score in each of the above categories, based on sub-indicators, before arriving at an aggregated score for overall independence. Unlike many other studies that quantify central bank independence, Gisolo's methodology included the possibility of assigning negative values on most indicators.

In Gisolo's ranking, the CBJ was found to be among the least independent of his sample of central banks with an overall score of –0.25, relative to an average score of 1.92, and a top score of 4.25 (Algeria).

Gisolo's overall assessment of CBJ's independence is driven by the low (and negative) scores assigned to the CBJ's political independence. As Gisolo indicated (2009: 35), the overall ranking is largely driven by the provisions for the hiring and dismissal of the governor and the board. This seems to overwhelm the high (sometimes full) scores assigned to economic and instrument independence, particularly the freedom from budget deficit finance, where the CBJ is awarded the full score, consistent with more recent developments. Therefore, this ranking of the CBJ as among the least independent in the MENA region appears to be rather harsh given the critical importance of instrument independence – including limits on lending to the government – in determining actual independence, as several studies have shown (Cukierman, 1992; Fry, 1998; Fry *et al.*, 2000).

In sum, the monetary framework has witnessed clear positive developments since the early 1990s, in that the CBJ is now enjoying a higher degree of actual independence. Although the central bank law itself has not changed, the overall legal framework that governs central bank operations has improved with the 2001 public debt law, which prohibited direct lending to the government. This represents a significant improvement over previous legislation.

4 Monetary policy instruments and operations

The main change in the operation of monetary policy in Jordan was the adoption of indirect control instruments in the early 1990s, which improved the ability of the CBJ to conduct monetary policy and supported its increased autonomy.

In September 1993, the CBJ introduced an auction system for its own certificates of deposits (CDs). Initially, the CBJ was using M2 as an intermediate target to achieve its final objective of maintaining price stability and the exchange rate peg. The CBJ aimed to maintain bank reserves at the required minimum level at all times (IMF, 1995). By mid-1995, the CBJ had expanded the use of CDs to implement monetary policy and shifted to using the CD auction rate as its operational target. At the same time, the CBJ intervened in the foreign exchange market to maintain the exchange rate peg. By targeting the CD rate, the CBJ tried to influence bank lending and deposit rates so as to induce changes in demand for the JD relative to the USD and maintain exchange rate stability. Thus after 1995, the intermediate target of monetary policy changed from M2 to the banking system's interest rates.

The CBJ influences CD interest rates by varying its offerings of CDs at auction, and this would directly impact retail interest rates in the banking system; however, in recent years, banking sector interest rates have been less responsive to CBJ policy rates (Poddar *et al.*, 2006).

The 3-month CD rate was maintained at between 9 and 9.55 per cent from 1995 to 1998 to coincide with the tight monetary policy pursued by the CBJ throughout the 1990s. The CBJ used its CDs as the main instrument to control the money supply and absorb excess liquidity. A decade of tight monetary policy resulted in a reduction of inflation to very low levels: by 1999 inflation stood at 1 per cent, after averaging 4 per cent between 1991 and 1999, while real GDP growth was 5 per cent on average over the same period.

The change in the CBJ's policy framework from targeting M2 to targeting interest rates coincided with the change in the nature of the exchange rate peg from pegging the JD to the SDR within a narrow margin to fixing it completely to the USD; the JD has remained unchanged against the USD at the rate JD 0.71/USD until now.

In 1998, the CBJ introduced another indirect instrument to its kit: it launched an overnight deposit facility, which gave the CBJ a tool for managing liquidity on a daily basis and provided a floor for interbank rates. In 2000, the CBJ started adjusting the overnight rate in line with the changes in the US federal funds rate. Thus since 2000, the CBJ has moved away from solely targeting CD auction rates to a corridor system with the overnight window as the floor and the 7-day repo facility, which had been introduced in 1994, as the ceiling (Poddar *et al.*, 2006: 7). In May 2007, the CBJ simplified its interest rate structure, by replacing the 7-day repo facility with an overnight facility to ensure symmetry with the overnight deposit window, and thus reducing the interest rate corridor width by 125 basis points. Poddar *et al.* (2006) argued that the CBJ still had some independence in setting the interest rate spread between the level of domestic interest rates and that in the US, as the result of imperfect asset substitutability. Further empirical analysis also supports this conclusion as will be discussed in section 5. Figure 5.1 shows the evolution of the central bank's CD rate since 1999, relative to that of the federal funds rate. The CBJ policy rate remained stable at 6 per cent in 2000 and fell to 3.9 per cent in 2001 despite the increase in the federal funds rate of 1.27 percentage points. Recently, the decoupling of the CD rate from the US federal funds rate became more pronounced, as the CBJ kept interest rates considerably higher than in the US due to its concern over inflationary pressures emanating from the pass-through of food and fuel price shocks in 2007 and early 2008, and to avoid pressure on the balance of payments after the eruption of the global financial crisis in late 2008 (IMF, 2008, 2009).

Since 2000, the main features of the monetary framework have remained broadly unchanged. But two developments are worth mentioning: the monetary stance of the CBJ became more accommodating in the early 2000s, and the government enacted a new public debt law, which introduced ceilings on foreign and domestic public debt and tightened the limits on government borrowing from the central bank, thereby enhancing its actual independence.

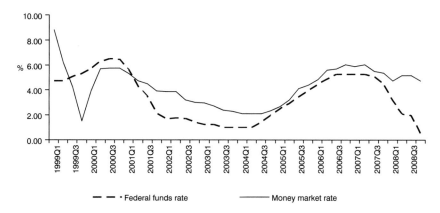

Figure 5.1 Money market rate and Federal funds rate

In 1999, the average 3-month CD rate was reduced to 6 per cent from 9.5 per cent in 1998 and it continued to decline, reaching 2.9 per cent in 2004. The discount rate followed the same pattern and stood at 3.8 per cent in 2004, down from 9 per cent in 1998. Similarly, banking sector interest rates showed a falling trend after 1999. Starting in 2005, the CBJ reversed the declining trend in interest rates due to concerns over high credit growth, and the emergence of inflationary pressures in 2006 (IMF, 2007).

Kanakria (2002) attributed the change in the stance of monetary policy to the unprecedented level of foreign reserves at the CBJ, which reached seven months of imports at the end of 1999. This signalled confidence in the JD and allowed the CBJ to lower interest rates on CDs, which fed into banks' interest rates.

Compared with the monetary framework, the area of public finance has witnessed more significant changes since 1999, as the government enacted a new public debt law and replaced direct borrowing from the banking system, including the CBJ, with the issue of Treasury bills to finance its deficit.

A new law for public debt management was passed in 2001 and was later complemented by a Memorandum of Understanding (MoU) between the CBJ and the Ministry of Finance in March 2008. The 2001 law prohibited the government from direct domestic borrowing from commercial banks or any other institutions and limited domestic borrowing to the issuing of securities, while the more recent MoU eliminated the interest-free overdraft facility at the CBJ, which had funded the government's short-term cash needs.

The public debt law also deals with the government's debt to the CBJ by freezing it at the stock outstanding in April 2001 at the time when the new law entered into force. The 2008 MoU set out a clear strategy for the settlement of the outstanding overdraft by securitising the debt and sharing the government's borrowing plans with the CBJ on a quarterly basis to help coordinate liquidity management.

In addition, Articles 21–23 of the law limit the stock of both foreign and domestic debt at any point in time to 60 per cent of GDP each (at current prices of the latest year for which data is available) and the total outstanding public debt to 80 per cent of GDP. The public debt ceiling stated in the 2001 law is expected to be reached by 2011 through fiscal adjustment and the introduction of new debt instruments, as well as improvements in the capacity of public debt management (IMF, 2008).

The government started holding regular Treasury bill (TB) auctions in the fall of 1999 and the stock of government securities (bills and bonds) grew from JD 330 million in 1999 to JD 1500 million in 2004 and JD 4133 million by October 2008 (CBJ data). By the latter date, government issues of bills and bonds represented 62 per cent of the total stock of domestic debt outstanding, amounting to JD 5.3 billion ($7.5 billion), while CDs issued by the CBJ accounted for 32 per cent and the remainder was made up of corporate securities (4 per cent), bonds issued by public entities (2 per cent) and development bonds (less than 1 per cent).

Treasury bonds accounted for most of the government's domestic debt (about 80 per cent), while T-bills constituted the rest. T-bonds are currently issued with 3- and 5-year maturities. The average remaining maturity on the current stock of T-bonds was roughly 2 years, and it carried a weighted average yield of 7.4 per cent. T-bills are currently issued with a 1-year maturity, while CDs are issued with 3- and 6-month maturities, typically on a bi-weekly basis. Banks are the primary holders of domestic debt issued by the government, as they hold about 94 per cent of outstanding T-bills and 65 per cent of T-bonds, while the rest are held by the Social Security Corporation (SSC), which holds 4 per cent and 28 per cent of the respective totals. A much smaller percentage of these markets are held by corporate savings plans.

There is strong demand for government securities from the banking sector, as they offer relatively high returns; short-term T-bills offered over 100 basis points more than the deposit window rate at the central bank in early 2008. Rates on government securities are typically higher than CDs as well. In the absence of other alternative investments, commercial banks tend to hold government securities to maturity. Public debt securities are issued using a multiple (or discriminatory) price auction. Banks, the SSC and other financial companies (including insurance companies) are eligible to bid directly in the auction; other investors must channel their bids through a bank.

Since the early 2000s, the structure of public debt has increasingly moved from external to domestic debt, and the share of foreign currency debt has fallen from over 80 per cent of the total in 2001 to below 50 per cent in 2008. This development has strengthened the balance sheet of the public sector and reduced its vulnerability to external shocks and exchange rate pressures. Historically, the government had relied on concessional foreign debt and borrowing from the CB to finance the budget deficit. The government believed that domestic borrowing through T-bills was too costly compared with the other sources of finance. However, as the government borrowed abroad, the CBJ was forced to use CDs to sterilise the impact of government borrowing on domestic liquidity, with additional interest cost. The total cost of borrowing, if one considers both the direct cost of borrowing abroad and the cost of sterilisation using CDs, would be lowered if the government used T-bills to borrow directly from the banking system. Initially, the government had been reluctant to do so because the cost of CDs does not appear directly in its balance sheets and is borne entirely by the CBJ. In practice, however, sterilisation costs reduce CBJ profits and compromise the strength of its balance sheet.

In 2002, the CBJ started to reduce the stock of CDs on offer in order to contain the cost of sterilisation, as it had been making losses from issuing CDs. However, the impact of this policy was to direct the excess liquidity still available in the banking system to the overnight deposit window at almost the same interest rate. This policy may also have been more costly to the CBJ, as the very liquid nature of overnight deposits allowed commercial banks to reduce the level of frictional balances that they might have kept otherwise. In response, the CBJ implemented an alternative policy of reducing both the volume of CDs and the overnight interest rate, which sets the floor for the CD rate determined by auction. This contributed to channelling excess liquidity back to CDs at a lower cost to the CBJ.

In contrast with the mostly subservient nature of the relation between the CBJ and the government during the 1980s, the evolution of the monetary framework and the increased discipline of fiscal policy necessitate greater coordination between the government and the central bank. This issue became particularly important with the elimination of the government's overdraft facility at the CBJ, as the government started to increase its reliance on short-term T-bills to replace that facility.

In the medium term, it may be more efficient to replace the CBJ CDs with government T-bills as a tool for monetary management. As the government introduces a short-term T-bill (perhaps 3-month bills), the CBJ could use it to conduct open-market operations; however this would require close coordination between the CBJ and the Ministry of Finance. This would reduce the combined cost of borrowing and sterilisation, and would contribute to the development of a secondary bond market.

5 Monetary policy autonomy

Recent literature has documented that operating a flexible exchange rate is not the enabling factor in implementing an independent monetary policy, as countries operating a flexible exchange rate regime were as much (if not more) responsive to world interest rates as those operating a fixed regime (Frankel, 1999; Frankel *et al.*, 2002; Fratzscher, 2002). Monetary independence, or the lack thereof, is measured by the influence of world interest rates on domestic interest rates. Jordan has operated a fixed exchange rate to the USD since 1995, which has been successful in providing a credible anchor for monetary policy. The exchange rate peg has served Jordan well in maintaining price stability and attracting foreign capital and investment, particularly from the region. This section will examine whether Jordan is also able to maintain a degree of autonomy in operating monetary policy, given its fixed exchange rate peg.

The literature has proceeded on the assumption that monetary independence should allow countries to avoid responding to world interest rates, and any influence from foreign interest rates has been taken as an indicator of the loss of independence of the domestic monetary policy. The current work, however, employs a more nuanced definition of monetary independence. World interest rates cannot be ignored as an important determinant in the design of monetary policy in emerging markets and ignoring them would be misleading; the definition of monetary independence applied here, and put forward in earlier work (Maziad, 2008), accepts the fact that as emerging markets integrate further into the global economy, the impact of world interest rates is going to increase. However, this natural phenomenon does not necessarily preclude the operation of a monetary policy that is geared towards achieving domestic objectives. In a sense, the point is not whether developing countries are responding to world interest rates, but whether they are still able to respond to domestic objectives at the same time.

To analyse the response of monetary policy in Jordan to US interest rates and domestic conditions, cointegration analysis and a Vector Error Correction Model (VECM) were estimated using quarterly data from 1999 to 2008. The objective of this analysis is to investigate the degree of monetary policy autonomy in Jordan, as defined above.

The domestic variables used to assess monetary independence are the inflation differential and the output gap differential[9] between Jordan and the US. The output gap differential was constructed using quarterly GDP data. GDP for each country was regressed on a linear and quadratic trend function and the output gap was obtained as the residuals of this regression. Each output gap series was then standardised by dividing the quarterly observations by the series' own standard deviation. The difference between these standardised output gaps for the Jordanian economy and the US economy is the variable used in the analysis to assess the response of monetary policy to the real economy. The reason for this procedure is that output gaps in emerging market countries are typically larger in both directions than those in developed countries such as the US; the standardisation process makes it possible to capture the relationship between the two business cycles which could have been masked by the larger magnitude of variation in Jordan had the series not been scaled using the standard deviations.

Using the Johansen cointegration technique, a long-run relationship was found between the variables in the system.[10] A cointegrating relation exists between the domestic interest rate (r), the US interest rate (r^*), the inflation differential (π), and the output gap differential (y), of the following form (t-stats are provided in brackets):

$$r = 1.39 + 0.74 \ r^* + 0.83 \ \pi + 0.77 \ y$$
$$(26.9) (17.8) (9.1)$$

As expected, the policy rate in Jordan responds to changes in the US interest rate. At the same time, monetary policy also reacts to domestic variables, namely the inflation and output gap differentials. Given the definition of monetary policy independence put forward, the CBJ has some autonomy in designing monetary policy in response to domestic variables. Essentially, the results point to the latitude that the CBJ has in setting the interest rate spread between the JD and the USD.

An alternative specification of the model, using explicitly the interest rate spread, confirmed the results, showing that the domestic variables influence the interest rate spread with broadly similar long-run coefficients.[11]

A VECM model was then estimated to distinguish the short-run responses of monetary policy to the different variables and to identify the speed of adjustment to the long-run equilibrium. A VECM is a restricted VAR designed for use with nonstationary series that are known to be cointegrated. The VECM has cointegration relations built into the specification so that it restricts the long-run behaviour of the endogenous variables to converge to their cointegrating relationships while allowing for short-run adjustment dynamics. The cointegration term is known as the error correction term since the deviation from long-run equilibrium is corrected gradually through a series of partial short-run adjustments. The estimated VECM was of the following form, where the lag length was identified using the Akaike criteria:

$$\Delta r_t = \sum_{p=1}^{P} D_p \Delta r_{t-p} + \sum_{k=0}^{Q} B_k \Delta r_{t-k}^* + \sum_{l=0}^{L} G_l' \Delta X_{t-l} - \delta[r_{t-1} - c - \beta r_{t-1}^* - \gamma' X_{t-1}] + u_t$$

where X is a vector of exogenous variables, including the inflation (π) and output gap (y) differentials as discussed above, u is an error term, and δ is the speed of adjustment to the long-run equilibrium. Table 5.3 provides the detailed results from the VECM estimation.

The short run dynamics indicate that the domestic interest rate adjusts relatively fast to the long-run equilibrium, where the speed of adjustment (δ) was estimated at 0.5. The coefficients on most of the lagged variables were statistically insignificant, except for those on the first lag of the inflation differential and output gap differential, which were statistically significant at the 5 per cent level.

The results of the VAR/VECM analysis were used to obtain the impulse response functions and the variance decomposition of the response of the domestic policy rate to the different variables in the system over a forecast horizon of 10 quarters. The results of the impulse response functions show that the domestic policy rate responds gradually to innovations in US interest rates until it peaks at about 7 quarters, after which the impact fades, while the response to the inflation differential is initially stronger, peaking at the 4th quarter. Based on the VAR analysis, the policy reaction to the output gap differential seems small (Figure 5.2).

The variance decomposition results show the share of the fluctuation in the domestic policy rate that can be attributed to individual shocks (or variables in the system). Table 5.4 provides the variance decomposition results obtained from the VECM analysis, with the columns showing the percentage of the variation due to each shock, and the rows adding up to 100 per cent in each period. The results suggest that in the 2nd quarter, innovations to the US interest rates can explain about 3.5 per cent of the variance in the domestic interest rate, reaching a peak of 57 per cent after 8 quarters. On the other hand, domestic variables, that is the inflation and output gap differentials combined, explain about 18 per cent of the

Table 5.3 VECM estimation

Vector error correction estimates – *t-stats in [ ]*	
Cointegrating equation:	
r	1
r*	−0.736006
	[−26.8556]
π (−1)	−0.834533
	[−17.8792]
y (−1)	−0.766947
	[−9.07574]
C	−1.399098
Error correction:	
Error correction term	−0.498103
	[−2.08138]
D(r_JOR(−1))	0.114278
	[0.69715]
D(r_JOR(−2))	−0.05902
	[−0.40443]
D(r_JOR(−3))	−0.08108
	[−0.65818]
D(r_US(−1))	−0.089543
	[−0.25957]
D(r_US(−2))	0.241891
	[0.75967]
D(r_US(−3))	0.384351
	[1.48891]
D(π (−1))	−0.339432
	[−2.01728]
D(π (−2))	−0.129941
	[−0.85263]
D(π (−3))	−0.031617
	[−0.34991]
D(y (−1))	−0.30641
	[−2.06503]
D(y (−2))	−0.159538
	[−1.44195]
D(y (−3))	−0.123202
	[−1.65448]
C	0.128831
	[1.88310]
R-squared	0.779269
Adj. R-squared	0.642626
Sum sq. resids	2.945599
F-statistic	5.702961
Log likelihood	−6.34972

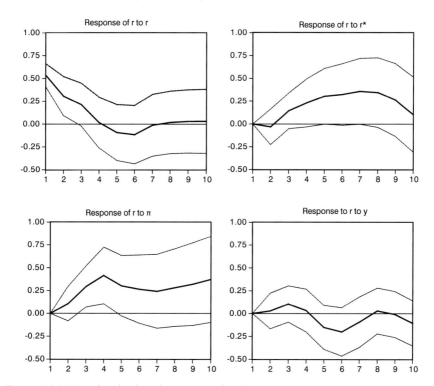

Figure 5.2 VAR estimation impulse response function

Table 5.4 VECM variance decomposition of policy rate in Jordan

Period	S.E.	r	r*	π	y
1	0.37	100.00	0.00	0.00	0.00
2	0.48	94.65	3.46	1.39	0.50
3	0.65	64.49	21.10	12.22	2.20
4	0.90	43.17	38.17	16.98	1.68
5	1.12	33.34	47.34	17.66	1.67
6	1.32	27.31	52.74	18.36	1.60
7	1.54	23.11	56.04	18.67	2.17
8	1.75	19.88	57.12	20.65	2.35
9	1.94	18.07	57.09	22.52	2.32
10	2.09	16.83	56.77	24.31	2.08

Cholesky ordering: r, r^*, π, y

variation in domestic interest rates by the 4th quarter. The variance decomposition results confirm the VAR impulse response analysis, where the impact of the output gap differential is small, especially compared with the policy response to the inflation differential.

Compared with other emerging markets operating a fixed exchange rate regime, the impact of the US interest rate appears moderate, while the speed of adjustment is relatively high. Frankel *et al.* (2002) analysed the degree of monetary policy independence in a sample of 46 industrial and developing countries. They applied OLS with fixed effects to panel data and controlled for periods of transition and currency crisis, distinguishing between different exchange rate regimes and between different time periods. Their results indicated that during the 1990s, on average the long-run coefficients on the US interest rate were 1.81 for fixed regimes, 0.81 for intermediate regimes and 0.91 for freely floating regimes.

In a sample of 19 emerging markets spanning the period from 1990 to 2005, the same type of analysis was conducted using OLS estimation of single-equation ECMs on individual country–exchange rate episodes, distinguishing between fixed and flexible exchange rate regimes. In that analysis, the long-run coefficient on the US interest rate was statistically significant in almost all the cases and averaged 1.5 for fixed exchange rate episodes, while the speed of adjustment for that group averaged 0.3 (Maziad, 2008).

Thus the present results indicate that the influence of US interest rates on policy in Jordan is smaller than in other emerging markets operating a fixed exchange rate, while monetary policy in Jordan is also responsive to domestic inflation and the output gap differential. One caveat is that, although a country like Jordan may be able to deviate from US interest rates by maintaining interest rates above those in the US, deviations in the opposite direction may be difficult. In other words, monetary policy independence could be asymmetric. Over the period studied, the output gaps in the US and in Jordan were positively correlated with a correlation coefficient of 0.25 (t-statistic 1.55),[12] which may have made it easier to follow US monetary policy without sacrificing domestic policy objectives; in addition, concerns over inflationary pressures in Jordan led the CBJ to widen the margin between the interest rates in the two countries, which implies policy independence in the current analysis. While it would still be possible to narrow the interest rate margin, as the CBJ did during the period from 2002 to the end of 2005 (see Figure 5.1), it might not be feasible, in the context of a fixed exchange rate, to loosen monetary policy to the point where interest rates are below those in the US due to concerns over inflationary expectations, potential loss of reserves, and the credibility of the peg.

6 Conclusion

This chapter has examined central bank independence and monetary policy operations in Jordan, as well as the issue of monetary autonomy in the context of Jordan's exchange rate peg. The Jordanian monetary framework has evolved considerably since the 1988–89 balance of payments crisis, when the domestic currency lost more than half of its value. In the aftermath of the crisis, the authorities embarked on a process of monetary and fiscal reforms, which restored confidence in the currency and assisted in the maintenance of a fixed exchange rate regime for over a decade and a half. In addition, over the past 18 years, the CBJ has gradually acquired a higher degree of central bank independence than it had enjoyed earlier in its history.

The legal and actual independence of the CBJ has increased and its ability to achieve monetary stability improved with the adoption of more sophisticated indirect control policy instruments. At the same time, the government is working towards greater fiscal consolidation and improving its debt management abilities. This development along with the CBJ's acquired skills and experience in managing monetary policy has enhanced its actual independence, thus emphasising the need for better coordination between fiscal and monetary policies.

The empirical analysis presented in this chapter points to the ability of the CBJ to shape monetary policy in response to domestic policy objectives, even in the presence of a strong influence from US interest rates. The VAR/VECM results suggest that the CBJ responds gradually to changes in US interest rates over a period of about 8 quarters, while also accommodating domestic variables: the inflation and output gap differentials between Jordan and the US. After an extended period of successfully operating a fixed exchange rate regime, the CBJ has built a credible track-record of maintaining low and stable inflation without restricting economic growth. With that experience, the CBJ could be able to make the transition to a more flexible monetary policy framework in the medium-term, if the authorities wished to do so, such as an inflation targeting framework that could grant it more independence in operating monetary policy.

Notes

1 There is little published research on central banking in Jordan. This chapter therefore draws heavily on publications of the Central Bank of Jordan (CBJ), publicly accessible IMF reports, a series of interviews conducted by the author with central bank and government officials in June 2004, and the returns to a questionnaire administered by the author to CBJ officials in 2004. The discussion of the central bank law relies on the 1971 CBJ law and its amendments in 1989 and 1992. All data is obtained from the IFS or the CBJ unless otherwise indicated.

2 IFS data shows that the JD remained stable against SDR but it depreciated by 4 per cent against the USD in April 1986.

3 Along with the emerging currency crisis, a major trade crisis also erupted in 1988 with the country's largest trading partner, Iraq. In 1983, the Economic Security Committee (ESC) introduced a policy of providing letters of credit to the Iraqi government to finance imports from Jordan to the tune of USD 100 million annually on average. In 1988, corruption and lack of oversight resulted in Iraqi importers overspending their credit by USD 240 million, which resulted in overall Iraqi debt to Jordan rising to almost USD 600 million. The credit scandal caused the government to freeze all letters of credit in order to investigate the legitimacy of the claims of Jordanian traders (Carroll, 2003; Satloff, 1992). The crisis dealt an additional blow to Jordan's fragile external position and contributed to the already growing speculation against the currency.

4   Severe pressures on the currency erupted when King Hussein announced in July that Jordan would disengage from the West Bank, which led Palestinians to panic and dump large holdings of JD, especially in the West Bank. Amid this confusion, the CBJ refused to provide foreign currency to the private sector, and in February 1989 the government began officially to devalue the JD and announced that it was floating the currency for a brief period before embarking on a stabilisation programme (Satloff, 1992).

5   Political independence refers to the capacity of the central bank to choose the final goals of monetary policy, such as inflation or the level of growth, while economic independence is the capacity to choose the instruments with which to pursue these goals. The measurement of political independence typically analyses the procedures for hiring and dismissing the central bank's governor and its board, while economic independence measures the ability of the central bank to operate its monetary policy instruments freely, for example to set the interest rate and not to finance the budget deficit. The literature also distinguishes between goal/target independence and instrument independence. See, for example Grilli, Masciandaro, and Tabellini (1991), Cukierman (1992), and Bofinger (2001).

6   This is consistent with Gisolo (2009: 35), where Jordan's central bank independence was ranked relatively low compared with other MENA countries on account of the strong government involvement in the appointment and dismissal of the governor and the board.

7   The ongoing financing of the budget deficit was reflected in the return to a questionnaire on central bank independence administered to CBJ staff in early 2004, in which they responded that there was no limit on CBJ lending to the government during the 1980s. Later, during interviews conducted in June 2004, CBJ staff confirmed that the existence of a provision for exceptional loans was interpreted as 'no limits' on lending despite the statutory limitation of 20 per cent of revenues. Central bank finance of the deficit is a key element in determining actual CBI, which in the case of Jordan seems to have been low until the early 1990s.

8   Gisolo (2009) studied the following countries: Algeria, Cyprus, Egypt, Israel, Jordan, Lebanon, Libya, Malta, Morocco, Palestine, Tunisia, and Turkey.

9   The inflation differential was used in earlier research but including the output gap differential in assessing monetary policy independence is an innovation.

10   The standard Augmented Dickey–Fuller test was run to test for the order of integration. The null hypothesis of unit root could not be rejected for both interest rate series and could only be rejected at the 5–10 per cent level for the inflation and output gap differentials.

11   The cointegration analysis was run on an alternative specification, using the interest rate spread, the inflation differential, and the output gap differential. The results were broadly similar to those presented in this chapter.

12   A seasonally adjusted output gap series for Jordan showed a correlation coefficient of 0.67 (t-statistic: 5.54).

References

Abu-Hammour, M. (2005), 'Jordan's Economic Reform', speech at the Eighth Annual Meeting of Middle Eastern and North African Bank Chief Executives, February, Abu Dhabi.

Arnone, M., Laurens, B., Segalotto, F., and Sommer, M. (2007), 'Central Bank Autonomy: Lessons from Global Trends', IMF working paper 07/88.

Bofinger, P. (2001), *Monetary Policy: Goals, Institutions, Strategies, and Instruments*, Oxford University Press.

Carroll, K. (2003), *Business as Usual? Economic Reform in Jordan*, Lexington Books.

CBJ (1971), Law No. 23 of 1971, amended by Law No. 37 of 1989, amended by Law No. 16 of 1992, Central Bank of Jordan.

——(1989), *The Central Bank of Jordan over Twenty-five Years: A Special Volume* (in Arabic), Central Bank of Jordan.

Cukierman, A. (1992), *Central Bank Strategy, Credibility and Autonomy*, Cambridge, MA: MIT Press.

Frankel, J. (1999), 'No single currency regime is right for all countries or at all times', NBER working paper 7338.

Frankel, J., Schmukler, S., and Serven, L. (2002), 'Global transmission of interest rates: monetary independence and currency regime', NBER working paper 8828.

Fratzscher, M. (2002), 'The Euro bloc, the Dollar bloc, and the Yen bloc: How much monetary policy independence can exchange rate flexibility buy in the interdependent world', European Central Bank working paper 154.

Fry, M.J. (1998), 'Assessing central bank autonomy in developing countries: Do actions speak louder than words?', *Oxford Economic Papers*, 50: 307–34.

Fry, M.J., Julius, D., Mahadeva, L., Roger, S., and Sterne, G. (2000), 'Key issues in the choice of monetary policy framework', in L. Mahadeva and G. Sterne (eds), *Monetary Policy Frameworks in a Global Context*, London: Routledge.

Gisolo, E. (2009), 'The degree of legal central bank independence in MENA countries' in D. Cobham and G. Dibeh (eds.), *Monetary Policy and Central Banking in the Middle East and North Africa*, Routledge.

Grilli, V., Masciandaro, D., and Tabellini, G. (1991), 'Political and monetary institutions and public financial policies in the industrial countries,' *Economic Policy,* 13: 341–92.

IMF (1995), *Jordan – Background Information on Selected Aspects of Adjustment and Growth Strategy*, IMF Staff Country Report 95/97, International Monetary Fund.

——(2007), *Jordan: Post-Program Monitoring Discussions – Staff Report*, IMF Country Report 07/284, International Monetary Fund.

——(2008), *Article IV Consultation*, IMF Country Report 08/291, International Monetary Fund.

——(2009), *Article IV Consultation*, IMF Country Report 09/159, International Monetary Fund.

Jordanian Ministry of Finance (2001), *Public Debt Management Law No. 26* of 2001.

Kanakria, E. (2002), 'Economic reform programme in Jordan and its impact on public finance', Arab University of Jordan, Unpublished paper (in Arabic).

Maziad, S. (2008), *Monetary Frameworks in Emerging Market Countries: Exchange Rate Arrangements and Central Bank Independence*, PhD Dissertation, School of Economics and Finance, University of St. Andrews, Scotland, UK.

Poddar, T., Sab, R., and Khachatryan, H. (2006), 'The monetary transmission mechanism in Jordan', IMF working paper 06/48.

Satloff, R. (1992), 'Jordan's Great Gamble: Economic Crisis and Political Reform' in Barkey, H. (ed.), *The Politics of Economic Reform in the Middle East*, St. Martin's Press, New York.

6 From occupation to an independent monetary policy

Achievements and aspirations in Palestine

Jihad K. Wazir, Mohammad Atallah and Shaker A. Sarsour

1 Introduction

The Palestine Monetary Authority (PMA) was set up as an independent institution in 1995, initially by presidential decree, with its authority and autonomy over money and banking markets later established in law number (2) of 1997. The overall purpose of the PMA is to work to maintain the stability and effectiveness of the Palestinian financial system, and to promote the sustained economic and financial growth of the Palestinian economy through effective and transparent regulation and supervision of the operations of the banks. The longer term aspiration is for the PMA to become the central bank for an independent Palestinian state.

The PMA has made significant progress in establishing effective regulation and banking supervision, and overseeing the payments system in Palestine. However, it does not as yet operate a monetary policy, essentially because the PMA cannot issue a national currency without Israeli agreement, and because there is as yet no Palestinian state. The currencies used in the Palestinian Territory (the West Bank and Gaza; PT) were stipulated in Annex IV of the Paris Protocol on Economic Relations between the Government of Israel and the PLO (part of the so-called Oslo agreements) signed in 1994. The Protocol laid down that 'the New Israeli Shekel (NIS) shall be legal tender and will serve as means of payment in the Palestinian Territory'. The Oslo accords also allowed the US dollar and the Jordanian dinar to function as legal tender. About 50 per cent of bank customer deposits in Palestine are in US dollars, around 22 per cent are in Israeli shekels, about 26 per cent in Jordanian dinars, and the rest are in other currencies. The US dollar and the Jordanian dinar (which is pegged to the dollar) are the primary deposit currencies, while the Israeli shekel is used for most retail transactions. As Israel is the largest trading partner of the Palestinian Territory, transactions between banks operating in the PT and those in Israel were about 20 billion shekels in 2007.

In 2006 the PMA adopted a Strategic Transformation Plan (STP) (Abed, 2006), which is designed to turn the current institution from a banking supervision agency into a full-fledged modern central bank. The STP involves substantial internal modernisation and restructuring, including the adoption of a clear focus on the twin functions of monetary stability and financial stability, and the creation of a Research and Monetary Policy Department. It also envisages the adoption of a real time gross settlement (RTGS) payments system. This development of the PMA into a modern central bank would be facilitated if the new central bank law which has been drafted but not yet enacted was brought into operation.

Given the absence of a Palestinian currency it is not surprising that there are relatively few studies on monetary policy in Palestine. A number of authors have considered what would be the appropriate exchange rate regime when a currency is eventually issued, notably Naqib (1999), Erickson von Allmen and Fischer (2001), Cobham (2004) and Beidas and Kandil (2005). But there is little on the instruments which monetary policy in Palestine might use or on the domestic targets it might pursue.

In this chapter we explore a number of actions and initiatives which the PMA is taking to strengthen its capacity to operate a monetary policy when the time comes. In section 2 we show that the new central bank law would indeed greatly increase the independence of the PMA. Section 3 discusses methods of estimating the amount of notes and coin in circulation in Palestine, which would be an essential prerequisite to the introduction of a new currency. Section 4 considers the idea for the PMA to issue its own certificates of deposit, which would provide a basic instrument for interbank operations and, ultimately, for the operation of monetary policy through market interest rates. Section 5 discusses the question of dollarisation, which has been posed by the recurrent difficulties in ensuring an adequate supply of shekel currency in Gaza. Section 6 summarises and concludes.

2 Central bank independence

The analytical and empirical aspects of central bank independence (CBI) have been intensively explored during recent decades. Analytical research by economists such as Cukierman (1992) has argued that the degree of central bank independence is an important determinant of countries' inflation rates. On the empirical side economists including Bade and Parkin (1982), Grilli, Masciandaro and Tabellini (1991) and Cukierman, Webb and Neyaptı (1992) have measured the degree of central bank independence by constructing indices which take account of relations between government and central banks, the objectives of the central bank, policy formulation, the conditions under which the government can borrow from the central bank, the method of appointment of the central bank governor, and other factors. On such indices it appears that higher central bank independence is associated with lower inflation in developed, but not necessarily in developing, countries.

The most comprehensive assessment of CBI for Middle East and North African countries is that of Gisolo (2009) who used the index of Gutierrez (2003), which evaluates CBI in terms of six dimensions: central bank objectives, policy formation, political autonomy (governor), political autonomy (board members), economic autonomy and economic accountability, with a scoring on each element (sub-dimension) which goes from –1 to +1. Gisolo's analysis covered the PMA, on the basis of the 1997 central bank law. Table 6.1 shows his results for Palestine,

Table 6.1 CBI in Palestinian territory under the 1997 law and the new law

Index	Weight	Palestinian Territory		Israel	Jordan
		1997 law	*New law (not yet enacted)*	*Israel*	*Jordan*
Central bank objectives					
Economic policy	1	0.25	1	0.25	0.25
Financial system	0.2	0	0	0	0
Total		0.25	1	0.25	0.25
Policy formulationx					
Monetary policy	1	1	1	0.5	0.5
Foreign exchange policy	0.6	0.6	0.3	0.3	0.3
Coordination of policies	1	0.25	0.25	0	0.25
Resolution of conflicts	0.8	0.2	0.4	0	0.2
Total		2.05	1.95	0.8	1.25
Political autonomy (governor)					
Appointment of governor	1	−1	0.25	0.25	−1
Term of the governor	1	−1	1	1	−1
Dismissal of governor	1	0.5	0.5	−1	0.5
Government representation	0.8	−0.8	0	0	0
Total		−2.3	1.75	0.25	−1.5
Political autonomy (board members)					
Appointment of board members	1	−1	0.25	0.25	−1
Terms of board members	1	−1	−1	1	−1
Dismissal of board members	1	0.5	0.5	−1	−1
Total		−1.5	−0.25	0.25	−3
Economic autonomy					
Credit to the government	1	0.25	1	−1	0.25
Quasi fiscal activities	0.4	0	0	0	0
Monetary instruments	1	1	1	0	1
Solvency	1	1	1	0.25	0.25
Total		2.25	3	−0.75	1.5
Accountability					
Publication of statements	0.2	0	0	0.05	0
Audit	0.8	0.8	0.8	0.6	0.8
Total		0.8	0.8	0.65	0.8
TOTAL SCORE		1.55	8.25	1.45	−0.7

Source: Authors' calculation of the index under the new law (not yet enacted). Gisolo (2009) for the 1997 law index and Israel and Jordan.

Israel and Jordan, together with our assessment of what the independence of the PMA would be if the new law were to be enacted.[1]

The new assessment makes clear that the new law would guarantee much more independence for the PMA. Indeed, at 8.25 its independence would be well above that for any other MENA central bank included in Gisolo's sample, where the highest overall scores were 4.0 for Algeria and 3.25 for Tunisia. The 1997 law incorporates a higher score with respect to policy formulation, mainly because the 1997 law gives the PMA the right to set exchange rate policy whereas the new law would require the PMA to consult on this with the Ministry of Finance. On all the other dimensions the new law indicates a higher score, with particularly large differences on central bank objectives (price stability is now enshrined as the primary goal), the political autonomy of the governor and to a lesser extent board members, and economic autonomy (the new law would prohibit any lending to the government whereas the existing law allows for temporary lending, though this facility has not been used in recent years).

3 Towards an independent monetary policy: estimating the notes and coin in circulation

Palestine has not had its own national currency for more than fifty years. Before 1967 the Jordanian dinar (JD) was the official currency, and there was a monetary authority (the Central Bank of Jordan) and a number of financial intermediaries (Arab banks and Palestinian money changers). After the Israeli occupation of the West Bank and Gaza Strip in 1967, the Israeli shekel[2] and the Jordanian JD were both official currencies. There was no monetary authority and few financial intermediaries (the Arab banks were closed and the Israeli banks did not service Palestinian customers, who had to rely on Palestinian money changers). In addition, the Israeli civil administration, which managed Palestinian Territory matters at this time, tended to discourage domestic or foreign debts. Thus during this period the PT had no monetary (or financial) policy of the conventional type.

Even after the signing of the provisional peace treaty in 1994 with Israel, the arrival of the Palestinian National Authority and the foundation of the PMA, as laid down in the Paris Protocol, the Palestinian territory did not possess its own currency. The Protocol covered the establishment of a Palestinian Monetary Authority with full central bank duties and jurisdiction, except for the issue of a currency, despite the obvious economic importance and political significance of an independent currency in terms of monetary policy and as a symbol of national sovereignty.

There are three (or more) currencies now used in Palestine: the Jordanian dinar (JD), Israeli shekel (NIS), and US dollar (USD). We have data on the amount of each currency held in bank deposits, but no data on the notes and coin in circulation in Palestine. The estimation of this amount is essential if a new currency is to be introduced at some point: the PMA would need to determine the amount of cash to be issued, especially in the early stages, where the cash issued was equivalent to cash in circulation outside the banking system, and particularly if the intention was to replace all the cash in circulation outside the banking system with the new national currency in one stroke, and not in phases.[3]

The most accurate way to identify this component (cash in circulation) would be via a large-sample survey, but this would be expensive and would require considerable time and effort by a team of specialists, and is therefore not feasible at present. However, it is possible to use indirect alternative methods to estimate the cash in circulation, by exploiting similarities in the conditions and patterns of economic activity in the countries whose currencies circulate in the Palestinian territory, particularly Jordan and Israel. It has to be borne in mind that these countries enjoy relative economic and political stability, national currencies and clear geographical borders, features which are not present in the Palestinian case.

There are three different indicative ratios for each of Jordan and Israel which could be used to estimate the amount of cash in circulation outside the banking system in Palestine: first, the ratio of cash in circulation to demand deposits in Jordan (Israel); secondly, the velocity of money in Jordan (Israel); and thirdly, the ratio of cash in circulation to GDP in Jordan (Israel). In each case we assume that the same ratio holds in Palestine, and apply it to the known total of bank deposits and/ or nominal GDP, as appropriate, to find the implied cash in circulation in Palestine.

The results derived from these three approaches are shown in Table 6.2. Here it is immediately obvious that the second and (in the Israeli case) third approaches produce results that are inconsistent with the Palestinian reality: the amount of cash implied by the Jordanian velocity is implausibly small and that implied by the Israeli velocity is actually negative (this is because the exercise predicts a level of money which is less than the known total of demand deposits), while the Israeli cash to GDP ratio also implies an extremely small amount of cash. On the other hand, the cash to demand deposit ratios predict broadly similar amounts of cash in both cases. Given these findings we now examine in more detail the factors underlying the cash to demand deposit ratio predictions.

Cash in circulation in a specific year is estimated as follows:

$$CC/DD * DD_{Pal} = CC_{Pal}$$

where:

CC_{Pal} = cash in circulation in Palestine outside the banking system,

DD_{Pal} = demand deposits in Palestine in all currencies, converted into US dollars,

CC/DD = ratio of cash in circulation to demand deposits in Jordan (Israel), where for Jordan $DD_{Pal} + DD_{Jor} = DD$, and for Israel $DD_{Pal} + DD_{Isr} = DD$: since we have data only for total holdings of currency in both Jordan (Israel) and Palestine we take the ratio of this amount to total demand deposits in both Jordan (Israel) and Palestine.

Table 6.3 shows the data on money supply in each of Jordan and Israel, together with the corresponding demand deposits in Palestine and three key ratios, for the years 1996–2008. While there is a trend increase in both countries in the outstanding totals of both cash and overall deposits, there is also a trend fall in the

Table 6.2 Currency in circulation in Palestine according to the three different approaches (million USD)

Year	On the basis of Jordanian data			On the basis of Israeli data		
	Approach 1 CC/DD	Approach 2 V = GDP/M1	Approach 3 CC/GDP	Approach 1 CC/DD	Approach 2 V = GDP/M1	Approach 3 CC/GDP
1996	735.34	597.1	711.02	345.7	−336.1	85.19
1997	721.72	712.7	770.66	375.5	−331.2	94.47
1998	783.17	603.5	723.20	419.0	−368.5	103.14
1999	1,020.6	682.0	866.70	511.8	−409.8	120.78
2000	1212.7	666.2	919.61	677.2	−587.2	109.00
2001	954.5	470.2	707.78	613.2	−530.0	106.64
2002	935.0	195.5	581.91	694.1	−585.7	92.80
2003	1034.3	396.7	723.78	840.9	−796.5	109.24
2004	1019.5	373.8	712.72	1107.1	−929.5	129.34
2005	981.9	677.5	828.81	1099.7	−961.7	156.25
2006	1030.7	647.4	889.32	921.3	−949.4	154.16
2007	1343.2	472.9	964.48	1122.9	−1,157.4	189.82
2008	1765.7	702.6	1,218.08	1396.3	−1,152.4	271.43

Table 6.3(a) Money supply components in Jordan during 1996–2008

Jordan (millions of Jordanian dinars)

Year	Currency in circulation (CC)	Demand deposits (DD)			Money supply (M1)	(CC)/(M1)	(DD)/(M1)	(CC)/ (DDtotal)
		DDj[a]	DDp[b]	DDtotal				
1996	952.2	587.0	128.1	715.1	1,539.2	61.86	38.14	1.332
1997	987.6	654.8	123.7	778.5	1,642.4	60.13	39.87	1.269
1998	952.8	672.4	94.1	766.5	1,625.2	58.63	41.37	1.243
1999	1,106.6	670.5	99.2	769.7	1,777.1	62.27	37.73	1.438
2000	1,239.9	786.8	115.7	902.5	2,026.7	61.18	38.82	1.379
2001	1,202.4	917.3	112.4	1029.7	2,119.7	56.73	43.27	1.169
2002	1,252.7	1,063.5	127.2	1190.7	2,316.2	54.08	45.92	1.052
2003	1,443.7	1,476.1	158.1	1634.2	2,919.8	49.45	50.55	0.888
2004	1,414.4	1,778.5	195.7	1974.2	3,192.9	44.30	55.70	0.721
2005	1,657.2	2,404.1	218.6	2622.7	4,061.3	40.80	59.20	0.633
2006	2,027.4	2,539.1	207.8	2746.9	4,566.5	44.40	55.60	0.735
2007	2,172.4	2,660.7	226.2	2886.9	4,833.1	44.95	55.05	0.750
2008	2,664.9	2,908.2	245.7	3153.9	5,573.1	47.82	52.18	0.846

Table 6.3(b) Money supply components in Israel during 1996–2008

Israel (millions of new Israeli shekels)

Year	Currency in circulation (CC)	Demand deposits (DD)			Money supply (M1)	(CC)/(M1)	(DD)/(M1)	(CC)/(DDtotal)
		DDi[a]	DDp[b]	DDtotal				
1996	7,769	11,921	496	12,417	19,690	39.46	60.54	0.626
1997	8,766	12,646	626	13,272	21,412	40.94	59.06	0.660
1998	10,064	14,432	701	15,133	24,496	41.08	58.92	0.665
1999	12,189	16,065	844	16,909	28,254	43.14	56.86	0.721
2000	12,374	15,033	1100	16,133	27,407	45.15	54.85	0.770
2001	14,567	18,319	1108	19,427	32,886	44.30	55.70	0.751
2002	15,574	18,900	1076	19,976	34,474	45.18	54.82	0.781
2003	16,178	21,210	1255	22,465	37,388	43.27	56.73	0.722
2004	17,883	21,406	1497	22,903	43,024	45.52	54.48	0.783
2005	20,858	27,665	2149	29,814	50,937	42.99	57.01	0.709
2006	21,405	31,069	1599	32,668	55,089	40.79	59.21	0.657
2007	24,568	37,039	2401	39,440	64,591	39.88	60.12	0.627
2008	29,884	42,497	2785	45,282	70,092	41.30	58.70	0.669

Sources: www.bankisrael.gov.il , www.cbj.gov.jo

Notes

a DDj is the amount of demand deposits in Jordan, and DDi is the amount of demand deposits in Israel

b DDp is the amount of demand deposits in Jordanian dinars (or new Israeli shekels) in the Palestinian Territory

ratio of cash to deposits in both countries, with a stronger decline in Jordan than in Israel. This can be understood in part as the result of a trend in Jordan towards the more intensive use of banking systems and greater use of electronic payment instruments, which means that Jordan has been 'catching up' on Israel. In Jordan this ratio (CC/DD) fell from 1.33 in 1996 to 0.85 in December of 2008, while in Israel the corresponding ratio fluctuated between 0.63 and 0.78 and ended 2008 at 0.67. It is probable that Palestine has been experiencing a comparable change to that in Jordan: there has been a gradual spread of awareness and banking culture among Palestinians and increasing use of electronic payment methods such as ATMs, credit cards, and electronic point of sale systems. On the other hand, the constraints of occupation suggest that Palestine may lag a little behind Jordan in this respect.

Table 6.4 shows what the money supply would have been in the Palestinian Territory in each year from 1996 to 2008 if the ratio of currency in circulation had been the same as in Jordan, on the one hand, or Israel, on the other. However, there is another factor which has affected the Jordanian ratio in the last few years: the immigration of a large number of Iraqi refugees in 2003 and the next few years who brought with them significant amounts of bank deposits. It is clear from Table 6.3 that there were unusually sharp declines in the Jordanian CC/DD ratio in 2003, 2004 and 2005, followed by a slight reversal from 2006.

For the future introduction of a national currency in Palestine what matters is, of course, the currency in circulation at that point, rather than in the past. If we take the 'Iraqi effect' in Jordan into account, but assume both that there was some continuation of the trend decline in the 'real' CC/DD ratio in Jordan and that Palestine was lagging a little behind Jordan in this respect, a realistic maximum for the CC/DD ratio in Palestine at the end of 2008 would be 1.0. On the other hand it seems clear that the Palestinian use of cash must be higher than that in Israel. Given the fluctuations in the Israeli cash to demand deposit ratio, we take 0.7 as the minimum for Palestine. On this basis the minimum cash in circulation outside the banking system in Palestine (based on the ratio of 0.7) amounted in December 2008 to 1461.0 million dollars, while the maximum limit (based on the ratio of 1.0) was 2087.1 million dollars.

A further question of interest is the currency structure of the cash in circulation, as between shekels, dollars, dinars and other currencies. Is this comparable to the structure of cheques cleared, or the structure of cash in the vaults of Palestinian banks, or is it comparable to the structure of demand deposits? Table 6.5 shows the structure of each of these three. It is clear that the shekel has a much larger share in cheques cleared (67 per cent) than in demand deposits (36 per cent) or vault cash (53 per cent), and it seems likely that the currency structure of cash in circulation is broadly similar to this. This is also consistent with casual observation, which suggests relatively low shares of each of the Jordanian dinar and US dollar in daily transactions but relatively high shares in savings, and the opposite for the Israeli shekel. On the other hand a significant proportion of private employees are paid in dollars, and a large part of the remittances sent back to Palestine by emigrants

Table 6.4 Money supply estimates for Palestine (million USD)

| Year | Currency in circulation according to first approach | | Demand deposits (DD) in Palestine | Money supply in Palestine according to | |
	DDpal *(CC/DD)jor	DDpal *(CC/DD)isr		MS = DDpal + [DDpal*(CC/DD)jor]	MS = DDpal + [DDpal*(CC/DD)isr]
1996	735.34	345.7	552.24	1287.8	897.9
1997	721.72	375.5	568.91	1290.9	944.4
1998	783.17	419.0	630.04	1413.2	1049.0
1999	1,020.6	511.8	709.88	1730.7	1221.7
2000	1212.7	677.2	879.43	2092.2	1556.6
2001	954.5	613.2	816.52	1771.0	1429.7
2002	935.0	694.1	888.75	1823.7	1582.9
2003	1034.3	840.9	1164.70	2199.0	2005.6
2004	1019.5	1107.1	1413.96	2433.4	2521.1
2005	981.9	1099.7	1551.12	2533.0	2650.9
2006	1030.7	921.3	1402.35	2433.1	2323.7
2007	1343.2	1122.9	1790.93	3134.1	2913.8
2008	1765.7	1396.3	2087.11	3852.8	3483.4

Table 6.5 Composition of demand deposits, vault cash, and clearing cheques in Palestine, December 2008 (million USD)

	Demand deposits (DD)		Vault cash		Clearing cheques	
	Value	*%*	*Value*	*%*	*Value*	*%*
Israeli shekels (NIS)	776.50	37.2	182.76	52.79	389.74	66.67
Jordanian dinars (JD)	346.35	16.6	74.96	21.65	53.61	9.17
US dollars (USD)	760.94	36.5	81.69	23.6	136.33	23.32
Other currencies	203.32	9.7	6.77	1.96	4.92	0.84
Total	2087.11	100	346.18	100	584.6	100

is in dollars, and these phenomena are consistent with the large share of the dollar (23 per cent of cheques cleared).

Table 6.6 shows the composition of the money supply in Palestine at end-2008 based on the currency structure of cheques cleared, for the minimum (0.7) and maximum (1.0) limits for the ratio of currency in circulation to demand deposits. On this basis the minimum and maximum totals are respectively a little above the (Israel-based and Jordan-based) numbers given for 2008 in Table 6.4, while the share of the shekel in the total money supply is around 51 per cent, that of the dollar just over 30 per cent and that of the dinar around 13 per cent.

It should also be noted that if a national currency were to be introduced it would be important to be able to estimate the division of the cash in circulation between the various types and sizes of money (big notes, small notes, coins of different values) as well as the overall money supply. Moreover, if the overall money supply turned out to be more or less than the money demanded, market forces will work to restore the balance between supply and demand, mostly without the need for intervention by the monetary authorities. But if demand for a specific note or coin was out of line with supply, that can only be fixed by the intervention of the monetary authorities. At present there is no data available on the note and coin breakdown of the existing cash in circulation. If and when the issue of a national currency is planned, it will be necessary to conduct a sample survey to obtain such information.

4 Towards an independent monetary policy: the issue of certificates of deposit

A certificate of deposit (CD) is a short-term negotiable financial instrument originally issued by banks but more recently issued by emerging economy central banks to their commercial banks.[4] The primary objective of a CD instrument for a central bank is to facilitate the management of liquidity in a situation where there is persistent excess liquidity. A CD instrument is only one of many instruments available within a comprehensive monetary and financial framework that would include government-issued bond instruments within an established primary and secondary capital market structure. However, the Palestinian financial infrastructure is yet to develop all of the necessary institutional frameworks, the capital market suffers from a lack of depth and a high degree of segmentation, and the PMA has not yet developed a monetary policy framework of its own.

Nevertheless, with or without a national currency, it is envisaged that the PMA's role in macroeconomic management would be strengthened by the development of domestic interbank money and foreign exchange markets. Apart from a limited volume of transactions between banks, there are currently no active interbank money markets, nor an active interbank foreign exchange market. As a result, banks mainly place their excess funds with the PMA or abroad. This contributes to significant inefficiencies and costs. In addition, the lack of such markets exacerbates liquidity and foreign exchange risks.

Table 6.6 Composition of money supply in Palestine according to currencies, December 2008 (million USD)

	Currency in circulation		Demand deposits DD	Money supply	
	Minimum	Maximum		Minimum MS (% of total)	Maximum MS (% of total)
Israeli shekels (NIS)	974.0	1391.5	776.5	1750.5 (49.3)	2168.0 (51.9)
US dollars (USD)	340.7	486.7	760.9	1101.6 (31.0)	1247.6 (29.9)
Jordanian dinars (JD)	134.0	191.4	346.3	480.0 (13.5)	537.7 (12.9)
Other currencies	12.3	17.5	203.3	215.6 (6.1)	220.8 (5.3)
Total	1461.0	2087.1	2087.1	3548.1 (100.0)	4174.2 (100.0)

The policy decision to introduce a CD instrument would have an impact on the risk profile of the PMA with respect to its credit risk and operational risk, and an impact on financial market development and the provision of intraday liquidity for the payment system. Similarly, such an instrument will also have an impact on the banks' ability to manage balance sheet risks because it will address the current deficiencies and problems associated with the pricing and distribution of liquidity.

Another element underlying the idea of issuing CDs is the PMA's implementation of the first integrated national payments and securities settlement system project in the West Bank and Gaza. A key component of this project is the activation of a real time gross settlement (RTGS) facility. The PMA will evaluate the options for liquidity management in the RTGS facility which will include the mobilisation of compulsory reserves, the acceptance of cash collateral for payment system purposes and the issuing of the PMA's own securities. The system will operate in the current multicurrency environment and will be able to accommodate a future national Palestinian currency. The PMA will also adopt measures to encourage an interbank money market which will be closely integrated with the settlement system.

An RTGS system could work with all settlement taking place via banks' reserves, which would mean that reserve requirements would need to be kept high. But efficiency would suggest that, as occurs in most RTGS systems, it would be better to have intraday liquidity provided by the central bank. However, such liquidity needs to be collateralised, to prevent risk to the central bank. In this context, the creation of CDs would provide a form of collateral which banks can place with the central bank against intraday loans when necessary. At the same time, it would help facilitate the development of an interbank market by enabling banks to lend to each other against CD collateral. By this measure the PMA would therefore be taking the lead in developing a wholesale money market and contributing to the wider development of financial markets in Palestine.

By introducing the CD instrument, the PMA would also be introducing an incipient monetary policy instrument that could potentially influence interest rates in the local market even without the introduction of Palestinian currency, by setting a voluntary benchmark rate that ostensibly would be difficult for banks to ignore.[5]

Finally, the existence of CDs would in the normal way strengthen the PMA's ability to manage liquidity in the market by absorbing excess liquidity from the system.

5 Towards an independent monetary policy: the issue of dollarisation

In 2007, the Israeli Government took the decision to declare Gaza 'hostile territory', a decision that left Israeli banks dealing with Palestinian banks in Gaza open to potential litigation over continued financial links to banks in Gaza. Soon after, the two major Israeli banks which traditionally had correspondence relationships with Palestinian banks announced their intention to sever all banking relationships not only with Gaza banks but also with those in the West Bank. This made it extremely difficult for Palestinian banks to settle shekel-based business transactions both between Israeli and Palestinian traders as well as internally between themselves, by using shekel-denominated settlement of accounts. In addition, the Israeli military has repeatedly refused to allow timely and sufficient transfers of shekel currency from the Palestinian banks in the West Bank to their branches in Gaza, which has significantly reduced the shekel liquidity in Gaza branches available for use in the Gaza economy and further eroded the viability of the shekel currency in the Palestinian Territory.

Palestinian banks also rely on Israeli banks for deposit and withdrawal of physical cash in shekel currency, so that the severing of these relationships implies that the shekel will cease to be a viable currency for transactions in the Palestinian Territory, in violation of existing agreements. These measures by Israeli banks are more surprising in the light of the international recognition of the strong steps taken by the PMA and the Palestinian banks to ensure full compliance with international standards and conventions on anti-money laundering (AML). In the short term, the actions by the Israeli banks threaten to compromise the Palestinian financial sector and even shake confidence in the banking institutions. And while the PMA has been working with the central bank of Israel (BoI) to temporarily stay the Israeli banks' decision to sever these banking relationships, in the meantime the PMA and the BoI are trying to find alternative arrangements to prevent a serious economic impact on both sides. In the medium to long term, these developments justify the PMA's plans to investigate alternative currency arrangements as well as the option of issuing a Palestinian currency once Palestinian statehood is reached.

In the short term, if the shekel ceases to be a viable currency, other currencies will have to substitute for the shekel. The US dollar and the Jordanian dinar are the obvious alternatives to consider. The Jordanian dinar would be perhaps the easiest currency to adopt, given that the JD was legal tender in the West Bank during the Jordanian control of the West Bank between 1948 and 1967, that there are close economic and family ties between Palestinians in the West Bank and the East Bank of the river Jordan, i.e. the Hashemite Kingdom of Jordan, and that the JD is still used in the West Bank and to some extent in Gaza. Palestinians are familiar with the Jordanian paper currency and to a lesser extent with its coins. The Jordanian dinar was traditionally used for purchases of high-value items such as property since it has traditionally been viewed as a very stable currency. That confidence in the stability of the JD harks back to the days of the hyperinflation of the Israeli shekel in the 1970s, during which Palestinians under Israeli occupation found the JD a more reliable and stable store of value. However, today, given the sensitive and complex political dynamics of the Israeli, Palestinian, and Jordanian triangle, the choice of 'dinarisation' is fraught with political implications that neither the Jordanian nor the Palestinian side is willing to undertake at the current stage.

The other option would be to further 'dollarise' the Palestinian economy, given that currently approximately 50 per cent of bank deposits are in US dollars. Many local companies, businesses, manufacturers and institutions such as the UN and many local and international NGOs pay salaries in US dollars. Shops and supermarkets readily accept dollars in daily transactions and some of the newly published laws relating to tax collection use the US dollar as the currency of payment.

Dollarisation has many policy implications and there is a significant literature both for and against dollarisation (Balino *et al.*, 1999; Berg and Borensztein, 2000; Armas *et al.*, 2006). Its proponents argue that it promises a way of avoiding currency and balance of payments crises and removes the risks associated with possible sharp depreciation and unexpected capital outflows resulting from expectations or fears of possible devaluation. It also leads to closer integration with international markets and lower transaction costs resulting from stable dollar-denominated pricing. Considering the bad record of many developing countries in promoting low inflation and achieving price stability, dollarisation is viewed as a more stable alternative, particularly for developing countries with small economies, which would include the Palestinian Territory.

Critics of dollarisation argue that monetary policy is fundamentally a national issue to be decided by national governments. Dollarisation also means a loss of seigniorage revenue.[6] In the Palestinian case, if the decision was taken to go for full dollarisation, it would be very difficult to reverse it with the introduction of a Palestinian currency. However, in the short term, dollarisation cannot be ruled out.[7]

To encourage a further shift into the US dollar, the PMA would need to coordinate with the Ministry of Finance on the possibility of changing the national budget from being denominated in shekels to being denominated in US dollars. This would mean that the Government would pay civil service salaries and suppliers in US dollars, which would dramatically boost the process of dollarisation. There are also a number of practical and operational issues that would need to be addressed including the import of US coins or 'change', which are not commonly available in the local market, as well as the possibility of issuing Palestinian coins as an alternative to the costly import of US quarters, nickels and dimes, as was done in East Timor following their dollarisation after independence.[8] In addition, the monetary operations division in the PMA will need to manage the introduction of new dollar bills in different denominations as well as the replacement of old or worn out bills. The division will also need to establish vaults and procedures for storing and maintaining the cash in clean and safe conditions, and there will be a need to educate the public on the features of the various bills and coins.

6 Conclusion

Since its establishment in 1995, the Palestine Monetary Authority has been aiming to transform itself into a full central bank. To this end, the PMA adopted its Strategic Transformation Plan in 2006 and initiated a process of restructuring and internal reform aimed at transforming the current institution into a full-fledged, modern central bank. The plan envisages a set of steps and actions, which include both the internal restructuring of the PMA and working for a new central bank law. As shown in section 2, the new law (still not yet enacted) will ensure a much greater degree of independence for the PMA than the 1997 law. However, it should be noted that this is a *de jure* and not a *de facto* independence, because of the absence of a Palestinian national currency. The main difference between the two laws, as discussed in section 2, is that the new law declares price stability to be the main objective of the PMA, whereas under the 1997 law the main objective was monetary stability and sustainable economic growth. Moreover, there is also a large discrepancy between the two laws in the area of political autonomy.

Section 3 considered the problems in estimating the money supply in Palestine, which is a complex matter because of the absence of a national currency, the regular use of three currencies (JD, USD, and NIS) and the unavailability of data on currency in circulation in the Palestinian Territory. It discussed a method for determining the amount of a Palestinian national currency to be issued, if and when that occurs, using indicative ratios from Jordan and Israel to estimate the money supply in the Palestinian Territory.

Section 4 discussed the PMA's plans to issue certificates of deposit, which will enable it to establish an elementary monetary policy instrument that could potentially influence interest rates and help in managing the liquidity in the local market, even without the introduction of a Palestinian national currency. Finally, section 5 discussed the question of dollarisation in Palestine, which has been posed by the recurrent difficulties in providing adequate supplies of shekel notes in Gaza.

Overall, the PMA is making progress towards its aim of becoming a fully-operative, *de facto* independent, central bank capable of implementing its own monetary policy. But this transformation is significantly affected by political conditions, and it is still far from complete.

Notes

1 Weights for each criterion are assigned (as in Gisolo, 2009) on the basis of the importance given to them in the compliance assessment pursued by the European Central Bank (ECB) with respect to accession countries.

2 In 1985 the New Israeli Shekel replaced the old shekel (in both Israel and the Palestinian Territory). The old shekel had itself replaced the Israeli lira (which came into existence in 1948) in 1980.

3 Earlier work on seigniorage in the Palestinian territory includes Hamed and Shaban (1993), Arnon and Spivak (1996) and Hamed (2000).

4 See Laurens *et al.* (2005) for a wider perspective on the move towards money market operations in monetary policy in developing/emerging countries.

5 There is some (unpublished) evidence that the Palestinian financial system is insulated to a certain extent from outside influences, so that there is some limited independence for Palestinian interest rates.

6 However, Cobham (2004) has argued that on the desirable condition of low inflation the seigniorage is unlikely to be large enough to justify, on its own, the issue of a separate currency in Palestine.

7 It should also be noted that in the long term it is likely that the largest share of a future Palestinian state's trade would be with the EU rather than the US (see Erickson von Allmen and Fischer, 2001).

8 See Banking and Payments Authority of East Timor (2004).

References

Abed, G. (2006), 'Strategic Transformation Plan', Ramallah: Palestine Monetary Authority.

Armas, A., Ize, A., and Yeyati, E. (eds) (2006), *Financial Dollarisation: the policy agenda.* New York: Palgrave Macmillan.

Arnon, A., and Spivak, A. (1996), 'On the introduction of a Palestinian currency', *Middle East Business and Economic Review*, 8 (1): 1–14.

Bade, R., and Parkin, M. (1982), 'Central bank laws and monetary policy', mimeo, University of Western Ontario.

Balino, T., Bennett, A., and Borensztein, E. (1999), 'Monetary policy in dollarized economies', IMF occasional paper 171.

Banking and Payments Authority of East Timor (2004), Public Instruction Number 01/2004 Concerning the Issuance and Use of Coins in Timor-Leste.

Beidas, S., and Kandil, M. (2005), 'Setting the stage for a national currency in the West Bank and Gaza: the choice of exchange rate regime', IMF working paper 05/70.

Berg, A., and Borensztein, E. (2000), 'The pros and cons of full dollarisation', IMF working paper 00/50.

Cobham, D. (2004), 'Alternative currency arrangements', in D. Cobham and N. Kanafani (eds), *The Economics of Palestine: Economic Policy and Institutional Reform for a Viable Palestinian State*, London: Routledge.

Cukierman, A. (1992), *Central Bank Strategy, Credibility and Independence: Theory and Evidence.* Cambridge, MA: MIT Press.

Cukierman, A., Webb, S., and Neyaptı, B. (1992), 'Measuring the independence of central banks and its effect on policy outcomes', *World Bank Economic Review*, 6: 353–398.

Erickson von Allmen, U., and Fischer, F. (2001), 'The choice of future exchange rate regime in the West Bank and Gaza', in R. Valdivieso, U. Erickson von Allmen, G. Bannister, H. Davoodi, F. Fischer, E. Jenkner and M. Said, *West Bank and Gaza: Economic Performance, Prospects and Policies*, Washington DC: IMF.

Gisolo, E. (2009), 'The degree of legal central bank independence in MENA countries: international comparisons and macroeconomic implications', in D. Cobham and G. Dibeh (eds), *Monetary Policy and Central Banking in the Middle East and North Africa*, London: Routledge.

Grilli, V., Masciandaro, D., and Tabellini, G. (1991), 'Political and monetary institutions and public financial policies in the industrial countries', *Economic Policy*, 13: 342–392.

Gutierrez, E. (2003), 'Inflation performance and constitutional central bank independence: Evidence from Latin America and Caribbean', IMF working paper 03/53.

Hamed, O. (2000), 'Monetary policy in the absence of a national currency and under currency board in West Bank and Gaza Strip', Palestine Economic Policy Research Institute (MAS) Discussion Paper.

Hamed, O., and Shaban, R. (1993) 'One-sided customs and monetary union: the case of the West Bank and Gaza Strip', in S. Fischer (ed.), *The Economics of Middle East Peace*, Cambridge, MA: MIT Press.

Laurens, B. and staff team (2005), *Monetary Policy Implementation at Different Stages of Market Development*, IMF Occasional Paper 244 Washington DC: IMF.

Naqib, F. (1999), 'The economic of currency boards: the case of the Palestinian economy in the West Bank and Gaza Strip', paper presented at the Sixth Annual Conference of the ERF, Egypt.

7 The banking sector and macroeconomic performance

The case of Turkey

Berksoy Bilgin and F. Gülçin Özkan

1 Introduction

A key issue that has emerged from the experience of the recent global financial crisis is that a properly functioning banking sector is essential for overall economic health. Indeed, the financial crisis started with a liquidity squeeze following the collapse of a number of banks in the US and then spread to other parts of the world. The contribution of the functioning and the nature of the financial systems in precipitating the financial crisis in the US and the UK, the two largest economies that have been greatly affected by the crisis, has been intensely debated. Although emerging economies have been much more resilient during the 2008–2009 global crisis, a number of these countries have faced collapsing currencies and financial turmoil as recurring events since the early 1990s. The Turkish case was particularly notable. Turkey was hit by a combination of currency and financial crises in 2000–2001, which then turned into the most severe real downturn the country had experienced in its post-war history, with an output contraction of nearly 10 per cent of GDP (see Özatay and Sak, 2002; Özkan, 2005). A closer look at the Turkish experience as well as that of other emerging market countries throughout the 1990s and early 2000s highlights the importance of the institutional framework of financial systems as a determinant of overall financial fragility in these economies.

A salient feature of the functioning of the financial system in Turkey is that, due to the lack of well-developed domestic debt markets, the banking system has been the main financial intermediary and a major lender to the government. For example, the ratio of banking sector credit to the public sector as a percentage of total bank credit was 64.7 during 2001–2003.[1] One important factor that is likely to have played an important role in such reliance on the national banking system as an important source of public borrowing is the volatility of international capital flows into and out of Turkey, which was high throughout the 1990s. In addition, external borrowing is usually on a short-term basis, making both the scale and the terms of such borrowing move closely with market sentiment. A further difficulty associated with external borrowing is the inability to borrow in domestic currency in international markets, a widely recognised phenomenon associated with emerging market countries and referred to as 'original sin'.[2] These difficulties and costs associated with external borrowing highlight the importance of domestic debt markets in Turkey. When combined with the above-mentioned dominance of the banking sector in lending to the government, it is clear that the banking sector plays a significant role in public finances and thereby macroeconomic outcomes in Turkey.

In this chapter we examine two channels through which the behaviour of the banking sector is likely to influence macroeconomic policy outcomes. The first is related to fiscal policy and derives from the banking sector's role as the main financial intermediary, as explained above. In countries where the banking sector is the primary holder of domestic debt instruments, as it is in Turkey, the sector has a significant role in shaping the terms of domestic borrowing. To explore this channel, we use a formal model developed by Özkan *et al.* (2010) which provides an analytical framework that integrates the role of a dominant financial sector into an otherwise standard macroeconomic policy model. We present the main predictions of this model in summary form together with informal evidence from Turkey on the predicted relationships between individual characteristics of the banking sector and macroeconomic performance.

The second channel between the banking sector and macroeconomic policy that we explore is related to the more traditional role of the banking sector working through the bank lending channel. In contrast to the first channel, this is related to the functioning of monetary policy. Through the lending channel, banks are instrumental in translating the changes in monetary policy into changes in loan supply and thus into the cost of borrowing for bank-dependent borrowers. To explore this channel, we examine the empirical relationship between monetary policy changes and the volume of bank lending in Turkey.

Overall, our results suggest that the banking sector has played an important role in both fiscal and monetary policy outcomes in Turkey. The remainder of the chapter is structured as follows. Section 2 sets out the main elements of the analytical framework developed by Özkan *et al.* (2010) to explore how financial sector characteristics shape the terms of domestic borrowing. Evidence from the Turkish experience on the role of the banking sector for both fiscal and monetary policy outcomes is presented in Section 3. Section 4 concludes the paper.

2 Theoretical framework

This section presents an analytical framework developed by Özkan *et al.* (2010) that uses a simple dynamic game-theoretic model with three players: monetary and fiscal authorities and the financial sector. In the model, interactions between the two macroeconomic policy-making authorities determine the stance of policy and thus the public sector borrowing requirement; and the interactions between the fiscal authority and the financial sector determine the cost of that borrowing. In what follows we briefly describe the main elements of this model.

The basic model

Policymakers' preferences

Consider a policymaker whose preferences can be summarised by the following loss function:[3]

$$L_t^G = \frac{1}{2}\sum_{t=1}^{T=2}\beta_G^{t-1}\left[\delta_1\pi_t^2 + (x_t - \bar{x}_t)^2 + \delta_2(g_t - \bar{g}_t)^2\right] \tag{1}$$

where L_t^G denotes the welfare losses incurred by the government, δ_1 and δ_2 represent, respectively, the government's relative dislikes for the deviations of inflation (π_t) and public spending as a share of output (g_t) from their target levels (0 and $\bar{g}_t$ respectively) relative to the deviations of output (x_t) from its target level ($\bar{x}_t$) and β_G is the government's discount factor.

The preferences of the central bank (CB) can be described as:

$$L_t^{CB} = \frac{1}{2}\sum_{t=1}^{T=2}\beta_{CB}^{t-1}\left[\mu_1\pi_t^2 + (x_t - \bar{x}_t)^2\right] \tag{2}$$

where L_t^{CB} denotes the welfare losses incurred by the CB, μ_1 is the CB's inflation stability weight, β_{CB} is the CB's discount factor. In addition, the CB is more conservative than the elected government; $\mu_1 > \delta_1$ and it does not discount the future at as high a rate as the elected government; $\beta_{CB} > \beta_G$.

Equations (1) and (2) suggest that policymakers' welfare losses increase in the deviations of inflation, output and public spending from their target levels (or 'bliss' points). The target level of inflation is taken to be zero to indicate the desirability of price stability. A non-zero output target represents the bliss point for output in the absence of non-tax distortions, for example, due to labour or commodity market imperfections. Both the weights, μ_1, δ_1, and δ_2, and the bliss points for output and public spending, $\bar{x}_t$ and $\bar{g}_t$, reflect the political and institutional structure of the economy.

Output is given by the following supply function:

$$x_t = \alpha\left(\pi_t - \pi_t^e - \tau_t\right) \tag{3}$$

where π_t^e is expected inflation and τ_t is the tax rate levied on the total revenue of the firm and all other variables are as defined above.

Demand for funds

The fiscal and monetary authorities operate independently with the government in charge of fiscal policy-making while monetary policy decisions are taken by an independent CB. There are three sources of finance to pay for public expenditures: tax revenues, money creation and government-issued debt. The government thus faces the following budget constraint at time t:

$$g_t + (1 + r_{t-1})d_{t-1} = \tau_t + k\pi_t + d_t \tag{4}$$

where d_{t-1} denotes the amount of single-period debt issued (as a ratio of output) in period $t-1$ and to be re-paid in period t, r_{t-1} represents the rate at which it is borrowed, d_t is the new debt issued in period t and k is the real money holdings as share of output.[4] All other variables are as defined earlier.

It follows that the borrowing requirement, d_t, would be determined by the preferences of the monetary and fiscal policymakers as described above and the interactions between the two.

Supply of loanable funds

Now we turn to the determination of the supply of loanable funds available to the government. The importance of banks as dominant buyers of government paper in Turkey was stated above. As explained, this is mainly due to the relatively underdeveloped nature of the financial markets, which results in banks playing a major role in mobilising savings for the use of governments. It has been argued that stable interest income on government securities makes them attractive for banks, which can use these securities to balance more volatile investments (see OECD, 2001). Given the dominance of banks as investors in government securities in Turkey, the banking sector is taken to be the main lender.

Now consider a financial sector that is composed of n banks. Banks compete with each other both in collecting deposits and in lending the collected funds. The relationship between the supply of deposits facing bank i and the deposit rate offered by the bank is summarised as:

$$z_t^i = \frac{1}{n}\left(A + \eta r_t^{zi}\right) + \omega \sum_{j=1, j \neq i}^{n}\left(r_t^{zi} - r_t^{zj}\right) \tag{5}$$

where z_t^i is the deposit supply facing bank i, r_t^{zi} is the deposit rate offered by bank i, r_t^{zj} is the vector of deposit rates paid by all other banks and A, η and ω are positive parameters characterising the structure of the deposit market. The sensitivity of deposit supply with respect to the deposit rate is measured by parameter η and the parameter ω measures the competitiveness of the banking sector. Clearly, the higher ω is, the more competitive is the banking sector in the deposit market.

The representative bank's profit function can then be written as:

$$V_t^{Bi} = r_t b_t^i - r_t^{zi} z_t^i - \frac{c}{2}\left(b_t^i - \phi z_t^i\right)^2 \tag{6}$$

where V_t^{Bi} is bank i's profit at time t, b_t^i is bank i's bond holdings in the form of government securities, r_t is the rate of interest on these securities, z_t^i is the deposit supply facing bank i, r_t^{zi} is the deposit rate offered by bank i and c is the cost associated with illiquidity.[5] These costs are assumed to rise at an increasing rate as illiquidity rises. The maximum that a bank can lend is then the difference between the amount of deposits that it collects and the amount that it needs to hold as required reserves, which is captured by ϕ in equation (6) (the reserve requirement ratio can be expressed as $(1 - \phi)$).

The representative bank also chooses how much to lend to the government, b_t^i, which determines the demand for bonds. This will clearly depend upon the return on government bonds as well as the structure of the banking sector.

Determination of the cost of borrowing

In period $t = 1$ the banking sector chooses the amount of government bonds to hold and therefore directly influences the strategic choices facing the government. The CB chooses π_1 so as to minimise its welfare losses (equation (2)) and the government chooses τ_1, g_1 and d_1 to minimise its own welfare losses (equation (1)). The resulting borrowing requirement in $t = 1$ is given by:

$$d_1 = \Phi\left[\bar{g}_1 - F\bar{g}_2 + \frac{1}{\alpha}\bar{x}_1 - \frac{F}{\alpha}\bar{x}_2 + (1 + r_0)d_0\right] \tag{7}$$

where Φ and F are positive coefficients.[6] (The details of this derivation can be found in Özkan *et al.*, 2010.)

As seen from equation (7), the demand for borrowing (the supply of bonds) is determined by the borrowing rate, r_1 (since F is a function of r_1), as well as the spending and output targets and the scale of initial borrowing.

The demand for bonds, on the other hand, is determined as an outcome of each bank's own profit-maximising actions. Bank i chooses its own deposit rate and the amount of its bond holdings so as to maximise profits, taking the bond rate and the deposit rate offered by all other banks as given.[7]

Combining the relevant first order conditions and re-arranging yields the following demand for bonds on the part of bank i:

$$b_1^i = \frac{[(c\eta^2 + c\eta n_1)\phi^2 + nn_1 + 2n\eta]r_1 + (\eta + n_1)cA\phi}{cn(n_1 + 2\eta)} \tag{8}$$

where $n_1 = \omega(n-1)n$.

The expression for b_t^i in equation (8) is bank i's demand for bond holdings in terms of the bond rate, r_1. This is an increasing function of the bond rate, $\partial b_1^i / \partial r_1 > 0$ for $n>1$. It follows that this relationship is shaped by the number of banks operating in the financial system, n; the scale of the costs of illiquidity, c; the determinants of the deposit supply, A, η and ω; and the reserve requirement ratio, $(1-\phi)$.

How is the cost of public borrowing determined in this framework? It is straightforward to solve for the bond rate, r_1, by combining the banks' total demand for bonds, $b_1 = nb_1^i$ with the government's demand for borrowing (supply of bonds), d_1. In equilibrium, the demand for bonds b_1 is exactly matched by the supply d_1, thereby eliminating any excess demand for borrowing and thus any excess supply of bonds. This suggests that in equilibrium:

$$E_1^d(r_1) = d_1(r_1) - b_1(r_1) = 0 \tag{9}$$

where $E_1^d(r_1)$ denotes excess demand for borrowing expressed in terms of the bond rate and $d_1(r_1)$ and $b_1(r_1)$, are, respectively, the demand for borrowing (supply of bonds) and the demand for bonds.

Substituting $d_1(r_1)$ and $b_1^i(r_1)$ into equation (9) yields

$$
E_1^d(r_1) = \Phi(\overline{g}_1 - F\overline{g}_2 + \frac{1}{\alpha}\overline{x}_1 - \frac{F}{\alpha}\overline{x}_2 + (1 + r_0)d_0)
$$

$$
- \frac{[(c\eta^2 + c\eta n_1)\phi^2 + nn_1 + 2n\eta]r_1 + (\eta + n_1)cA\phi}{c(n_1 + 2\eta)} = 0
$$

(10)

Equation (10) suggests that the cost of public borrowing in equilibrium would be determined by a combination of factors related to the institutional and political structure of the economy – exhibited by the preferences of policymakers (as indicated by terms in the first line) as well as the structure of the banking sector (denoted by expressions in the second line).

We now turn to the relationship between the cost of borrowing r_1 and its determinants, which underlies equation (10).

3 Evidence on the role of the banking sector in macroeconomic outcomes

Banking sector and public debt dynamics

The macroeconomic policy model presented in Section 2 spelt out the optimisation behaviour for each of the banking sector and the policymakers. The banking sector maximises profits subject to the supply of deposits and the demand for public borrowing. Similarly, policymakers maximise their welfare given the structure of the economy – output supply and the budget constraint – and the supply of funds provided by the banking sector. Combining the decision-making of the banking sector with that of the fiscal and monetary authorities allows us to solve for the equilibrium cost of borrowing. Clearly, factors that raise the demand for borrowing – the first line in equation (10) – would also lead to an increase in the cost of borrowing. In contrast, factors that increase the supply of bonds – likely to be associated with the structure of the banking sector – would have a favourable impact on the terms of borrowing. Table 7.1 lists some of the likely determinants of the demand for and the supply of government bonds and the direction of the expected impact on the equilibrium cost of borrowing utilising equation (10) (the derivation of the comparative statistics presented in the second column of Table 7.1 is provided in Appendix A).

We now turn to the empirical content of these relationships with specific reference to the Turkish economy.

Table 7.1 Determinants of the cost of borrowing

Determinant of the cost of borrowing	The effect on the cost of borrowing
The number of banks	$\partial r_1/\partial n < 0$
The depth of the deposit market	$\partial b_1/\partial A > 0$ and $\partial b_1/\partial \eta > 0$
The cost of illiquidity	$\partial r_1/\partial c > 0$
Reserve requirements	$\partial r_1/\partial (1 - \phi) > 0$
The government's time preference	$\partial r_1/\partial \beta_G < 0$

Competition in the banking sector

Table 7.1 suggests that the more competitive the banking sector, that is, the higher the number of operating banks n, the lower will be the cost of borrowing in equilibrium. This relationship derives from the banking sector's predominant role in the government securities market. Clearly, a rise in the number of banks is associated with a rise in the demand for government securities with favourable consequences for the terms of borrowing.

Figure 7.1 plots both the number of bank branches and the cost of domestic borrowing in Turkey since 1989. An upward trend in the number of bank branches and a downward trend in the cost of borrowing are visible, especially since the mid-1990s.

The depth of the deposit market

As set out in the formal model presented earlier, an important determinant of banks' demand for government securities is the depth of the deposit market. The deeper the deposit base, the better are banks able to channel resources towards meeting the public sector's borrowing requirement. Figure 7.2 plots this relationship for Turkey for 1989–2007. The figure suggests that the fall in the cost of borrowing has gone hand in hand with a rise in the deposit market volume throughout this period, especially since 1995.

The cost of illiquidity

The arguments set out above suggest that the cost to banks of running out of liquidity affects how much they lend to the government. A higher cost of obtaining funds would therefore be associated with reduced willingness to lend on the part of banks and thus a higher cost of public debt in equilibrium. As is evident from Figure 7.3, the cost of borrowing and the interbank rate appear to be very closely correlated.

Reserve requirements

Another factor that is likely to impact upon the availability of lending is the severity of reserve requirements. A rise in the ratio of deposits that banks are required

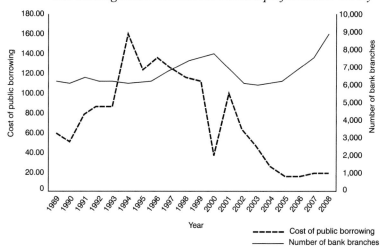

Figure 7.1 Number of bank branches

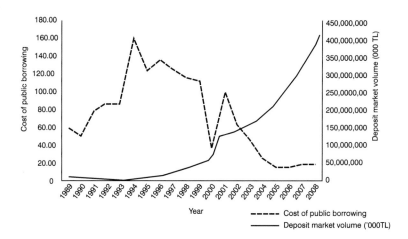

Figure 7.2 Deposit market volume

to hold as reserves reduces the amount available to be lent to the government, pushing the interest rate up in equilibrium. Figure 7.4 plots this relationship for Turkey over the last two decades and reveals a close relationship between the reserve requirements and the cost of borrowing, as expected.

The time preference

In addition to the features of the banking sector, policy-making institutions also play a role in determining the conditions in the public securities market. One such factor is related to the policymaker's time preference, which in turn is closely related to political stability. The lower the political instability, the more stable

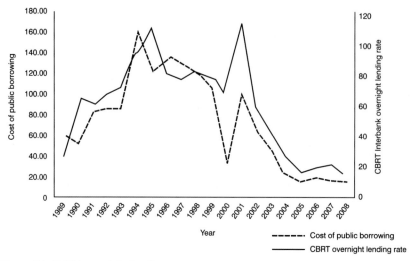

Figure 7.3 CBRT overnight lending rate

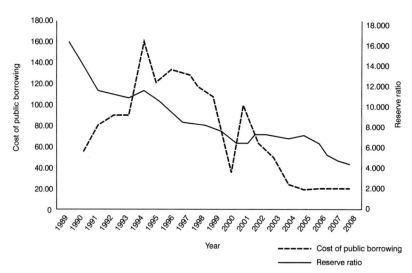

Figure 7.4 Reserve ratio

the environment, the greater would be the incumbent's concern with the future implications of current borrowing, and the lower borrowing in equilibrium. This, in turn, would have a favourable impact on the terms of borrowing.

Figure 7.5 presents some supporting evidence for this relationship. The rate of fall in the cost of borrowing was especially pronounced from 2002 with the election of a single-party government – the first since the late 1980s – and the associated political stability.

Figures 7.1–7.5 suggest that there was a marked decline in the cost of domestic borrowing in Turkey since the early 1990s. In addition, the movements in variables depicted in these figures also suggest that the evolution of the cost of borrowing and the movements of its determinants identified above are in line with the proposition that the latter play an important role in the determination of the former. Given the significance of bank lending to the public sector in Turkey over this period, an interesting issue is whether such holdings of government securities in the banking sector impacted upon the ability of banks to create money in the banking system as a multiple of the monetary base. To examine this, movements in both the cost of public borrowing and the money multiplier (M2/monetary base) are plotted in Figure 7.6 over 1989–2008. There appears to be a negative relationship between the two series especially since the early 2000s. When there is a significant need for public sector borrowing from the banking sector, which is expected to underlie a higher borrowing cost, banks would hold a sizable government securities portfolio and that would restrict the extent of money creation. Figure 7.6 clearly displays periods of a high borrowing cost coinciding with a lower money multiplier, in 1995–2000, and lower borrowing cost and higher money multiplier, in 2002–2008.

Banking sector and monetary policy

The previous section explored linkages between the structure of the banking sector and macroeconomic policy outcomes in the context of the government securities market. As explained above, the existence of such a link is due to the special position of the banking sector as primary holders of government debt in Turkey. We now explore the second channel through which the banking sector's

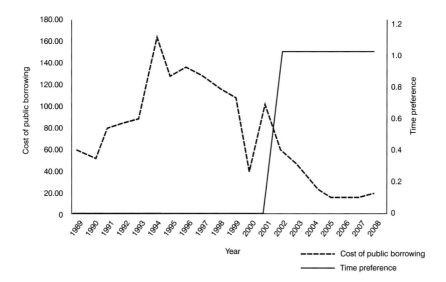

Figure 7.5 Time preference

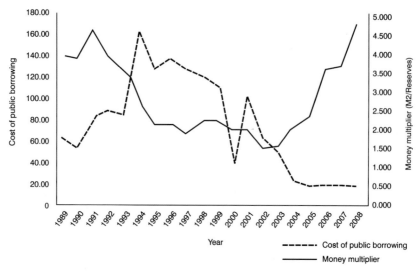

Figure 7.6 Money multiplier

behaviour impacts upon macroeconomic policy, namely the bank lending channel. It is widely agreed that banks play a special role in the transmission of monetary policy through their lending behaviour (see, for example, Bernanke and Blinder, 1992). Banks are an important source of intermediated credits in many countries and their response to monetary policy changes through varying the supply of loans is likely to have real effects (see Bernanke and Gertler, 1995). For example, if the monetary authority introduces a contractionary policy stance draining reserves from the banking system, banks face a reduction in the supply of loanable funds. As banks cannot easily replace this reduction by other sources of external funds, they will be forced to reduce lending to bank-dependent borrowers. When combined with borrowers' inability to replace such a reduction in loan supply with other sources of finance, the initial reduction in the supply of loanable funds is likely to reduce real economic activity. Central to both these mechanisms are financial frictions and information asymmetries. That both banks and borrowers find it difficult to access alternative sources of funds is, in turn, related to financial market imperfections which drive a wedge between internal and external financing. It therefore follows that for a bank lending channel to exist it must be the case that banks and borrowers are unable to switch frictionlessly between different sources of funds (see, for example, Kashyap and Stein, 2000).

It is also well known that uncovering the extent of this bank lending channel using aggregate data is not easy. Although it is straightforward to establish empirically that a reduction in aggregate bank lending usually follows a monetary tightening, it is not clear whether this is due to a fall in aggregate loan supply or in loan demand (see, for example, Kakes and Sturm, 2002; Kashyap and Stein, 2000; Ashcraft, 2006). In order to address this problem a number of recent studies utilise disaggregated data to explore the impact of monetary policy shocks on the loan supply of individual banks (Kashyap and Stein, 2000; Kishan and Opiela, 2000; Altunbaş et al. 2002; Gambacorta, 2005; Ashcraft, 2006). We adopt this approach here and examine evidence on the bank lending channel in Turkey using individual bank level data.

The empirical model and the data

We explore evidence of the bank lending channel in Turkey by estimating the following empirical specification which is based on Kashyap and Stein (2000), Altunbaş et al. (2002) and Gambacorta (2005):

$$\Delta L_{it} = \beta_i + \beta_1 \Delta L_{it-1} + \sum_{j=0}^{t} \beta_2 \Delta r_{t-j} + \sum_{j=0}^{t} \beta_3 Cap_{it-j} + \sum_{j=0}^{t} \beta_4 S_{it-j}$$
$$+ \sum_{j=0}^{t} \beta_5 Liq_{it-j} + \sum_{j=0}^{t} \beta_6 Sec_{it-j} + \sum_{j=0}^{t} \beta_7 y_{t-j} + u_{it} \tag{11}$$

where $i = 1, ..., N$ and $t = 1, ..., T$ and N is the number of banks; L is bank loans; r is the monetary policy instrument; Cap is bank capitalisation; S is bank size, measured by the scale of total assets; Liq is the ratio of liquid assets to total assets; Sec is the bank's financial security holdings and y is real GDP. Utilising individual bank level data, loan growth is regressed on changes in the policy rate, the bank's size, its capitalisation, its liquidity ratio and its holdings of financial securities. The growth rate of real GDP is also included to control for changes in loan demand. The central bank of Turkey's policy rate is used as the monetary policy indicator.

Our sample consists of 32 commercial banks in Turkey.[8] We utilise quarterly data for these banks for the period 2002–2008 obtained from the databases of the Banks Association of Turkey and the State Planning Organisation. We chose the post-2002 period due to the introduction of a major banking reform in Turkey in 2001.[9] More details on the definitions of regressors and data sources are provided in Appendix B. Equation (11) is estimated using the random effects panel data approach.

Empirical results

Our estimation results are presented in Table 7.2. Results listed in the second column of the table reveal that bank lending in Turkey responds to the monetary policy instrument, giving support to the existence of the bank lending channel in Turkey in the sample period. The coefficient of r_t, the policy rate, is negative and significant at the 1 per cent level. In addition, a rise in both the size, S_{it}, and the ratio of liquid assets, Liq_{it}, is associated with a rise in bank lending. That is, banks that increase in size are likely to expand their lending. Banks that experience a rise in their holdings of liquid assets are also likely to increase their lending. In contrast, it appears that a rise in the holdings of financial securities is associated with a fall in bank loans. In terms of the role of demand factors, to the extent that

Table 7.2 Estimation of lending behaviour; full sample and for small and large banks separately

Independent variables	Full sample		Small banks		Large banks	
ΔL_{it-1}	−0.067**	(0.037)	−0.067	(0.043)	0.091	(0.07)
Δr_t	−0.023***	(0.007)	−0.026***	(0.009)	−0.005	(0.004)
Δr_{t-1}	0.018**	(0.008)	0.022**	(0.011)	−0.002	(0.005)
ΔCap_t	0.071	(0.048)	0.063	(0.058)	−0.006	(0.054)
ΔCap_{t-1}	−0.052	(0.033)	−0.052	(0.039)	0.016	(0.054)
S_{it}	0.465***	(0.077)	0.448***	(0.093)	0.869***	(0.12)
S_{it-1}	−0.463***	(0.077)	−0.445***	(0.094)	−0.874***	(0.119)
ΔLiq_{it}	0.555***	(0.195)	0.515**	(0.235)	0.974***	(0.291)
ΔLiq_{it-1}	−0.346*	(0.201)	−0.359	(0.245)	−0.656**	(0.292)
ΔSec_{it}	−0.07***	(0.017)	−0.069***	(0.019)	−0.146**	(0.058)
ΔSec_{it-1}	0.028	(0.018)	0.031	(0.021)	−0.084**	(0.04)
Δy_t	0.157	(0.106)	0.228	(0.143)	−0.097*	(0.056)
Δy_{t-1}	−0.224	(0.113)	−0.243	(0.15)	−0.187***	(0.065)
N	644	476			168	
R^2	14.37	14.10			53.02	

Notes: This table reports results from estimating equation (11) for 32 commercial banks in Turkey, for the period 2002–2008 using quarterly data. The dependent variable is the change in bank loans. The standard errors are reported in parentheses. ***, ** and * indicate significance at the 1%, 5% and 10% level, respectively. Results presented here are estimated using a random effects model. Small banks are those that have an average bank size below the third quartile. This means that 8 of the 32 banks are classified as large, and 24 as small. All specifications include time dummies (coefficient estimates are not reported).

GDP is a good proxy for loan demand, a rise in loan demand is associated with a rise in the volume of bank lending although this variable is not significant at conventional significance levels.[10]

An interesting aspect of the bank transmission of monetary policy is the extent to which bank lending is related to bank-specific characteristics. The existing literature has focused on three bank features as potential determinants of bank lending behaviour: size, liquidity and capitalisation. Size may be important because a reduction in loanable funds resulting from a contractionary monetary policy action poses a greater restriction on smaller banks, leading to a greater response to a monetary shock. Similarly, banks with a lower liquidity ratio may find themselves more financially constrained and therefore may respond differently to a monetary policy change from banks with a higher liquidity ratio. Also, poorly capitalised banks are expected to be in a less flexible position to maintain their loan portfolios in the face of a monetary shock (see, for example, Kashyap and Stein, 1995; Gambacorta, 2005). In order to test these propositions we estimate our empirical specification for six separate sub-samples; for small banks and large banks; for banks with low liquidity and high liquidity ratios; and for poorly-capitalised banks and well-capitalised banks. The thresholds used to distinguish between groups are as follows. We define 'small banks' as those that have an average bank size below the third quartile and 'large banks' as those that have the average size of banks above the third quartile. The distinction between 'low-liquidity' and 'high-liquidity' banks and 'poorly-capitalised' and 'well-capitalised' banks are based on the same thresholds.

Our estimation results for the small and large banks are reported in Table 7.2 alongside the results from the full-sample. Table 7.3 reports estimation results from the sub-samples of 'low-liquidity' and 'high-liquidity' banks and 'poorly-capitalised' and 'well-capitalised' banks.

Estimates presented in the third and the fourth columns in Table 7.2 provide supporting evidence for the proposition that bank size matters for the responsiveness of bank loans to monetary policy shocks. The estimated coefficient of the monetary policy indicator, r_t, in the third column for small banks is negative and significant, as in the full sample. In contrast, this coefficient is insignificant in the fourth column, suggesting that large banks' lending behaviour is not sensitive to monetary policy changes. This result is in line with those from Kashyap and Stein (1995) and Kishan and Opiela (2000). It is argued that large banks are able to draw on other sources of finance more easily than small banks, making their lending less sensitive to monetary policy changes.

Table 7.3 presents supporting evidence for the hypothesis that the sensitivity of bank lending to monetary policy shocks is related to liquidity and capitalisation. As with the findings regarding size reported in Table 7.2, the estimates in Table 7.3 suggest that banks that have lower liquidity are more responsive to monetary policy changes than those with higher liquidity. Likewise, poorly-capitalised banks appear to have greater sensitivity to monetary shocks as compared with well-capitalised banks.[11]

4 Conclusions

This chapter has explored the role of the banking sector in macroeconomic policy outcomes in Turkey. We have examined two channels through which the behaviour of the banking sector is expected to impact upon macroeconomic policy outcomes. The first is related to the banking sector's role as the dominant holders of public debt in Turkey, a feature which results in banks having a significant role in shaping the terms of domestic borrowing. The analytical framework features a simple two-period game theoretic model with three players; monetary and fiscal authorities and the financial sector. Interactions between the two macroeconomic policy-making authorities determine the stance of policy and thus the public sector borrowing requirement, and the interactions between the fiscal authority and the financial sector determine the cost of that borrowing. We then investigate the empirical content of the model's main predictions for Turkey by studying the relationship between the observed cost of borrowing in Turkey and its determinants, as suggested by the

Table 7.3 Estimation of bank lending behaviour; low- and high-liquidity banks and poorly- and well-capitalised banks

Independent variables	Low-liquidity banks		High-liquidity banks		Poorly-capitalised banks		Well-capitalised banks	
ΔL_{it-1}	-0.003*	(0.043)	-0.199**	(0.08)	-0.159***	(0.043)	-0.000	(0.081)
Δr_t	-0.027***	(0.006)	-0.012	(0.02)	-0.022***	(0.007)	-0.018	(0.019)
Δr_{t-1}	0.029***	(0.008)	-0.008	(0.026)	-0.02**	(0.009)	0.014	(0.025)
ΔCap_t	0.013	(0.059)	0.115	(0.109)	-0.06	(0.057)	0.159	(0.098)
ΔCap_{t-1}	-0.124**	(0.052)	-0.014	(0.06)	-0.205***	(0.044)	0.068	(0.061)
S_{it}	0.574***	(0.091)	0.365*	(0.196)	0.411***	(0.1)	0.535***	(0.152)
S_{it-1}	-0.576***	(0.092)	-0.345*	(0.194)	-0.419***	(0.1)	-0.52**	(0.152)
ΔLiq_{it}	0.571***	(0.163)	-0.033	(1.124)	0.359	(0.458)	0.565*	(0.299)
ΔLiq_{it-1}	-0.31*	(0.168)	-1.313	(1.191)	-0.169	(0.454)	-0.651**	(0.317)
ΔSec_{it}	-0.083***	(0.016)	-0.017	(0.044)	-0.07***	(0.024)	-0.068**	(0.03)
ΔSec_{it-1}	0.0168	(0.023)	0.059	(0.037)	-0.026	(0.024)	0.08**	(0.03)
Δy_t	0.174	(0.097)	0.109	(0.327)	0.122	(0.105)	0.124	(0.312)
Δy_{t-1}	-0.114*	(0.102)	-0.589*	(0.334)	-0.223*	(0.116)	-0.117	(0.309)
N	486.00		158.00		146.00			
R^2	20.96		19.45		24.32			

Notes: Please see the notes under Table 7.2. As with size, low-liquidity banks are those that have an average liquidity ratio below the third quartile and high-liquidity ones are those above the third quartile. Similarly, poorly-capitalised and well-capitalised banks are those that have an average bank capitalisation lower than the third quartile and higher than the third quartile, respectively. Such a classification procedure yields 8 low-liquidity banks versus 24 high-liquidity ones and 8 poorly-capitalised banks versus 24 well-capitalised ones.

formal model presented in the first part of the chapter. We show that the evolution of the set of financial and macroeconomic factors that are identified by the theoretical framework and the terms of public borrowing in Turkey is consistent with the former playing an important role in the determination of the latter over the sample period. More specifically, we have shown that reductions in the cost of borrowing in Turkey over the sample period were associated with increases in the number of banks and the volume of bank deposits and with reductions in the interbank rate, reserve requirements and political instability.

The second channel between the banking sector and macroeconomic policy that we have explored is related to the more traditional role of the banking sector working through the bank lending channel. Through the lending channel, banks are instrumental in translating the changes in monetary policy into changes in loan supply and thereby into the cost of borrowing for bank-dependent borrowers. We present an empirical investigation of the bank lending channel in Turkey, using data from 32 deposit banks in the Turkish banking system for the post-banking reform period, 2002–2008. Our analysis provides supporting evidence for the existence of a lending channel in Turkey over the period analysed. Overall, our results suggest that the banking sector plays an important role in both fiscal and monetary policy outcomes in Turkey.

Appendix A: Derivation of the relationships between the determinants of and the cost of borrowing

Table 7.1 presents determinants of the cost of borrowing and their impact on the equilibrium cost of borrowing. The signs presented in Table 7.1 are derived as follows.

1 *Competition in the banking sector*: The argument provided in the text regarding the derivation of the equilibrium cost of borrowing, r_1, suggests that the sign of $\frac{\partial r_1}{\partial n}$ would be determined by the signs of $\frac{\partial r_1}{\partial E_1^d}$, $\frac{\partial E_1^d}{\partial b_1}$ and $\frac{\partial b_1}{\partial n}$. Equation (8) in the text suggests that $\frac{\partial b_1}{\partial n} =$

$$[(2n-1)(c\phi A\omega\eta + c\phi^2\eta^2\omega r_1) + (n-2)n^3\omega^2 r_1 + r_1 n^2\omega^2 + 4r_1\eta^2 + 4r_1\eta n_1]/[c(n_1+2\eta)^2]$$

(note that $b_1 = n\, b_1^i$). Thus it follows that $\frac{\partial b_1}{\partial n} > 0$ given that $n \geq 2$ and b_1^i, c, ϕ, A and r_1 are all non-negative. Also given that $\frac{\partial E_1^d}{\partial b_1} < 0$ and $\frac{\partial r_1}{\partial E_1^d} > 0$, it can easily be established that $\frac{\partial r_1}{\partial n} < 0$, as listed in Table 7.1.

2 *The depth of the deposit market*: Differentiating b_1 with respect to A yields $\frac{\partial b_1}{\partial A} = \frac{\phi(\eta + n_1)}{(n_1 + 2\eta)}$, which suggests that $\frac{\partial b_1}{\partial A} > 0$ given all parameter restrictions.

Therefore, as under 1 above, it is straightforward to establish that $\dfrac{\partial r_1}{\partial A} < 0$ since $\dfrac{\partial b_1}{\partial A} > 0$ and $\dfrac{\partial r_1}{\partial b_1} < 0$

Another indicator of the depth of the deposit market is given by parameter η. Differentiating in equation (8) with respect to parameter η yields:

$$\frac{\partial b_1}{\partial \eta} = \phi\big[(n-2)r_1\phi\omega^2 n^3 + 2r_1\phi\eta n_1 + r_1\phi\omega^2 n^2 + 2r_1\phi\eta^2 + (n-n^2)A\omega\big]/(n_1 + 2\eta)^2$$

It therefore follows that $\dfrac{\partial b_1}{\partial \eta} > 0$ for $n \geq 2$ and

$$(n-2)r_1\phi\omega^2 n^3 + 2r_1\phi\eta n_1 + r_1\phi\omega^2 n^2 + 2r_1\phi\eta^2 > An_1.$$

3   *The cost of illiquidity*: Taking the derivative of b_1 with respect to c gives $\dfrac{\partial b_1}{\partial c} = \dfrac{-r_1 n}{c^2}$, which is unambiguously negative given that both n and c are non-negative parameters. Hence, $\dfrac{\partial r_1}{\partial b_1} < 0$ establishes that $\dfrac{\partial r_1}{\partial c} > 0$.

4   *Reserve requirement ratio*: Differentiating b_1 with respect to ϕ yields $\dfrac{\partial b_1}{\partial \phi} = (\eta + n_1)(A + 2\phi\eta r_1)/(n_1 + 2\eta)$, which is unambiguously non-negative Thus, this result when combined with $\dfrac{\partial r_1}{\partial b_1} < 0$ suggests that $\dfrac{\partial r_1}{\partial(1-\phi)} > 0$.

5   *The government's time preference*: The derivative of d_1 with respect to β_G is $-\dfrac{F}{\beta_G}\Phi^2\left[\left(\bar{g}^2 + \dfrac{1}{\alpha}\bar{x}^2\right) + (1+r_1)\left(\bar{g}_1 + \dfrac{1}{\alpha}\bar{x}_1 + (1+r_0)d_0\right)\right]$. Given that all parameters in this expression are positive this derivative is unambiguously negative. It therefore follows that $\dfrac{\partial r_1}{\partial\beta_G} < 0$.

Appendix B: Data

Individual bank level data are obtained from the Banks Association of Turkey. The banks that are used in our empirical analysis are: ABN Amro Bank, Adabank, Akbank, Alternatif Bank, Anadolubank, Arap-Türk Bankası, Bank Mellat, Birleşik Fon Bankası, Citibank, Denizbank, Deutsche Bank, Eurobank Tekfen, Finansbank, Fortisbank, Habib Bank, HSBC, ING Bank, JP Morgan, Millennium Bank, Société Générale, Şekerbank, Tekstil Bankası, Turkish Bank, Türkland Bank, TEB, Ziraat Bankası, Garanti Bankası, Halkbank, İş Bankası, Vakıfbank and Yapı Kredi Bankası. Some banks do not have full data series for all variables.

Definitions of variables that are used in the empirical analysis are as follows.

* Total liquidity = deposits and placements with banks and other financial institutions + securities held for trading (net) + loans, advances and financing

+ cash and short-term funds and statutory deposits with the central bank + accounts receivable from money market + derivatives for risk hedging purposes + securities available for sale (net) + securities held to maturity (net).

- Total holdings of financial securities = securities held for trading (net) + derivatives for risk hedging purposes + securities available for sale (net) + securities held to maturity (net).
- Cash holdings = cash and short-term funds and statutory deposits with the central bank.
- Bank capitalisation = total shareholders' equity/total assets.

Notes

1 This ratio was 57.1 in Argentina, 54.3 in Mexico, and 51.1 in Brazil over the same period (see Kumhof and Tanner, 2005, and Özkan *et al.*, 2010).
2 See, for example, Eichengreen and Hausmann (2005).
3 Similar variants of this model are used by Beetsma and Bovenberg (1997, 1999) and İsmihan and Özkan (2010).
4 While seigniorage revenues, $k\pi t$, tend to be negligible in industrial economies, emerging market countries with less developed financial systems routinely resort to seigniorage as a source of revenue (see, for example, IMF, 2001).
5 See Cukierman (1991).
6 Note that $\Phi = \dfrac{1}{1+(1+r_1)F}$, $F = (1+\tilde{\phi})\tilde{D}^*$, $\tilde{D}^* = (1+r_1)\beta_{FA}\tilde{D}$ and $\tilde{D} = \left(\dfrac{\delta_2}{\alpha^2} + \dfrac{\delta_2\delta_1}{\mu_1^2} + 1\right)\tilde{\lambda}^2$.
  See Özkan *et al.* (2010).
7 It follows that the deposit rate offered by bank *i* will also be related to the bond rate.
8 There are 49 banks operating in Turkey as of July 2009. Thirty-two of these are commercial banks, thirteen are development and investment banks and four are participation banks (Banks Association of Turkey, 2009).
9 For details on the 2001 banking sector reform see, for example, OECD (2003).
10 Şengönül and Thorbecke (2005) and Brooks (2007) also provide evidence supporting the existence of the bank lending channel in Turkey for the period 1997–2001 and in the aftermath of the May–June 2006 financial turbulence, respectively.
11 We also tested for the proposition that bank ownership impacts upon bank lending behaviour. We found that the ownership structure, that is whether a bank is privately or publicly owned, and domestically or foreign owned, does not impact upon its lending behaviour. The same result holds for whether a bank is listed or not (these results are not reported here).

References

Altunbaş, Y., Fazylow, O., and Molyneux, P. (2002), 'Evidence on the bank lending channel in Europe', *Journal of Banking and Finance*, 26(11): 2093–2110.
Ashcraft, A.B. (2006), 'New evidence on the lending channel', *Journal of Money, Credit and Banking*, 38(3): 751–775.
Banks Association of Turkey (2009), *The Financial System and Banking Sector in Turkey*, September 2009, available at http://www.tbb.org.tr/english/duyurular/The%20 Financial%20System%20and%20Banking%20Sector%20in%20Turkey.pdf.
Beetsma, R., and Bovenberg, L. (1997), 'Central bank independence and public debt policy', *Journal of Economic Dynamics and Control*, 21: 873–894.

——(1999), 'Does monetary unification lead to excessive debt accumulation?', *Journal of Public Economics*, 74: 299–325.

Bernanke, B., and Blinder, A. (1992), 'The federal funds rate and the channels of monetary transmission', *American Economic Review*, 82(4): 901–921.

Bernanke, B., and Gertler, M. (1995), 'Inside the black box: the credit channel of monetary policy transmission', *Journal of Economic Perspectives*, 9(4), 27–48.

Brooks, P. (2007), 'Does the bank lending channel of monetary transmission work in Turkey?', IMF working paper 07/272.

Cukierman, A. (1991), 'Why does the Fed smooth interest rates?', in M.T. Belongia (ed.), *Monetary Policy on the 75th Anniversary of the Federal Reserve System*, Norwell, MA: Kluwer.

Eichengreen, B., and Hausmann, R. (eds) (2005), *Other People's Money: Debt Denomination and Financial Instability in Emerging Market Economies*. Chicago: University of Chicago Press.

Gambacorta, L. (2005), 'Inside the bank lending channel', *European Economic Review*, 49: 1737–1759.

IMF (2001), 'The decline of inflation in emerging markets: can it be maintained?', in IMF *World Economic Outlook*, September 2001.

İsmihan, M., and Özkan, F.G. (2010), 'A note on public investment, public debt and macroeconomic performance', *Macroeconomic Dynamics*, forthcoming.

Kakes, J., and Sturm, J. (2002), 'Monetary policy and bank lending: evidence from German banking groups', *Journal of Banking and Finance*, 26: 2077–2092.

Kashyap, A., and Stein, J. (1995), 'The impact of monetary policy on bank balance sheets', *Carnegie-Rochester Conference Series on Public Policy*, 42: 151–195.

——(2000), 'What do one million observations on banks have to say about the transmission mechanism of monetary policy?' *American Economic Review*, 90: 407–428.

Kishan, R., and Opiela, T. (2000), 'Bank size, bank capital and the bank lending channel', *Journal of Money, Credit and Banking*, 32(1): 121–141.

Kumhof, M., and Tanner, E. (2005), 'Government debt: a key role in financial intermediation', IMF working paper 05/57.

OECD (2001), *Economic Surveys: Turkey*.

——(2003), *Economic Surveys: Turkey*.

Özatay, F., and Sak, G. (2002), 'Banking sector fragility and Turkey's 2000–01 financial crisis', *Brookings Trade Forum*, 121–172.

Özkan, F.G. (2005), 'Currency and financial crises in Turkey 2000–2001: bad fundamentals or bad luck?', *The World Economy*, 28(4): 541–572.

Özkan, F.G., Kıpıcı, A., and İsmihan, M. (2010), 'The banking sector, government bonds and financial intermediation: the case of emerging market countries', forthcoming, *Emerging Markets Finance and Trade,* available at http://www.york.ac.uk/depts/econ/documents/dp/0811.pdf.

Şengönül, A., and Thorbecke, W. (2005), 'The effect of monetary policy on bank lending in Turkey', *Applied Financial Economics*, 15: 931–934.

Part II

Monetary policy strategies

8 Monetary policy strategies and exchange rate regimes on the southern and eastern shore of the Mediterranean

Developments and prospects

Thierry Bracke, Michal Franta and Jan Stráský[1]

1 Introduction

At first glance, monetary policy and exchange rate strategies differ considerably across the countries on the southern and eastern shore of the Mediterranean Sea. Different historical traditions, different economic structures, and different trade orientations have resulted in a variety of choices of monetary and exchange rate regimes, ranging from very tightly pegged or managed exchange rates to floating exchange rates with monetary policy formulated on the basis of domestic targets.

Within this variety of regimes, there is nevertheless a clear trend across the region towards floating exchange rates and towards monetary policy based on domestic targets. Two central banks in the region, the Bank of Israel and the Central Bank of the Republic of Turkey, introduced an inflation targeting approach several years ago. Central banks in three more countries, notably Egypt, Morocco, and Tunisia, have announced their intention to do so. The shift towards domestic monetary policy targets in the Mediterranean region is in line with a global trend across a range of industrial and emerging market economies, and is the outcome, in most cases, of protracted difficulties in managing fixed exchange rate regimes and/or managing inflation expectations under such regimes.

A shift to an inflation targeting monetary policy strategy may deliver considerable benefits, but it is institutionally, economically, and technically demanding. Successful inflation targeting requires a sound institutional framework (e.g. effective central bank independence), a flexible and stable macroeconomic context (e.g. effective monetary policy transmission), and an advanced state of technical know-how (e.g. sufficient forecasting capacities). Testing these economic, institutional and technical preconditions for inflation targeting in selected economies is the first objective of this chapter. We focus specifically on the three central banks that have concrete plans for the adoption of inflation targeting, i.e. those of Egypt, Morocco, and Tunisia.

We complement this check of 'preconditions' with empirical results from small dynamic macroeconomic models, which we have estimated with Bayesian techniques using quarterly data for the three economies. The model illustrates the impact of external and domestic shocks under the assumption that an implicit inflation targeting regime is in place. A comparison of our results with those of established inflation targeters helps assess whether economic structures are fit for an inflation targeting approach.

The main findings from our two complementary approaches are the following.

- On the economic, institutional, and technical preconditions, all three countries have over the past few years made considerable progress by modernising central bank legislation, improving the central banks' statistical, analytical and technical capacity, and modernising communication tools. Still, despite progress, further work remains to be done for the preconditions to be met.
- On the macroeconomic model results, we find that the price formation and monetary transmission processes in these countries are compatible with an inflation targeting framework. The model produces reasonable estimated coefficients that are compatible with the empirical regularities observed in countries with an established inflation targeting framework. At the same time, these countries have experienced several structural breaks, which may have changed monetary policy transmission channels, thereby seriously hindering inference from our estimation results. The global economic and financial crisis of 2008–2009 may represent yet another structural break for these economies, even though available data so far suggest that the impact of the global crisis has been comparatively mild when compared with that for other emerging or developing countries.

In reviewing the readiness of selected Mediterranean countries to adopt inflation targeting, this chapter does not purport to provide recommendations regarding the usefulness of such a policy step or to advocate alternative monetary or exchange rate regimes for any of the countries concerned.

The remainder of the chapter is structured as follows. After recalling the current state of monetary and exchange rate regimes across Mediterranean countries in Section 2, the chapter examines the preconditions for inflation targeting in Egypt, Morocco, and Tunisia in Section 3, and presents some preliminary results from a Bayesian-estimated model of inflation targeting in these three countries in Section 4. Section 5 concludes.

2 Monetary policy strategies and exchange rate regimes

Countries on the southern and eastern shore of the Mediterranean have adopted a wide range of exchange rate and monetary policy strategies. A vast majority of countries, including Algeria, Egypt, Jordan, Lebanon, Libya, Morocco, Syria, and Tunisia, pursue some form of exchange rate management vis-à-vis the US dollar or a basket of currencies. This exchange rate anchoring has brought important benefits, such as enhanced monetary policy credibility, price stability, and a disciplining effect on fiscal and structural policies. But experience over the past few years has also pointed to the constraints of an external anchor, as exchange rate fixity coupled with growing capital account liberalisation has severely curtailed the room for independent monetary policy (impossible trinity).[2] In addition, large exchange rate movements between major currencies such as the euro and the US dollar have at times complicated monetary policy management in those countries anchoring their currency to the US dollar. Indeed, while the US dollar has a predominant role in exchange rate anchoring across the region, trade linkages are typically more intensive with the European Union than with the United States.

Partly in response to these constraints, several countries have adjusted their exchange rate regimes and moved towards greater exchange rate flexibility. Egypt, for instance, has allowed its currency to become more flexible against its anchor currency, the US dollar, and Tunisia shifted in 2005 from a crawling peg to a managed floating regime. These reforms in exchange rate regimes are part of broader ongoing central bank reforms, and even wider economic policy reforms aimed at enhancing economic flexibility and at unlocking the growth potential of the economies in the region. In many cases, central banks have been playing a central role in driving and stimulating these reforms.

Two countries, Israel and Turkey, have switched to freely floating exchange rate regimes and adopted an inflation targeting approach over the past years. This has been part of a global trend away from intermediate exchange rate regimes. The decisions of the central banks of Israel and Turkey to adopt inflation targeting followed a period of macroeconomic instability, characterised by protracted inflation, difficulties in managing the exchange rate, and, in the case of Turkey, a severe financial crisis. The inflation targeting frameworks were introduced gradually in both cases (e.g. in Israel, continued foreign exchange interventions between the introduction of the first target in 1991 and 1997; in Turkey, 'implicit' inflation targeting between 2002 and 2005).

In both cases, the introduction of inflation targeting helped central banks to quickly enhance their credibility and initiate a disinflation process. At the same time, the experience in Israel and Turkey has also underlined some limitations of the inflation targeting approach. In Israel, inflation targets were often over- or undershot due to the high, exchange rate-induced, volatility of inflation. In Turkey, the economy was hit by a series of external shocks that prevented inflation from staying within the announced targets over most of the past three years and – after a rapid process of disinflation to single-digit levels – from coming down further to levels consistent with price stability. Also, following the global financial crisis, the two central banks have since late 2008 resumed relatively large-scale and systematic foreign exchange interventions, thereby apparently – at least temporarily – abandoning the paradigm that foreign exchange interventions under inflation targeting occur only on an exceptional basis.

3 Initial conditions for inflation targeting in Egypt, Morocco and Tunisia

The inflation targeting literature identifies various preconditions for successful inflation targeting.[3] These preconditions can be grouped under economic, institutional, and technical conditions. Economic conditions relate to the flexibility of the exchange rate, the soundness of fiscal policy, the existence of sound, deep and stable financial systems, and the effectiveness of the monetary transmission mechanism. Institutional conditions have to do with the independence, accountability and governance of the central bank. Technical conditions pertain to central banks' capacity to model and forecast inflation, and to communicate effectively about monetary policy decisions.

Such preconditions provide important guideposts for assessing the readiness for inflation targeting, even though their relevance is subject to some debate. Most preconditions – such as central bank independence, sound fiscal policies and good forecasting capacities – are not specific to inflation targeters and are arguably relevant for any systematic monetary policy framework (Amato and Gerlach, 2000). Other preconditions are subject to 'endogeneity', i.e. they tend to be fulfilled endogenously after the establishment of inflation targeting. Indeed, the adoption of an inflation targeting framework may act as a commitment device, strengthening the institutional underpinning and credibility of the central bank (IMF, 2006). However, this endogeneity argument is not uncontested, and it is definitely preferable to advance as much as possible with regard to the various technical, economic and institutional requirements before engaging in inflation targeting.

With these considerations in mind, this section reviews the economic, institutional, and technical preconditions for inflation targeting in Egypt, Morocco, and Tunisia. These three countries have indicated their intention to move towards an inflation targeting regime. Evidence on the two countries in the region that have already adopted inflation targeting – Israel and Turkey – is presented, where relevant, for comparison purposes.

Economic preconditions

Inflation targeting calls for a sufficient degree of control over inflation and requires a stable macroeconomic and financial framework. Three key elements reviewed here are: (i) well-functioning and flexible foreign exchange markets, (ii) deep and stable financial markets, allowing for an efficient monetary policy transmission and (iii) a relatively limited occurrence of supply-side shocks or fiscal policy shocks to inflation.

Flexible and efficient foreign exchange markets

Egypt, Morocco, and Tunisia all have exchange rate regimes that involve some degree of exchange rate pegging. The de facto regimes are a managed float in Egypt and Tunisia and a peg to a euro/US dollar basket in Morocco.

There are several signs that the de facto flexibility of the exchange rate has increased somewhat over recent years, in particular for the Egyptian pound and the Tunisian dinar. The short-term flexibility can be measured by the historical volatility of the daily exchange rate. This volatility has risen slightly in the Egyptian pound/US dollar currency pair, from 1 per cent on average in 2006 to more than 3 per cent on average over the first four months of 2008, but remains below the volatility levels of fully flexible currencies (e.g. 10 per cent in the US dollar/euro rate) (see Figure 8.1a). The Moroccan dirham registers only very limited volatility against the currency basket targeted by the authorities. The Tunisian dinar is the most flexible among the three currencies, but even its volatility against a hypothetical basket of currencies,[4] which was around 4 per cent over the first months of 2008, remains below that of the currencies of inflation targeting economies such as Israel and Turkey.

In addition, when longer horizons are considered, there are signs that the authorities are allowing for larger exchange rate fluctuations. One indicator

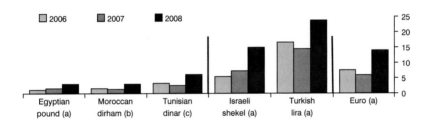

(a) Volatility of daily exchange rate movements (average historical volatility of daily exchange rates against US dollar/against basket for Morocco and Tunisia, annualised, in per cent)

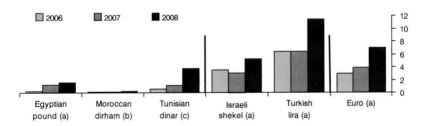

(b) Variability of the exchange rate over one year (coefficient of variation of the exchange rate against US dollar/against basket for Morocco and Tunisia, in per cent)

Figure 8.1 Exchange rate flexibility in selected Mediterranean economies

Sources: Bloomberg and authors' calculation

Notes
a   Against US dollar
b   Against disclosed basket (80% EUR, 20% USD)
c   Assuming a basket of 2/3 EUR, 1/3 USD

is provided by the coefficient of variation, a measure of the dispersion of the exchange rate around its mean. During the year 2008, this indicator was at 1.6 per cent for the Egyptian pound against the US dollar, close to 0 per cent for the Moroccan dirham against a EUR/USD basket and 3.7 per cent for the Tunisian dinar against a EUR/USD basket (see Figure 8.1b). These values are higher than in previous years, but still far below those for the Israeli shekel and the Turkish lira, which recorded coefficients of variation well above 5 per cent in 2008.

Central banks play a diminishing but still pervasive role in foreign exchange markets. Comprehensive evidence on the direct involvement of central banks in these markets is scant. One indication in the case of Morocco comes from data on foreign exchange (FX) markets, which distinguish FX transactions among commercial banks from FX transactions involving the central bank. These data point out that, within an overall growing market, the role of the central bank was gradually diminishing up to 2008. As of early 2008, the central bank accounted for roughly one quarter (about 50 billion dirhams out of a total of 200 billion dirhams) of all FX transactions (see Figure 8.2a).[5] Another indirect indication of the role of central banks in FX markets comes from data on FX reserve accumulation. In all three countries, reserves have grown at double-digit annual growth rates in the period 2005–2007, though reserve accumulation stopped or even reversed in 2008 as a result of the global financial crisis (see Figure 8.2b). That said, these figures do not by themselves imply heavy interventions in the foreign exchange markets. Changes in reserves may partly be driven by income and valuation effects (see e.g. the euro area, where reserves measured in US dollars increased due to such effects) or by precautionary, rather than intervention, motives (see e.g. the case of Turkey, which until the first half of 2008 continued to accumulate reserves almost exclusively for precautionary purposes).[6]

Deep and stable financial markets

Deep and stable financial markets are important for monetary policy transmission. In an environment of liquid and complete financial markets, changes in central bank policy rates can more efficiently be transmitted to the full term structure. This is crucial for an impact on the effective cost of investment and the return on saving, and thus affects saving-investment decisions reflected in aggregate demand.

Sound financial systems allow the economy to cope with policy-motivated increases in the real interest rate. In order to sustain the inflation target in the face of adverse shocks, the central bank may be required to tighten monetary policy and curb aggregate demand. If the banking system is in a weakened state, the central bank's ability to raise interest rates is limited, as it may lead to a collapse of the financial system. Such a situation can also lead to a currency collapse and a reversal of capital flows out of the country (a sudden stop).[7]

Financial market deepening has progressed relatively slowly over recent years in the countries under consideration (Figure 8.3). As of end-2006, bank assets ranged from 77 per cent of GDP in Tunisia to 127 per cent of GDP in Egypt, a

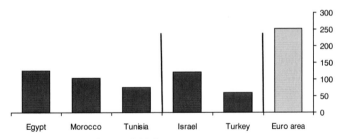

(a)   Transactions in Moroccan FX markets
       (turnover in terms of buy and sell
       transactions of local against foreign
       currency, in billion dirham, 12-month
       cumulated figures, Jan 2001–Nov 2009)

(b)   FX reserves, annual per cent change
       (in per cent, based on US dollar
       data)

Figure 8.2 Indicators of central bank involvement in foreign exchange markets

Source: Bank-Al Maghrib, IMF (International Financial Statistics)

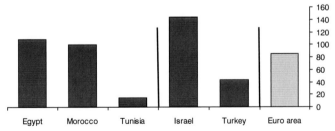

(a)   Bank assets in per cent of GDP (2007)

(b)   Stock market capitalisation in per cent of GDP (2007)

Figure 8.3 Indicators of financial market depth in Egypt, Morocco and Tunisia

Source: IMF, S&P Global Stock Market Factbook 2008, authors' calculations

range that is comparable to that in the inflation targeters in the region (Turkey 61 per cent and Israel 121 per cent). Financial depth in terms of non-bank financial intermediation is more heterogeneous. The stock market, for instance, is still at an early stage of development in Tunisia, with capitalisation at 15 per cent of GDP as of end-2007. Stock market capitalisation is far more advanced in Morocco (100 per cent of GDP) and Egypt (109 per cent of GDP), though the increasing capitalisation over recent years in these two countries is more a reflection of price effects (buoyant share price increases) than of genuine market deepening.

Limited access to finance and a still large stock of non-performing loans may limit the effectiveness of monetary policy transmission.[8] Considerable parts of the household and corporate sectors have limited access to banking and financial market instruments, which limits their potential sensitivity to interest rate changes. Effective monetary policy transmission may also be hampered by the existence of large stocks of non-performing loans – close to 20 per cent of total loans in Egypt and Morocco, and well over 10 per cent in Tunisia as of end-2006. Interest rate increases may lead to a materialisation of credit risks and therefore worsen the non-performing loan portfolio. That said, several measures have been adopted and are being implemented to address these non-performing loan problems.

Nature of shocks to inflation

A third set of economic conditions pertains to the nature of inflationary shocks. Managing inflation and inflation expectations is likely to be more challenging in an economy with frequent and large supply-side shocks, fiscal shocks and/or external shocks.

The high weight of volatile items and administered prices in CPI baskets is one element complicating monetary policy conduct. Food and energy-related items, in particular, play a dominant role in the CPI baskets of the three countries under review. Food prices, for instance, account for around 40 per cent of the baskets in all three countries. In Egypt food prices contributed around 8.6 percentage points to the inflation rate of 16.4 per cent (year-on-year) as of April 2008. Also price subsidies, which are still prevalent across most economies, may add to price volatility beyond the control of monetary policy.

Fiscal policy can be another important source of inflationary shocks. Large and persistent shocks to government spending can compromise monetary policy and endanger the fulfilment of the inflation target. A simple indication of the incidence of fiscal policy shocks is given by the coefficient of variation of government expenditure. This coefficient of variation is highest in Egypt (see Figure 8.4). A related challenge to inflation targeting may come from fiscal dominance. This arises when monetary policy is constrained by solvency considerations of the public sector.[9] Fiscal dominance can also refer to the case of external debt and concerns about its sustainability. Blanchard (2004) shows that raising real interest rates to resist inflationary pressures can lead to higher default risk and hence capital outflows, depreciation, and, ultimately, *higher* inflation.

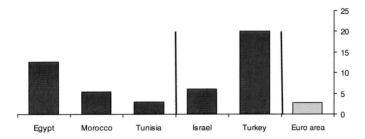

(a)   Variability of government expenditure (coefficient of variation of expenditure to
      GDP ratio, yearly data 1995–2008)

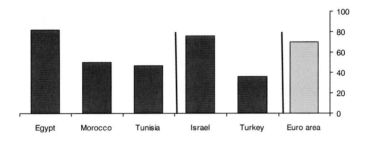

(b)   Gross government debt (in per cent of GDP, 2008)

Figure 8.4 Fiscal indicators in Egypt, Morocco and Tunisia

Source: IMF (World Economic Outlook), authors' calculations

Empirical work has come to differing conclusions about the importance of fiscal dominance issues in the countries under consideration. Hassan (2003), for instance, provides some empirical evidence on fiscal dominance in Egypt. Jbili and Kramarenko (2003) find that a number of countries from the Middle East and Northern Africa need to reduce fiscal dominance problems before engaging in inflation targeting. Panel data evidence from an estimated version of an optimising model in de Resende (2007), by contrast, suggests that Morocco, Tunisia, and Israel exhibit a degree of fiscal dominance comparable to that of the United Kingdom and the United States.[10]

Finally, external shocks may interfere with monetary policy conduct. Countries with a high degree of openness to trade may, ceteris paribus, be more sensitive to imported inflation. Among the three countries, Tunisia records a high degree of trade openness (Figure 8.5a). Moreover, volatility of international capital flows may complicate monetary policy management. One indication of that is given by the variability of capital inflows, which is relatively high in the cases of Egypt and Morocco, in particular (Figure 8.5b).

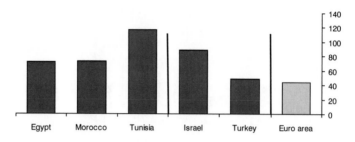

(a)   Trade openness (exports and imports in per cent of GDP, 2007)

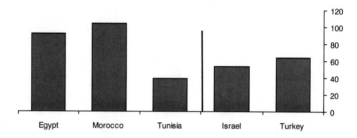

(b)   Variability of capital inflows (coefficient of variation of capital inflows in per cent of GDP, yearly data 1995–2008)

Figure 8.5   External indicators in Egypt, Morocco and Tunisia

Source: IMF (World Economic Outlook), authors' calculations

Institutional preconditions

Various institutional arrangements are necessary for the successful control of inflation. First, a public commitment to price stability as the only long-run goal of monetary policy. Although this is often explicitly mentioned in central bank laws in many countries, what matters most is the de facto commitment of governments and the general public. Second, central bank independence, including a prohibition of government financing and the power to set policy instruments without government interference. On the personal level, the members of the policy-setting body should be insulated from political processes by long-term appointments and protection from arbitrary dismissal. Third, central bank disclosure and transparency, including the dissemination of information on monetary policy decisions and the reasoning behind such decisions.

Over recent years, Egypt, Morocco and Tunisia have made significant progress in all these areas. This has happened, inter alia, in the context of a modernisation of central bank laws in all three cases. Egypt promulgated a law on the Central Bank, the Banking Sector and Money in 2003 and adopted new central bank statutes in 2004. Morocco adopted a new law on the statute of the Bank Al-Maghrib in 2005.

Tunisia introduced in 2006 and 2007 some amendments to the organic law on the Central Bank of Tunisia.

The amendments to central bank laws in Egypt (2003), Morocco (2005) ,and Tunisia (2006) have all introduced price stability as the primary objective of monetary policy (see Table 8.1). All three central banks also have secondary objectives pertaining to general support of the government's economic and financial policy (Morocco) or the promotion of sound banking and payment systems (Egypt and Tunisia).

Central bank independence

The degree of central bank independence varies across countries but has generally been enhanced over the past years (see Table 8.1).

*   *Institutional independence* is helped by strict limitations on the functions and powers of government officials (e.g. the strict listing of the powers of the 'commissaire du gouvernement' at the Bank Al-Maghrib) or bodies comprising government officials (e.g. the limiting of the role of the Coordinating Council at the Bank of Egypt to the setting of monetary policy objectives). The fact that, in all three cases, central bank accountability has been shifted from governments to heads of state is generally considered as a sign of growing independence (Boughrara *et al.*, 2009). At the same time, none of the three central banking laws has explicit references to autonomy, independence or a prohibition from taking instructions.
*   *Personal independence* is promoted by clear clauses on the terms for central bank governors and board members (all three countries) and limitations on the legal grounds for removing governors (e.g. '*faute grave*' in the case of Bank Al-Maghrib).
*   *Financial independence*, while difficult to assess, is helped by the clear disclosure of financial data by the three central banks, including for instance through the publication of central bank balance sheets (Egypt, Morocco, Tunisia), the disclosure of central bank profit and loss accounts (Morocco, Tunisia), and the external audit performed on the central bank (e.g. Morocco).

Practices regarding the prohibition of monetary financing differ across countries. In the case of Morocco, for instance, the extension of central bank credit to government is prohibited according to the statutes, while in Egypt and Tunisia such credit is not ruled out. In Egypt, though, there is de facto no recourse to such monetary finance.

A full assessment of central bank independence is, however, complicated as it depends not only on legal frameworks, but also on actual practices. As pointed out by Gisolo (2009) in his review of central bank independence in the Mediterranean region, the degree of actual independence may differ from what the law suggests.

Table 8.1 Selected aspects of central bank objectives and independence

	Primary objective	Secondary objective(s)	Autonomy	Provison of direct credits to the government	Term and reappointment of Governor and Board members
Countries planning to introduce inflation targeting					
Egypt	Yes (Art. 5)	Banking system soundness (Art. 5)	– [a]	Yes, with limitations and not used (Art. 27)	4 years / Yes (Art. 10 and 11)
Morocco	Yes (Art. 6)	The Bank 'accomplishes its mission in the context of the government's economic and financial policy' (Art. 6)	– [a]	No	6 years / Yes (Art. 38)
Tunisia	Yes (Art. 33)	Sound functioning of payment systems, their efficiency and security	– [a]	Yes	6 years / Yes (Art. 9)
Inflation targeters					
Israel	Yes [b] (Art. 3)	High level of production, employment, national income and capital investment (Art. 3)	– [a]	No [c]	5 years (Governor), 4 years (Deputy Governor) / Yes (Art 12)
Turkey	Yes (Art. 4)	Support the growth and employment policies of the Government (Art. 4)	'Absolute autonomy in exercising the powers and carrying out the duties granted by this Law' (Art. 4)	No (Art. 56)	5 years (Governor), 3 years (Board members) / Yes (Art. 25)

Source: Central banks, authors' compilation

Notes

a No explicit reference to the 'taking of instructions' or 'autonomy' of the central bank.

b The central bank specifies 'price stability and financial stability' as main objectives. The central bank law refers to 'the stabilization of the value of the currency in Israel and outside Israel'.

c Credit to government is prohibited by 'the non-printing law' of 1985.

Transparency

In terms of disclosure and transparency, central banks have made considerable progress over recent years. All three banks, for instance, have started to report regularly on the outcome of their monetary policy deliberations, providing an overview of their decisions and the underlying reasoning (see Table 8.2). One central bank, the Bank Al-Maghrib, produces a quarterly monetary report, which includes a discussion of economic developments, a review of monetary policy actions, and a 12-month-ahead inflation forecast, thereby effectively emulating conventional inflation targeting practices.

Technical preconditions

Inflation targeting requires a fully equipped central bank with well-developed statistical and forecasting capacities. Reliable data on current inflation, good indicators of inflation expectations, and well-founded inflation projections are among the most essential inputs into the monetary policy decisions of inflation targeting central banks.

The countries under review have improved the quality and coverage of their economic and financial statistics. All three countries have joined the IMF's Special Data Dissemination Standard (SDDS) – Tunisia in 2001 and Egypt and Morocco in 2005 – which has helped foster the quality and improve the dissemination of the statistics. Data on consumer price inflation are available on a monthly basis in all three countries and meet international standards in terms of timeliness, coverage, and compilation methods (see Table 8.3 for an overview).

Reliable indicators of inflation expectations are more difficult to find for the countries concerned. Such indicators are useful in an inflation targeting framework as they provide guidance to the monetary authorities about the risk of policy slippages due to a lack of well-anchored inflation expectations. In Egypt, Morocco, and Tunisia, published data on inflation expectations are not available at the moment. This contrasts with the experience in Israel and Turkey, where some indicators of inflation expectations are publicly available.

Finally, the three central banks are expanding their forecasting and modelling capacities. Economic research is intensifying within the central banks, and in some cases external expertise is being sought to develop and enhance macroeconomic modelling techniques. At the same time, public information on research results is so far limited, making a comprehensive assessment very difficult.

4 A Bayesian-estimated macroeconomic model of Egypt, Morocco, and Tunisia

The model and the estimation strategy

This section presents evidence from an estimated macroeconomic model. Similar models have been used in Canada and New Zealand, the pioneers of inflation targeting, and in other countries that introduced inflation targeting in the 1990s

Table 8.2 Selected aspects of central bank communication

	Announce monetary actions via press release	Inflation/monetary policy reports			Other means of communication		
		Frequency	Review of performance and actions	Inflation outlook	Annual reports and other periodical publications	Publication of MPC minutes	Publication of models for inflation outlook
Countries planning to introduce inflation targeting							
Egypt	Yes	No[a]	No	No	Yes	No	No
Morocco	Yes	Quarterly	Yes	One-year range with discussion	Yes	No	No
Tunisia	Yes	No	No	No	Yes	No	No
Inflation targeters							
Israel	Yes	Monthly	Yes	Two-years range with discussion	Yes	Yes	Yes, some
Turkey	Yes	Quarterly	Yes	Up to three-years range with discussion	Yes	No	No

Source: Carare *et al.* (2002), central banks, authors' compilation

Note

a But the central bank publishes a quarterly 'Economic Review', which presents economic developments and results from research conducted at the Bank

Table 8.3 Main features of consumer price statistics in selected Mediterranean economies

	Periodicity (in weeks)	Timeliness	Advance release calendar	Population coverage	Geographical coverage	Frequency of weight updates (in years)
Countries planning to introduce inflation targeting						
Egypt	Monthly[a]	4	Yes (1 quarter)	All households	Whole country	5
Morocco	Monthly	3	Yes (1 year)	All households	Whole country	5
Tunisia	Monthly	2	Yes (1 quarter)	All households	Cities only	Around 8[b]
Inflation targeters						
Israel	Monthly	2	Yes (1 quarter)	All households	Whole country	2
Turkey	Monthly	<1	Yes (1 year)	All households	Whole country	1

Source: IMF Dissemination Standards Bulletin Board, authors' compilation

Notes
a Bimonthly for rural regions
b Since its establishment, the CPI weights have been updated in 1962, 1970, 1977, 1983, 1990, and 2000 bases

(the Czech Republic and South Africa, among others). Berg, Karam, and Laxton (2006a, 2006b) document this modelling strategy in detail, including its relation to other approaches to macroeconomic modelling.

The model consists of four equations describing price-setting behaviour, aggregate demand, exchange rate determination and the monetary policy rule. As in Svensson (2000), the variables referring to the rest of the world are approximated by the US. World output is approximated by US GDP and the world real interest rate in the uncovered interest parity (UIP) condition is approximated by the US real interest rate. All variables are measured in deviations from their long-run trends approximated by the Hodrick–Prescott filter with $\lambda = 1600$.

The Phillips curve relates CPI inflation to past and expected inflation, the output gap and the change in the real exchange rate:

$$\pi_t = \alpha_\pi \pi4_{t+4} + (1 - \alpha_\pi)\pi4_{t-1} + \alpha_{ygap} ygap_{t-1} + \alpha_z(z_t - z_{t-1}) + res_t^\pi \quad (1)$$

where π_t is the annualised quarter-on-quarter CPI inflation rate, $\pi4_t$ is the annual CPI inflation rate defined as $\pi4_t = 0.25(\pi_t + \pi_{t-1} + \pi_{t-2} + \pi_{t-3})$, is the lagged value of the domestic output gap (in percentage of capacity output) and z_t is an appropriately scaled logarithm of the real effective exchange rate.

Annual inflation four quarters ahead hence represents model-consistent expectations of annual inflation and the Phillips curve incorporates the effect of inflation expectations on inflation. The coefficient α_π measures how much a central bank can influence future inflation through influencing inflation expectations. A value of close to 1 implies an economy that can be steered relatively easily by the central bank, and where disinflation is relatively less costly.

The aggregate demand equation is specified using the output gap as the dependent variable. The output gap is assumed to be determined by its lagged and lead value, the difference between the lagged actual and the equilibrium real interest rate ($RR_{t-1} - RR_{t-1}^{Eq}$), the lagged gap between the actual and the equilibrium real exchange rate ($zgap_{t-1}$) and the world output gap ($ygap_t^*$):

$$ygap_t = \beta_{ygap}^{Lead} ygap_{t+1} + \beta_{ygap}^{Lag} ygap_{t-1} - \beta_{rrgap}\left(RR_{t-1} - RR_{t-1}^{Eq}\right) + \beta_{zgap} z_{t-1} + \\ + \beta_{ygap*} ygap_t^* + res_t^{ygap} \quad (2)$$

The equation is a standard open-economy aggregate demand equation, including (i) the real interest rate effect on domestic demand, (ii) the real exchange rate effect on the demand for imports and exports, and (iii) the rest-of-the-world income effect on demand for domestic exports.

The uncovered interest rate parity condition allows for deviations from the rational expectations formation (Ez_{t+1}), as possible departures from the rational expectations hypothesis are often considered more suitable for emerging market economies. The current period real exchange rate is set equal to a weighted average of expected future and past exchange rates plus a standard term capturing the real interest rate differential:

$$z_t = \delta E_t z_{t+1} + (1-\delta)z_{t-1} - \left(RR_t - RR_t^*\right)/4 + res_t^z \tag{3}$$

where $E_{z_{t+1}}$ is the expectation of the real exchange rate in $t + 1$ conditional on information in time t, the parameter δ (assumed to be between 0 and 1) is the weight on the expected future exchange rate, RR_t is the domestic real interest rate, and RR_t^* is the world real interest rate.

Finally, the monetary policy rule is a version of the inflation-forecast-based rule where the central bank adjusts short-term nominal interest rates. In deviations from equilibrium, the monetary policy rule can be written as:

$$RS_t = \gamma_R^{Lag} RS_{t-1} + (1 - \gamma_R^{Lag})\left(\gamma_\pi E_t \pi 4_{t+1} + \gamma_{ygap} ygap_t\right) + res_t^{RS} \tag{4}$$

where RS_t is the short-term nominal interest rate. A central bank reacts to the deviation of inflation from its (implicit or explicit) target and to the output gap. Furthermore, the model assumes interest rate smoothing – the central bank adjusts the nominal interest rate in a sequence of gradual steps with infrequent changes of direction. The monetary policy rule is not explicitly micro-founded, but can be motivated by assuming a central bank's loss function that penalises deviations of both inflation and output gap from their long-run values.

This model is transparent and simple and yet rich enough to analyse issues relevant to a small open economy. Although the model abstracts from many important issues, including the supply side, fiscal policy, and the current account, it still allows consideration of the monetary transmission mechanism and the trade-offs faced by a country wishing to implement inflation targeting. Moreover, the flexibility of the model allows for explicit treatment of additional issues. Laxton and Pesenti (2003) extend it to cover, among other things, capital accumulation, the labour market, and the traded and non-traded sectors. Karam and Pagan (2008) have recently used this model as a starting point for the analysis of external debt accumulation. Substantial limitations in data availability for emerging market economies add to the appeal of this simple modelling framework, making it a suitable starting point for a first attempt at quantitative assessment of monetary policy.

The model leaves room for judgement and serves as a tool for coherent assessment of future developments. The model is specified in terms of deviations of economic variables from their equilibrium values (the gap form) and hence requires input about past and future equilibrium values, policy actions, and the sources of shocks. The model is not fully micro-founded, but it contains standard specifications with well-established economic interpretations, is based on a general equilibrium framework, and invokes the rational expectations assumption.[11]

The point of our estimation exercise is to check whether it gives meaningful estimates of the transmission mechanism that can be compared with the existing literature. These include the degree of forward-looking behaviour in the Phillips curve and in aggregate demand, the degree of the exchange rate pass-through, and the relative importance of the real interest rate and the real exchange rate in influencing aggregate demand. Finally, we should also get some idea about the magnitude and relative importance of the shocks hitting these countries.

Our analysis should be read with several caveats in mind. The reliability of parameter estimates is negatively affected by short data series and the possible presence of structural change, for which we do not test here. On the other hand, Bayesian methods that do not rely exclusively on observed data seem particularly suitable for economies with short data series. Implicitly, we also assume that an inflation-forecast-based policy rule is a suitable description of the data in the time when no such policy has been in place. However, the finding that such a model can be estimated suggests that a systematic monetary policy stabilising the price level has been in place and the data do not contradict the prior information including the assumed model structure.

We estimate the model using Bayesian techniques. These techniques combine prior information about the estimated parameters with the observed data to produce a new (posterior) estimate of the parameter. Sims (2002) argues that the main advantage of the Bayesian estimation is that the researcher must explicitly formulate his or her priors, which improves the transparency of the modelling and estimation process. The central insight of this method is formalised by the Bayes theorem:

$$p(\theta \mid Y) = \frac{p(Y \mid \theta)p(\theta)}{p(Y)} \tag{5}$$

where $p(\theta \mid Y)$ denotes the posterior probability density function that takes observed data Y into account. The term $p(Y \mid \theta)$ stands for the likelihood of observed data given the vector of model parameters θ, $p(\theta)$ represents the prior probability density function and is a marginal density that is computed as:

$$p(Y) = \int p(\theta, Y)d\theta$$

Intuitively, the Bayesian estimation is a method half-way between calibration (choice of the prior distribution) and maximum likelihood estimation (inferring parameters from observed data using the likelihood function). Technically, the likelihood of observed data given the vector of parameters, $p(Y \mid \theta)$, is obtained using a Kalman filter. The combination of likelihood function and prior density in the numerator of equation (5) is simulated using a sampling procedure.

The usual measures of the goodness of fit, such as the R-squared, as well as other diagnostic tests for the validity of the classical model assumptions, are not available in Bayesian estimation. With some degree of simplification, this is due to the fact that, unlike the classical estimation that builds on the concept of a 'true' data-generating process, in the Bayesian approach the model is always conditional upon, and hence inseparable from, the data set used in estimation. While it is possible to compare the fit of several models, conditional on an identical data set, we only estimate one model for each country and such an exercise is thus beyond the scope of this chapter.

The calculations reported here were obtained using DYNARE, a Matlab pre-processor and toolbox for estimating and solving rational expectations models.[12] The implementation of Bayesian estimation uses the Metropolis–Hastings sampling algorithm that 'constructs a Gaussian approximation around the posterior mode and allows for an efficient exploration of the posterior distribution at least in the neighbourhood of the mode' (An and Schorfheide, 2006: 18). We simulate the posterior probability density using 200,000 replications with the acceptance rate between 0.25 and 0.30. This value lies within the range 0.2 to 0.4 which is usually used in practical applications (see Harjes and Ricci, 2008, among others). Intuitively speaking, an appropriate choice of the acceptance rate ensures that the algorithm calculating the posterior mode properly reflects the tails of the posterior distribution and does not get stuck in the subspace of the parameter range. The convergence of the algorithm is assessed by the method suggested by Brooks and Gelman (1998).

The priors are based on available research and conventional findings of similar macroeconomic work. We mainly draw on Harjes and Ricci (2008) for the selection of priors. Since macroeconomic aggregates are likely to be more volatile in Morocco and Tunisia than in South Africa, we impose higher values for the standard deviations of some estimated shocks. Prior distributions are chosen on the basis of admissible parameter values, the values used in the literature for other countries and values reflecting the stylised facts of the transmission mechanism. In Tables 8.4 to 8.6 we report the types of prior distribution, the means, and the standard deviations of the model parameters.[13]

We estimate the model for Egypt, Morocco, and Tunisia, using quarterly time series data from 1994. Data are taken from the IMF's *International Financial Statistics*. The dataset for Egypt covers the period from 1994Q1 to 2007Q2, that for Morocco from 1994Q1 to 2006Q4, and that for Tunisia from 1994Q1 to 2007Q2. Since quarterly data on Tunisian GDP are available only from 2000 onwards, we derived the quarterly data for 1994 to 1999 from annual values using the variation in the data on industrial production. For the same reason, we use annual GDP data for Egypt and decompose them into quarterly series using data on electricity utilisation. The quarterly time series are interpolated from annual flows using the proportional Denton method. While the data on industrial production and electricity utilisation serve as 'indicator series' that provide the pattern for interpolation, the observed annual data constrain the annual totals.[14]

Estimation results

The results for Egypt, Morocco, and Tunisia suggest important similarities in the transmission mechanisms (see Table 8.7).[15] The Phillips curve coefficient on expected CPI inflation is between 0.65 for Egypt and 0.69 for Tunisia. Although higher than in other models reported for comparison in Table 8.7, estimates in the range of 0.6 to 0.7 are not unusual. For example, Galí and Gertler (1999) using US quarterly data from 1960Q1 to 1997Q4 report estimated values of the parameter between 0.59 and 0.87. For a restricted version of their Phillips curve with the coefficients on expected and lagged inflation summing to unity, they report values

Table 8.4 Estimation results (priors and posteriors) for Egypt

Parameter	Prior distribution			Posterior distribution		
	Mean	Distribution	Standard deviation	Mean	90% confidence interval	
α_π	0.25	beta	0.1	0.649	0.529	0.777
α_{ygap}	0.30	gamma	0.1	0.324	0.187	0.454
α_z	0.15	beta	0.05	0.146	0.064	0.226
β_{ygap}^{Lead}	0.05	beta	0.02	0.053	0.019	0.085
β_{ygap}^{Lag}	0.70	beta	0.05	0.665	0.584	0.743
β_{rrgap}	0.12	gamma	0.03	0.133	0.077	0.182
β_{zgap}	0.05	gamma	0.01	0.058	0.040	0.075
β_{ygap^*}	0.20	gamma	0.05	0.195	0.117	0.268
δ	0.50	beta	0.1	0.544	0.407	0.695
γ_R^{Lag}	0.50	beta	0.1	0.739	0.661	0.817
γ_π	2.00	gamma	0.3	1.882	1.416	2.344
γ_{ygap}	0.30	beta	0.1	0.276	0.123	0.430

Note: Parameters in the table correspond to coefficients in the equations introduced in the model description.

Table 8.5 Estimation results (priors and posteriors) for Morocco

Parameter	Prior distribution			Posterior distribution		
	Mean	Distribution	Standard deviation	Mean	90% confidence interval	
α_π	0.25	beta	0.1	0.677	0.535	0.820
α_{ygap}	0.30	gamma	0.1	0.226	0.113	0.334
α_z	0.15	beta	0.05	0.158	0.060	0.258
β_{ygap}^{Lead}	0.05	beta	0.02	0.052	0.019	0.084
β_{ygap}^{Lag}	0.70	beta	0.05	0.631	0.542	0.714
β_{rrgap}	0.12	gamma	0.03	0.130	0.076	0.182
β_{zgap}	0.05	gamma	0.01	0.061	0.041	0.080
β_{ygap^*}	0.20	gamma	0.05	0.181	0.109	0.254
δ	0.50	beta	0.1	0.566	0.435	0.720
γ_R^{Lag}	0.50	beta	0.1	0.781	0.712	0.854
γ_π	2.00	gamma	0.3	1.830	1.366	2.303
γ_{ygap}	0.30	beta	0.1	0.231	0.100	0.363

Note: Parameters in the table correspond to coefficients in the equations introduced in the model description.

Table 8.6 Estimation results (priors and posteriors) for Tunisia

		Prior distribution		Posterior distribution		
Parameter	Mean	Distribution	Standard deviation	Mean	90% confidence interval	
α_π	0.25	beta	0.1	0.686	0.565	0.811
α_{ygap}	0.30	gamma	0.1	0.255	0.152	0.357
α_z	0.15	beta	0.05	0.128	0.056	0.198
β_{ygap}^{Lead}	0.05	beta	0.02	0.048	0.018	0.077
β_{ygap}^{Lag}	0.70	beta	0.05	0.612	0.534	0.691
β_{rrgap}	0.12	gamma	0.03	0.126	0.075	0.174
β_{zgap}	0.05	gamma	0.01	0.060	0.043	0.078
β_{ygap*}	0.20	gamma	0.05	0.166	0.101	0.229
δ_R	0.50	beta	0.1	0.708	0.610	0.809
γ_R^{Lag}	0.50	beta	0.1	0.868	0.828	0.909
γ_π	2.00	gamma	0.3	1.774	1.317	2.214
γ_{ygap}	0.30	beta	0.1	0.234	0.098	0.365

Note: Parameters in the table correspond to coefficients in the equations introduced in the model description.

of 0.77 and 0.62, depending on the exact estimation methodology.[16] Furthermore, one has to keep in mind that the values of α_π reported in Table 8.7 for Canada and the Czech Republic come from calibrated models. The value for Israel obtained by the GMM estimation using quarterly data from 1992Q1 to 2005Q3 is already much closer to the range of our estimated values.

All in all, the estimated coefficient suggests that inflation is influenced considerably by expectations about future inflation and that the increases in the real interest rate needed to reduce inflation can be relatively moderate, provided that they are perceived as permanent. This result highlights the importance of anchoring inflation expectations in the three countries and the role of credibility in monetary policy strategy. In the terminology of Berg, Karam and Laxton (2006b), Egypt, Morocco, and Tunisia appear to be 'speedboat' economies, where the wheel needs only to be turned slightly, albeit persistently, to achieve disinflation.[17] The weight put on the expected output gap in the aggregate demand equation, β_{ygap}^{Lead}, on the other hand, suggests only a limited degree of forward-looking behaviour and the real interest rate channel of monetary policy transmission, β_{rrgap}, is almost identical in all three countries. Similarly, the degree of exchange rate pass-through, which can be judged from the size of the coefficient on the real exchange rate in the Phillips curve, α_z, is only marginally higher in Morocco (0.16) than in Egypt (0.15) and Tunisia (0.13).

The estimation results also point to some differences among countries. The weight of the output gap in the Phillips curve is higher in Egypt (0.32) than in

Table 8.7 Comparison of selected parameters for Egypt, Morocco, Tunisia, South Africa, Canada, the Czech Republic and Israel

	Egypt	Morocco	Tunisia	South Africa	Canada	Czech Republic	Israel
α_π	0.649	0.677	0.686	0.434	0.20	0.33	0.53
α_{ygap}	0.324	0.226	0.255	0.228	0.30	0.50	–
α_z	0.146	0.158	0.128	0.146	0.10	–	–
β_{ygap}^{Lead}	0.053	0.052	0.048	0.043	0.10	–	–
β_{ygap}^{Lag}	0.665	0.631	0.612	0.746	0.85	0.90	–
β_{rrgap}	0.133	0.13	0.126	0.086	0.10	0.13	–
β_{zgap}	0.058	0.061	0.06	0.027	0.05	0.15	–
β_{ygap^*}	0.195	0.181	0.166	0.143	0.25	0.21	–
δ	0.544	0.566	0.708	0.434	0.50	0.50	0.45
γ^{Lag}	0.739	0.781	0.868	0.700	0.50	0.50	0.60
γ_π	1.882	1.830	1.774	1.932	2.00	5.00	1.50
γ_{ygap}	0.276	0.231	0.234	0.283	0.50	1.00	0.50
res^π	2.853	3.951	2.133	2.657	–	–	–
res^{ygap}	1.179	2.279	1.585	0.579	–	–	–
res^z	1.477	0.673	0.645	6.291	–	–	–
res^{RS}	1.069	0.767	0.372	1.286	–	–	–

Notes: Values for Canada are taken from Berg, Karam, and Laxton (2006a), for the Czech Republic from Coats, Laxton, and Rose (2003), and for Israel from Argov *et al.* (2007). Model specifications for Canada, Czech Republic and Israel differ from the rest of the countries. Values for Morocco, Tunisia and South Africa are Bayesian estimates. Models for the Czech Republic and Canada are calibrated. Values for Israel are GMM estimates from single equation estimation.

the other two countries, Tunisia (0.26) and Morocco (0.23). These comparisons can be used to judge the relative importance of the domestic as opposed to imported inflation for the overall CPI dynamics. The transmission of domestic and imported inflation to the CPI seems fastest in Egypt. The foreign exchange markets, as captured in the UIP condition, also differ across countries. The coefficient capturing forward-looking expectations in foreign exchange markets reaches 0.54 in Egypt and 0.57 in Morocco, but 0.71 in Tunisia. These fractions can be interpreted as a crude measure of foreign exchange market efficiency. The higher the share of forward-looking foreign exchange market participants, the higher the market's efficiency. These results are, however, still preliminary and need to be corroborated by further evidence.

The estimation results for Egypt, Morocco, and Tunisia can also be compared with results from econometric studies on other countries with an inflation targeting framework. Table 8.7 thus provides a comparison of our posterior means with estimation results for South Africa,[18] Canada, the Czech Republic[19] and Israel.[20] This comparison yields three insights:[21]

- First, we see that the forward-looking component of inflation expectations (a_π) is relatively high in Egypt, Morocco, and Tunisia. One should, however, keep in mind that a simple identification of expectations with realised future values may be too strong an assumption for these countries. On the other hand, the low calibrated value for Canada suggests that the size of this coefficient is not in itself a problem for inflation targeting.
- Second, the Egyptian, Tunisian, and Moroccan economies exhibit a similar degree of exchange rate pass-through to CPI inflation (a_z) to that in South Africa. Since Egypt, Morocco and Tunisia are likely to face high unexpected exchange rate shocks, this is perhaps not surprising.
- Third, the effect of the exchange rate gap on domestic demand (β_{zgap}) is higher for Egypt, Morocco and Tunisia than for the rest of the sample (with the exception of the Czech Republic). The effect of world demand on domestic demand (β_{ygap*}) is higher than in South Africa but smaller than the calibrated values for Canada and the Czech Republic. The ratio of the real interest rate effect to the real exchange rate effect in aggregate demand is between two and three, suggesting enough room for stabilisation through variation in short-term real interest rates.

The impulse response functions (not reported) are fairly standard for open economy models of this type. They show typical paths of endogenous variables after one-off shocks to aggregate supply, aggregate demand, the policy rate, and the real exchange rate. The magnitudes of the shocks are those estimated using the actual country data and, hence, differ for Morocco and Tunisia, as the estimated variance of the shocks is higher in Morocco. This includes shocks to the policy rate which in Egypt and Morocco are more than twice the size of those in Tunisia.

5 Conclusions

Monetary policy frameworks in the Mediterranean countries are still heavily dominated by external anchors, but have started shifting towards more flexibility and more domestically-oriented targets. Three countries – Egypt, Morocco, and Tunisia – have formally announced their intention to move towards inflation targeting. While precise timelines and calendars have so far not been published, the three central banks are advancing the technical and operational preparations for the transition to inflation targeting.

Central banks in all three countries do not yet fully meet all the economic, institutional and technical conditions for inflation targeting, but they are making steady progress. In terms of *economic preconditions*, the central banks have gradually started to liberalise their foreign exchange markets, and financial markets are quickly becoming deeper, but the uneven access of the private sector to bank credit and to financial markets, coupled with the still large stock of non-performing loans, could limit the effectiveness of monetary policy transmission. In terms of *institutional preconditions*, central banking frameworks have advanced considerably over recent years through amendments to central bank laws. In terms of *technical preconditions*, the central banks have considerably enhanced their statistical apparatus and are gradually expanding their technical expertise in modelling and inflation forecasting.

Results from a Bayesian-estimated model estimated for three countries (Egypt, Morocco, and Tunisia) suggest that basic macroeconomic relations observed in their economies are compatible with an inflation targeting framework. A conventional small macroeconomic model, developed and commonly used by inflation targeters in advanced and emerging market economies, seems to fit well the economies under review. The model produces reasonable estimated coefficients and its impulse response functions are compatible with the empirical regularities observed in countries with an established inflation targeting framework. Specifically, the estimated Taylor rules for all countries ensure model stability as they fulfil the so-called Taylor principle. The estimated Phillips curves have output gap coefficients implying the usual cost of disinflation (the sacrifice ratio). There are, however, also country-specific differences, namely in the fraction of backward-looking agents in the economy as reflected in the Phillips curve and the UIP condition estimates.

Our estimation exercise should perhaps best be viewed as a simple test of whether, despite the evidence on monetary policy strategies followed in the past, the data contradict the four-equations model structure that we impose on them as part of the prior information used in the Bayesian estimation. Our results do not suggest any such contradiction and we interpret this finding as supporting the introduction of inflation targeting. However, our estimation results do not allow us to capture possible structural breaks that may have occurred in monetary policy transmission in the countries concerned.

In the end, the genuine readiness of policymakers to accept the full implications of inflation targeting will be as decisive for success as the fulfilment of preconditions and the model results. Full support from the entire spectrum of policymakers for the central bank's continued focus on price stability as the overriding monetary policy objective may prove to be the most important ingredient of success for any move towards inflation targeting.

Notes

1 This chapter reflects the view of the authors, not those of the European Central Bank. We are grateful to Livia Chiţu for excellent research assistance and to Alexander Jung, Christian Mank, Frank Moss, Michael Sturm and Jean-Pierre Vidal for useful comments. An early version of the chapter benefited from helpful comments by participants at the fifth high-level Euro-Mediterranean seminar of Eurosystem and Mediterranean central banks, which was jointly organised by the Central Bank of Egypt and the European Central Bank in Alexandria, Egypt, on 27 November 2008.

2 Mundell (1968) elaborated the concept of the impossible trinity. Adding the trade dimension, Padoa-Schioppa (1990) extended this notion to an 'impossible quartet'.

3 See Eichengreen *et al.* (1999), Masson *et al.* (1997), Debelle *et al.* (1998) and Agénor (2000).

4 The hypothetical basket used is 2/3 euro, 1/3 US dollar. This is based on IMF (2007), which states that the weight of the euro is 'at least two thirds'.

5 In 2008 and 2009, foreign exchange market activity collapsed, presumably as a result of the global financial crisis, and central bank involvement in the foreign exchange market again became important.

6 The Central Bank of the Republic of Turkey (2005) distinguishes intervention activities from pre-announced reserve purchases to build up a buffer of foreign exchange reserves. The Bank of Israel has also recently engaged in a programme of regular reserve purchases, which are clearly distinct from foreign exchange interventions.

7 Mishkin (2004) calls this scenario a 'twin crisis', for it comprises two separate crises, currency and financial. Burnside, Eichenbaum and Rebelo (2001) point out that the bailout of the banking system often required when a twin crisis occurs increases government liabilities that will have to be monetised in the future, thus undermining the inflation targeting regime.

8 Empirical estimates of monetary policy transmission channels for Egypt (Al-Mashat and Billmeier, 2008) and for Morocco and Tunisia (Boughrara, 2003) point to relatively weak monetary policy transmission across the region. Boughrara, Boughzala and Moussa (2009) develop a model for the Tunisian economy, which illustrates that a possible sharp increase in non-performing loans in the event of interest rate responses to inflationary shocks may constitute a major obstacle to the introduction of inflation targeting.

9 Sargent and Wallace (1981) were the first to note that 'a permanently higher government deficit must eventually be accommodated by increases in monetary base', i.e. at least partially monetised. Their original model deals with the special case where the real interest rate is constant and higher than a constant real growth rate. A newer re-statement of the primacy of fiscal over monetary policy is the fiscal theory of the price level proposed by, among others, Woodford (1995).

10 The overall finding of the study is that the null hypothesis of an identical degree of fiscal dominance in OECD and developing countries can be safely rejected. This result is, however, not driven by the Mediterranean countries in the sample.

11 Berg, Karam and Laxton (2006a) argue that in practice specific microfoundations are not helpful in modelling observed macroeconomic magnitudes. This observation is in line with the pragmatic approach adopted by many policy-making institutions.

12 The codes and documentation for DYNARE are available at http://www.cepremap. cnrs.fr/dynare

13 Note that there should be at least as many shocks as observable variables in the system. We thus added to the model five parameters that relate the observable foreign output gap, foreign real interest rate, real exchange rate gap, equilibrium real interest rate and annual inflation target to an assumed AR(1) process and included these five additional equations in the Bayesian estimation.

14 In addition, we use data on foreign output and the real interest rate, proxied by US GDP and the interest rate on 3-month US Treasury Bills deflated by actual CPI. The nominal interest rate for both Morocco and Tunisia is the money market rate reported in the IFS. In Morocco, it refers to the inter-bank lending rate, in Tunisia to the upper margin on overnight inter-bank deposits. The real exchange rate for all three countries is the real effective exchange rate weighted by manufactured trade in 1999 to 2001 and deflated by relative CPI.

15 We present results for the estimated coefficients. Results in terms of impulse response functions are not presented here, but available from the authors upon request.

16 The difference in estimates results from the exact specification of the orthogonality conditions used in the GMM estimation. They argue in favour of the former, i.e. a higher value of the coefficient.

17 Economies where big and persistent changes in the policy rate induce only small and delayed changes in current inflation are called 'aircraft carrier' economies in Berg, Karam and Laxton (2006b). Although some papers link the value of the coefficient

to the degree of central bank credibility, values around 0.5 can be observed even in developed economies.

18 The South African results are taken from Harjes and Ricci (2008), who use a virtually identical macroeconomic model and the same Bayesian estimation method.

19 For Canada and the Czech Republic, we report calibrated values that are used in very similar model specifications for policy analysis.

20 The results for Israel are GMM estimates from a small macroeconomic model.

21 The estimates for Morocco, Tunisia and South Africa can be compared directly as they come from a very similar model estimated by the same econometric technique. The values in the last three columns serve as examples of countries that have already adopted inflation targeting. The point estimates should be always considered in terms of their respective confidence intervals, so the apparent similarities should not be exaggerated.

References

Agénor, P.-R. (2000), 'Monetary policy under flexible exchange rates: An introduction to inflation targeting', World Bank, Policy working paper 2511.

Al-Mashat, R., and Billmeier, A. (2008) 'The monetary transmission mechanism in Egypt', *Review of Middle East Economics and Finance,* 4(3), article 2.

Amato, J., and Gerlach, S. (2000), 'Inflation targeting in emerging market and transition economies: Lessons after a decade', *European Economic Review,* 46: 781–790.

An, S., and Schorfheide, F. (2006), 'Bayesian analysis of DSGE models', Federal Reserve Board, Philadelphia, working paper 06–5.

Argov, E., Binyamini, A., Elkayam, D., and Rozenshtrom, I. (2007), 'A small macroeconomic model to support inflation targeting in Israel', Monetary Department, Bank of Israel.

Berg, A., Karam, P., and Laxton, D. (2006a), 'A practical model-based approach to monetary policy analysis – Overview', IMF working paper 06/80.

——(2006b), 'Practical model-based monetary policy analysis – A how-to guide', IMF working paper 06/81.

Blanchard, O. (2004), 'Fiscal dominance and inflation targeting: Lessons from Brazil', National Bureau of Economic Research, working paper 10389.

Boughrara, A. (2003), 'What do we know about the monetary policy and transmission mechanisms in Morocco and Tunisia?', Paper presented to the 10th Annual Conference of the ERF held in Marrakech (Morocco).

Boughrara, A., Boughzala, M., and Moussa, H. (2009), 'Inflation targeting and financial fragility in Tunisia', in·D. Cobham and G. Dibeh (eds), *Monetary Policy and Central Banking in the Middle East and North Africa,* London: Routledge.

Brooks, S.P., and Gelman, A. (1998), 'Alternative methods for monitoring convergence of iterative simulations', *Journal of Computational and Graphical Statistics,* 7: 434–455.

Burnside, C., Eichenbaum, M., and Rebelo, S. (2001), 'Prospective deficits and the Asian currency crisis', *Journal of Political Economy,* 109: 1155–1197.

Carare, A., Schaechter, A., Stone, M. and Zelmer, M. (2002). 'Establishing Initial Conditions in Support of Inflation Targeting', IMF Working Papers 02/102 Washington DDC: IMf.

Central Bank of the Republic of Turkey (2005), 'General framework of inflation targeting regime and monetary and exchange rate policy for 2006', available at www.tcmb.gov.tr/yeni/announce/2005/ANO2005–45.pdf, December 2005.

Coats, W., Laxton, D. and Rose, D. (2003), *The Czech National Bank's Forecasting and Policy Analysis System,* Prague: Czech National Bank.

Debelle, G., Masson, P., Savastano, M., and Sharma, S. (1998), 'Inflation targeting as a framework for monetary policy', IMF, *Economic Issues*, no. 15.

Eichengreen, B., Masson, P., Savastano, M., and Sharma, S. (1999), 'Transition strategies and nominal anchors on the road to greater exchange-rate flexibility', *Essays in International Finance*, no. 213, Princeton University.

Gali, J., and Gertler, M. (1999). 'Inflation dynamics: A structural econometric analysis', *Journal of Monetary Economics*, 44(2): 195–222.

Gisolo, E. (2009), 'The degree of legal independence of the Mediterranean central banks: international comparison and macroeconomic implications', in D. Cobham and G. Dibeh (eds), *Monetary Policy and Central Banking in the Middle East and North Africa*, Routledge.

Harjes, T., and Ricci, L.A. (2008), 'A Bayesian-estimated model of inflation targeting in South Africa', IMF working paper 08/48.

Hassan, M. (2003), 'Procyclicality, fiscal dominance, and the effectiveness of fiscal policy in Egypt', paper presented at the 9th Banca d'Italia workshop on public finances, Banca d'Italia, Rome.

IMF (2006), 'Does inflation targeting work in emerging markets?', *World Economic Outlook*, September 2006, Chapter IV.

——(2007), 'Tunisia. Selected issues: Inflation forecasting and exchange rate pass-through', IMF Country Report 07/319.

Jbili, A., and Kramarenko, V. (2003), 'Choosing exchange regimes in the Middle East and North Africa', International Monetary Fund, available at http://www.imf.org/external/pubs/ft/med/2003/eng/jbili/jbili.htm.

Karam, P., and Pagan, A. (2008), 'A small structural monetary policy model for small open economies with debt accumulation', IMF working paper 08/64.

Laxton, D., and Pesenti, P. (2003), 'Monetary policy rules for small, open, emerging economies', *Journal of Monetary Economics*, 50: 1109–1146.

Masson, P.R., Savastano, M.A., and Sharma, S. (1997), 'The scope for inflation targeting in developing countries', IMF working paper 97/130.

Mishkin, F.S. (2004), 'Can inflation targeting work in emerging market countries?', NBER working paper 10646.

Mundell, R. (1968), *International Economics*, Macmillan: New York.

Padoa-Schioppa, T. (1990), 'Financial and monetary integration in Europe: 1990, 1992 and beyond', *Occasional Paper*, no. 28. Washington: Group of Thirty.

Resende, C. de (2007), 'Cross-country estimates of the degree of fiscal dominance and central bank independence', Bank of Canada working paper 2007-36.

Sargent, T., and Wallace, N. (1981), 'Some unpleasant monetarist arithmetic', *Federal Reserve Board of Minneapolis Quarterly Review*, 7: 1–13.

Sims, C. (2002), 'The role of models and probabilities in the monetary policy process', *Brookings Papers on Economic Activity*, 2: 1–62.

Svensson, L.E.O. (2000), 'Open-economy inflation targeting', *Journal of International Economics*, 50: 155–183.

Woodford, M. (1995), 'Price level determinacy without control of a monetary aggregate', *Carnegie Rochester Conference Series on Public Policy*, 43: 1–46.

9 Channels and environments of monetary policy and their implications for its conduct in GCC countries

Wassim Shahin

1 Introduction

This chapter addresses the transmission mechanism channels and the environments of monetary policy in the Gulf Cooperation Council (GCC) countries to study their implications for monetary policy strategy and conduct. These countries comprise Bahrain, Kuwait, Oman, Qatar, Saudi Arabia and the United Arab Emirates (UAE). The monetary policy pursued in these countries revolves around pegging their national currencies to the US dollar, except for Kuwait which has been pegging against an undeclared basket of currencies since 2007. In this respect, GCC members believe that the peg provides an anchor for monetary policy aimed at achieving price stability. To preserve the national currency–dollar fix, domestic interest rates have been adjusted in line with US interest rates. This monetary policy framework prevents both the exchange rate and to a lesser extent the interest rate from acting as channels for the transmission of monetary policy. In addition, this group of countries is working on establishing a Gulf Monetary Union in the next decade, with a common currency. This union may require a different monetary policy framework, which will affect the transmission mechanism of monetary policy.

Given its purpose, the present chapter draws on a large theoretical and empirical literature that addresses the various transmission mechanisms of monetary policy. The financial and economic environments necessary for policy effectiveness are then highlighted. After theoretically reviewing the channels and the environments, the chapter studies the economic and financial characteristics necessary for successful transmission mechanisms in developing and transition economies including the GCC countries. The salient features are specifically highlighted for the GCC countries and compared with the general environments necessary for efficient transmission mechanisms, in order to determine which channels may be more suited for policy making in these countries. The purpose is to recommend an effective monetary policy strategy for the GCC countries using a transmission mechanism framework, after analysing their current practices in comparison with the suggested ones. The rest of the chapter is organised as follows. Section 2 reviews the theoretical and empirical literature on the transmission mechanism channels of monetary policy. These channels operate under three broad headings, namely the liquidity effect, the credit view and other asset prices. Specifically, the section reviews the theoretical and empirical underpinnings governing the effects of interest rates and other asset price channels such as exchange rates, Tobin's Q theory and financial wealth on consumption, investment and general economic activity. Next, the analysis studies the impact of bank lending, firm's balance sheets and asymmetric information on investment and output. This section also highlights, at a theoretical level, the financial and economic environments necessary for the efficiency of monetary policy transmission mechanism channels. Specifically, the section reviews for each channel discussed the tools available to central banks to conduct monetary policy, the operational independence and transparency of these banks, the efficiency of primary and secondary financial markets, the conditions regarding interest rates and exchange rate policies and environments necessary for successful transmission channels, along with the regulatory, supervisory, and institutional arrangements. Section 3 addresses the conditions regarding the environment of transmission mechanisms in developing and transition economies with a special emphasis on the GCC, based on the same theoretical analysis of the previous section. GCC countries share many of the characteristics of the developing/transition economies which means that they need to be dealt with as a subgroup of these economies. The purpose is to analyse the financial and economic environments of the identified transmission mechanism channels in the GCC countries and link these environments to the ones necessary for successful monetary policy conduct and to the effectiveness of monetary policy. Section 4 discusses some macroeconomic data on the GCC economies, examines the existing monetary policy framework in these countries, and highlights a monetary policy strategy for the GCC based on the analysis and the recommendations derived in the previous section. The suggested strategy is compared with the existing one in the GCC group and recommended for possible adoption by the attempted GCC monetary union. Section 5 contains concluding remarks.

2   Transmission mechanisms of monetary policy and the environments necessary for their effectiveness

The literature on the transmission mechanism of monetary policy or the search for a channel through which money affects economic activity started with the work of Keynes in the 1930s on the interest rate or the cost of capital channel.[1] The timing, historical and statistical evidence provided by Friedman and Schwartz (1963a, 1963b), Friedman and Meiselman (1963) and the more advanced empirical research of the St. Louis model in the study by Andersen and Jordan (1968) shed additional light on the positive and significant relationship between money and output. The findings of these studies led to an intensification of the search for the transmission mechanisms of monetary policy. The current view of these mechanisms classifies these channels under three broad headings, namely, traditional interest rate effects, other asset price effects and the credit view (Mishkin 2007, 2010).[2] Other studies in the literature speak of two main broad channels, the liquidity view and the credit channel (Ohanian and Stockman

1995, Hubbard 1995). On an alternative decomposition of the analysis in the literature, monetary policy is believed to operate in the first steps in each channel through real and nominal interest rates, stock prices and bank deposits. Further decomposition into second and third steps in each channel shows that in several cases, especially in the credit view, monetary policy affects gross domestic product in as much as it can influence moral hazard and adverse selection through agency theory effects, exchange rates and bank loans. Therefore, I will categorise the transmission mechanisms of monetary policy as having to pass through five main steps with these steps differing between mechanisms and in order of occurrence: nominal and real interest rates, bank loans, moral hazard and adverse selection, exchange rates and stock prices. A discussion of each follows with an emphasis on the theoretical environment necessary for their effectiveness.

The liquidity effect

The practice of monetary policy in countries using an interest rate of some type as an operating target, intermediate target or anchor of policy is based on the presence of a liquidity effect. This effect refers to the inverse relationship between a change in a monetary aggregate that affects reserve conditions in the economy and interest rates. A distinction is made between nominal and real interest rates as well as between short-term and long-term ones. The liquidity effect refers to short-term interest rates and may affect nominal rates, real rates or both. Analysis and discussion of the liquidity effect still centres around theoretical issues as well as empirical ones. Theoretical issues are analysed to determine the conditions under which a liquidity effect exists and its implications. These implications, as explained in Ohanian and Stockman (1995), diverge as different models may imply different welfare effects of monetary policies as well as different effects on interest rates, different implications for optimal monetary policy and different interpretations of the data.

To take a representative example, consider the case of traditional sticky-price models in comparison with neo-classical flexible-price ones. With sticky prices, a permanent increase in money supply raises real money supply by the same amount. Given that real income rises by less than this amount, the nominal interest rate will have to fall to re-equilibrate the money market. This would also cause a decline in real interest rates. In most neo-classical flexible-price models on the other hand, the increase in the nominal money supply causes an increase in the price level sufficient to keep real money supply, real income and nominal interest rates unchanged with a decline only in real interest rates. Thus, monetary policy becomes more effective in a liquidity effect framework the stickier are prices.

The issue of whether prices are sticky or flexible has been the subject of macroeconomic debates motivating a large body of empirical work to determine the impact and speed of price adjustment, and, thus, the effects of monetary policy on economic activity. In a study by Christiano, Eichenbaum, and Evans (1999) on monetary policy shocks, it was shown that following an unanticipated monetary policy tightening, aggregate price indices remain sticky and rigid for around

18 months and start declining afterwards. Boivin, Giannoni, and Mihov (2009) examined sticky prices and monetary policy using disaggregated US data and found that disaggregated prices appear to be sticky in response to macroeconomic and monetary disturbances but flexible in response to sector-specific shocks. Therefore, according to Pagan and Robertson (1995), four concerns are crucial in evaluating those studies that have examined the liquidity effect: the various definitions of monetary aggregates, the different models used, the different empirical techniques and estimation procedures, and the difference in the sample period. In summary, most economists agree on the presence of a liquidity effect in the transmission mechanism of monetary policy although the theoretical explanations of such effects remain controversial due to the variety of models and assumptions. A case in point is the controversy in the macroeconomic literature on the issue of price rigidity. The size and timing of the effect is also not clear due to the empirical limitations mentioned earlier.

The liquidity view is based on the fact that interest rates are flexible and move with the state of reserve conditions in the economy. In addition, some degree of partial or full price-stickiness is necessary. The success of this mechanism as shown in Table 9.1 requires a financial, regulatory and supervisory environment in which central banks are capable of changing reserves or the rate at which financial instruments such as repos are traded, so as to affect market interest rates (interbank, lending and deposit rates). This requires first a central bank with a high degree of autonomy, transparency and operational independence. Second, there is a need for proper institutional, regulatory and supervisory arrangements for secondary markets especially in government securities. Third, the financial environment should be characterised by a strong interbank loan market to ensure that interbank interest rates are affected. Fourth, existing primary and secondary markets for government securities should be efficient in the sense of depth (large volumes), breadth (wide range of ownership) and resiliency. The task of affecting interest rates in industrial economies is mostly accomplished through open-market operations in government securities, which justifies the need for efficient primary and secondary markets. Central banks have also used other tools of policy to affect reserves, such as repurchase operations and discount rates (Blommestein and Thunholm 1997).

The credit view (and agency theory)

The credit view of the monetary transmission mechanism channel is sometimes perceived as an addition or an augmentation to the liquidity effect in the debate on whether monetary policy actions by central banks have consequences other than those for open-market interest rates (Hubbard 1995). The exploration of this view was motivated by the fact that cyclical movements in aggregate demand especially in investment may not be caused only by small changes in real interest rates, especially in models of partial sticky prices. This credit channel can be broadly divided into two categories. The first is the traditional view based on the existence of bank-dependent borrowers affected by an increase in the ability of banks to

Table 9.1 Environment necessary for effectiveness of monetary policy transmission mechanisms

Liquidity view (Nominal and real interest rates)	Credit view		Asset prices view	
	Traditional loan	Agency theory	Exchange rates	Other asset prices
Flexible interest rates	High level of indirect finance in financial intermediation	Prevalence of information asymmetries	Flexible de facto exchange rate arrangements	Wide range of public firms
Full or partial price-stickiness	Developed loan market and credit facilities	Ability to reduce information asymmetries by affecting stock prices, nominal interest rates	Large degree of trade openness	Well-developed financial markets characterised by depth (large volume), breadth (wide ownership) and resiliency
Large degree of central bank autonomy, transparency and operational independence	High level of firm external finance from banks compared with internal finance	Ability to reduce agency costs through the enforcement of restrictive covenants and the introduction of proper regulation to increase financial transparency	Proper institutional regulatory and supervisory arrangements for spot, forward and derivative currency markets trading	High capitalisation
Proper institutional, regulatory and supervisory arrangements for secondary markets	Presence of bank-dependent borrowers for consumption spending and residential investment		Efficient market with immediate and unlimited trade in foreign exchange	Transparent system for financial market regulation
Efficient interbank market to affect interbank loan rate			Central bank ability to predict real exchange rate appreciation	Proper institutional regulatory and supervisory arrangements for primary and secondary markets
Efficient primary and secondary markets for government securities characterised by depth (large volume), breadth (wide range of ownership) and resiliency				
Such markets are necessary for successful open-market operations			High ratio of central bank net foreign reserves to central bank liabilities in domestic currencies	Central bank ability to predict stock price bubbles
Presence of other tools of policy in addition to OMOs such as repurchase operations with government securities and discount window operations				

Source: Compiled by author

lend. An increase in bank reserves through monetary policy actions impacts the supply of loans, causing an increase in investment as well as consumption spending. In this view, regulatory actions by central banks such as credit controls can also be used to explain spending decisions by firms and consumers.

The second broad view is more micro in nature, relating to agency theory and informational imperfections in credit and insurance markets. Asymmetric information and moral hazard increase agency costs and the spread between the cost of internal finance and external finance including bank lending. A reduction in the cost of external finance through monetary policy actions aimed at reducing information asymmetries and increasing borrowers' net worth is a key element of the credit view.

This view is based on the existence of bank-dependent investors/consumers in the economy. Therefore, indirect finance through banks ought to play a major role in financial intermediation. In addition to the prevalence of indirect finance, as shown in Table 9.1, a successful credit mechanism requires a developed loan market and credit facilities, a high degree of firm external finance from banks in comparison with debt and equity financing and a low level of internal firm finance, as well as the presence of borrowers who are bank dependent for their consumption spending and residential investment.

The success of a transmission mechanism through agency theory effects rests on the ability of the central bank to reduce information asymmetries by affecting stock prices and nominal interest rates. In addition, agency costs could be reduced through the enforcement of restrictive covenants and the introduction of proper regulation to increase financial transparency.

The effects of exchange rates (and other asset prices)

The traditional role of exchange rates in affecting economic activity operates through the impact of these rates on net exports. It is believed that a decline in exchange rates or an increase in the value of the domestic currency reduces exports and increases imports, and causes a decline in the growth of gross domestic product. Monetary policy actions that affect interest rates tend to affect exchange rates by changing the attractiveness of portfolio investments in various currencies. The academic literature believes that a smaller amount of output volatility is due to external shocks (and thus changes in exchange rates) in advanced industrial economies than in developing ones. The latter economies, being characterised by openness and thinner and developing financial markets, are more vulnerable to changes in exchange rates. Developing financial markets are associated with lower exchange rate flexibility, which makes for higher external shocks. Therefore, developing economies, unlike some industrial countries, tend to include the exchange rate explicitly in their policy reaction functions.

Strong and robust financial markets are also necessary for a transmission mechanism through other asset prices besides those on debt instruments. Stock prices affect economic activity by impacting investment, firm balance-sheets, household liquidity and household wealth (Mishkin 2007, 2010). Monetary policy responses to fluctuations in asset prices usually depend on the nature of the shock as central banks do not generally target stock market prices. In addition, if the central bank has no informational advantage over the private sector, it is as likely as the private sector to mispredict a stock price bubble. Therefore, the empirical evidence on the link between monetary policy and stock prices is still relatively weak, as movements in stock prices appear to be more related to economic fundamentals and expectations about the future of a certain economy. In addition, monetary policy responses to permanent shocks differ from those to temporary shocks, as stock market collapses can damage economic activity.

An efficient transmission mechanism operating through exchange rates requires flexible de facto exchange rate arrangements. In such situations, the exchange rate is able to change as the result of monetary policy actions to achieve the desired policy goals. For this to happen, as Table 9.1 states, there is a need for a large degree of trade openness and an efficient foreign exchange market with instantaneous and unrestricted trading. In addition, there is a need to intervene successfully in foreign exchange markets based on a high ratio of net foreign reserves to central bank and commercial bank liabilities in domestic currency. Needless to say, proper institutional, regulatory and supervisory arrangements for trading foreign currencies in spot, forward and derivative markets are necessary.

A transmission mechanism through asset price channels such as stock prices requires most importantly the presence of a large number of firms that rely on equity financing for a substantial part of their operations. Such financing cannot be concentrated in a very few firms. In addition, a well-developed and efficient market for stocks ought to exist in terms of depth (volume), breadth (wide range of ownership) and resiliency. Three other issues are also of crucial importance: a transparent and equitable system of financial market regulation, including proper institutional, regulatory and supervisory arrangements, and the ability of the central bank to predict stock price bubbles so as to avoid them disturbing the transmission mechanism process.

3 The environment of monetary policy transmission mechanisms in developing and transition economies and in GCC countries

The present section discusses the environment of the monetary policy transmission mechanisms in developing and transition countries and in the GCC economies. The GCC countries share many of the characteristics of the transition economies which means that they need to be treated as a subgroup of these economies with their salient features. After highlighting the characteristics of the developing/transition economies that are shared with the GCC countries, I adjust the analysis provided in the previous section to the salient features of these economies pertinent to the transmission mechanism. The purpose is to compare the theoretical environment necessary for successful transmission mechanism channels and the one existing in transition environments and GCC countries to determine the GCC-relevant channels. The main points of the analysis are reported in Tables 9.2 and 9.3.

Table 9.2 Environment of transmission mechanisms of monetary policy in developing/transition economies

Liquidity view (Nominal and real interest rates)	Credit view	Asset prices view	
	Traditional loan	Exchange rates	Other asset prices
Authority-determined interest rates	Prevalence of indirect finance in financial intermediation	Mostly fixed de facto exchange rate arrangements	Limited range of public firms
Full or partial price stickiness	Usually developed loan markets with degree being country specific	Large degree of trade openness, capital flows and remittances	Inefficiency in depth and especially in breadth
Central bank autonomy and independence is country specific. Mostly limited independence with autonomy sometimes depending on choice of instrument used	Firms rely on bank finance and internal/self-finance	Mostly proper institutional regulatory and supervisory arrangements for spot trading only	Low turnover and capitalisation
Institutional, regulatory and supervisory arrangements usually exist	Large presence of bank-dependent borrowers	Absence of forward and currency derivatives in domestic currency	Appropriate regulation when markets exist
Inter-bank loan rate is largely authority-determined like other interest rates		Market efficiency is country specific	Limited ability to predict bubbles
Developing primary and secondary markets of government securities characterised sometimes by captive buyers with inefficiency in breadth, making open-market operations in secondary markets ineffective.		Real exchange rate appreciation in countries with relatively high inflation rates	
Other tools of policy used to replace open-market operations such as liquidity and reserve requirement ratios and discount window		Ability of central bank to defend arrangement is country specific	
Open-market type operations or primary market interventions such as: • Use of primary issues of government securities to influence liquidity conditions • Use of primary issues of central bank securities • Auction of central bank deposits			

Source: Compiled by author

Table 9.3 Monetary policy instruments (affecting liquidity and interest rates) in the GCC

Bahrain	Kuwait	Oman	Qatar	Saudi Arabia	UAE
Overnight lending repo facility against government securities	Repos in negotiable bonds	Repos in T-Bills and CDs	Repos in domestic government securities	Repos in government development bonds and T-Bills predominantly overnight	Repos in CDs
Deposit and lending standing facilities for adjusting liquidity needs of commercial banks. Interest rate on standing facilities in the CBB. Policy interest rates	CBK issues negotiable bonds to banks to manage domestic liquidity levels	CDs issued by Central Bank to absorb excess liquidity	Money Market Instrument (QMR) (tool for monetary policy that allows banks to deposit at and borrow from QCB)	Overnight reverse Repos to absorb liquidity	CDs issued by Central Bank to absorb excess liquidity. Interest rates on CDs determine both debit and credit interest rates.
Required Reserves with the CBB (around 6%)	Required Reserve Ratio (around 6%)	Required Reserves Ratio (8%)	Required Reserves Ratio (2.75%)	Cash Reserve Ratio of 7% on current account liabilities and 2% on savings/time deposits	Minimum Reserve Requirement (14% on current and savings and 1% on time deposits). Banks are required to keep at CB 30% of their dirham deposits abroad.
Foreign exchange facility for buying and selling dinars	Loan to deposit ceiling	Reverse Swap Facility in US dollars		Statutory Liquidity Ratio where banks are required to maintain a minimum of liquid assets equal to 20% of demand and time liabilities	Swap arrangements to inject dirham liquidity where banks sell foreign currency denominated assets at spot price. These assets are to be repurchased at future dates of one week, month, 3 months
		Direct lending in US dollars		Foreign exchange swaps	Advances and overdraft facility for banks
				Placement of public funds with banks	

Source: Compiled by author based on central banks reports of GCC countries. www.cbb.gov.bh, www.cbk.gov.kw, www.qcb.gov.qa, www.cbo-oman.org, www.sama.gov.sa, www.centralbank.ae

The liquidity effect

The main differences between the environment in this view and the theoretically necessary one are in interest rates, the market for government securities and the ability of central banks to influence reserves and liquidity conditions through open-market operations. Therefore, other tools and methods are necessary and used in developing/transition economies. In these economies, interest rates are, in general, largely fixed by the monetary authority and adjusted depending on policy objectives. Such adjustments may sometimes affect the operational independence of the central bank if changing the level of interest rates is motivated by fiscal policy needs such as minimising interest payments on government debt or making the primary issuance of such debt more attractive. Having authority-determined interest rates affects the efficiency of the interbank loan market and its loan rate as the anchor through which the state of reserve conditions is determined. Markets for government securities are largely inefficient, especially in the breadth or wide range of ownership. In many cases, holders of such securities in the primary market are largely captive buyers, mostly banks which, due to the lack of investment opportunities in the domestic currency on the asset side, subscribe to these securities, relying on the spread between their return and that on deposits in domestic currency. These characteristics influence the efficiency of open-market operations in the secondary market, especially in terms of volume and the ability to inject reserves to all sectors in the economy.

The necessity to conduct these operations so as to influence reserve conditions in the economy and make the authority-determined interest rate as close to market levels as possible has caused several developing and transition economies to rely on other tools of monetary policy such as ones used in 'open-market type operations'. These types of operations as defined in Quintyn (1997) refer to the use of primary issues of securities through auctions, or auctions of central bank credit or deposits at the central bank to achieve monetary policy objectives. Thus, open-market type operations are primary market operations whereas open-market operations refer to transactions in secondary securities markets. The process of open-market type operations is initiated by central banks for specific purposes and has taken the form of issuing government or central bank securities for monetary purposes or auctioning deposits at the central bank (Sundararajan and Dattels 1997). The advantages and disadvantages of each method are discussed in Quintyn (1997) and can be summarised as follows. Issuing government securities in primary market operations contributes to the development of an efficient market but requires a high degree of coordination with fiscal policymakers and may affect the operational autonomy of central banks. Issuing central bank securities facilitates operational independence but may lead to a reduction in central bank profits, whereas auctioning of central bank deposits guarantees operational independence and avoids competition with treasury securities, but may not assist in the development of a securities market unless the securities are negotiable (Quintyn 1997: 168).

Interest rates throughout the GCC countries are largely authority-determined and allowed to move depending on movements in the US federal funds rate.

An efficient secondary market for government securities is also absent which limits the scope for using these operations to influence reserve conditions in the economy. However, countries in the GCC have relied on other tools of policy to achieve monetary policy objectives. A summary of the various tools is found in Table 9.3.

A common feature among the six GCC countries is the use of repurchase agreement (repo) and reverse repos in various type of securities to affect liquidity conditions and influence interest rates. Whereas Bahrain, Qatar and Saudi Arabia rely on repos in existing government securities to affect liquidity, Kuwait, Oman and the UAE have conducted open-market type operations by issuing central bank bonds. The central bank of Kuwait has issued negotiable bonds to banks to manage domestic liquidity levels. The central banks of Oman and the UAE have issued CDs to banks to absorb liquidity and have conducted repo operations with these CDs. In the UAE, interest rates on these CDs determine debit and credit interest rates.

Various GCC countries have also adopted traditional monetary policy tools such as required reserve ratios and central bank discount lending facilities to influence bank liquidity and interest rates. These required reserve ratios vary across countries and are adjusted occasionally. Regarding lending facilities, the central bank of Bahrain provides deposit and loan standing facilities for commercial banks to adjust their liquidity, as well as foreign exchange facilities for buying and selling dinars. The central bank of Oman provides banks with direct lending in US dollars as well as a reverse swap facility in these dollars to affect liquidity. Qatar has created a money market instrument, the Qatar monetary rate (QMR), to allow banks to deposit and borrow at this rate from the central bank. Saudi Arabia and the UAE allow foreign exchange swaps to inject domestic liquidity. In addition Saudi Arabia places public funds in various commercial banks whereas the UAE provides advances and various overdraft facilities for commercial banks.

The presence of all these policy tools should enable the central banks of the GCC countries to influence interest rates and reserve conditions in the economy.

The credit channel

In the credit market of developing economies, there is a prevalence of indirect finance in the process of financial intermediation. Very few firms rely on direct finance as stock markets and corporate bond markets are inefficient. The state of development of loan markets is country specific but this market is one of the most developed ones in these countries. It is the primary source of external firm finance. Regarding agency effects, as stated earlier, their success may be limited in developing and transition economies largely due to the inability of central banks to affect stock prices because financial markets are largely inefficient, as will be seen next.

The credit channel is important in developing countries for the reasons discussed earlier. For the GCC group, the increase in oil revenues since 2000 has fuelled bank deposits and stimulated credit activities in these countries. Growth rates in private sector lending by banks have been high though not uniform across countries. For 2005 these rates stood at 36 per cent in Saudi Arabia, 39 per cent in

Qatar, 43 per cent in UAE, 20 per cent in Bahrain and Kuwait, and 11 per cent in Oman (Devaux 2006). Similar growth rates hold for bank loans in consumer and property sectors. The growth in retail sector loans also increased from moderate to very strong. According to Crowley (2008), the GCC nations had above average credit growth for the Middle East and Central Asia region and accounted for the majority of the total increase in credit in the region, especially Saudi Arabia and the UAE. These figures were higher for the GCC countries (except for Oman) over 2002–2006 compared with 1997–2001. Private sector credit growth exceeded GDP growth also in four of the countries (but not in Kuwait and Oman) between 1998 and 2006. GCC countries had also by far the highest ratio of private sector credit to GDP in the region in 2006. I have computed more recent and different figures in Table 9.5 and Figure 9.1, which show the ratio of non-government domestic credit to GDP from 1999 to 2008 in various GCC countries.[3] This ratio increased between 2006 and 2008 from 52.5 per cent to 83.9 per cent for Bahrain, from 106.2 per cent to 110.4 per cent for Kuwait, from 66.9 per cent to 84.8 per cent for Oman, from 85.7 per cent to 102.8 per cent for Qatar, from 38.3 per cent to 38.8 per cent for Saudi Arabia and from 74.9 per cent to 93.9 per cent for the UAE. The role of banking intermediation is expected to strengthen as a result of the possible monetary union and the opening up of banks to competition.

The exchange rate channel (and other asset price effects)

The exchange rates in many developing/transition economies, as shown in Table 9.2, are mostly fixed de facto to a currency or a basket of currencies even though the de jure arrangements may be different. There exists a large degree of trade openness as these countries are heavily involved in international trade and many

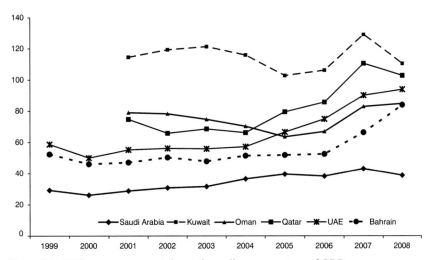

Figure 9.1 GCC non-government domestic credit as percentage of GDP

Source: International Monetary Fund, *International Financial Statistics*, Various Issues.

are characterised by high levels of remittances and capital flows. There exist proper institutional, regulatory and supervisory arrangements for spot market activities but there are typically no forward markets in these currencies. Market efficiency is country specific but in most cases there is instantaneous and unrestricted trade in foreign exchange. There has been some real exchange rate appreciation especially in countries with fixed exchange rate arrangements and relatively high inflation rates in comparison with the country to which currencies are fixed. The ability of various central banks to defend the peg is country specific (Stone *et al.* 2009).

Regarding the other asset prices channel, there are very few public firms with shares traded on stock markets. These markets are inefficient in terms of volume and capitalisation and in terms of the range of ownership. There are proper institutional arrangements and transparency of regulation in countries where trading activities exist. However, as in other countries, the central bank's ability to predict bubbles remains limited.

The relationship between this channel and economic activity is mixed. However, there exists enough evidence of a strong relationship between exchange rates and growth and inflation in many studies that have included the GCC in their data set (Husain, Mody and Rogoff 2005). Table 9.4 summarises the practice of the official policies (*de jure*) from the 1970s to 1998 and the actual (*de facto*) policies from 1990 to 2010 of the GCC group.[4] For five of the countries, namely Bahrain, Oman, Qatar, Saudi Arabia, and the UAE, the de facto classification of exchange rate regimes has been conventional fixed peg arrangements against a single currency at least since 1990. Kuwait changed its official and actual arrangement in May 2007 from a peg against the US dollar to one against an undisclosed basket of currencies.

Are all the mechanisms relevant for the GCC?

The previous discussion clearly shows that the transmission mechanism channel operating through stock prices is not present in the developing transition economies or in the GCC. Therefore, I rule it out from the analysis in the next section. In addition, agency theory effects need a more advanced economic structure than exists in these countries. The other three mechanisms seem to work under some conditions. The liquidity view operating through interest rates can be functional even in the absence of efficient open-market operations, for the reasons discussed earlier. There is a need to allow the interest rate to float freely or to be authority-determined close to its market level so that it can reflect the actual reserve conditions in the economy. The creation of special tools of monetary policy such as open-market type operations should help achieve a transmission mechanism through interest rate channels. The credit view seems also to be operational as there exist bank-dependent borrowers among firms and individuals. In addition, this channel benefits from the absence of equity financing by firms due to the inefficient stock market. The absence of financial intermediation through direct finance creates a necessity for a strong channel of indirect financial intermediation and self-finance.

Table 9.4 Exchange rate arrangements of GCC countries

	Official announced (de jure)	Actual arrangement (de facto)
Bahrain	Limited flexibility vis-à-vis a single currency	Classified under Other Conventional Fixed Peg Arrangements where the country pegs its currency at a fixed rate to a major currency or a basket of currencies and where the exchange rate fluctuates within a narrow margin of at most +/–1% around a central rate.
Kuwait	Pegged against a currency composite	Classified under Other Conventional Fixed Peg Arrangements. The peg has been against a composite until 2001 but changed later to against a single currency. The peg is against a single currency. In May 2007, currency pegged again to an undisclosed basket of currencies.
Oman	Pegged against a single currency	Classified under Other Conventional Fixed Peg Arrangements. The peg is against a single currency.
Qatar	Limited flexibility vis-à-vis a single currency	Classified under Other Conventional Fixed Peg Arrangements. The peg is against a single currency.
Saudi Arabia	Limited flexibility vis-à-vis a single currency	Classified under Other Conventional Fixed Peg Arrangements. The peg is against a single currency.
UAE	Limited flexibility vis-à-vis a single currency	Classified under Other Conventional Fixed Peg Arrangements. The peg is against a single currency.

Source: Compiled by author from International Monetary Fund, International Financial Statistics, Various Issues

The third channel through which a successful mechanism can be achieved is the exchange rate channel. Developing transition economies and the GCC are largely open with a high degree of capital flows and remittances. The ability to influence the exchange rate or defend the peg to a currency or basket of currencies is country specific and therefore should be analysed on a country-by-country basis.

4 Recommended monetary policy strategy for GCC countries

The analysis in the previous section shows that the GCC countries command three transmission mechanisms that could be used as channels through which central banks can affect real economic activity, namely, the liquidity channel (through interest rates), the traditional credit channel (through total loans) and the exchange rate channel. These channels have not been tested in this study. However, given the theoretical characteristics of the environment necessary for such successful mechanisms, it is evident that there are enough features, tools and evidence to conclude that central banks in the GCC should be able to affect interest rates and exchange rates. In addition, the credit channel through bank loans seems to be developing fast on the basis of the growth figures in loans expressed in all six countries and discussed in the previous section.

This section first presents some data reflecting the macroeconomic environment in the GCC economies conditioning the conduct of monetary policy. Then, the actual monetary policy practice in the GCC countries is examined. The analysis continues by addressing several possible monetary policy strategies that could be pursued in these countries before finally recommending one strategy based on the relative viability of the channels of monetary policy that may possibly remain viable after the creation of the Gulf Monetary Union.

The GCC macro-economy

The GCC and the free trade area among its members were established in 1981 by the six countries concerned which share many economic, social and geographic characteristics. A common market was launched in 2008 to reduce trade barriers. The deadline for the launching of the Gulf monetary union was postponed from 2010 until late in the next decade and it is thought that at least ten years may be needed before a unified currency is introduced. However, Oman in 2008 and the UAE in 2009 made a decision not to join the monetary union. The six countries are currently trying to meet convergence criteria that would help them establish a union and converge their economies further. These countries have over the last ten years, in addition to the financial developments discussed in the previous section and Table 9.3, experienced some good positive macroeconomic outcomes concerning total non-government domestic credit (addressed earlier), oil revenue, inflation and economic growth, as listed in Table 9.5.

The first common feature among these countries is that their economies are dominated by oil production. Over the last five years, oil revenue as percentage of GDP has constituted an average of 47.4 per cent for Kuwait, 45.7 per cent for Saudi Arabia, 30.4 per cent for the UAE, 29.0 per cent for Qatar, 25.2 per cent for Bahrain and 23.8 per cent for Oman. Oil revenue as percentage of GDP seems to have also stabilised in two countries between 1999 and 2008, namely Bahrain and Oman. This ratio has risen on balance in Saudi Arabia, the UAE and Kuwait up to 2007, but declined recently in Qatar. Four of the countries, namely Bahrain, Kuwait, Oman and Saudi Arabia, experienced stable growth and inflation figures over the last decade but particularly over the last five years. The moderate to high economic growth rates coupled with relatively low inflation figures also reflect a decline in inflation and growth volatility. Qatar, which has had the highest rate of inflation (9.9 per cent on average over the last five years) also commands the highest average growth rate (13.5 per cent) whereas the UAE commands a relatively high inflation rate of 8.3 per cent compared with the average growth rate of 6.2 per cent. The inflation figures for these two countries are out of line with the convergence criterion for this variable. The average figures for interest rates are also converging on the low side, benefiting from low interest rate levels in the United States. These rates, as will be explained shortly, are adjusted to the US rates to preserve the peg of the domestic currencies to the US dollar. What is of interest is the growth in non-government domestic credit to GDP explained in the previous section. These figures are expected to remain mostly on the rise due to the stable and increasing growth rate figures; Crowley (2008) confirms in an empirical study that economic growth is the driving force behind private sector credit growth. Therefore, a larger role for domestic credit is expected. However, the rise in this ratio is not necessarily enough on its own to posit the existence of a significant credit channel.

Monetary policy framework

This subsection highlights the monetary policy practice in the six GCC countries. The framework shows that for the whole group, the policy pursued is based on preserving the exchange rate peg to the US dollar (except for Kuwait since 2007)[5] and allowing domestic interest rates to adjust in line with the US federal funds rate.

In Bahrain, the Central Bank (CBB) maintains a fixed exchange rate regime between the Bahrain dinar and the US dollar. The peg provides an anchor for monetary policy which contributes to the control of inflation and the preservation of the external value of the Bahrain dinar. The fixed exchange rate implies that CBB policy rates are closely aligned to US interest rates. In Kuwait, the Central Bank (CBK) maintains a fixed exchange rate regime with an undeclared basket of currencies of countries that have major trade and financial relations with the state of Kuwait. This system provides the CBK with more relative flexibility in drawing up and executing monetary policy. Kuwait's interest rate does not, for example, solely follow movements in the federal funds rate any more as its discount rate was only cut by 0.25 per cent when the former was cut by 0.75 per cent. In Oman, the monetary policy operations of the Central Bank (CBO) are constrained by the limitations on monetary policy independence imposed by the fixed peg of the

Table 9.5 Data on GCC countries

Country/year	Non-government domestic credit as % of GDP	Exchange rate (against US dollar)	Interest rate in %	Inflation rate in %	Growth rate in %	Oil revenue as % of GDP
Bahrain						
1999	52.33	0.376	4.80	-1.344	4.32	14.92
2000	46.08	0.376	5.82	-11.17	5.23	25.52
2001	47.09	0.376	2.71	-1.175	4.618	22.43
2002	50.32	0.376	1.34	-0.496	5.193	21.65
2003	47.86	0.376	1.48	1.679	7.245	22.81
2004	51.44	0.376	1.54	2.248	5.644	22.34
2005	51.83	0.376	3.14	2.618	7.853	25.00
2006	52.47	0.376	4.37	2.041	6.653	23.77
2007	66.33	0.376	4.485	3.252	8.069	23.50
2008	83.90	0.376	1.65	3.533	6.119	28.56
2009	n.a.	0.376	1.60	3.00	3.04	n.a.
Average 2005–2009	63.63	0.376	3.04	2.88	6.34	25.20
Kuwait						
1999	n.a.	0.3044	5.76	3.083	-1.779	36.96
2000	n.a.	0.3068	5.89	1.569	4.685	48.16
2001	114.54	0.3067	4.47	1.448	0.22	43.9
2002	119.31	0.3039	3.15	0.797	3.01	38.06
2003	121.29	0.298	2.42	0.986	17.329	42.08
2004	115.93	0.2947	2.65	1.257	10.244	47.61
2005	102.81	0.3075	3.47	4.12	10.623	51.85
2006	106.18	0.29911	4.983	3.092	5.143	55.7
2007	129.01	0.2844	4.9415	5.465	2.509	54.48
2008	110.43	0.2679	3.1435	10.5	6.325	27.41
2009	n.a.	0.28449	1.7285	4.65	-1.51	n.a.
Average 2005–2009	112.10	0.280	3.65	5.56	4.61	47.36

Country/year	Non-government domestic credit as % of GDP	Exchange rate (against US dollar)	Interest rate in %	Inflation rate in %	Growth rate in %	Oil revenue as % of GDP
Oman						
1999	n.a.	0.3845	8.12	0.512	-0.613	20.12
2000	n.a.	0.3845	7.62	-1.197	4.638	23.07
2001	79	0.3845	4.5	-0.841	5.572	25.13
2002	78.28	0.3845	2.89	-0.334	2.063	28.55
2003	74.72	0.3845	2.37	0.166	0.354	27.96
2004	70.26	0.3845	2.32	0.673	3.413	30.6
2005	63.5	0.3845	1.269	1.853	4.891	26.6
2006	66.87	0.3845	1.6695	3.441	5.999	22.8
2007	82.84	0.3845	1.948	5.894	7.738	23.0
2008	84.80	0.3845	1.9855	12.611	7.779	22.9
2009	n.a.	0.3845	2.411	3.323	4.066	n.a.
Average 2005–2009	74.50	0.3845	1.85	5.42	6.09	23.82
Qatar						
1999	n.a.	3.64	6.5	2.163	5.504	33.01
2000	n.a.	3.64	n.a.	1.679	10.939	38.28
2001	74.7	3.64	n.a.	1.436	6.318	40.1
2002	65.79	3.64	n.a.	0.244	3.2	25.7
2003	68.54	3.64	3.49	2.263	6.323	23.0
2004	66.18	3.64	3.67	6.797	17.723	42.4
2005	79.44	3.64	4.18	8.814	9.24	40.15
2006	85.67	3.64	4.44	11.828	15.03	26.75
2007	110.55	3.64	3.26	13.764	15.348	27.35
2008	102.78	3.64	3.07	15.049	16.395	21.57
2009	n.a.	3.64	3.72	0	11.467	n.a.
Average 2005–2009	94.61	3.64		9.88	13.49	28.95

Continued

Table 9.5 continued

Country/year	Non-government domestic credit as % of GDP	Exchange rate (against US dollar)	Interest rate in %	Inflation rate in %	Growth rate in %	Oil revenue as % of GDP
Saudi Arabia						
1999	29.25	3.75	6.14	−1.307	−0.748	23.76
2000	26.13	3.75	6.67	−1.1	4.865	35.67
2001	28.83	3.75	3.92	−1.138	0.547	34.16
2002	30.80	3.75	2.23	0.23	0.128	27.86
2003	31.61	3.75	1.947	0.587	7.659	25.03
2004	36.54	3.75	2.318	0.355	5.268	35.15
2005	39.54	3.75	4.17	0.632	5.553	42.66
2006	38.26	3.75	5.284	2.31	3.158	45.25
2007	43.02	3.75	4.86	4.107	3.314	39.00
2008	38.75	3.75	3.163	9.871	4.448	55.93
2009	n.a.	3.75	1.226	4.5	−0.88	n.a.
Average 2005–2009	39.89	3.75	3.73	4.28	3.11	45.71
United Arab Emirates						
1999	58.68	3.6725	4.94	2.095	3.139	22.47
2000	50.00	3.6725	6.2	1.357	12.382	21.72
2001	55.21	3.6725	3.6	2.736	1.695	19.23
2002	56.14	3.6725	1.8325	2.927	2.649	18.53
2003	55.85	3.6725	1.396	3.161	11.885	12.50
2004	57.17	3.6725	1.6325	5.022	9.691	18.60
2005	66.53	3.6725	5.25	6.187	8.192	22.43
2006	74.86	3.6725	4.61	9.272	9.388	31.91
2007	90.13	3.6725	4.665	11.115	6.338	29.10
2008	93.93	3.6725	3.05	12.26	7.412	38.14
2009	n.a.	3.6725	2.1	2.549	−0.172	n.a.
Average 2005–2009	81.36	3.67	3.93	8.27	6.22	30.39

Source: International Monetary Fund, International Financial Statistics. Various Central Bank Reports

Omani riyal to the US dollar. The fixed exchange rate automatically conditions the monetary policy framework whose main objective is to protect and defend the peg. Therefore, as the federal funds rate eased sharply from 5.25 per cent to 2 per cent between August 2007 and April 2008, Oman had to import that easy monetary policy stance as reflected in the sharp easing of the CBO's policy rates and interbank money market rates. The weighted average interest rate on CBO CDs declined from 3.63 per cent in December 2006 to 1.975 per cent in December 2007 and the overnight domestic interbank lending rate fell from 3.39 per cent to 1.47 per cent in the same period. In Qatar, the objective of the Qatar Central Bank (QCB)'s monetary policy is to keep the Qatari riyal (QR) stable against the US dollar. Aspects other than the exchange rate are of no high priority in relation to monetary policy (e.g. cyclical developments in Qatar). The QCB's monetary policy is subordinated to its exchange rate policy. It is drawn up and implemented so as to manage the short-term interbank interest rates to sustain the fixed parity between the QR and the US dollar. QCB overnight interest rates are closely related to the federal funds rate. In Saudi Arabia, monetary policy is tied to exchange rate policy with the policy objective being to maintain the peg of the Saudi riyal to the US dollar. Thus, the role of monetary policy is circumscribed by the exchange rate regime with riyal interest rates tracking US dollar rates. In the UAE, monetary policy is also tied to exchange rate policy (Al Thani 2003). The fixed peg of the dirham to the US dollar implies that domestic interest rates have to be aligned to those of the dollar across the maturity curve, reducing if not eliminating their effectiveness as monetary policy instruments. In December 2007, for example, the interest rate on CD repos was reduced from 4.5 per cent to 4.25 per cent in line with the new level of the federal funds rate. This rate reached 1 per cent in January 2009 in line with US rates.

Several possible monetary policy strategies

There are three possible targets for policy: two price-type targets, interest rates and exchange rates, and one quantity-type target or total credit. What follows shows the various possibilities that could be adopted given these targets.

First, consider the current monetary policy framework where the target is the exchange rate. The interest rate has to adjust following the other country's rate to preserve the peg. In this case, the central bank can influence the economy through the credit channel of transmission mechanisms.

Second, if the central bank opts to target interest rates, total domestic credit and reserve conditions have to adjust to the interest rate target. The exchange rate has to float, which means it becomes the transmission mechanism of monetary policy.

Third, if the central bank targets total domestic credit, interest rates have to alleviate reserve pressure leaving room for the manipulation of the economy through exchange rates, which here also become the transmission mechanism of monetary policy.[6]

Many call for the GCC countries to adopt inflation targeting. It would be hard to have de facto pegged exchange rate arrangements and inflation targets as inflation targeting requires nominal exchange rate flexibility. Exchange rate fluctuations may be unavoidable. In this case, either inflation targets have to be large ranges allowing central banks to conduct currency market intervention or exchange rates should be allowed to crawl within a wide band. The interest rate has to adjust with a view to preserving the exchange rate wide band but also achieving the inflation target wide range. This scenario leaves the central bank with the possibility to influence the economy through the total credit channel.

Suggested monetary policy strategy

The several scenarios discussed in the previous subsection should be assessed on the basis of the effectiveness of exchange rates, total credit and interest rates as transmission mechanisms of policy. Are the three channels equally effective in transmitting policy impulses to the goal variables?

The evidence on the exchange rate transmission channel seems to be significant for several emerging countries. In Argentina, for example, this channel appears to be significant in the transmission of nominal shocks to inflation and the real economy (Pesce 2008). The same applies for Turkey (Basci, Özel, and Sarikaya 2008). The pass-through from exchange rates to inflation is rather small, however, for Peru, about 10 per cent within a year (Rossini and Vega 2008). However, in a study examining the latest status of monetary policy transmission mechanisms in emerging market economies, Mohanty and Turner (2008) show that the macroeconomic changes in the global economy reflected in market-oriented monetary policy operating systems imply that flexible exchange rate arrangements open up an additional channel of monetary policy transmission. This channel strongly influences demand in small open economies, constitutes a key variable for private sector expectations about inflation and produces large balance-sheet effects in economies where firms have foreign currency assets and liabilities. In one of the most reliable studies on the relationship between the nature of the exchange rate arrangements and economic growth (Husain, Mody and Rogoff 2005), which differs from previous ones in that it draws on new data and advances in exchange rate regime classification, the findings imply that for developing economies with little access to international capital markets, pegged exchange rate regimes deliver relatively low inflation and high exchange rate durability without sacrifices in economic growth. As countries become more financially developed, they gain from moving to more flexible exchange rate regimes by achieving higher growth without higher inflation. However, for emerging markets, exchange rate arrangements do not seem to have a systematic effect on output growth. With regard to the GCC, the monetary policy instruments highlighted in Table 9.3 along with the improving role of domestic credit in economic activity may cause these countries to benefit from more flexible exchange rate arrangements in terms of higher growth without higher inflation.

Several of the developments in the financial structure of many emerging economies which have made exchange rates more significant transmission channels of policy have also made interest rates more effective channels. The interest rate channel seems to have gained importance in several Asian economies such as Thailand and Hong Kong, and to varying extents in central and eastern Europe (Mohanty and Turner 2008). Interest rates are also important transmitters of nominal shocks to the real economy and inflation in several Latin American countries such as Argentina (Pesce 2008), with the impact being uncertain in other countries such as Peru (Rossini and Vega 2008).

The lending channel seems to provide mixed results in the emerging market literature. While it has been weakening in many countries such as Poland, the Czech Republic, Thailand and Singapore, it is gaining in importance in China and India (Mohanty and Turner 2008). This channel is also becoming weaker within the United States (Cetorelli and Goldberg 2008) as banking becomes more globalised.

Would the achievement of the Gulf monetary union influence the transmission mechanism of monetary policy? That is, would the achievement of the convergence criteria change the structure of the GCC economies, causing a change in the transmission mechanism process? Would creating a single currency alter the effectiveness of the exchange rate channel? A comparison could be found by viewing whether the monetary transmission mechanism in the Euro area changed after the establishment of EMU and the use of the common currency. In a study by Weber, Gerke, and Worms (2009), it is shown that the monetary transmission process for 1980–1996 does not significantly differ from that for 1999–2006, while the period 1996 to 1999 may be characterised as a transition period.

In sum, according to the various studies analysed, exchange rates and interest rates seem to transmit policy decisions more strongly to the goal variables than the credit channel of the transmission mechanism. In addition, enough instruments exist to support the central banks' ability to affect interest rates. Therefore, total credit does not seem to be the most effective transmission mechanism of monetary policy. However, based on the current monetary policy framework pursued by the GCC, given a pegged exchange rate regime and interest rates adjusting to preserve the peg, the various GCC economies seem to be relying on a lending transmission mechanism channel. In order to rely on the most possible effective transmission mechanism, there may be a need to change the current monetary policy framework especially after the establishment of the Gulf monetary union. A recommended monetary policy strategy for the GCC is to use a more flexible exchange rate arrangement which would allow the exchange rate channel to become a more effective transmission mechanism. Interest rates in such a system can act as an implicit operating anchor of policy, with total credit as the intermediate policy target if any. The transmission of monetary policy can then take effect through some type of flexible exchange rate arrangement with a representative interest rate adjusting implicitly as a policy anchor. The absence of a pure freely floating regime will keep interest rates responding to the interest rates of the countries to which the managed floating is aligned. Thus, a target range for the representative interest rate becomes the implicit policy anchor with the range being narrower the more flexible is the float.

5 Concluding remarks

This chapter has analysed the theory of the transmission mechanism channels and the environment of monetary policy in industrial, transition and GCC economies for the purpose of recommending a monetary policy strategy for the GCC countries. After a theoretical presentation of various channels, the analysis highlighted the environment of the monetary policy transmission mechanism necessary for the success of each channel. The analysis was then applied to the GCC countries based on their monetary policy tools. It was shown that given the environment of these economies, three channels of transmission remain possibly viable: the liquidity channel operating through interest rates, the asset price channel operating through exchange rates and the traditional credit channel operating through bank loans. An evaluation of each channel was conducted based on the experience of several countries and on empirical studies determining the significance of various mechanisms largely in transition and emerging economies. It was observed that the exchange rate channel and to a lesser extent the interest rate one are more significant than the credit channel. The current monetary policy framework revolves around pegging the domestic currency to the US dollar and having the interest rate adjust to achieve the peg. Such a policy prevents the exchange rate and to a lesser extent the interest rate from acting as the transmission mechanism of policy, leaving this role for the credit channel. Given that this channel was shown to be less effective in many other countries, a suggested monetary policy strategy of adopting some type of flexible exchange rate arrangement while using the interest rate as an implicit policy anchor (with the possibility of a credit aggregate as an intermediate target) was recommended. The larger the exchange rate flexibility, the narrower is the range of the implicit anchor. Given that the GCC economies are becoming more financially developed and with the advent of the Gulf monetary union, these countries may benefit from more flexible exchange rate arrangements in terms of higher growth without higher inflation.

Notes

1 The quantity theory of money which was based on the equation of exchange and the work of the classical as well as the Cambridge economists stipulates that money affects output subject to a stable velocity. However, the channel through which money influences the economy was specified neither in this theory nor in the theories on which the quantity theory was built. In this sense, the literature on the transmission mechanism of monetary policy or the search for a channel through which money affects economic activity started with the work of Keynes in the 1930s.

2 In both references, Mishkin classifies the mechanisms under three headings: the traditional interest rate effects including real and nominal interest rates, other asset price effects including exchange rates, Tobin's Q and wealth effects, and the credit view including the bank lending channel, the balance-sheet channel, the cash flow channel, the unanticipated price level channel, and household liquidity effects.

3 The non-government domestic credit figures include claims on other resident sectors for Bahrain; claims on other sectors, financial corporations, public non-financial corporations and private sector for Kuwait, Oman and Qatar; claims on public enterprises and private sector for Saudi Arabia; and claims on official entities, private

sector and other financial institutions for the UAE. I excluded domestic credit to the government for all countries as this figure biased the results in the sense that it is computed as the difference between government debt held by the banking system and government deposits at the central bank. Since 2005, with the increase in oil prices, government deposits at the central bank have increased significantly, causing domestic credit to the government to be negative, and in the case of Saudi Arabia total domestic credit (to private and public sectors) became negative in 2008.

4 The sources of information are the IMF Annual Reports, various issues, and the study of Bubula and Ötker-Robe (2002) which constructed a database on actual exchange rate regime classifications from 1990 to 2001 for almost all IMF member countries using the IMF nomenclature adopted in 1999.

5 However, the movement of the Kuwaiti dinar against the dollar has so far been relatively limited.

6 Targeting growth rates for money instead of credit is not considered as the chapter uses a transmission mechanism approach in the analysis. The only quantity aggregate in the transmission mechanism process is credit.

References

Al Thani, F. (2003), 'Monetary policy in Qatar and Qatar's attitude toward the proposed single currency for the Gulf Cooperation Council', *BIS Papers,* 17: 108–114.

Andersen, L. and Jordan, J. (1968), 'Monetary and fiscal actions: a test of their relative importance in economic stabilisation', *Federal Reserve Bank of St. Louis Review*, 50 (6): 11–23.

Basci, E., Özel, Ö., and Sarikaya, C. (2008), 'The monetary transmission mechanism in Turkey: new developments', *BIS Papers* no. 35: 475–499.

Blommestein, H., and Thunholm, E. (1997), 'Institutional and operational arrangements for coordinating monetary, fiscal, and public debt management in OECD countries' in V. Sundararajan, P. Dattels and H. Blommestein (eds), *Coordinating Public Debt and Monetary Management*, Washington DC: International Monetary Fund.

Boivin, J., Giannoni, M., and Mihov, I. (2009), 'Sticky prices and monetary policy: evidence from disaggregated US data', *American Economic Review*, 99: 350–384.

Bubula, A., and Ötker-Robe, I. (2002), 'The evolution of exchange rate regimes since 1990: evidence from de-facto policies', IMF working paper 02/155.

Cetorelli, N., and Goldberg, L. (2008), 'Banking globalisation, monetary transmission and the lending channel', National Bureau of Economic Research working paper 14101.

Christiano, L., Eichenbaum, M., and Evans, C. (1999), 'Monetary policy shocks: what have we learned and to what end?', in *Handbook of Macroeconomics*, Volume 1A, ed. J. Taylor and M. Woodford. New York: Elsevier Science.

Crowley, J. (2008), 'Credit growth in the Middle East, North Africa and Central Asia region', IMF working paper 08/184.

Devaux, P. (2006), 'Oil bonanza and banking activity in the GCC countries', *Conjuncture*, December, pp. 15–25, BNP PARIBAS Etudes Economiques.

Friedman, M., and Schwartz, A. (1963a), *A Monetary History of the United States, 1867– 1960*. Princeton, NJ: Princeton University Press.

——(1963b), 'Money and business cycles', *Review of Economics and Statistics*, 45 (supp.): 32–64.

Friedman, M., and Meiselman, D. (1963), 'The relative stability of monetary velocity and the investment multiplier in stabilisation policies', in *Stabilization Policies: Commission on Money and Credit*, Englewood Cliffs, NJ: Prentice Hall.

Hubbard, G. (1995), 'Is there a credit channel for monetary policy?', *Federal Reserve Bank of St. Louis Review*, 77 (3): 63–77.

Husain, A., Mody, A., and Rogoff, K. (2005), 'Exchange rate regime durability and performance in developing versus advanced economies', *Journal of Monetary Economics*, 52: 35–64.

International Monetary Fund, *Annual Reports*, various issues.

——*International Financial Statistics*, CD-ROM.

Mishkin, F. (2007), 'The transmission mechanism and the role of asset prices in monetary policy' in F. Mishkin, *Monetary Policy Strategy*, Cambridge, MA: MIT Press.

——(2010), *The Economics of Money, Banking and Financial Markets*, 9th Edition, Pearson–Addison Wesley.

Mohanty, M., and Turner, P. (2008), 'Monetary policy transmission in emerging market economies: what is new?', *BIS Papers* no. 35: 1–59.

Ohanian, L., and Stockman, A. (1995), 'Theoretical issues of liquidity effects', *Federal Reserve Bank of St. Louis Review*, 77 (3): 3–25.

Pagan, A., and Robertson, J. (1995), 'Resolving the liquidity effect', *Federal Reserve Bank of St. Louis Review*, 77 (3): 33–54.

Pesce, M. (2008), 'Transmission mechanisms for monetary policy in emerging market economies: what is new?' *BIS Papers* no. 35: 131–137.

Quintyn, M. (1997), 'Government versus central bank securities in developing market-based monetary operations' in V. Sundararajan, P. Dattels and H. Blommestein (eds), *Coordinating Public Debt and Monetary Management*, Washington DC: International Monetary Fund.

Rossini, R., and Vega, M. (2008), 'The monetary policy transmission mechanism under financial dollarisation: the case of Peru 1996–2006', *BIS Papers* no. 35: 395–412.

Stone, M., Roger, S., Seiichi, S., Nordstrom, A., Kisinbay, T., and Restrepo, J. (2009), 'The role of the exchange rate in inflation-targeting emerging economies', International Monetary Fund Occasional paper 267.

Sundararajan, V., and Dattels, P. (1997), 'Coordinating public debt and monetary management in transition economies: issues and lessons from experience', in V. Sundararajan, P. Dattels and H. Blommestein (eds), *Coordinating Public Debt and Monetary Management*, Washington DC: International Monetary Fund.

Weber, A., Gerke, R., and Worms, A. (2009), 'Has the monetary transmission process in the euro area changed? Evidence based on VAR estimates', BIS working paper 276.

Useful websites

Central Bank of Kuwait, www.cbk.gov.kw

Central Bank of Oman, www.cbo-oman.org

Central Bank of Qatar, www.qcb.gov.qa

Central Bank of Saudi Arabia, www.sama.gov.sa

Central Bank of the UAE, www.centralbank.ae

10 Assessing inflation and output variability using a New Keynesian model

An application to Egypt

Rania A. Al-Mashat[1]

1 Introduction

Inflation targeting (IT) is one of the operational frameworks for monetary policy aimed at attaining price stability. In contrast to alternative strategies, notably money or exchange rate targeting, which seek to achieve low and stable inflation through targeting intermediate variables – for example, the growth rate of money aggregates or the level of the exchange rate of an 'anchor' currency – IT involves targeting inflation directly.

A relatively long list of requirements has been identified in the literature for countries to successfully operate an IT framework, with increased exchange rate flexibility being essential to eliminate confusion surrounding the central bank's nominal anchor. However, in many cases, particularly in emerging markets, IT is sought without completely fulfilling the exchange rate requirements, on the grounds that there is a high pass-through from exchange rate swings to inflation in these countries and hence if the overriding concern is reducing inflation variability and, in turn, output variability there will be a tendency to maintain some exchange rate rule.

Although a functioning exchange rate transmission channel may add to the effectiveness of monetary policy under IT, actively manipulating the exchange rate along with inflation is likely to worsen the performance of monetary policy. However, this does not imply that central banks should not pay attention to the exchange rate. While inflation targeting may be a framework that is typically free from formal exchange rate commitments, it is nonetheless not free from exchange rate considerations. The apparent reluctance of policy makers to take a completely hands-off approach to the exchange rate may reflect neither an irrational fear nor an unconditional distaste for floating per se. There are many good reasons for any open economy to be concerned about certain types or magnitudes of exchange rate movements such as the high degree of exchange rate pass-through, effects on the external sector, financial stability and market functioning.

Against this background, research in this area has focused on introducing an exchange rate term in the conventional Taylor rule, which has been commonly used to reflect the central bank's reaction function under an IT regime. However, the results from applying this methodology have not been conclusive, which invites the application of reduced form structural models.

This chapter builds on previous work in this strand of the literature by presenting a small open economy structural gap model with forward looking expectations and with an endogenous monetary policy response, which can be classified as a reduced form New Keynesian Model (NKM). Unlike in other structural gap models, the exchange rate equation is a modification of the standard uncovered interest rate parity equation while the monetary policy reaction function in the model represents that of a central bank under inflation targeting but captures the implications of a managed exchange rate regime. The aim of this chapter is to examine the consequences of various approaches to the conduct of monetary policy by presenting the variability of inflation and output in the light of alternative degrees of exchange rate intervention under an IT regime, applying the model to the Egyptian case.

The results reveal that a fixed exchange rate regime generates the highest output and inflation variability, in addition to the worst loss function for the economy under the specified model. As the exchange rate is allowed more flexibility, the variability of output and inflation declines. While a full-fledged inflation targeting regime does not represent the best outcomes in terms of output and inflation variability, a situation of increased exchange rate flexibility in the context of a framework close to inflation targeting provides the best combination. The remainder of the chapter is structured as follows. In the next section, the role played by the exchange rate in inflation targeting countries is discussed with a particular focus on open and emerging economies. In Section 3, we examine how the introduction of the exchange rate in the central bank's reaction function has been accommodated. Initially, the augmented 1993 Taylor rule is examined and then a reduced form NKM is considered. The suggested modification to the standard model is explored in Section 3. Section 4 assesses the inflation and output variability under varying degrees of inflation targeting and exchange rate management, and Section 5 concludes.

2 The role of the exchange rate under inflation targeting

For decades the vast majority of emerging countries had rigid exchange rate regimes – either pegs (adjustable or hard) or managed floats – given the exchange rate's importance in affecting inflation, exports, imports and economic activity. This, however, has changed as an increasingly large number of countries have moved towards adopting flexible exchange rate regimes, which coincided with the launch of IT as a way of conducting monetary policy. The conjunction of IT and flexible rates has brought up a host of policy relevant issues, including those related to the role of the exchange rate in monetary policy, and the relationship between exchange rate changes and inflation.

As described in Schaechter, Stone, and Zelmer (2000), earlier experiences of IT countries involved a combination of exchange rate and inflation targeting. For example, Chile spent more than ten years in a transition from quasi inflation targeting to fully fledged inflation targeting. During this period, the monetary policy framework was based on a crawling peg exchange rate regime as well as announcements of an inflation target. The aim of announcing inflation targets was to gradually reduce inflation by providing an anchor for monetary policy that supplemented the existing crawling exchange rate band. In Israel, the long transition to inflation targeting similarly began with the move to a crawling exchange rate band that required inflation targets to define the upward slope of the crawl.[2]

Emerging market economies tend to be relatively more vulnerable to the various consequences of exchange rate fluctuations than industrial economies as the pass-through in the former has been historically large, particularly in countries that have experienced currency crises. In addition, exchange rate fluctuations could generate uncertainties that impede trade. These external sector consequences of exchange rate fluctuations are expected to be more relevant for economies that are more open to and dependent on trade (Ho and McCauley, 2003). Moreover, large and abrupt depreciations may increase the burden of dollar-denominated debt, produce a massive deterioration of balance sheets, and increase the risks of a financial crisis along the lines discussed in Mishkin (2000). Moreover, one of the arguments frequently invoked in favour of exchange rate targeting is that markets often drive the exchange rate well away from the levels implied by fundamentals and that this has damaging effects on the economy as a whole (Kirsanova, Leith and Wren-Lewis, 2006).

Hence, under IT, since achieving the inflation target is the bottom line, then sufficiently large exchange rate movements can still be a threat for any positive degree of pass-through and given the relatively larger and often still increasing role of the external sector in these economies (Jonas and Mishkin, 2003).

Against this background, emerging market countries cannot afford to ignore the exchange rate when conducting monetary policy under inflation targeting, but the role they ascribe to it should be clearly subordinated to the inflation objective (Mishkin and Schmidt-Hebbel, 2001). In their study, Mohanty and Klau (2005) estimated monetary policy reaction functions – Taylor rules – for thirteen emerging and transition economies and found that in eleven cases the coefficient of the real exchange rate was significant (Table 10.1). This has motivated the introduction of the exchange rate in the central bank's reaction function.

3 Introducing the exchange rate in the central bank's reaction function

The importance of the exchange rate as a key variable in the transmission mechanism incorporated within many policy-evaluation models has inspired the estimation of an alternative version of the Taylor rule (1993) which attempts to explain the central bank's reaction function. As described in Svensson (1999), the standard Taylor rule suited closed economies but in many instances could not fully capture important considerations facing central banks in emerging economies. As Svensson points out, including the exchange rate in the discussion of inflation targeting has several important consequences.

First, the exchange rate allows additional channels for the transmission of monetary policy. In a closed economy, the standard transmission includes an

Table 10.1 Interest rate response to changes in the real exchange rate (obtained from estimated Taylor rule equations)

Country	Short-term	Long-term
India	0.18	0.60
Korea	0.29	0.67
Philippines	0.09	0.13
Taiwan	0.03	0.18
Thailand	0.31	0.74
Brazil	0.10	0.36
Chile	0.00	0.00
Mexico	0.79	1.58
Peru	0.38	2.71
Czech Republic	−0.03	−0.19
Hungary	0.15	0.60
Poland	0.05	0.20
South Africa	0.12	6.00

Source: Mohanty and Klau (2005)

aggregate demand channel and an expectations channel. Regarding the first channel, monetary policy affects aggregate demand with a lag via its effect on the short real interest rate (and possibly the availability of credit). Aggregate demand then affects inflation, with another lag via an aggregate supply equation (a Phillips curve). The expectations channel allows monetary policy to affect inflation expectations which, in turn, affects inflation, with a lag via wage and price setting behaviour. On the other hand, in an open economy, the real exchange rate will affect the relative price between domestic and foreign goods, which in turn will affect both domestic and foreign demand for domestic goods, and hence contributes to the aggregate demand channel for the transmission of monetary policy. There is also a direct exchange rate channel for the transmission of monetary policy to inflation which through the exchange rate affects the domestic currency prices of imported final goods. Typically, the lag of this direct exchange rate channel is considered to be shorter than that of the aggregate demand channel. Hence, by inducing exchange rate movements, monetary policy can affect inflation with a shorter lag.

The modified Taylor rule

In expanding the standard Taylor rule to account for the exchange rate, Taylor (2001) documents the results from several studies, which typically consider policy rules of the following form:

$$i_t = f\pi_t + gy_t + h_0 e_t + h_1 e_{t-1} \tag{1}$$

where i_t is the short-term nominal interest rate set by the central bank, π_t is the rate of inflation, and y_t is the deviation of real GDP from potential GDP. The variable e_t is the real exchange rate. The policy parameters are f, g, h_0, and h_1. If $f > 1$, $g > 0$, and $h_0 = h_1 = 0$, then equation (1) is the standard Taylor rule proposed in 1993 with no reaction to the exchange rate.

In his paper, after presenting parameter values proposed in Ball (1999), Obstfeld and Rogoff (1995) and Svensson (2000), Taylor concludes by asking why reacting to the exchange rate does not yield a greater improvement in the performance of these studies and why performance actually deteriorates in some cases. He argues that there 'may be some deviations of the exchange rate from purchasing-power parity that should not be offset by changes in interest rates; the required changes in interest rates will have adverse affects on real output and inflation that may be worse than the swings in the exchange rate themselves. In some situations the changes in the exchange rate might reflect changes in productivity that should not be offset. Even a random change in the exchange rate, due perhaps to fads or irrational expectations, may have small consequences relative to the cost of smoothing them out' (Taylor, 2001: 267). He also suggests that better models are needed as an attempt to capture the exchange rate in the central bank's reaction function in order to overcome these concerns.

The reduced form New Keynesian model (NKM)

Against this background, a strand of models has been developed which blends the New Keynesian emphasis on nominal and real rigidities and the role of aggregate demand in output determination, with the real business cycle tradition methods of dynamic stochastic general equilibrium and rational expectations. These models integrate Keynesian elements (imperfect competition, and nominal rigidities) into a dynamic general equilibrium framework that until recently was largely associated with the Real Business Cycle (RBC) paradigm. Galí (2002) emphasises that these models can be used (and are being used) to analyse the connection between money, inflation and the business cycle, and to assess the desirability of alternative monetary policies. In contrast with earlier models in the Keynesian tradition, the new paradigm has adopted a dynamic general equilibrium modelling approach. Thus, equilibrium conditions for aggregate variables are derived from optimal individual behaviour on the part of consumers and firms, and are consistent with the simultaneous clearing of all markets. From that viewpoint, the new models have much stronger theoretical foundations than traditional Keynesian models. In addition, the emphasis given to nominal rigidities as a source of monetary non-neutralities also provides a clear differentiation between NKMs and classical monetary frameworks (monetary models with perfect competition and flexible prices, and no frictions other than those associated with the existence of money).

Berg, Karam and Laxton (2006) sum up by explaining that NKMs are structural because each of the equations has an economic interpretation while causality and identification are not in question. Policy interventions have counterparts in changes in parameters or shocks, and their influence can be analysed by studying the resulting changes in the model's outcomes. Moreover, these are general equilibrium models because the main variables of interest are endogenous and depend on each other, and stochastic in that random shocks affect each endogenous variable. In addition, rational expectations are incorporated because expectations depend on the model's own forecasts, so that there is no way to consistently fool economic agents. Applying such models has proven extremely helpful in running policy experiments and testing the implications of various shocks with different magnitudes on the macroeconomic variables.

In connection to the key question of how the monetary authority attempts to control both the exchange rate and inflation, Benes and Varva (2004) present this in the framework of a simple reduced form NKM of monetary transmission. They argue that the coexistence of inflation targeting and exchange rate management can be achieved in two institutionally different ways with varying modelling implications. In one case, the monetary authority affects the exchange rate solely through manipulation of interest rates, and the exchange rate then responds to interest rate differentials according to interest rate arbitrage. In the other, the authority conducts exchange rate interventions independently of its interest rate management, violating the interest rate parity, if necessary. When the exchange rate is managed through interest rates simultaneously with inflation, the monetary authority has to consider both inflation (and output) and exchange rates in its interest rate rule. Less flexible exchange rate regimes are represented by a high weight on the deviation of the exchange rate from the desired level. The exchange rate itself is then modelled via the conventional uncovered interest parity (UIP) arbitrage relationship, and the exchange rate fluctuations remain limited by the appropriate management of policy rates. On the other hand, modelling of the situation when the exchange rate is managed through interventions becomes possible if the interest rates are set with respect to the inflation target while the interest rate parity has only a limited role in determining the exchange rate (depending on the flexibility of the regime). Although modelling of both practices is important, Benes and Varva (2004) focus on the exchange rate interventions independent of the interest rate management, arguing that: (i) managing the exchange rate via interest rates does not permit the analysis of the simultaneous functioning of fixed exchange rate and inflation targeting regimes, because in that case the interest arbitrage fixes policy rates at a parity implied by foreign interest rates; and (ii) realistic modelling of the simultaneous coexistence of IT and managed exchange rates (explicit or implicit) requires (at least partial) violation of the interest rate parity condition.

This chapter follows the methodology presented in Benes and Varva (2004), exploring the effect of different degrees of intervention in order to assess inflation and output variability under various degrees of exchange rate flexibility within an IT framework, with an application to the Egyptian case. The Central Bank of Egypt (CBE) has taken many important steps to upgrade Egypt's framework for conducting monetary policy over the last few years, with a view to adopting inflation targeting as a new paradigm once the prerequisites are fulfilled. The steps undertaken by the CBE to reform Egypt's monetary policy framework are outlined in the Appendix.

The model is highly aggregated and provides a stylised representation of the key monetary policy transmission mechanisms in the economy. It can be viewed as the smallest model necessary to explain the interaction of output, interest rates, exchange rates and inflation under an inflation targeting framework. The model is calibrated to match salient features of the economy under consideration, drawing on theory and a wide range of empirical estimates to choose parameter values for the model that result in appropriate aggregate properties, following the methodology outlined in Coats *et al.* (2003) and Berg *et al.* (2006). The calibration process is iterative: choosing reasonable parameter values, examining the properties of the model next, and changing the parameter values or the structure of the model, until the model behaves appropriately (Bulir and Hurnik, 2006).

Expectations play an explicit role in the model. First, expectations of future inflation are of importance as they affect price- and wage-setting behaviour today. Second, expectations of future interest rate developments affect today's exchange rate. Finally, expectations of future economic cycles will affect today's spending decisions.

The model aims to explain how deviations from equilibrium develop and dissipate over the medium- to long-term. There is a clear role for monetary policy in the model, which is to provide the economy with a nominal anchor. In other words, it prevents actual and expected inflation from drifting away from the target. When the central bank fulfils its role, the economy converges to a well-defined equilibrium. The model is designed such that the monetary authorities cannot boost output above its supply-determined level in the long run. In other words, in the long run, monetary policy is neutral and there is no trade-off between the levels of output and inflation.

The four standard behavioural equations in the model are described as follows:

(a) The aggregate demand (IS) equation

$$\hat{y}_t = \hat{a}_1 y_{t-1} - a_2 rmci_t + a_3 \hat{y}_t^{Foreign} + \varepsilon_t^{Demand} \qquad (2)$$

This aggregate demand or IS curve, which describes the dynamics of the output gap, relates the level of real activity to past real activity $\hat{y}_{t-1}$, and to the real interest rate and the real exchange rate which are both represented in the real monetary conditions index $rmci_t$. $\hat{y}$ is the output gap. The term $rmci_t$ provides the model's mechanism for the influence of monetary choices on the real economy, through the output gap, and then, through the Phillips curve, on inflation. The real interest rate gap describes the impact of monetary policy on the intertemporal substitution of economic agents. The positive real interest rate gap implies relatively costly current consumption which bears down on current consumption expenditures and increases saving and consequently future consumption. The real exchange rate describes an intratemporal substitution, that is, the substitution between domestic and foreign goods. The term is a demand shock which could represent changes in tastes and preferences or the effects of fiscal policy.

(b) The inflation adjustment equation (Phillips curve)

$$\pi_t = b_1\pi_{t-1} + (1-b_1)\pi_{t+n} + b_2 rmc_{t-1} + \varepsilon_t^P \tag{3}$$

The Philips curve characterises the dynamic response of inflation π_t to inflation expectations π_{t+n}, the output gap and the real exchange rate which are jointly represented in the real marginal cost rmc_t. Hence, rmc_t is the indicator of underlying inflationary pressures.[3] The Phillips curve suggests that inflation expectations are partially forward looking and partially backward looking. In addition, the curve satisfies the monetary policy neutrality condition as the parameters in front of the inflation expectation terms (partially forward and backward looking) sum to one. The monetary neutrality condition stresses that inflation can be at any level, and what anchors inflation is inflation expectations. As a consequence any monetary policy action does not impact real variables in the long run. A shock to the Phillips curve ε_t^P could represent the growing importance of cheaper imports from abroad or stronger competition in the product market.

(c) The uncovered interest rate parity (UIP) equation

$$s_t = s_{t+1}^e + \left(-i_t + i_t^{Foreign} + prem_t\right)/4 + \varepsilon_t^{UIP} \tag{4}$$

The UIP condition is an arbitrage condition that expresses the dynamic relationship between the expected exchange rate one quarter ahead (s_{t+1}^e) and the spread between domestic and foreign interest rates, $(i_t$ and $i_t^{Foreign}$, respectively) adjusted for the risk premium $(prem_t)$.[4] The UIP indicates that international investors will act to equalise effective rates of return on investments in different currencies, allowing for any country-specific risk premiums. The key point in terms of effective rates of return is that changes in the exchange rate must be taken into account. A foreign investor who expects a depreciation of the local currency will demand compensation for that in the form of a higher return from local assets. Similarly, a foreign investor who expects an appreciation of the local currency will need a smaller risk premium than would otherwise have been the case. Flood and Rose (2002) show that, while a strong consensus has developed in the literature that UIP works poorly, it predicts that countries with high interest rates should on average have depreciating currencies; they add that recent research has started to provide more compelling empirical results.[5] In its conventional form, UIP assumes a flexible exchange rate regime. Any deviation from such a regime requires a modification of the above-mentioned equation, which will be explained below. A shock to the UIP equation could represent a change in the risk premium associated with domestic financial assets.

(d) The monetary policy rule

$$i_t = d_1 i_{t-1} + (1 - d_1)\left(r_t^* + \pi_t^{Tar} + d_2(\pi_{t+n} - \pi_{t+n}^{Tar}) + d_3 \hat{y}_t\right) + \varepsilon_t^{MP} \tag{5}$$

The central bank's policy reaction function closes the system consistently, leading inflation to return to its target (π^{Tar}) and output to its non-inflationary potential, in the case of any shock or new information. The equation above is a forward-looking reaction function, in which decisions on where to set the policy instrument (the short-term interest rate) today are made by considering what is likely to happen in the future. It also suggests that if headline CPI inflation is above the target rate, then the central bank acts to push up the short-term interest rate, all else equal. Similarly, if there is perceived to be excess demand in the system at the decision point, the central bank acts to push up the short-term interest rate, all else equal. Even if inflation is below target, if there is strong enough excess demand in the system, the central bank acts to push up rates. The first term(s) in the reaction function provide both a long-term level for rates and some additional dynamic structure. In the long-term steady state, the nominal rate goes to the equilibrium real rate (r^*) plus the inflation target. In the short term, however, there is some inertia; all else equal, the interest rate moves to its equilibrium according to a first-order autoregressive process. Instruments other than the interest rate can be accommodated, and arguments other than inflation and output may belong in the reaction function. A variety of papers have explored, in particular, the question of whether the exchange rate belongs in the reaction function.[6] Against this background, a modified version of this equation will be examined below. Exogenous shocks ε_t^{MP} to the monetary policy rule represent interest rate responses to changes in variables that are not included in the monetary policy rule.

All model variables are in logarithms. The hat over a variable denotes the gap, which is the deviation of the variable from its potential. The potential was obtained using the recursive Kalman filter.[7] The main parameter values are presented in Table 10.2.[8] Even though the model is simple, its strength is in its focus on the role of monetary policy, a property that makes it well suited for the analysis carried out. Monetary policy affects inflation and the real economy through three main channels in the model. First, there is the traditional demand channel. An increase in the nominal interest rate also increases the real interest rate, due to nominal rigidities, which discourages expenditure. Less demand pressure, in turn, results in lower inflation through both lower wage inflation and profit margins (not modelled explicitly). Second, there is an exchange rate channel through which higher domestic nominal interest rates relative to those abroad cause the currency to appreciate, all else equal. Consequently, imported goods become cheaper and inflation falls. However, a stronger currency also has a negative effect on demand and output, via both an expenditure switching effect (towards imports), and reduced competitiveness for industries that compete internationally. Lower demand and output reduce inflation.

Table 10.2 Parameter calibrations

Parameter	Parameter ranges as described in Bulir and Hurnik (2002)	For Egypt
a_1	Output gap persistence varies between 0.1 (extremely low persistence) and 0.95 (high persistence). The linear homogeneity condition is $0 < a < 1$.	0.7
a_2	Pass-through from monetary conditions to real economy. The value varies between −0.1 (low impact) and −0.5 (high impact); the higher the parameter the more responsive is the output gap to changes in monetary policy and, hence, policy reactions need to be less pronounced. For the relative weight of the real interest rate and real exchange rate in real monetary conditions, the value varies between 0.3 (open economy) and 0.8 (closed economy).	0.15 and 0.075 for the real interest rate gap and the real exchange rate gap, respectively
a_3	Impact of foreign demand on the output gap typically varies from 0.1 to 0.5. Usually based on the export-to-GDP ratio.	0.2
b_1	Inflation persistence determines the share of forward-looking versus backward-looking agents in the goods markets. The value varies between 0.4 (low persistence) and 0.9 (high persistence); the higher is the share of forward looking agents (the lower is the parameter) the less persistent the model becomes and the less pronounced are the policy reactions required for a given disinflation goal.	0.4
b_2	Pass-through from output gap (real economy) to inflation (the 'sacrifice ratio'). The value typically varies between 0.05 (low impact and high sacrifice ratio) and 0.4 (strong impact and low sacrifice ratio). The higher the parameter the less costly is disinflation.	0.3
d_1	Policy rate persistence in the Taylor rule. The value varies between zero (no persistence in policy setting) and 0.8 ('wait-and-see' policy).	0.7
d_2	Weight put by the policy maker on deviations of inflation from the target in the policy rule. Ranges typically vary from 0.3 to 1.	1.5
d_3	Weight put by the policy maker on output gap in the policy rule. Ranges typically vary from 0.3 to 1.	0.5

Finally, there is the expectations channel. Expectations concerning future inflation and economic growth play an important role in price- and wage-setting. If monetary policy is credible, inflation will be expected to be equal or close to the inflation target. This in itself contributes to the stabilisation of inflation around the target. If the inflation-targeting framework lacks credibility, on the other hand, stabilising inflation is correspondingly more difficult.

In order to allow a degree of exchange rate management under the IT regime, the equations in the standard model outlined above have been modified. In particular, changes are introduced to the UIP equation and the monetary policy reaction function.

$$s_t = c_1 s_t^{Tar} + (1-c_1)\left[s_{t+1}^e + \left(-i_t + i_t^{foreign} + prem_t \right)/4 + \varepsilon_t^{UIP} \right] \tag{4'}$$

The standard UIP in (4) is extended in (4′) to capture a nominal exchange rate target. In its simplest form, the UIP relates the expected exchange rate change to the interest rate differential and risk premium, while in the proposed model the UIP takes into account an important aspect of monetary policy – the partially managed nominal exchange rate through intervention. The parameter c_1 in the exchange rate equation measures the extent to which exchange rate movement is driven by the interest rate differential following the standard UIP as opposed to exchange rate management through intervention. If c_1 equals one, monetary policy intervenes in the foreign exchange market to achieve the desired level of the nominal exchange rate s_t^{Tar}.

Moreover, in the proposed model within the monetary policy reaction function equation (5), there are two monetary policy variables – the nominal interest rate and the nominal exchange rate as described in equation (5′).

$$i_t = d_4 \left[d_1 i_{t-1} + (1-d_1)\left(r_t^* + d_2(\pi_{t+n} - \pi_{t+n}^{Tar}) + d_3 yF \right) + \varepsilon_t^{MP} \right] + \\ (1-d_4)\left[\Delta s_{t+1}^e + i_t^{foreign} + prem_t + \varepsilon_t^{UIP} \right] \tag{5'}$$

Under standard (pure) inflation targeting the monetary policy follows the inflation target using the interest rate rule, leaving the exchange rate to be determined by UIP. In this case the interest rate rule closes the model, by determining where the policy instrument has to be set to achieve the inflation target. On the other hand, in the case of a managed exchange rate there is a parameter (d_4) in the equation which can be changed to capture the control of monetary policy over money market rates. If this parameter is equal to one we assume that monetary policy is able to fully control money market rates. Values lower than one imply that monetary policy has only partial control and the domestic nominal interest rate is given by the expected nominal exchange rate appreciation and foreign interest rates adjusted by the risk premium.

Various combinations of the parameters c_1 and d_4 are explored below to determine and contrast the consequent inflation and output variability in an IT context.

4 Assessing inflation and output variability under varying degrees of inflation targeting and exchange rate management

As mentioned above, the parameters in the UIP equation and the monetary policy reaction function will be changed to present different degrees of exchange rate flexibility as well as varying degrees of IT. More explicitly the parameter c_1 will take on the values 0 to 0.9, with 0 representing a freely floating exchange rate while 0.9 represents intervention closest to an exchange rate peg. On the other hand, the parameter d_4 will take on values ranging between 1 which represents a full fledged IT regime and 0 which represents no IT. Different combinations of c_1 and d_4 are considered and the four-equation modified model described in the previous section is run under these different combinations. For each exchange rate and IT combination, the consequent inflation variability and output variability are documented. Tables 10.3 and 10.4 include the numerical values.

As is evident from Figures 10.1 and 10.2, the closer the system is to a fixed exchange rate regime the higher are the inflation variability and the output variability. The variability starts to decline as the exchange rate starts to become more flexible. This is, unsurprisingly, consistent with the situation where the monetary policy reaction function becomes closer to an IT regime. In pegged regimes, central banks are punished for their mistakes by financial markets, which act swiftly and with a force which is hard to counteract. On the other hand, mistakes in IT regimes are punished by consumers (and the public in general) through their expectations, which, however, evolve only gradually. In practice, then, monetary policy has many more opportunities to correct its mistakes when targeting inflation rather than the exchange rate. For IT, it is enough when the policy is correct on average, while for a peg a single mistake can have devastating consequences (Benes and Varva, 2004). The higher volatility of the variables under a fixed exchange rate regime does not come from the absence of the direct exchange rate–inflation channel of the transmission. It is the demand side (output gap) that stabilises the economy. In driving the demand, however, the real exchange rate does not help to stabilise the shock when the nominal exchange rate is fixed as much as when the exchange rate is flexible. Hence, the nominal (and real) interest rates have to move more to compensate for this. In other words, the conduct of monetary policy targeting inflation while maintaining a fixed exchange rate regime has to count on a larger volatility of its main macro variables, particularly output, keeping other relationships in the model as well as its calibration unchanged.

In addition to examining inflation and output variability, it is important to evaluate the loss function under the various exchange rate flexibility and IT scenarios. The loss function summarises the trade-off between inflation and output by providing a combination of inflation and output variability rather than emphasising the importance of one variable over the other. More explicitly, following Woodford (2001),

$$L = \frac{1}{T}\left[2\sum_{i=1}^{T}(\pi_i - \pi^*)^2 + \sum_{i=1}^{T}(y_i - y^*)^2 \right] \tag{6}$$

Table 10.3 Output variability

Degree of inflation targeting	Degrees of exchange rate flexibility									
Towards full-fledged IT →	Towards more flexible exchange rate →									
	0.0	0.1	0.2	0.3	0.4	0.5	0.6	0.7	0.8	0.9
1.0	0.8372	0.8579	0.8826	0.9125	0.9481	0.9886	1.0291	1.0587	1.0817	1.2030
0.9	0.8304	0.8461	0.8632	0.8817	0.9019	0.9253	0.9575	1.0138	1.1282	1.3737
0.8	0.8260	0.8332	0.8423	0.8555	0.8768	0.9131	0.9745	1.0751	1.2369	1.4985
0.7	0.8250	0.8190	0.8219	0.8383	0.8737	0.9335	1.0240	1.1529	1.3322	1.5829
0.6	0.8268	0.8042	0.8058	0.8333	0.8877	0.9699	1.0815	1.2258	1.4090	1.6426
0.5	0.8277	0.7909	0.7972	0.8393	0.9120	1.0119	1.1376	1.2896	1.4706	1.6867
0.4	0.8240	0.7812	0.7961	0.8527	0.9408	1.0540	1.1890	1.3443	1.5206	1.7204
0.3	0.8172	0.7756	0.8005	0.8700	0.9706	1.0939	1.2350	1.3913	1.5617	1.7471
0.2	0.8114	0.7737	0.8081	0.8887	0.9995	1.1306	1.2759	1.4317	1.5961	1.7687
0.1	0.8091	0.7748	0.8174	0.9074	1.0267	1.1640	1.3121	1.4667	1.6252	1.7865
0.0	0.8108	0.7782	0.8274	0.9253	1.0519	1.1942	1.3443	1.4972	1.6501	1.8014

Table 10.4 Inflation variability

Degree of inflation targeting Towards full-fledged IT	Degrees of exchange rate flexibility Towards more flexible exchange rate									
	0.0	0.1	0.2	0.3	0.4	0.5	0.6	0.7	0.8	0.9
1.0	2.8283	2.7151	2.6296	2.5840	2.5973	2.6957	2.9007	3.1737	3.3207	3.1081
0.9	2.6712	2.5595	2.4839	2.4494	2.4592	2.5095	2.5830	2.6495	2.6953	2.7849
0.8	2.5575	2.4591	2.3990	2.3733	2.3758	2.3995	2.4405	2.5041	2.6125	2.8149
0.7	2.5103	2.4199	2.3629	2.3337	2.3301	2.3535	2.4093	2.5063	2.6580	2.8857
0.6	2.5335	2.4205	2.3475	2.3131	2.3172	2.3604	2.4432	2.5672	2.7353	2.9538
0.5	2.5674	2.4132	2.3315	2.3096	2.3376	2.4073	2.5129	2.6501	2.8167	3.0126
0.4	2.5300	2.3775	2.3211	2.3315	2.3895	2.4821	2.6005	2.7389	2.8935	3.0622
0.3	2.4350	2.3419	2.3356	2.3842	2.4681	2.5747	2.6959	2.8265	2.9633	3.1042
0.2	2.3578	2.3432	2.3877	2.4673	2.5670	2.6775	2.7930	2.9098	3.0258	3.1399
0.1	2.3512	2.3999	2.4799	2.5765	2.6802	2.7853	2.8884	2.9876	3.0817	3.1706
0.0	2.4320	2.5139	2.6080	2.7060	2.8025	2.8946	2.9805	3.0596	3.1317	3.1972

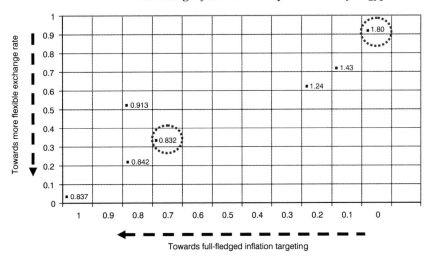

Figure 10.1 Output variability under varying degrees of exchange rate flexibility and inflation targeting

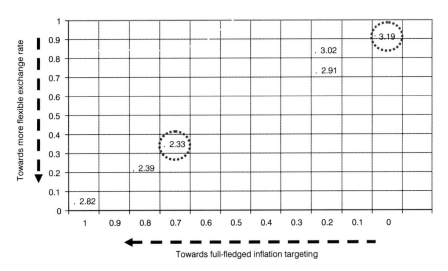

Figure 10.2 Inflation rate variability under varying degrees of exchange rate flexibility and inflation targeting

where L denotes the welfare loss to the economy, $(\pi_i - \pi^*)$ is the deviation of observed inflation at time i from its steady state value, $(y_i - y^*)$ is the deviation of real GDP at time from potential GDP and T is the time horizon required for all variables to reach their steady state values as identified in the model.

Previous results are confirmed in Table 10.5 and Figure 10.3, where the fixed exchange rate provides the highest loss in terms of inflation and output variability put together. It is, however, important to underscore that full-fledged IT does not guarantee the lowest inflation and output variability nor the lowest loss function based on equation (6). Therefore, given calculations related to the loss function, a framework close to IT with increased exchange rate flexibility is best suited for the case being examined. However, issues related to current account sustainability should not be neglected.

This is consistent with the discussion provided earlier which highlights the importance of exchange rate considerations in emerging markets which implement (or plan) to implement IT. Amato and Gerlach (2002) point out that some countries (e.g. Chile and Israel) formally incorporated an exchange rate target range/path in their inflation targeting framework, at least in the transition phase. Using the exchange rate to guide inflation may not be incompatible with inflation targeting after all. Accordingly, when implementing policy, central banks should consider the effects of exchange rate fluctuations on inflation and the output gap, but should not consider an independent role for the exchange rate since targeting an exchange rate is likely to worsen the performance of monetary policy.

Nonetheless, it is paramount that policy makers realise that limiting exchange rate movements runs the risk of transforming the exchange rate into a nominal anchor that takes precedence over the inflation target. It is also important for central banks to recognise that after a sustained period of low inflation engineered by an inflation targeting regime, the effect of the exchange rate on the expectations formation process and price setting practices of households and firms in the economy is likely to fall. Thus, inflation targeting is likely to help limit the pass-through from exchange rates to inflation.

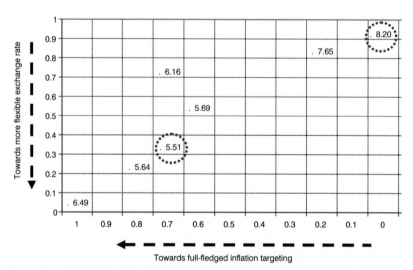

Figure 10.3 Magnitude of economic loss under varying degrees of exchange rate flexibility and inflation targeting

Table 10.5 Loss function $L = \dfrac{1}{T}\left[\dfrac{1}{2}\sum_{i=1}^{T}(\pi_i - \pi^*)^2 + \sum_{i=1}^{T}(y_i - y^*)^2\right]$

	Degrees of exchange rate flexibility									
	Towards more flexible exchange rate →									
	0.0	0.1	0.2	0.3	0.4	0.5	0.6	0.7	0.8	0.9
1.0	6.4938	6.2881	6.1418	6.0805	6.1427	6.3800	6.8305	7.4061	7.7231	7.4192
0.9	6.1728	5.9651	5.8310	5.7805	5.8203	5.9443	6.1235	6.3128	6.5188	6.9435
0.8	5.9410	5.7514	5.6403	5.6021	5.6284	5.7121	5.8555	6.0833	6.4619	7.1283
0.7	5.8456	5.6588	5.5477	5.5057	5.5339	5.6405	5.8426	6.1655	6.6482	7.3543
0.6	5.8938	5.6452	5.5008	5.4595	5.5221	5.6907	5.9679	6.3602	6.8796	7.5502
0.5	5.9625	5.6173	5.4602	5.4585	5.5872	5.8265	6.1634	6.5898	7.1040	7.7119
0.4	5.8840	5.5362	5.4383	5.5157	5.7198	6.0182	6.3900	6.8221	7.3076	7.8448
0.3	5.6872	5.4594	5.4717	5.6384	5.9068	6.2433	6.6268	7.0443	7.4883	7.9555
0.2	5.5270	5.4601	5.5835	5.8233	6.1335	6.4856	6.8619	7.2513	7.6477	8.0485
0.1	5.5115	5.5746	5.7772	6.0604	6.3871	6.7346	7.0889	7.4419	7.7886	8.1277
0.0	5.6748	5.8060	6.0434	6.3373	6.6569	6.9834	7.3053	7.6164	7.9135	8.1958

Degree of inflation targeting
Towards full-fledged IT ←

5 Conclusion

This chapter has presented a reduced form New Keynesian model, applicable to the case of Egypt, with modifications introduced to the standard uncovered interest rate parity condition and monetary policy reaction function so as to capture varying degrees of exchange rate flexibility under an inflation targeting regime. The results show that a fixed exchange rate regime generates the highest output and inflation variability, and the worst loss function for the economy, under the specified model. As the exchange rate is allowed more flexibility the variability of output and inflation declines. However, the optimal point involves less than perfect exchange rate flexibility.

Appendix: Steps towards reforming Egypt's monetary policy framework[9]

Over the last few years the Central Bank of Egypt (CBE) has taken many important steps to upgrade Egypt's monetary policy with a view to adopting IT as a monetary policy framework once the prerequisites are fulfilled. Under the new banking law, the CBE has been granted more independence and an explicit institutional framework was set up for interest rate determination. In addition, the CBE launched a comprehensive and far-reaching banking sector reform programme in 2004, which contained important steps to help overcome the previous shortcomings in the banking sector and fulfil the prerequisites for IT. It included the (non-performing-loans-related) restructuring and privatisation of banks with state participation, other regulatory reforms, the liberalisation of the foreign exchange and money markets, and ongoing efforts to strengthen the supervision of banks.

Restoring confidence in the foreign exchange market and replacing quantitative monetary instruments with price instruments were the cornerstones in the CBE's monetary policy reform programme. The exchange rate has been abandoned as the nominal anchor, and price stability has been declared the overriding policy objective. The CBE is committed to achieving, over the medium term, low rates of inflation, which it believes are essential for maintaining confidence and for sustaining high rates of investment and economic growth. Egypt made the transition to a unified, flexible exchange rate regime during 2004. The parallel market rate, which had a premium of over 15 per cent in late 2003, converged with the banking rate in the second half of 2004 as confidence was restored.[10]

A deep and well-developed banking sector is also important to allow for proper transmission of monetary policy actions. Monetary policy within an IT framework is highly market-oriented, and the banking sector is expected to function on market principles. The dominance of the state-owned banks in the market had tended to create rigidities in the interest rate structure in Egypt. Under the banking system reform programme, the banking sector has undergone substantial transformation which has entailed the exit of several weak banks, large-scale financial restructuring, the divestiture of state shares in private banks and the privatisation of a major state bank. These actions have reduced the share of banks with state participation significantly. The large stock of non-performing loans (NPLs) has been largely addressed through provisioning and cash settlements. The government and the CBE have been implementing programmes designed to clean up banks' balance sheets and settle the NPLs of public and private enterprises.

Moreover, several institutional and operational changes were initiated under the programme to help facilitate monetary policy formulation and assessment.

Institutionally

To carry out its better-defined mandate, the CBE established a Monetary Policy Committee (MPC), which convenes on Thursday every six weeks to decide on key policy rates. The MPC consists of nine members from the CBE's Board of Directors.

To enhance transparency, bolster the credibility of the CBE, and help anchor inflation expectations, MPC decisions are communicated to the market through a monetary policy statement, which is released on the CBE's web-site after each meeting.

Operationally

The exchange rate has been abandoned as the nominal anchor, and price stability has been declared the overriding policy objective.

On June 2, 2005 the CBE introduced an interest rate corridor with two standing facilities, an overnight lending facility and a deposit facility. The interest rates on the two standing facilities define the ceiling and floor of the corridor, respectively. By setting the rates on the standing facilities, the MPC determines the corridor within which the overnight inter-bank rate can fluctuate. In practice, steering the overnight inter-bank rate within this corridor is the operational target of the CBE.

Starting in August 2005, in addition to deposit auctions, central bank notes were added to the CBE's toolkit as the primary instrument for liquidity management via open market operations.

Notes

1 The views expressed in this chapter are those of the author and should not be attributed to the Central Bank of Egypt. The author would like to thank Jan Vlcek, the IMF consultant, for introducing the MATLAB codes and for extensive discussions. In addition, special thanks go to Nadia Mounir for excellent research assistance.
2 See also Roger and Stone (2005).
3 The term rmc_t encompasses the main price determinants in an economy and, in the absence of price inertia, any changes in costs of production have to be reflected immediately in price changes. Therefore, the real marginal costs are defined as the share of nominal marginal costs over final prices and can be used as an indicator of future inflationary pressures. In the case of an open economy the real marginal costs usually comprise the relative price of imports together with the real price of domestic intermediate products. The relative price of imports is captured by the real exchange rate gap. The real price of intermediate products is approximated by the domestic

output gap. The output gap can be viewed as an indicator of inflationary pressures stemming from diminishing returns to scale.

4   It is divided by 4 because the interest rates and the risk premium are measured at annual rates, while the exchange rate is quarterly.

5   There is a considerable amount of heterogeneity in results, which differ widely across countries.

6   For example, Parrado (2004) estimates a reaction function for Singapore in which the instrument is the change in the exchange rate. Kirsanova, Leith and Wren-Lewis (2006) show that it may be appropriate for the monetary authorities to respond to the terms of trade gap as well as the output gap, where their terms of trade gap concept has many similarities to the deviation of the real exchange rate from the fundamental equilibrium exchange rate.

7   The Kalman filter is an optimal recursive data processing algorithm. The Kalman filter processes all available measurements, regardless of their precision, to estimate the current value of the variables of interest, with use of (1) knowledge of the system and measurement device dynamics, (2) the statistical description of the system's noise, measurement errors and uncertainty in the dynamic models, and (3) any available information about initial conditions of the variables of interest.

8   The proposed parameter values are based on other countries' experiences using this type of model. Detailed explanations of the calibrated parameters which reflect certain stylised facts and dynamic inter-linkages of the main variables in the economy are found in Bulir and Hurnik (2002).

9   Al-Mashat (2007) assesses and contrasts Egypt's preparedness for IT with the experience of other emerging market inflation targeters in light of the 2004 Comprehensive Banking Sector Reform Programme.

10   In exploring the monetary transmission mechanism for Egypt, Al-Mashat and Billmeier (2008) find that, despite the shift away from the exchange rate as the nominal anchor, the exchange rate channel continues to play an important role in the transmission of monetary policy, as it greatly magnifies the impact of policy shocks.

References

Al-Mashat, R. (2007), 'Monetary policy in Egypt: a retrospective and preparedness for inflation targeting', Egyptian Center for Economic Studies, Cairo, working paper 134.

Al-Mashat, R., and Billmeier, A. (2008), 'The monetary transmission mechanism in Egypt', *Review of Middle East Economics and Finance*, 4 (3), article 2.

Amato, J., and Gerlach, S. (2002), 'Inflation targeting in emerging and transition economies: Lessons after a decade', *European Economic Review*, 46: 781–90.

Ball, L. (1999), 'Policy rules for open economies', in John B. Taylor (ed.), *Monetary Policy Rules*. Chicago: University of Chicago Press.

Benes, J., and Varva, D. (2004), 'Exchange rate pegs and inflation targeting: modeling the exchange rate in reduced form New Keynesian models', mimeo, Czech National Bank.

Berg, A., Karam, P., and Laxton, D. (2006), 'Practical model-based monetary policy analysis – a how-to guide', IMF working paper 06/81.

Bulir, A., and Hurnik, J. (2002), 'Handout for the modeling workshop', mimeo, IMF,

——(2006), 'The Maastricht inflation criterion: "saints" and "sinners"', Czech National Bank, working paper 8.

Coats, W., Laxton, D. and Rose, D. (2003), 'The Czech National Bank's forecasting and policy analysis system', Czech National Bank.

Flood, R., and Rose, A. (2002), 'Uncovered interest parity in crisis', *IMF Staff Papers*, 49: 252–66.

Galí, J. (2002), 'New Perspectives on Monetary Policy, Inflation, and the Business Cycle', National Bureau of Economic Research working paper 8767.

Ho, C., and McCauley, R. (2003), 'Living with flexible exchange rates: issues and recent experience in inflation targeting emerging market economies', BIS working paper 130.

Jonas, J., and Mishkin, F. (2003), 'Inflation targeting in transition countries: experience and prospects', National Bureau of Economic Research working paper 9667.

Kirsanova, T., Leith, C., and Wren-Lewis, S. (2006), 'Should central banks target consumer prices or the exchange rate?' *Economic Journal*, 116: 208–231.

Mishkin, F. (2000): 'Inflation targeting in emerging market countries', *American Economic Review*, 90: 105–9.

Mishkin, F., and Schmidt-Hebbel, K (2001), 'One decade of inflation targeting in the world: what do we know and what do we need to know?', National Bureau of Economic Research working paper 8397.

Mohanty, M., and Klau, M. (2005), 'Monetary policy rules in emerging market economies: issues and evidence', in R. Langhammer and L. Vinhas de Souza, (eds.), *Monetary Policy and Macroeconomic Stabilisation in Latin America,* Berlin: Springer-Verlag.

Obstfeld, M., and Rogoff, K. (1995), 'The mirage of fixed exchange rates', *Journal of Economic Perspectives*, 9: 73–96.

Parrado, E. (2004), 'Inflation targeting and exchange rate rules in an open economy', IMF working paper 04/21.

Roger, S. and Stone, M. (2005), 'On target? The international experience with achieving inflation targets', IMF working paper 05/163.

Schaechter, A., Stone, M., and Zelmer, M. (2000), 'Adopting inflation targeting: practical issues for emerging market countries', IMF Occasional Paper no. 202.

Svensson, L. (1999), 'Inflation targeting as a monetary policy rule', *Journal of Monetary Economics*, 43: 607–654.

——(2000), 'Open-economy inflation targeting', *Journal of International Economics*, 50: 117–53.

Taylor, J. (1993), 'Discretion versus policy rules in practice', *Carnegie–Rochester Conference Series on Public Policy* 39, 195–214.

——(2001), 'The role of the exchange rate in monetary-policy rules', *American Economic Review*, 91: 263–7.

Woodford, M. (2001), 'Inflation stabilisation and welfare', National Bureau of Economic Research working paper 8071.

11 Fiscal dominance

An obstacle to inflation targeting in Egypt

Hoda Abdel Ghaffar Youssef

1 Introduction

The successes of inflation targeting monetary policies, first in some developed countries and then in emerging market economies, have generated an interest among policymakers in exploring the feasibility of adopting this type of monetary policy in order to overcome inflationary trends. However, it is widely understood that a hasty adoption of such a policy without the fundamental conditions being met could lead to its failure and provoke serious consequences not only in terms of inflation but also for the credibility of the monetary authorities. There are many economic, institutional and technical requirements for the implementation of an inflation targeting regime. One of the most important is that the central bank should be independent of the executive authorities, which implies the absence of any kind of fiscal dominance. Indeed, the channels through which fiscal policy can affect monetary policy are multiple (monetary financing of public deficits, hesitation in raising interest rates when desirable, effects on aggregate demand, etc). Since fiscal disequilibrium can hinder inflation control, lead to severe restrictions on monetary policy, or even to its failure, it is essential for an inflation targeting regime to be underpinned by a sound fiscal stance.

In its monetary policy statement of June 2005, the Central Bank of Egypt (CBE) announced its intention to 'put in place a formal inflation targeting framework to anchor monetary policy once the fundamental prerequisites are met' (CBE, 2005). Hence, it is important to think about the basic conditions of such a move towards inflation targeting and to underline the most important ones without which an efficient conduct of this type of monetary policy cannot be ensured.

Central bank independence, a fundamental condition for a successful and efficient inflation targeting policy, cannot be guaranteed if the economy is suffering from fiscal dominance. It has often been argued that high inflation occurs when governments face large and persistent deficits that are financed through money creation (seigniorage), or as the result of open market operations in which the central bank purchases interest-bearing government debt. Inflation emerges as a fiscally driven monetary phenomenon. In other words, the budget deficit and its subsequent financing through money creation are regarded as exogenous to the monetary authority. Monetary growth is dominated by the government's financing requirements, and the price level increases as a result of that monetary expansion. A regime of that nature is one where there is fiscal dominance.

Hence, fiscal consolidation and the soundness of the public finances are not only a crucial element in the efficient struggle against inflation that arises from the monetary financing of public deficits, they also play a fundamental role in the determination of inflation expectations.

Given that many fiscal indicators have, for many years now, shown a serious disequilibrium in Egypt, this chapter aims to check whether the Egyptian economy suffers from fiscal dominance which is likely to affect the central bank's independence and credibility as well as its price stability goal and its inflation target. In order to do this, we try to evaluate empirically the impact on inflation of the monetary financing of public deficits, as represented by CBE lending to the government. Using an error correction model (ECM), we try not only to assess the empirical relationship between the fiscal deficit as a possible source of money creation and the price level, but also to identify the effect of fiscal dominance (through CBE lending to the government to finance the public deficit) on inflation.

The chapter is organised as follows. The next section contains a review of the literature on the impact of fiscal policy on monetary policy and inflation. Section 3 presents the main fiscal indicators for the Egyptian economy and analyses the structure of the budget in terms of both expenditures and revenues. In section 4, the data and the tests of the main statistical properties required for the ECM (unit root and cointegration tests) are described. We use this model to test for a long-run relationship between the financing needs of the government budget (as represented by CBE lending to the government) and the consumer price index (CPI). Finally, the chapter ends with some concluding remarks on the implications of our results and, more generally, the implications of the public finance position and the budget structure for inflation targeting.

2 The impact of fiscal policy on monetary policy: a literature review

The economic literature identifies various means through which fiscal policy can affect monetary policy and inflation. This effect can take place through the intertemporal government budget constraint, the effect of fiscal policy on monetary variables such as interest or exchange rates, or its effects on demand and expectations.

Regarding the government budget constraint, Sargent and Wallace's seminal paper (1981) underlines the difficulty of conducting an efficient monetary policy in an economic environment characterised by an unsustainable fiscal policy. The authors introduce the concept of 'monetary dominance' where the monetary authority sets an independent policy, as opposed to the concept of 'fiscal dominance'. In such a context, the government determines its budget independently, and announces the actual and future budget deficit as well as the revenues required to cover this deficit, either through government debt or through seigniorage. They show that, in the case of fiscal dominance, the monetary authority loses its capacity to control inflation. A reduction in monetary growth intended to curb inflation will raise the share of debt in the deficit financing, which raises the interest due and, subsequently, the future deficit. The financing of this deficit will then require more money creation, provoking higher inflation. In other words, a reduction in monetary growth could lead to higher inflation.

The fiscal theory of the price level (FTPL) describes a scenario in which the central bank can lose control of inflation. In its weak form, the FTPL points to an obvious link between monetary and fiscal policies. Since seigniorage is a possible revenue source, monetary and fiscal policy are jointly determined by fiscal budget constraints. The fiscal authority commits to a path for primary budget surpluses/ deficits, forcing the monetary authority to generate the seigniorage needed to maintain solvency. Hence, prices are driven by current and future money growth and inflation is a fiscally driven monetary phenomenon. Unlike the weak theory, where inflation is still (ultimately) a monetary phenomenon, the strong-form of FTPL maintains that fiscal policy affects the price level, but independently of future money growth and dependent on the changes in government debt or budget deficit. This is done through the intertemporal government budget constraint, i.e. the equality between the nominal debt (B_t) divided by the price level (p_t) and the present discounted value of future primary surpluses (S_t). Hence, the government intertemporal budget constraint requires that $B_t/p_t = S_t$. While the traditional view argues that the primary surplus must necessarily adjust in order to satisfy that equation and ensure solvency for any level of prices (Ricardian regime), advocates of the FTPL view the present value government budget constraint as an equilibrium condition. In this non-Ricardian regime, nothing requires the primary surplus necessarily to adjust to satisfy that equation: in equilibrium the price level will do the job which means that fiscal policy determines the price level.

The FTPL has been intensively analysed in the economic literature in recent years. Leeper (1991) talks about an active fiscal policy and a passive monetary policy. Sims (1994) and Woodford (1995, 1996) show that the price level that dominates is the only one that verifies the government's intertemporal budget constraint. Cochrane (1999, 2005) uses an analogy with a private stock, valued as a claim on corporate profits. He explains that, in the same manner, the fiscal theory determines the price level from the value of nominal government debt as a claim on government primary surpluses.

However, this theory has been criticised. Buiter (1999) believes that the policy conclusions that could be drawn from the FTPL could be harmful if it influenced the actual behaviour of the fiscal and monetary authorities, resulting in painful fiscal tightening, government default, or unplanned recourse to the inflation tax. McCallum (1998) denies the claim that the price level is fiscally determined in cases in which the central bank refuses to accommodate and keeps the monetary base on its predetermined path. As for empirical studies, they give mixed results.[1]

A number of research papers have attempted to test empirically for the existence of fiscal dominance. Most of the studies that have been done on developed countries find that the monetary policies adopted by these countries are not accommodating. Hence, they reject the hypothesis of fiscal dominance (see

Favero, 2002, on the Euro area). As for emerging countries, empirical studies tend to confirm that there is a strong positive association between deficits and inflation, and that fiscal dominance constrains the scope for an independent monetary policy (see Tanner and Ramos, 2002, and Moreira *et al.*, 2007, for Brazil, and Catão and Terrones, 2003, and Masson *et al.*, 1997, for comparisons of advanced and developing countries).

Fiscal policy can influence exchange rate policy as well. When a substantial part of the public debt is denominated in foreign currency, the monetary authority tries to avoid exchange rate depreciation. And in the case of a fiscal expansion, the rise in interest rates due to government borrowing attracts foreign capital, causing an exchange-rate appreciation in the short run. Hence, central banks can show some reluctance in raising rates in order to reduce the pressure on the exchange rate. Regarding emerging countries, the economic literature contains numerous research papers on the impact of fiscal policy on countries' vulnerability to foreign exchange crises. Kopits (2000) finds that sizable explicit or implicit government deficits and the market perception of a lack of fiscal sustainability render emerging market economies vulnerable to currency crises. He underlines the necessity of credible fiscal adjustment as a tool of crisis prevention.

Other studies (Blanchard, 2004; Favero and Giavazzi, 2004) have focused more particularly on the impact of fiscal policy under an inflation targeting monetary regime. When fiscal conditions are wrong (i.e. when debt is high, when a high proportion of debt is denominated in foreign currency, or when the risk aversion of investors is high), inflation targeting can clearly have adverse effects. An increase in real interest rates in response to higher inflation can increase the probability of default and is more likely to lead to a real depreciation, which in turn leads to a further increase in inflation. Hence, by increasing the probability of default, the high level of public debt would have produced the opposite of the conventional effect of a restrictive monetary policy. Such an environment is characterised by 'fiscal dominance', even if monetary policy is not accommodating. In this case, fiscal policy, not monetary policy, is the right instrument to decrease inflation.

Finally, the role played by fiscal policy in fighting inflation also operates through expectations. Celasun *et al.* (2004) look at the role of the imperfect credibility of stabilisation efforts in explaining the failure of inflation rates to decline during disinflation programmes. They find that expectations of future inflation play a much more important role than past inflation in shaping the inflation process, and that an improvement in primary fiscal balances significantly reduces inflation expectations. Drazen and Helpman (1990) analyse the development of inflation under both certainty and uncertainty about the composition or timing of fiscal stabilisation, and find that it depends on which policy tool is used (increasing taxes, increasing monetary growth rates or cutting expenditure).

3 The evolution of the main fiscal indicators in Egypt

Observation of the fiscal indicators for the Egyptian economy reveals that, after a net improvement following the implementation of the Economic Reform and

Structural Adjustment Programme (ERSAP) in 1991, the same indicators started to suffer from a disequilibrium which got progressively worse, especially from fiscal year FY98. The fiscal deficit increased to a peak of 10.2 per cent in FY02 before falling back to and remaining around 8 per cent in the following years. As for the public debt, it continued to grow, reaching 108 per cent in FY07 before declining to 90–95 per cent in FY08 and FY09 (see Figure 11.1).

The public deficit

Public expenditure

Data on public expenditure in Egypt shows that it decreased in the mid-1990s before jumping again from 25 per cent of GDP in FY98 to 33.8 per cent in FY09. During the last few years (from FY04 to FY09), the share of current expenditure was on average 88 per cent of total public expenditure, while capital expenditure represented only 12 per cent of the total. In FY99 and FY00, the decrease in the share of current expenditures allowed for an increased share of capital expenditure in the government budget. This suggests that the overall increase in public expenditure was partially done through a reduction in public investment, which is politically easier than cutting current expenditure (Figure 11.2).

The analysis of different categories of current expenditure reveals that subsidies have the biggest share (45 per cent in FY09). Since their share was only 7 per cent in FY91,[2] subsidies can be considered as an important source of the increase in

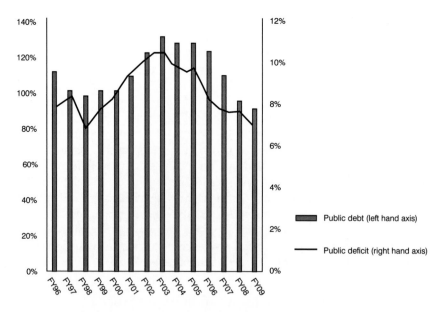

Figure 11.1 Evolution of main fiscal indicators FY96-FY07 (% of GDP)

Source: MOF and CBE

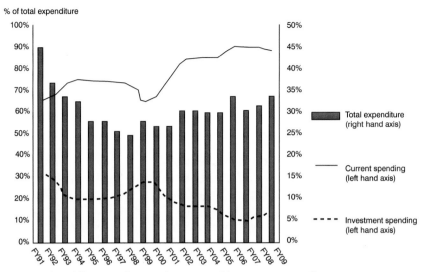

Figure 11.2 Public expenditure and current and investment expenditure

Source: MOF

the total expenditure. In FY09, they represent 14 per cent of GDP, a share that has been multiplied by more than three in 17 years (it was 4.2 per cent in FY92). Salaries occupy the second position in government current expenditure (25 per cent in FY09) while the public debt interest share is around 14 per cent. These two categories, which together consume around 40 per cent of the government budget, are hard to reduce in the short term, unlike capital expenditure which is more productive but easier to control or reduce from one year to another.

On the other hand, the analysis of the structure of revenues shows that the contribution of direct taxes to government revenues is relatively low, at an average of 28 per cent in the years FY05–09.[3] This results essentially from the existence of a large shadow economy together with the weakness of the tax administration (bureaucratic decisions and/or lack of necessary investment in human and material resources). In general, indirect taxes are less visible and, consequently, they are politically more attractive. With the progressive liberalisation of international trade, we observe a decrease in revenues coming from foreign trade as well.

Although it is not considered as an oil-producing country, Egypt is in fact an oil exporter and relies to a large extent on oil and gas revenues. Revenues also depend heavily on the profitability of the Suez Canal Authority. Historically, this has been an obstacle to fiscal consolidation because of the low interest in (non-oil) tax revenues and, consequently, the lack of incentive to develop an effective revenue administration. The relative importance of these revenues also creates more difficulties in predicting total government revenues and in linking key revenues to economic activity.

In 2004, some efforts were made to raise additional revenues. Egypt embarked on fiscal reforms intended to increase tax revenues and to make the tax administration more transparent and fair. The reforms involved tax cuts (the objective being to combat tax evasion, to widen the tax base and to improve tax collection). They were also supported by an awareness campaign and by the training of tax officers. In the years following the implementation of the reform, we can observe a positive effect reflected in the increase of tax revenues (Table 11.1).

The financing of the fiscal deficit

Historically, the public deficit was financed mostly through domestic resources (86 per cent on average between FY02 and FY07), with a small contribution from external borrowing (6 per cent), and the remaining deficit financed from other resources including privatisation proceeds. However, the last couple of years, FY08 and FY09, have seen a jump in the share of foreign borrowing (respectively 17 per cent and 32 per cent of total financing). Regarding the domestic financing, the government traditionally resorted to the banking system but has progressively increased the share from non-banking sources. The CBE is the main provider of bank financing, the remaining part being financed by commercial banks.

Seigniorage is one of the means by which governments can raise revenue to finance additional public expenditure. However, the chances of generating seigniorage revenues without causing inflation are very limited. Measured as the annual change in the monetary base divided by nominal GDP, seigniorage in Egypt has been around 12 per cent on average in recent years.[4] Relying on seigniorage as a source of revenue is counterproductive because of its effect on inflation. Therefore, public sector borrowing from the central bank and the banking system should be low or nonexistent. Instead, governments should work on broadening the tax base and should not rely on revenues generated by excessive currency issue.

Table 11.1 Structure of public revenues

% of total revenues	FY03	FY04	FY05	FY06	FY07	FY08	FY09
Tax revenues	51	54	57	56	56	55	57
Income taxes*	19	22	24	27	29	27	27
Sales taxes	21	21	24	20	19	20	22
Custom duties	8	7	6	5	5	6	5
Other tax revenues	3	3	3	2	2	2	1
Non-tax revenues	46	42	41	43	42	44	41
Grants	3	4	2	1	2	1	1

Source: Ministry of Finance and author's calculations.

Note: * Mostly from the Egyptian Gas and Petroleum Company (EGPC) and Suez Canal Authority (SCA)

BORROWING FROM THE BANKING SYSTEM

Bank financing of the fiscal deficit can take the form of borrowing from the central bank, which induces the creation of new money in the system, or from commercial banks, which is associated with the creation of interest-bearing debt and also induces money growth. In Egypt, M2 is the main indicator of money supply and domestic credit is one of the main causal factors in its change. Domestic credit can be divided into (i) credit to the government and (ii) credit to the private sector, public sector (public business and economic authorities) and households. The CBE data reveal that the share of net claims on government in total domestic credit has been 35 per cent on average in recent years. As for the share of credit to the government for budgetary support in total domestic liquidity, it has been around 32 per cent on average (Table 11.2). This significant share in domestic liquidity is an indicator of fiscal dominance in money growth in Egypt.

NON-BANK FINANCE

In Egypt, non-bank financing is raised mainly by borrowing from the National Investment Bank (NIB) and the Social Insurance Funds (SIFs) (through the NIB) and through the issue of Ministry of Finance securities (especially Treasury bills, Treasury bonds and notes issued to the CBE). This is an important source of finance for the deficit in Egypt. Theoretically, non-bank finance is less inflationary than bank borrowing. However, it has negative implications for domestic debt. Borrowing at high cost might lead to unsustainable levels of non-bank debt. Through its contribution to high debt servicing obligations, costly borrowing leads to an increase in fiscal deficits and so to more money creation which exerts upward pressure on inflation.

Public debt

There are of course valid reasons for a government to borrow and accumulate debt when this debt is used to fund spending that contributes to broader economic and

Table 11.2 CBE's claims on government

	FY02	*FY03*	*FY04*	*FY05*	*FY06*	*FY07*	*FY08*	*Average FY02–08*
LE millions	113231	131689	175579	218450	167685	170338	137743	
% of domestic liquidity	34.4	34.3	40.4	44.2	29.9	25.7	18.0	32
% of domestic credit	31.4	34.0	41.6	46.8	32.9	32.1	24.1	35

Source: CBE annual report 2007/2008

social objectives. However, excessive debt not only increases the risk of a fiscal crisis, it also imposes costs on the economy by keeping borrowing costs high, discouraging private investment, and limiting the flexibility of fiscal policy. It also has a significant impact on inflation due to the monetary financing of the debt. When public debt is excessively high, a substantial fiscal adjustment is needed to bring debt down. This can be done through an increase in public revenues, a decline in public expenditures, or a combination of the two. Another option is to use money creation whether directly through the issue of money by the central bank in favour of the government (seigniorage), or indirectly when the government issues securities that are mostly acquired by the central bank, which at the end of the day has the same inflationary consequences of money creation. In this case, the economy is described as suffering from fiscal dominance, and monetary policy is constrained to work towards avoiding the unsustainability of the public debt.

In Egypt, the persistent budget deficits resulted in a fast growth of public debt as a percentage of GDP. This growth started to accelerate in FY99 (Table 11.3), inducing an associated increase in debt servicing from EGP 15 billion in FY99 to EGP 53 billion in FY09 and EGP 71 billion in the FY10 budget.

4 Empirical analysis: cointegration and error correction modelling

Methodology and data

This study employs the econometric technique of cointegration and error correction modelling (ECM) in order to estimate the relationship between inflation and credit to the government for budgetary support. Cointegration analysis provides information about the long-term equilibrium relationship in a model (Engle and Granger, 1987), while the ECM allows for the estimation of both short- and long-term effects of the explanatory time series variables. A two-variable ECM is specified as follows:

$$\Delta Y_t = \beta_0 \Delta X_t - (1 - \alpha)[Y_{t-1} - \beta_1 - \beta_2 X_{t-1}] + z_t$$

where β_0 measures the short run impact of changes in X on Y, β_2 measures the long run impact and $(1 - \alpha)$ is the fraction of the previous period's disequilibrium error that is made up this period. The (–) sign before the coefficient indicates that this coefficient is expected to be negative and, most likely, less than one.

The basic model we use to test for the fiscal dominance hypothesis can be summarised as follows:

$$CPI = f(CG, RGDP, M2GDP)$$

where CPI is the consumer price index, CG is the variable representing claims on government, RGDP is the real GDP, and M2GDP is the money aggregate M2 as a

Table 11.3 Evolution of total public debt (% of GDP)

	FY98	FY99	FY00	FY01	FY02	FY03	FY04	FY05	FY06	FY07	FY08	FY09
Domestic debt*	66	71	72	81	87	89	90	95	96	87	75	73
External debt	33	31	28	28	33	42	38	31	27	23	20	17
Total public debt	99	101	100	109	121	131	128	126	124	110	95	90

Source: MOF and CBE

Note: *General government (government + NIB) and economic authorities

Table 11.4 Unit root test

Variables	ADF	Order of integration
LCPI	−1.5922	I(1)
D(LCPI)	−2.9385***	I(0)
LCG	−1.0925	I(1)
D(LCG)	−5.8714*	I(0)
LRGDP	−2.2643	I(1)
D(LRGDP)	−3.9297**	I(0)
LM2GDP	−2.1211	I(1)
D(LM2GDP)	−4.5536*	I(0)

Note: *, **, ***, significant at the 1%, 5%, 10% levels

percentage of nominal GDP. The function *f* is assumed to be increasing in CG and M2GDP and decreasing in RGDP.

All the series used in the model are annual (from 1960 to 2007) and are taken from the World Bank database *World Development Indicators.*[5] All variables in the equation are expressed in a log-linear form.

Unit root testing is carried out in order to determine the degree of stationarity. Using the augmented Dickey–Fuller (ADF) test, all series are found to be non-stationary (Table 11.4). Once expressed in first differences, all the series turn out to be stationary. Hence, all the series considered here are integrated of order one (or I(1)).

Cointegration and estimation of long-run coefficients

The first step in our analysis is to use the Johansen (1988) cointegration test to determine the long-run relationship between our non-stationary series. The Johansen test uses the trace statistic and the eigenvalue. We accept the existence of a cointegration relation if they are greater than the critical value. Table 11.5 presents the results of the Johansen likelihood ratio tests and the long-run cointegration relationship between the variables. At a 5 per cent level of significance, we reject the null hypothesis of the non-existence of cointegration (63.75852 > 47.85613 for the trace test and 41.62207 > 27.58434 for the max-eigenvalue test). They also indicate the existence of a single cointegrating vector (22.13645 < 29.79707 for the trace test and 13.47202 < 21.13162 for the max-eigenvalue test). Normalised on LogCPI, the estimated cointegrating vector is as follows (Table 11.6):

$$\text{LCPI} = 2.64 \, \text{LCG} - 6.09 \, \text{RGDP} + 1.49 \, \text{M2GDP} \tag{1}$$

Equation (1) suggests that, in the long run, CG and M2GDP both have a significant and positive effect on the general price level, while the effect of

Table 11.5 Johansen cointegration test

Unrestricted cointegration rank test (trace)

Hypothesised no. of CEs	Eigenvalue	Trace statistic	Critical value 5%	Prob.**
None *	0.6034	63.7585	47.8561	0.0008
At most 1	0.2587	22.1365	29.7971	0.2910
At most 2	0.1639	8.6644	15.4947	0.3973
At most 3	0.0135	0.6095	3.8415	0.4350

Notes
Trace test indicates 1 cointegrating equation at the 0.05 level
* denotes rejection of the hypothesis at the 0.05 level
** MacKinnon–Haug–Michelis (1999) p-values

Unrestricted cointegration rank test (maximum eigenvalue)

Hypothesised no. of CEs	Eigenvalue	Max-eigen statistic	Critical value 5%	Prob.**
None *	0.6034	41.6221	27.5843	0.0004
At most 1	0.2587	13.4720	21.1316	0.4098
At most 2	0.1639	8.0549	14.2646	0.3732
At most 3	0.0134	0.6095	3.8415	0.4350

Notes
Max-eigenvalue test indicates 1 cointegrating eqn(s) at the 0.05 level
* denotes rejection of the hypothesis at the 0.05 level
** MacKinnon–Haug–Michelis (1999) p-values

Table 11.6 Estimation of the cointegration equation

Normalised cointegration coefficient: 1 cointegration equation (standard error in parentheses)

LOG(CPI)	LOG(CG)	LOG(RGDP)	LOG(M2GDP)
1.000000	−2.6398	6.0887	−1.4854
	(0.3854)	(1.0971)	(0.4739)

Log likelihood: 316.9767 Number of included observations: 45

RGDP on the price level is found to be significant but negative. In other words, an increase in credit to the government and in money supply as a percentage of GDP increases the general price level, while an increase in real GDP would decrease the price level. This negative effect of RGDP on inflation can be explained by the fact that the Egyptian economy is not in a full employment position. In this case, the increase of the long-run aggregate supply means that the economy can meet a higher level of aggregate demand without putting upward pressure on the general price level.

The error-correction model (ECM)

Since the CPI series appeared to have a long-term relationship with the other variables, it is possible to make a distinction between the long-run and short-run behaviour of inflation by specifying an error-correction mechanism for the adjustment of actual inflation toward its long-run level. Results of the ECM are presented in Table 11.7, where 'RES' represents the residuals of the lagged value of the errors in the cointegration equation (1). On the one hand, the results show that the estimated error-correction term (−0.075) is negative, statistically different from zero at the 5 per cent level and lower than unity, which implies that the price level in Egypt is indeed affected by net claims on the government, broad money and real GDP. However, the low value of the error-correction term suggests that there is only a very slow adjustment toward the long-run equilibrium. On the other hand, the coefficients of the independent variables which represent the short-run relationship are not significant, which means that they do not influence the price level in the short-run.

Our results confirm the existence of the effects of credit to the government, M2 as a percentage of GDP and real output on the price level in Egypt – and consequently on inflation – in the long-run. These results are consistent with other studies that have employed similar techniques (cointegration analysis and vector error correction modelling) to test for fiscal dominance (see Nachega, 2005, on the Democratic Republic of Congo (DRC); Agha and Khan, 2006, on Pakistan; Metin, 1995, on Turkey; Helmy, 2008, and El-Sakka and Ghali, 2005, on Egypt). On the other hand, it seems difficult to observe a similar impact in the short term. This is also consistent with a number of studies that have analysed the relationship between money and prices and concluded that the correlation between money growth and inflation is greater the longer the time horizon over which both are measured and that, in the short run, this correlation is much less apparent (see, for example, King, 2002; De Grauwe and Polan, 2001; Chouraqui *et al.*, 1989).

Table 11.7 Results of the error correction model (ECM)

Dependent variable: DLOG(CPI)

DLOG(CPI) = C(1) + C(2) * RES + C(3) * DLOG(CG) + C(4) * DLOG(RGDP) + C(5) * DLOG(M2GDP)

Variable	Coefficient	Std. error	t-Statistic	Prob.
C(1)	3.2519	0.4041	8.0484	0.0000
C(2)	−0.0758	0.0096	−7.8818	0.0000
C(3)	0.3030	0.2143	1.4135	0.1650
C(4)	−0.1087	0.0543	−2.0013	0.0520
C(5)	−0.2078	0.1034	−2.0098	0.0511
R-squared	0.6109	Durbin–Watson:	1.6871	
Adjusted R-squared	0.5729			

Table 11.8 Granger casuality test

Null hypothesis	Obs	F-statistic	Prob.
DLCPI does not Granger cause DLCG	45	0.0467	0.9545
DLCG does not Granger cause DLCPI	45	4.2797	0.0207

We should also emphasise that the factors that are likely to influence the price level are so numerous that it is difficult to include all of them. The initial question behind this empirical work was to see if the Egyptian economy shows signs of fiscal dominance, which is incompatible with the conduct of an independent monetary policy based on inflation targeting. Given that the CBE financing of the budget deficit entails money creation, we used claims on the government as the variable representing the credit provided by the central bank to the government for budgetary support to see the impact of this credit on the price level and, consequently, on inflation. It is also worth noting that the analysis has been seriously limited by data availability.

Granger causality tests

We investigate the direction of causality between CG and CPI by testing for Granger causality between both variables. Our results (Table 11.8) show that we cannot reject the hypothesis that CPI does not Granger cause CG but we do reject the hypothesis that CG does not Granger cause CPI. Therefore it appears that Granger causality runs one way from CG to CPI and not the other way.

Stability tests

Since the period under consideration is rather long, it is of interest to divide the period into subperiods and perform stability tests to see whether there are significant differences in the estimated equation between the subsamples. We use the Chow breakpoint test which fits the equation separately for each subsample. A significant difference indicates a structural change in the relationship. In our analysis, we identify three key dates at which the relationship between our variables could have started to change. The first one is in 1991 with the beginning of the ERSAP programme, the second in 2003 with the adoption of the new law giving the CBE more independence and the floating of the Egyptian pound; and the third in 2005 with the announcement of the intention to adopt an inflation targeting regime. Table 11.9 presents the Chow test results for the first two dates, 1991 and 2003. The output shows that for both dates, the p-value reported for the Chow test statistic is more than 0.05. Hence, we cannot reject the null hypothesis of no breaks at specified breakpoints and we conclude that neither the implementation of ERSAP nor the new CBE law had a significant impact on the relation.

One major drawback of the Chow breakpoint test is that each subsample requires at least as many observations as the number of estimated parameters. Therefore, we use the Chow forecast test to test for structural change starting in

Table 11.9 Chow breakpoint test

Equation sample: 1962 2007			
Null hypothesis: No breaks at specified breakpoints			
Chow breakpoint test: 1991			
F-statistic	0.6668	Prob. F(5,36)	0.6510
Log likelihood ratio	4.0743	Prob. Chi-Square(5)	0.5388
Wald statistic	3.3340	Prob. Chi-Square(5)	0.6486
Chow breakpoint test: 2003			
F-statistic	0.7941	Prob. F(5,36)	0.5611
Log likelihood ratio	4.8126	Prob. Chi-Square(5)	0.4392

Table 11.10 Chow forecast test

From 2005 to 2007			
F-statistic	0.9171	Prob. F(3,38)	0.4418
Log likelihood ratio	3.2155	Prob. Chi-Square(3)	0.3596

2005. The results of the forecast test statistics in Table 11.10 do not reject the null hypothesis of no structural change in the relation even after the announcement of the intention to adopt an inflation targeting regime in 2005.

Finally, we test for parameter changes in our model based on a CUSUM test, which plots the cumulative sum of the recursive residuals together with the 5 per cent critical lines. Our test finds no parameter instability since the cumulative sum does not go outside the area between the two critical lines (Figure 11.3).

5 Implications of the structure of the government budget for monetary policy

This section is an attempt to highlight the main pressures on the government budget and their implications for the monetary policy conducted by the central bank and for inflation targeting in particular. It also presents some suggestions on how to deal with these pressures and prevent them from hampering the efficient conduct of monetary policy.

On the public expenditure side, there is a need to rethink the system of subsidies which is based on consumption. Some goods and services are considered as 'sensitive' and so are subject to strict price control. These subsidies are becoming increasingly inefficient and constitute a heavy burden on the government budget. The fiscal authorities should implement a global reform in order to reduce their cost and improve their targeting towards deprived social groups.

However, because administered or controlled prices are an important component of aggregate price indices, the reduction or the complete removal of these subsidies has an unavoidable effect on the short-run behaviour of inflation. This direct effect

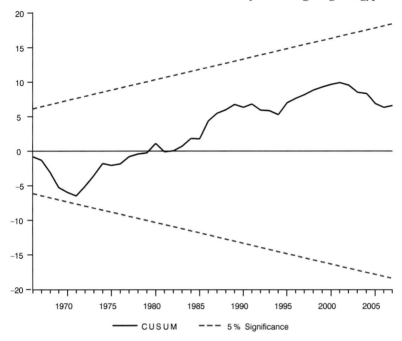

Figure 11.3 CUSUM test

should be a temporary one and should not provoke a strong reaction from the central bank, which should, however, remain cautious in case the initial increase in controlled prices induces second round effects. This can happen for example if the initial jump in prices induces a further increase in the public's longer-term inflation expectations, which would put additional upward pressure on inflation through higher nominal wages and higher costs of production. Hence, a proper inflation forecast would need to take account of the timing and extent of changes in those prices and requires a high degree of coordination between the monetary and fiscal authorities in order to guarantee that inflation expectations are anchored and the second round effects avoided. In order to do this, the central bank must acquire credibility through a clear and transparent communication strategy.

In the Egyptian case, the programme that has been implemented to progressively deregulate the administered prices was supposed to give more autonomy to the central bank. However, it did not result, as had been expected, in a slow down of inflation rates through increased confidence in monetary policy. On the contrary, price deregulation provoked an increase in inflation expectations which does not help the disinflation process.

Another challenge for monetary policy is the limited role of automatic fiscal stabilisers. They can be defined as features of the tax and transfer systems that tend by their design to offset fluctuations in economic activity, which means that they increase or decrease automatically to offset the current economic trend without government intervention. In general, these stabilisers work via income tax, transfers related to income support policies such as unemployment compensation or income supplements to the poor, or any other tool that is sensitive to the economic cycle. Hence, they allow for government deficits in recession periods to be offset by government surpluses in boom periods.

When automatic stabilisers do not exist or are weak, macroeconomic stabilisation occurs via discretionary measures (for example by adopting a new law), which is a time-consuming and irreversible process, not to mention the difficulties in detecting and correctly diagnosing cyclical fluctuations. Also the central bank is constrained to focus on economic stabilisation, which might sometimes be an obstacle to the achievement of its ultimate goal of price stability.

Finally, the relative rigidity of the structure of public expenditure leaves fiscal policy with little room to manoeuvre when responding to external shocks or setting new priorities. As noted above, this rigidity comes mainly from the non-reducible nature of certain categories of expenditures such as wages, subsidies and interest charges. Thus, the upward trend in expenditure does not result, strictly speaking, from discretionary action, but from the existence of some 'acquired rights' which cannot easily be modified in the short term. This lack of flexibility requires monetary policy to take a more active role. The additional pressure on the central bank makes it harder for the monetary authority to focus on achieving its inflation target.

Regarding the public revenues, the main challenge is to find a way to increase tax revenues without increasing the burden of taxes on the population, especially the poor. This can be done through the broadening of the tax base. As noted above, such taxes usually have a countercyclical effect and act as automatic stabilisers. For example, income taxes increase in periods of expansion and decline during recessions. In this regard, it is argued[6] that this stabilising effect is stronger when the tax system is more progressive. It follows that tax policies that do not rely on the principle of progressivity can adversely affect the ability of budgets to mitigate the impact of cyclical shocks which, once again, increases the burden on monetary policy.

In Egypt, the tax reforms introduced in 2004 have established a tax rate that is 'partly' progressive (it starts at 10 per cent and has a ceiling of 20 per cent), thus limiting the role of taxation in macroeconomic stabilisation. For fiscal policy to be more supportive of monetary policy, one of the methods suggested is to strengthen the role of automatic stabilisers, on both the expenditure and revenue sides. This can be done through a number of measures such as the establishment of a more progressive tax system and by strengthening the role and importance of the benefits and allowances that depend on economic conditions.[7] It is also quite important to give a higher priority to productive expenditures that contribute to future economic growth and help to strengthen the public sector's financial position.

6 Conclusion

From the above analysis, we conclude that fiscal policy has a great impact on the conduct of monetary policy in Egypt. This impact would be even greater if the monetary authorities had not just an unspecified objective of price stability but rather a formal and explicit commitment to achieving an inflation target. Hence, solvency is not the only constraint that should be considered by policy makers when conducting fiscal policy. There is a need to rethink fiscal policy and to correct imbalances before adopting an explicit policy of inflation targeting. This is very important in order to preserve the central bank's credibility, which could otherwise be undermined if fiscally driven conditions prevented it from achieving its target.

Notes

1 See Canzoneri *et al.* (1998), Cochrane (1998) and Sala (2004) for tests on US data, and see Afonso (2002) for tests on European economies. For evidence from emerging countries, see Loyo (1999) on Brazil.
2 According to the old classification then in use.
3 A new budget classification, based on the IMF 2001 GFS Standards, was adopted by the Egyptian Ministry of Finance by Law 97/2005, in order to bring Egyptian budgetary procedures into compliance with international standards. Therefore, data starting 2005/2006 are not comparable to previous years.
4 Source: author's calculations based on data from MOF for the FYs 2003 to 2008.
5 Despite some improvements in macroeconomic statistics in general, finding reliable and consistent data from national sources proved to be a challenging task.
6 Solow (2005).
7 It is important to note that the benefits and allowances system in Egypt does not include transfers of the 'unemployment compensation' type.

References

Afonso, A. (2002), 'Disturbing the fiscal theory of the price level: can it fit the EU-15?', working paper 2002/01, Department of Economics at the School of Economics and Management (ISEG), Technical University of Lisbon.

Agha, A., and Khan, M. (2006) 'An empirical analysis of fiscal imbalances and inflation in Pakistan', State Bank of Pakistan, *SBP Research Bulletin*, 2(2): 343–363.

Blanchard, O. (2004), 'Fiscal dominance and inflation targeting: lessons from Brazil', National Bureau of Economic Research working paper 10389.

Buiter, W.H. (1999), 'The fallacy of the fiscal theory of the price level', National Bureau of Economic Research working paper 6396.

Canzoneri, M., Cumby, R., and Diba, B. (1998), 'Is the price level determined by the needs of fiscal solvency?', National Bureau of Economic Research working paper 6471.

Catão, L. and Terrones, M. (2003), 'Fiscal deficits and inflation', IMF working paper 03/65.

CBE (2005), Monetary Policy Statement, Cairo, Egypt, June. http://www.cbe.org.eg/public/Monetary-Policy/Frameworks.htm.

Celasun, O., Gaston Gelos, R., and Prati, A. (2004), 'Obstacles to disinflation: what is the role of fiscal expectations?', IMF working paper 04/111.

Central Bank of Egypt (CBE), annual reports, various issues.

Chouraqui, J.-C., Driscoll, M., and Strauss-Kahn, M.O. (1989), 'The effects of monetary policy on the real sector: what do we know?', *Banca Nazionale del Lavoro Quarterly Review*, March, 3–46.

Cochrane, J. (1998), 'A frictionless view of U.S. inflation', National Bureau of Economic Research working paper 6646.

——(1999), 'Long term debt and optimal policy in the fiscal theory of the price level', *Econometrica*, 69(1): 69–116.

——(2005), 'Money as stock', *Journal of Monetary Economics*, 52 (3): 501–528.

De Grauwe, P., and Polan, M. (2001), 'Is inflation always and everywhere a monetary phenomenon?', Centre for Economic Policy Research (CEPR) discussion paper 2841.

Drazen, A., and Helpman, E. (1990), 'Inflationary consequences of anticipated macroeconomic policies' *Review of Economic Studies*, 57: 146–166.

El-Sakka, M., and Ghali, K. (2005) 'The sources of inflation in Egypt: A multivariate cointegration analysis,' *Review of Middle East Economics and Finance*, 3 (3): article 6, December.

Engle, R.F., and Granger, C. (1987), 'Cointegration and error correction: Representation, estimation and testing', *Econometrica*, 55(2): 251–276.

Favero, C. (2002), 'How do European monetary and fiscal authorities behave?', Innocenzo Gasparini Institute for Economic Research (IGIER) working paper 214.

Favero, C., and Giavazzi, F. (2004), 'Inflation targets and debt: Lessons from Brazil', National Bureau of Economic Research working paper 10390.

Helmy, O. (2008), 'The impact of budget deficit on inflation in Egypt', Egyptian Centre for Economic Studies, Cairo, working paper 141.

Johansen, S., (1988), 'Statistical analysis of co-integration vectors', *Journal of Economics Dynamic and Control*, 12(2–3): 231–254.

King, M. (2002), 'No money, no inflation – the role of money in the economy', *Bank of England Quarterly Bulletin*, 42: 162–177.

Kopits, G. (2000), 'How can fiscal policy help avert currency crises?', IMF working paper 00/195.

Leeper, E. (1991), 'Equilibria under "Active" and "Passive" monetary and fiscal policy,' *Journal of Monetary Economics*, 27(1): 129–147.

Loyo, E (1999), 'Tight money paradox on the loose: a fiscalist hyperinflation', mimeo, John F. Kennedy School of Government, Harvard University.

Masson, P., Savastano M., and Sharma S. (1997), 'The scope for inflation targeting in developing countries', IMF working paper 97/130.

McCallum, B. (1998), 'Indeterminacy, bubbles, and the fiscal theory of the price level determination', National Bureau of Economic Research working paper 6456.

MacKinnon, J., Haug, A., and Michelis, L. (1999). 'Numerical distribution functions of likelihood ratio tests for cointegration', *Journal of Applied Econometrics*, 14(5): 563–77

Metin, K. (1995), 'An integrated analysis of Turkish inflation', *Oxford Bulletin of Economics and Statistics*, 57 (4): 513–531.

Ministry of Finance (MOF), Egypt, various reports and publications.

Moreira, T., Souza, G., and de Almeida, C. (2007), 'The fiscal theory of the price level and the interaction of monetary and fiscal policies: The Brazilian case', *Brazilian Review of Econometrics*, 27 (1): 85–106.

Nachega, J.-C. (2005), 'Fiscal dominance and inflation in the Democratic Republic of the Congo', IMF working paper 05/221.

Sala, L (2004), 'The fiscal theory of the price level: Identifying restrictions and empirical evidence', Innocenzo Gasparini Institute for Economic Research (IGIER), Bocconi University, working paper 257.

Sargent, T., and Wallace, N. (1981), 'Some unpleasant monetarist arithmetic', *Federal Reserve Bank of Minneapolis Quarterly Review*, Fall: 1–17.

Sims, C. (1994), 'A simple model for study of the determination of the price level and the interactions of monetary and fiscal policy', *Economic Theory*, 4(3): 381–399.

Solow, R.M. (2005). 'Is fiscal policy possible? Is it desirable?' in *Structural Reform and Economic Policy*, International Economic Association Conference Volume no. 139. Palgrave Macmillan, New York.

Tanner, E., and Ramos, A. (2002), 'Fiscal sustainability and monetary versus fiscal dominance: Evidence from Brazil, 1991–2000', IMF working paper 02/5.

Woodford, M. (1995), 'Price level determinacy without control of a monetary aggregate,' *Carnegie-Rochester Series on Public Policy*, 43(1), 1–46.

——(1996), 'Control of the public debt: a requirement for price stability', National Bureau of Economic Research working paper 5684.

World Development Indicators, World Bank database.

12 Understanding the inflationary process in the GCC region

The cases of Saudi Arabia and Kuwait

Maher Hasan and Hesham Alogeel

1 Introduction

After two decades of impressive success in maintaining price stability, inflationary pressures have emerged since 2003 in all the Gulf Cooperation Council (GCC) countries, with the oil boom putting the control of inflation at the top of the agenda for policymakers in the region. Some have blamed these pressures mainly on the peg to the weakening US dollar, others on global shocks related to high food prices, local supply shortages related to rent, and demand shocks induced by large fiscal spending and an expansionary monetary stance imported from the US through the dollar peg. Accordingly, the remedies proposed include revaluation or adopting a more flexible exchange rate regime in order to gain monetary policy independence, higher subsidies, addressing supply bottlenecks, and containing government expenditures.

Although all these factors might have played a role in the recent inflationary pressures, the design of an appropriate policy response, especially the choice of exchange or monetary regimes, is likely to be guided by the forces driving inflation in the long run.[1] Understanding these driving forces is not only key to the adoption of appropriate policies to maintain price stability, but it is also essential for the assessment of the potential costs and benefits of the planned monetary union among GCC countries, with more homogeneous inflationary processes implying lower costs. This chapter seeks to contribute to the understanding of the factors that affect inflation in the GCC region by examining the inflationary processes in Saudi Arabia and Kuwait. Given the similarity of the economic structure of the GCC countries, it seems plausible to assume that the inflationary processes in Saudi Arabia and Kuwait could help us to gain a better understanding of the forces driving inflation in the other GCC countries.

The analysis concludes that external factors play an important role in explaining the inflationary process given the high dependence on imports and foreign workers to meet domestic demand. The analysis shows that, in the long run, inflation in trading partners is the main factor affecting inflation in Saudi Arabia and Kuwait, with a significant but lower contribution from the exchange rate pass-through. The weaker impact of the latter is due to the fact that while changes in the price level of trading partners are usually permanent,[2] changes in exchange rates are not, which enables part of the exchange rate impact to be absorbed. Positive demand shocks and excess money supply exert upward pressures on inflation in the short run, but tend to dissipate quickly as the real exchange rate and the money market reach a new equilibrium.

The rest of the chapter is organised as follows. Section 2 provides a brief review of the literature. Section 3 describes the economic model and methodology. The empirical analysis and results are discussed in section 4, followed by the conclusions in section 5.

2 Brief review of the literature

There is a huge body of literature on inflation and its determinants in both developed and developing countries. The literature considers inflation as the outcome of four main factors: supply side factors that come from cost-push or mark-up relationships; foreign factors; monetary factors; and demand factors. In addition, the literature considers inflation expectations as another source of inflation. For example, De Brouwer and Ericsson (1998) used the mark-up model to empirically model the inflation process in Australia. Juselius (1992a) investigated the long-run foreign transmission effects for Danish and German prices, exchange rates, and interest rates, finding strong evidence of the dependence of Danish prices on West German price levels. Lim and Papi (1997) found strong evidence for a key role for money and the exchange rates in explaining the inflation process in Turkey during 1970–95, and Bonato (2008) found a strong relation between money and inflation in Iran. Empirical analysis has often identified country-specific factors that affect inflation, for example, Sekine (2001; Japan), Khan and Schimmelpfennig (2006; Pakistan) and Diouf (2007; Mali).

Few studies have analysed the inflation process in the GCC countries, with hardly any emphasis on the long-run factors. For example, Darrat (1985) analysed the role of money in explaining inflation in Libya, Nigeria, and Saudi Arabia, finding that higher money supply and lower real income growth are associated with higher inflation in each country. Al-Mutairi (1995) constructed a VAR model to examine the impact of money supply, government expenditure and import prices on inflation in Kuwait. He found that government expenditure plays a dominant role in explaining the variation in the price level, followed by import prices and the money supply. Keran and Al-Malik (1979) analysed the monetary sources of inflation in Saudi Arabia and found, relative to the US, a greater influence of world prices on inflation and a lower influence of domestic monetary developments. Al-Raisi and Pattanaik (2003) examined the pass-through from the exchange rate to prices in Oman and found only a very weak pass-through effect. Specifically, they found that a depreciation of 10 per cent in the nominal effective exchange rate (NEER) will increase the CPI by only 0.4 per cent.

3 Economic model and methodology

Several factors make the domestic price level in the GCC countries highly sensitive to external factors. The GCC countries' tradable sector includes mainly hydrocarbon products, reflecting the region's comparative advantage. The region also has a very open trade system with most consumer products imported from outside the region. Figure 12.1 compares Saudi Arabia and Kuwait with their five largest trading partners[3] in terms of the share of domestic demand that is met through imports. It shows clearly the dependence of the two countries on imports. While the ratio is high also in Germany and to a lesser extent in Italy and the UK, this reflects the importance of imported intermediate inputs and raw materials, while imports are mainly for final consumption or investment in Saudi Arabia and Kuwait. Figure 12.2 shows that non-oil exports in Germany and Italy are in the range of 20–50 per cent of domestic demand, which suggests that a large proportion of imports is used as inputs for exports, while the ratio is less than 10 per cent for Kuwait and Saudi Arabia,[4] which implies that imports are for final consumption.

In addition, the two countries' flexible labour policies[5] have increased their dependence on foreign labour, which adds to the sensitivity of price levels to external factors. This stems from the fact that inflation in expatriates' home countries and the exchange rate influence the purchasing power of their remittances

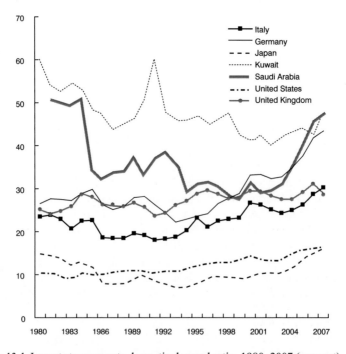

Figure 12.1 Imports to aggregate domestic demand ratio, 1980–2007 (per cent)

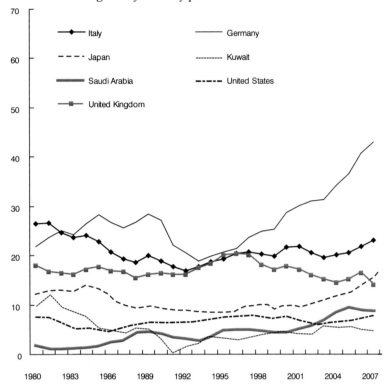

Figure 12.2 Non-oil exports to aggregate domestic demand ratio, 1980–2007 (per cent)

and hence the level of salaries required to attract them to Saudi Arabia or Kuwait, or to retain them there.

The domestic price level is also affected by changes in the price of nontradables which largely reflect domestic factors. However, several policies have limited the effect of domestic factors on inflation. The flexible labour policy has mitigated the impact of any shortages in local labour supply and enhanced the supply response of nontradables.[6] The generous subsidy arrangements, e.g. in education, health services, electricity and water, have also played an important role in limiting the impact of domestic and external factors on nontradable and to a lesser extent on tradable prices. In addition, the monetary discipline embodied in the pegged exchange rate regime has prevented the active use of monetary policy for achieving real sector objectives, and the open capital account has facilitated the dissipation of any excess money supply through capital outflows.

The choice of an economic model to analyse the inflationary process in the GCC region should be guided by these characteristics of the region which emphasise the role of external factors on inflation.[7] Hence, to take into account all the factors which affect the domestic price level, we will assume that the price level is such that

$$P = f\left(NEER, P^*, P^{oil}, M, AD\right) \tag{1}$$

where P is the domestic price level measured by the CPI, $NEER$ is the nominal effective exchange rate and it captures the exchange rate pass-through effect, P^* is the price level in trading partners and captures imported inflation, P^{oil} is the price of oil, included to capture transportation costs, M is the nominal money supply and AD is aggregate domestic demand.

If one were to assume that only external factors affect inflation in (1), an error correction model (ECM) could be used to assess the long-run effect of these factors as well as the short-term dynamics, as follows:[8]

$$\Delta p_t = c + \delta(p_{t-1} - \alpha_1 neer_{t-1} - \alpha_2 p^*_{t-1} - \alpha_3 p^{oil}_{t-1}) \tag{2}$$
$$+ \sum_{i=1}^{k} b_{1i} \Delta p_{t-i} + \sum_{i=1}^{k} b_{2i} \Delta neer_{t-i} + \sum_{i=1}^{k} b_{3i} \Delta p^*_{t-i} + \sum_{i=1}^{k} b_{4i} \Delta p^{oil}_{t-i}$$

where k is the number of lags to be included and the lower case represents the natural logarithm of the variables. With the exception of the $NEER$ which is measured as the price of foreign currency per unit of local currency (thus an increase in $NEER$ represents an appreciation of the local currency), all other variables are expected to have a positive impact on inflation. According to relative purchasing power parity (PPP), the effect of both foreign price changes and exchange rate changes on p is equal to one. However, there are many reasons why this might not hold, at least in the short run. These include transportation costs and the presence of non-traded goods in the consumer basket, the price level of which is largely subject to domestic factors such as monetary factors and domestic demand. Hence, estimates based on (2) would be biased and inefficient if money and domestic demand affect the inflationary process.

The monetary stance in Saudi Arabia and Kuwait has been more or less accommodative to money demand as determined by economic activity. Given the pegged exchange rate regimes which are furthermore highly credible in light of the large foreign reserves and the open capital accounts, there is little scope for an active rolé for monetary policy to stimulate or restrain economic activity. However, the peg regime does not prevent an occasional, limited, unanticipated deviation of money supply from money demand (excess money supply). This deviation could be measured by estimating a money demand equation where the deviation of money supply from long-run money demand represents an excess money supply. Assuming that money demand is a function of real GDP, the GDP price deflator and the interest rate, and estimating the long-run relationship between money demand and these variables, the excess money supply can be then measured as:

$$excm_t = m_t - \hat{m}_t \tag{3}$$

where m is the log of money supply and $\hat{m}$ is the estimated long-run money demand.

In the short run, excess aggregate demand may also exert positive pressures on inflation. Excess demand could be measured through the output gap such that:

$$excd_t = RGDP_t - \overline{RGDP}_t \tag{4}$$

where $RGDP_t$ is the real GDP and $\overline{RGDP}_t$ is the potential GDP. Although it is hard to observe potential GDP, there are different ways to estimate it. De-trending and Hodrick–Prescott (HP) filters are two common ways to estimate potential GDP. However, the large contribution of the oil sector in the GDP of Saudi Arabia and Kuwait affects the accuracy of this measure. This stems from the fact that changes in real GDP due to changes in the level of oil production, if they are not translated into higher government expenditures, would not have an impact on domestic demand and hence would not exert inflationary pressures. Alternatively, one could use real non-oil GDP to calculate the output gap. However, the inclusion of oil-related activities (refining, petrochemicals) affects the accuracy of non-oil GDP for measuring excess domestic demand and the unavailability of a long enough time series prevents its use in the case of Kuwait. To address these concerns, we assess excess domestic demand[9] such that

$$excd_t = d_t - \hat{d}_t \tag{5}$$

where d_t is the real domestic demand (i.e. government and private consumption and investment) and $\hat{d}_t$ is the potential (long-run) demand estimated by linear de-trending or using an HP filter.[10]

Excess demand (deviation of aggregate demand from its long-run level) could result from several factors. These include expansionary fiscal policy, monetary shocks, and the deviation of the real exchange rate from its equilibrium level. Expansionary fiscal policy increases demand directly while an expansionary monetary stance encourages private sector demand by lowering the cost of credit. The excess demand variable also captures the impact of any deviation of the real exchange rate from equilibrium. For example, an undervalued real exchange rate stimulates demand for nontradables.

Given all the factors discussed above, the general inflation equation could be expressed as:[11]

$$\begin{aligned}
\Delta p_t = {}& c + \delta_1 (p_{t-1} - \alpha_1 neer_{t-1} - \alpha_2 p^*_{t-1} - \alpha_3 p^{oil}_{t-1}) \\
& + \sum_{i=1}^{k} b_{1i}\Delta p_{t-i} + \sum_{i=1}^{k} b_{2i}\Delta neer_{t-i} + \sum_{i=1}^{k} b_{3i}\Delta p^*_{t-i} + \sum_{i=1}^{k} b_{4i}\Delta p^{oil}_{t-i} \\
& + \delta_2 excd_{t-1} + \delta_3 excm_{t-1} + \sum_{i=1}^{k} b_{5i}\Delta gdp_{t-i} + \sum_{i=1}^{k} b_{6i}\Delta m_{t-i} + b_7 D_t
\end{aligned} \tag{6}$$

Equation (6) is equation (2) augmented by excess money supply and demand shocks. The first line captures the long-run dynamic of the inflation process, while the second and third lines capture the short-run dynamic including the impact of domestic factors on inflation. An alternative specification could include money supply as a variable affecting the long-run dynamic of the inflation process. We will examine this hypothesis in the empirical analysis. Changes in real GDP and money could be included to capture the impact of the supply response and changes in money supply on inflation.[12] D is a dummy variable that could be used to account for specific events such as the invasion of Kuwait in 1990 and the Gulf War in 1991.

This model is similar to Juselius's (1992b) model which assumed that the inflationary process in Denmark was driven by the external, internal and monetary sectors. Juselius estimated the deviation from the steady state in each sector separately and then used that along with other possible determinants for inflation to estimate a short-run inflation dynamic model. For the external sector she assumed that PPP held, based on Juselius (1992a). While the model in (6) is similar to that of Juselius (1992b) in the sense that it takes into account the three sectors in addition to other possible determinants for inflation, it does not assume that PPP holds and it assesses excess demand differently.[13] This makes it possible to assess the long-run impact of the external factors on the inflationary process conditional on domestic or short-term factors, while relaxing the PPP assumption[14] which lacks strong supporting empirical evidence.

The choice of the two countries to be included in the analysis was guided by the likely stability in the inflationary process and the availability of data. Unlike the UAE and Qatar, Saudi Arabia and Kuwait did not go through large structural economic changes during the period we investigate, both having a well-developed oil industry and infrastructure and experiencing rather gradual diversification. The availability of relatively long time series data in the two countries is also critical for the long-run nature of the analysis we would like to conduct. Moreover, Saudi Arabia and Kuwait were the two largest economies in the GCC region for most of the period we investigate. While short-term factors could result in the divergence of inflation among the GCC countries, in the long run the similarity in the economic structure of the GCC countries is likely to entail similar inflationary processes.

4 Data and estimation[15]

Inflationary developments

The GCC region has witnessed two episodes of relatively high inflation; both of which coincided with oil booms (Figure 12.3). The first episode was in the 1970s with the first oil boom while the second one started in 2003. With the exception of UAE and Qatar, the second episode has been relatively milder. The Saudi economy experienced very high inflation during the 1970s. Although its level of inflation might be exaggerated by data measurement problems, the trend is consistent with

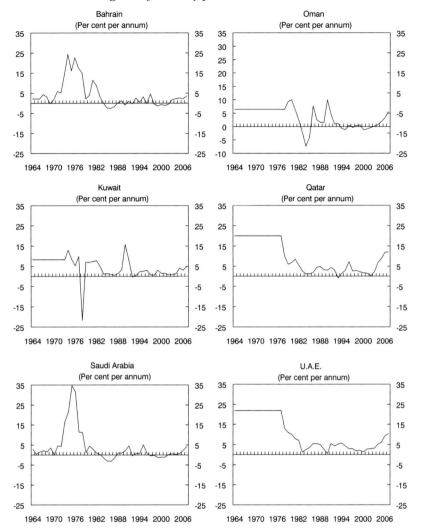

Source: World Economic Output

Figure 12.3 GCC: Inflation, 1964–2007

other GCC countries. During the 1980s and the 1990s, inflation in Saudi Arabia fluctuated between mild deflation and inflation, reaching 5 per cent in 1991 and 1995. Inflation remained steady during the 2000s and started to pick up in 2003, reaching 4.1 per cent in 2007 and 9.9 per cent in 2008.

Inflationary trends in Kuwait were similar to those in Saudi Arabia. While the level of inflation in Kuwait was lower during the 1970s, it was on average slightly higher during 1984–2004 (excluding 1990–91 (the Gulf War)) than the Saudi level. The sharp deflation in 1978 is likely to have been related to problems with the splicing of a CPI series that started in 1978 onto the previous series. This is corroborated by examining the wholesale price index (WPI) inflation which declined by 1 per cent only in 1978.[16] Inflation in Kuwait increased significantly during the invasion in 1990 and the liberation and reconstruction in 1991. As in other GCC countries, inflation started to pick up in 2003, averaged 5 per cent in 2007 and reached 10.5 per cent in 2008.

Order of integration

To determine the order of integration for the variables considered in the analysis, unit root tests for the logs of the variables (except for the interest rate) and their first differences were conducted, to test for the null orders of I(1) and I(2), respectively. Table 12.1 lists the augmented Dickey–Fuller (ADF) statistics. As expected, most of the variables are I(1). The output gap, interest rate, demand gap, and excess money supply are stationary (I(0)), as expected. Money supply is I(2) in the case of Kuwait.

Estimates of the inflation model (Saudi Arabia)

We start by examining a model where money supply is included in the error correction vector to assess the long-run impact of money. This resulted in non-sensible signs for the coefficients of the variables examined[17] and model selection criteria which did not support the inclusion of money, in the case of both Saudi Arabia and Kuwait.[18] Juselius (1994) suggested using real money to overcome the I(2) problem or estimating the excess money supply from a money demand function. While real money is I(1), including it does not solve the previous problems.[19] Alternatively, we use excess money supply to assess the impact of money; since it is stationary, it can be included in the short-term dynamics.[20] Appendix 2 provides details of the estimation of excess money supply for Saudi Arabia and Kuwait.

As discussed in the previous section, the use of real GDP or non-oil GDP to proxy demand shocks might provide a less accurate measure of excess demand, given the high level of oil GDP and the large share of oil-related activities in the non-oil GDP. Alternatively, we use a 'demand gap' to assess demand shocks. The data for demand is available from 1981. While using demand would come at the cost of losing about 15 years of data, the gain from enhancing the accuracy is likely to be high. In addition, starting from 1981 means excluding the period of the 1970s during which the very high inflation may reflect data problems or structural breaks in the data-generating process, given the significant stability in the price level since then. Moreover, the fact that the exchange rate systems were different in the 1960s and 1970s (Bretton Woods) argues for avoiding a structural break in the relation between inflation and the NEER. Figure 12.4 shows inflation in Saudi Arabia and its theoretical determinants. The co-movements of Saudi inflation and trading partners' inflation are clear from the figure. The figure also indicates that the volatility of the NEER is relatively high and that the recent level of domestic demand is significantly higher than its trend.

Table 12.1 Unit root tests

Variable	Description	Saudi Arabia[a]		Kuwait[b]	
		I(1)	I(2)	I(1)	I(2)
p	Consumer price index (CPI)	−1.98	−3.12**	−2.03	−3.63**
$neer$	Nominal effective exchange rate	−2.43	−3.81***	−1.64	−4.00***
p^*	Trade partner's CPI[c]	−2.22	−3.84**	−2.58	−4.52***
p^{oil}	Nominal oil prices[d]	−1.35	−6.27***	−1.35	−6.27***
$excm$	Excess money	−2.18**	−4.57***	−2.64***	−5.77***
dhp	Excess demand using HP-filter	−4.8***	…	−4.67***	…
$dgap$	Excess demand using de-trending	−2.17**	…	−1.75*	…
$gdpgap$	Output gap using de-trending method	−3.68***	…	−1.84*	…
$gdphp$	Output gap using HP-filter	−4.05***	…	−4.78***	…
m	Nominal money supply (M3)	−0.75	−3.05**	2.39	2.1
gdp	Real GDP	−2.54	−3.66***	−0.48	−5.33***
p^{def}	GDP deflator index	−1.7	−3.70***	−1.88	−4.81***
r	Interest rate (federal funds rate)[5]	−3.68**	…	−3.68**	…
p^{wpi}	Wholesale price index	−3.03**	−3.10**	−1.52	−3.27**

Notes

Asterisks *, **, and *** denote rejection at the 10%, 5% and 1% critical values respectively.

a   The sample is from 1966 to 2007 for all variables except for excess demand which is from 1981 to 2007. A dummy variable is added in testing unit root of p and m for Saudi Arabia to count for possible structural change from 1966–1980. An ADF test without a dummy for the period 1980–2007 indicates that p is I(1). The WPI sample is from 1985 to 2007.

b   The data sample for Kuwait is from 1974 to 2007 for all variables except excess demand which is from 1979 to 2007.

c   For p*, we include a trend in the ADF test.

d   The sample period is from 1966 to 2007.

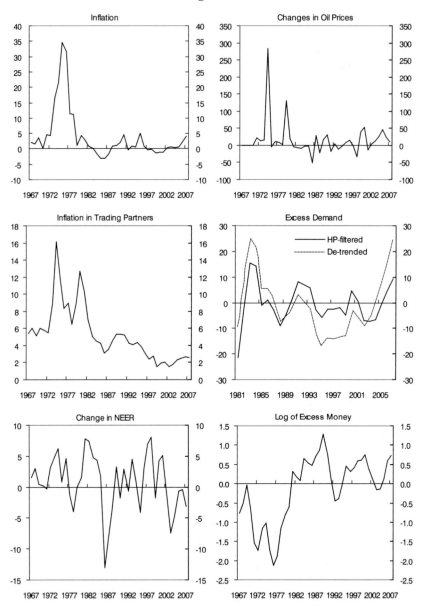

Sources: Country authorities and fund staff estimates

Figure 12.4 Saudi Arabia: Inflation and its theoretical determinants (1967–2007; in per cent)

Table 12.2 summarises the cointegration test results for Saudi Arabia and Kuwait. It indicates the existence of one cointegrating vector.[21] Table 12A.1 (in Appendix 1) summarises the results from the ECM. It shows that the long-run inflation equation could be written[22]

$$p = 2.4 - 0.194 \cdot neer + 0.833 \cdot p^* + 0.015 \cdot p^{oil} - 0.024 \cdot time$$
$$[-2.62] \qquad [3.46] \qquad [0.69]$$

while the short-term inflation equation could be written as

$$\Delta p_t = -0.590 \cdot (p + 0.194 \cdot neer - 0.833 \cdot p^* - 0.015 \cdot p^{oil} - 2.4 + 0.024 \cdot time)_{t-1}$$
$$[-5.68] \qquad [2.62] \qquad [-3.46] \qquad [-0.69]$$

$$+ 0.025 \cdot Excd_{t-1} + 0.011 \cdot Excm_{t-1}$$
$$[0.66] \qquad\qquad [1.70]$$

$$- 0.43 \cdot \Delta p_{t-1} - 0.046 \cdot \Delta p_{t-2} - 0.077 \cdot \Delta neer_{t-1} + 0.05 \cdot \Delta neer_{t-2} + 2.20 \cdot \Delta p^*_{t-1} + 0.29 \cdot \Delta p^*_{t-2}$$
$$[-2.39] \qquad [-0.23] \qquad [-1.12] \qquad [0.66] \qquad [3.94] \qquad [0.41]$$

$$- 0.006 \cdot \Delta p^{oil}_{t-1} - 0.004 \cdot \Delta p^{oil}_{t-2} - 0.241 \cdot \Delta gdp_{t-1} - 0.25 \cdot \Delta gdp_{t-2} + 0.094 \cdot \Delta m_{t-1} + 0.153 \Delta m_{t-2}$$
$$[-0.49] \qquad [-0.29] \qquad [-2.89] \qquad [-3.39] \qquad [1.73] \qquad [1.82]$$

$$- 0.315 + 0.007 \cdot time$$
$$[-4.50] \qquad [4.22]$$

All variables are significant and have the expected signs, except oil prices and excess demand which are insignificant. The results indicate that the main driving force for inflation is trading partners' inflation. A 1 per cent increase in trading partners' price level results in a 0.83 per cent increase in the price level in Saudi Arabia. The impact of the second driving force, the pass-through effect, is relatively moderate. A 1 per cent increase in the NEER (appreciation) results in a 0.19 per cent decline in the price level in Saudi Arabia. This moderate pass-through effect is consistent with the empirical evidence in other countries (see Mishkin, 2008). For example, Gagnon and Ihrig (2004) estimated the pass-through effect for 20 industrial countries using data spanning the period from 1971 to 2003, and found that it ranged from 0.02 (Sweden) to 0.53 (Greece) with an average of 0.23. Campa and Goldberg (2006) found similar results for a different set of countries. The insignificance of oil prices could be due to the authorities' policy of pricing domestically refined oil products. During periods of low oil prices the authorities raise domestically refined oil products prices (reduce subsidies) to compensate for low oil exports. On the other hand, in 2006, while international oil prices were increasing, the authorities reduced domestic gasoline prices to help cope with the impact of the sharp correction in the stock market and as a way to share rising oil wealth.[23]

Table 12.2 Cointegration test for inflation equation

| | Null hypothesis | | | | | | | | |
| | r = 0 | | | r ≤ 1 | | | r ≤ 2 | | |
	Eigenvalue	Trace stat. (95% CV)	Max stat. (95% CV)	Eigenvalue	Trace stat. (95% CV)	Max stat. (95% CV)	Eigenvalue	Trace stat. (95% CV)	Max stat. (95% CV)
Saudi Arabia	0.7	68.73*	45.76*	0.3	22.97	14	0.2	8.98	8.89
		(47.86)	(27.58)		(29.80)	(21.13)		(15.49)	(14.26)
Kuwait	0.76	74.72*	45.91*	0.44	28.81	18.63	0.25	10.19	9.18
		(47.86)	(27.58)		(29.80)	(21.13)		(15.49)	(14.26)

Notes
The VEC in both countries has two lags. The ECM is linear with intercept and no trend. Sample sizes are 1966–2007 for Saudi and 1974–2007 for Kuwait. A war dummy is introduced for Kuwait. Asterisks * indicate rejection of the hypothesis at 95% CV.

The results also indicate that the speed of adjustment is relatively high.[24] It takes about nine months to eliminate one-half of the deviation from long-run equilibrium. The results indicate that domestic factors play a relatively limited role in driving the inflation. In addition to excess money supply, lagged increases in money supply create inflationary pressures. The negative impact of growth in real GDP on inflation might reflect the impact of an increase in nontradable supply on inflation. Relative PPP implies the coefficients of *neer* (α_1) and $p^*(\alpha_2)$ should be -1 and 1, respectively, but the results do not support the PPP assumptions and a test for the PPP hypothesis was strongly rejected (see Table 12A.4 in Appendix 1). Figure 12.5 shows the long-run and short-run predicted inflation compared with the actual level of inflation. The model tracks actual inflation well. Diagnostic tests for the residuals suggest there is no serial correlation and the normality hypothesis is not rejected (see Table 12A.4).

Table 12.3 summarises the results for alternative specifications and shows that the results for trading partners' inflation and the pass-through effect are robust to alternative specifications. These include removing the time trend from the model[25] (model 2), using real money instead of nominal money to estimate excess money supply (model 3), using detrending instead of the HP filter to estimate excess demand (model 4), changing the period to 1966–2007 and 1968–2007 and using real GDP (models 5 and 6)[26] or real non-oil GDP (model 7) to proxy excess demand (output gap), and using the WPI[27] instead of the CPI (model 8). Models 2 and 4 indicate that excess demand is significant and that 1 per cent excess demand increases inflation by 0.1 per cent in the short run. Despite the small size of the excess demand coefficient, the large level of excess demand over the last few years, induced by strong public and private spending, has contributed to the recent inflationary pressures. As is clear from Figure 12.4, excess demand in 2007 was about 10 per cent using the HP-filter method and about 30 per cent using the de-trending method. This, together with a monetary stance that is accommodative to money demand as determined by economic activity, explains part of the recent inflationary trends. The relatively larger impact of trading partners' inflation during the 1966–2007 period could be due to the high (exaggerated) inflation during the 1970s, which coincided with high inflation in trading partners. This might have inflated the impact of trading partners' inflation as indicated by the fact that the coefficient of p^* is greater than one.[28] The results for the 1966–2007 period might also have been affected by the unavailability of demand data for that period and the use of a GDP-based output gap instead.

Estimates of the inflation model (Kuwait)

As for Saudi Arabia, we use excess demand instead of a GDP-based output gap to proxy demand shocks. Data for demand are available from 1979. While using demand comes at the cost of losing about 5 years of observations, it is likely to enhance accuracy. Starting from 1979 helps avoid the problem arising from the splicing of the two CPI series in 1978. Given that money is I(2), we use only excess money with no lagged changes for money supply. Figure 12.6 shows the

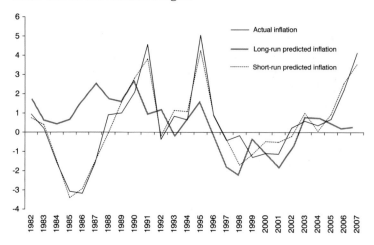

Figure 12.5 Saudi Arabia: actual inflation and predicted long- and short-run inflation

Sources: Authorities data and fund staff estimates

inflation in Kuwait and its theoretical determinants. As was the case for Saudi Arabia, the co-movements of Kuwait's inflation and trading partners' inflation are very clear. The relatively high inflation in 1990–1991 reflects the impact of the invasion in 1990 and the war in 1991 and we will use a dummy variable to account for that. As was the case for Saudi Arabia, the figure shows relatively high excess demand in 2007.

Table 12A.2 (in Appendix 1) summarises the results from the ECM. All variables are significant and have the expected signs. From Table 12A.2 the long-run inflation equation could be written as

$$p = 1.53 - 0.15 \cdot neer + 0.78 \cdot p^* + 0.055 \cdot p^{oil}$$
$$[-2.42] \qquad [50.89] \quad [3.16]$$

while the short-term inflation equation could be written as

$$\Delta p_t = -0.592 \cdot (p - 1.53 + 0.15 \cdot neer - 0.78 \cdot p^* - 0.055 \cdot p^{oil})_{t-1} + 0.10 \cdot Excd_{t-1} + 0.032 \cdot Excm_{t-1}$$
$$[-5.31] \qquad\qquad [2.42] \qquad [-50.89] \quad [-3.16] \qquad\qquad [3.04] \qquad\qquad [1.78]$$

$$+ 0.203 \cdot \Delta p_{t-1} - 0.204 \cdot \Delta p_{t-2} - 0.012 \cdot \Delta neer_{t-1} - 0.086 \cdot \Delta neer_{t-2} + 1.11 \cdot \Delta p^*_{t-1} + 0.12 \cdot \Delta p^*_{t-2}$$
$$[1.03] \qquad [-1.53] \qquad [-0.23] \qquad\qquad [-1.56] \qquad\qquad [4.34] \qquad [0.42]$$

$$+ 0.004 \cdot \Delta p^{oil}_{t-1} - 0.009 \cdot \Delta p^{oil}_{t-2} + 0.067 \cdot \Delta gdp_{t-1} + 0.005 \cdot \Delta gdp_{t-2} - \quad 0.034 \quad + 0.055 \cdot D$$
$$[0.36] \qquad\qquad [-0.75] \qquad\qquad [2.85] \qquad\qquad [0.25] \qquad\qquad [-2.79] \quad [3.68]$$

Table 12.3 Comparing alternative models in Saudi data[1]

	Model 1	Model 2	Model 3	Model 4	Model 5	Model 6	Model 7
							LWPI
Long-run equation:							
LCPIG(−1)	1.0000	1.0000	1.0000	1.0000	1.0000	1.0000	1.0000
LNEERC(−1)	0.1935	0.1996	0.1333	0.1399	0.3166	0.2410	0.1563
	[2.6196]	[2.2589]	[1.6264]	[1.3472]	[0.8527]	[1.0055]	[4.5723]
LPP(−1)	−0.8330	−0.8742	−0.5786	−1.0511	−1.6108	−1.2363	−0.6007
	[−3.4613]	[−11.3910]	[−8.1456]	[−11.1059]	[−8.4896]	[−14.6809]	[−27.4123]
LNOIL(−1)	−0.0152	0.0426	−0.0378	0.1112	0.3056	0.1001	0.0089
	[−0.6937]	[1.8517]	[−2.4215]	[3.3657]	[3.412]	[2.3924]	[1.1248]
Time	0.0244	NO	NO	NO	NO	NO	NO
C	−2.4521	−1.7825	−2.5294	−0.9516	−0.1197	−0.7310	−2.6002
Short-run dynamic:	D(LCPIG)	D(LCPIG)	D(LCPIG)	D(LCPIG)	D(LCPIG)	D(LCPIG)	D(LCPIG)
Adjustment speed	−0.5904	−0.3612	−0.5346	−0.3003	−0.1123	−0.1903	−1.4414
	[−5.6842]	[−5.1745]	[−5.3616]	[−4.2414]	[−3.0332]	[−5.7904]	[−4.5177]
C	−0.3150	−0.1290	−0.1013	−0.1268	−0.1307	−0.1623	−0.0849
	[−4.5000]	[−5.31396]	[−5.3417]	[−4.4810]	[−3.1447]	[−5.7877]	[−3.5854]
Time	0.0074	NO	NO	NO	NO	NO	NO
	[4.2202]						

Continued

Table 12.3 continued

Demand	DHP	DHP	DHP	DGAP	GDPHP	GDPHP	DHP
	0.0254	0.0902	0.0427	0.0909	-0.3127	-0.2383	-0.0373
	[0.6639]	[2.1732]	[1.2025]	[2.1920]	[-3.5752]	[-3.8778]	[-0.4159]
	Nominal	Nominal	Real	Nominal	Nominal	Real	Nominal
Excess money	0.0108	0.0133	0.0153	0.0121	-0.0096	-0.0020	-0.2333
	[1.6976]	[1.7518]	[1.6475]	[1.4221]	[-0.9479]	[-0.1874]	[-1.8372]
Sample period:	1981–2007	1981–2007	1981–2007	1981–2007	1966–2007	1966–2007	1985–2007
R-squared	0.9272	0.8807	0.8778	0.8453	0.9344	0.9560	0.8785
Adj. R-squared	0.7979	0.7018	0.7223	0.6133	0.8916	0.9273	0.7791
Log likelihood	99.3566	92.9316	92.6193	89.5543	99.4668	107.2552	64.7188
Akaike AIC	-6.3351	-5.9178	-5.9707	-5.6580	-4.2803	-4.6798	-5.2113

Note: 1 T-statistics in [ ].

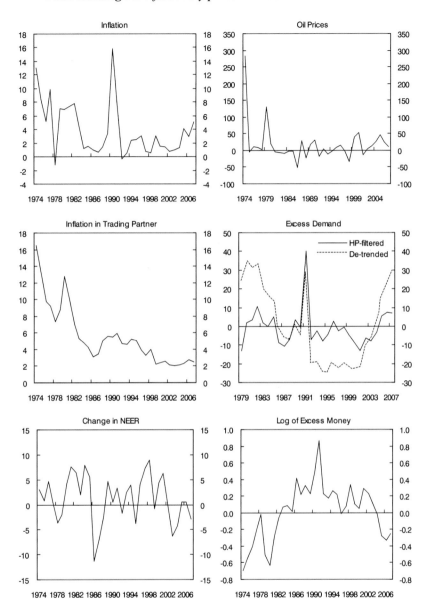

Figure 12.6 Kuwait: Inflation and its theoretical determinants (1974–2007; in per cent)

Sources: Authorities data and fund staff estimates

The results indicate that the main driving force for inflation is trading partners' inflation, followed by the pass-through effect. The size of the impact of trading partners' inflation and the pass-through effect is very close to that of Saudi Arabia, confirming the similarity between the two economies. The results also indicate that the speed of adjustment is relatively high and close to that of Saudi Arabia. Both excess demand and excess money supply are significant. Demand that exceeds the long-run (trend) level by 1 per cent increases inflation by 0.1 per cent in the short run. Similarly money supply in excess of equilibrium money demand by 1 per cent increases inflation by 0.03 per cent in the short run. Given the recent increase in domestic demand, the model suggests that part of the inflation in the last few years was driven by strong domestic demand. Figure 12.7 shows the long-run and the short-run predicted inflation compared with the actual level of inflation. The model tracks the inflation path very well.

Table 12.4 summarises the results from alternative specifications including using real money instead of nominal money to estimate excess money supply (model 2),[29] using de-trending instead of an HP filter (model 3), changing the period to 1974–2007 (model 4), and using WPI instead of CPI (model 5). The results are quite robust to these different specifications. Using detrending produces slightly better results. Adding 1974–1978 observations to the sample and using WPI inflation in 1978 to address the problem of linking the two CPI series[30] does not alter the results regarding the impact of trading partners' inflation and the pass-through effect, but produces less favourable results as indicated by model selection criteria. The oil price variable is insignificant in the WPI model and model selection criteria suggest it should be removed. As was the case for Saudi Arabia, the PPP assumption is strongly rejected by a log likelihood ratio test.

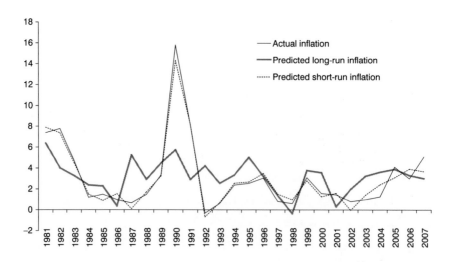

Figure 12.7 Kuwait: Actual inflation and estimated long-run and short-run inflation

Sources: Authorities data and fund staff estimates

Table 12.4 Kuwait: Comparing alternative models[1]

	Model 1	Model 2	Model 3	Model 4	Model 5
					LWPI
Long-run equation:					
LCPI(−1)	1	1	1	1	1
LNEER(−1)	0.1514	0.1602	0.2075	0.1234	0.1864
	[2.4188]	[4.6219]	[3.4708]	[1.8650]	[1.6222]
LP*(−1)	−0.7843	−0.7508	−0.8298	−0.8011	−0.9335
	[−50.8870]	[−89.1691]	[−52.6992]	[−47.3708]	[−23.8789]
LNOIL(−1)	−0.0546	−0.0173	−0.0070	−0.0104	NO
	[−3.1636]	[−3.1157]	[−0.3079]	[−0.9379]	
C	−1.5346	−1.8329	−1.7363	−1.4890	−1.2846
Short-run dynamic:	D(LCPIG)	D(LCPIG)	D(LCPIG)	D(LCPIG)	D(LCPIG)
Adjustment coefficient	−0.5925	−0.7335	−0.6008	−0.4137	−0.2667
	[−5.3101]	[−3.4292]	[−7.9228]	[−2.3448]	[−1.9581]
C	−0.0336	−0.0289	−0.0337	−0.0212	−0.0433
	[−2.7895]	[−2.4091]	[−4.0159]	[−0.9241]	[−1.2757]
WAR	0.0552	0.0572	0.0581	0.0992	0.0995
	[3.6797]	[3.2234]	[5.4287]	[3.5827]	[3.0777]
	DHP	DHP	DGAP	GDPHP	DGAP
Demand	0.1015	0.1294	0.1011	0.0039	0.0401
	[3.0378]	[3.7102]	[6.6672]	[0.0599]	[1.0389]

Continued

Table 12.4 continued

	Model 1	Model 2	Model 3	Model 4	Model 5
	Nominal	Real	Nominal	Nominal	Nominal
Excess money	0.0319	0.0417	0.0432	-0.0320	0.0222
	[1.7825]	[1.3730]	[2.8978]	[-1.2555]	[0.7261]
Sample period	1979–2007	1981–2007	1979–2007	1974–2007	1979–2007
R-squared	0.9622	0.9715	0.9789	0.8519	0.8087
Adj. R-squared	0.9215	0.9258	0.9562	0.7300	0.6557
Sum sq. resids	0.0011	0.0008	0.0006	0.0052	0.0074
F-statistic	23.6320	21.2663	43.0772	6.9854	5.2857
Log likelihood	102.8564	103.1332	111.0209	94.1023	75.6601
Akaike AIC	-6.2755	-6.3802	-6.8586	-4.9439	-4.4757
Schwarz SC	-5.5618	-5.5643	-6.1450	-4.2568	-3.8572

Note: 1 T-statistics in [ ]

While the lack of detailed GDP data makes it difficult to use the model to predict inflation in 2008, trading partners' inflation, NEER and oil price data enable us to predict the long-run (equilibrium) inflation. The models predict that the equilibrium inflation would increase by 300 and 240 basis points for Saudi Arabia and Kuwait, respectively, in 2008. This is in line with the recent developments in inflation in the two countries. The lower increase in Kuwait is due, in part, to the fact that the Kuwaiti dinar NEER appreciated by 2.5 per cent in 2008 while the riyal NEER depreciated by 3.9 per cent.

While the results for Saudi Arabia and Kuwait are consistent with the assumption that external factors are the main driving forces for inflation in the two countries, one could ask why the impact of the pass-through effect is relatively moderate and significantly smaller than trading partners' inflation, given that the underlying arbitrage mechanisms for each of these effects are the same.[31] The difference could be due to the fact that changes in the price level of trading partners are usually *permanent*[32] making it essential for importers to pass their impact through to consumers, in order to preserve profitability over the long run. On the other hand, changes in exchange rates are usually *transitory*. Hence, exporters, aiming at protecting their market share in the Saudi and Kuwaiti markets, might be willing to absorb part of the exchange rate impact by adjusting their profit mark-ups, i.e. 'pricing to market', instead of raising prices, as they believe that exchange rate changes are temporary. Similarly importers in Saudi Arabia and Kuwait, who exert some monopolistic power due to agency laws, and retailers might also adjust their profit mark-ups to preserve their market share,[33] on the grounds that today's market share determines tomorrow's profits. In addition, competition induced by globalisation, along with stable and low global inflation, enhances the scope for containing the impact of changes in the exchange rate through substitutions. Crossborder production (where production happens in several stages in a number of different countries) limits the pass-through impact on the final products. Moreover, subsidies, especially those for basic commodities in Saudi Arabia and Kuwait which are particularly affected by changes in exchange rates, limit the impact of the pass-through effect.[34] The fact that a large part of the Saudi and Kuwaiti labour market participants are government employees, along with the stickiness of private sector wages, at least in the short run, suggests that changes in the NEER would have large effects on real income and nontradable prices. For example, an appreciation of the NEER would reduce import prices and hence the prices of CPI tradable components, but would allow consumers with a given riyal or dinar budget to spend more on both tradables and nontradables, which would push up the prices of the latter. The increase in nontradables prices would offset part of the decrease in the CPI due to the NEER appreciation and hence limit the pass-through effect. Finally, many economists (e.g. Mishkin, 2008; Taylor, 2000) have argued that the establishment of a strong nominal anchor in many countries in recent years has created a stable and predictable monetary policy environment. This has reduced the sensitivity of domestic prices to nominal shocks and led to the very low and declining pass-through of the exchange rate to inflation (Box 1).

There is strong empirical evidence, from case studies of highly open economies, of a weak and declining pass-through effect (Mishkin, 2008; see also Laflèche, 1996/1997; Cunningham and Haldane, 2000; Gagnon and Ihrig, 2004; Burstein, Eichenbaum, and Rebelo, 2007). For example, recent empirical analysis by the Hong Kong Monetary Authority indicates that the long-run exchange rate pass-through in Hong Kong, which has similar openness and exchange rate regime to Saudi Arabia and Kuwait, is about 0.2 (Yam, 2008). After Sweden and the United Kingdom's withdrawal from the Exchange Rate Mechanism of the European Monetary System in September 1992, both countries experienced low inflation despite large depreciation in their currencies. The US dollar NEER has depreciated by more than 30 per cent between 2002 and June 2008 but inflation remained low. The riyal NEER appreciated by an annual average of 3.9 per cent during the 1972–1976 period while inflation averaged 21.7 per cent. In 2002, 2003 and 2004, the riyal NEER depreciated by 2.0, 7.0 and 5.0 per cent respectively, while inflation was 0.2, 0.6 and 0.4 per cent respectively.

Episodes of a strong correlation between currency depreciation and high inflation have been associated with unstable and weak nominal anchors. For example, until the past decade, several Latin American countries faced a combination of chronically high inflation and exchange rate depreciation (Mishkin, 2008).[37] Following the break up of the Bretton Woods system, Sweden's currency depreciated by an average of 5 per cent per year between 1973 and 1985 against the deutschmark, and its annual inflation rate was on the order of 4 percentage points higher than German inflation over the same period.

Box 12.1 Empirical evidence on the exchange rate pass-through

The relatively strong impact of trading partners' inflation is consistent with recent empirical evidence. For example, Wang and Wen (2007) examined a sample of 18 OECD countries and found that the cross-country correlation of inflation averaged 0.57. The correlation was even higher for a G7 sample with an average of 0.62 (the minimum value is 0.26 (between Germany and the US), the maximum is 0.92 (between France and Italy)).[35] They also found that country pairs with higher cross-country correlations in inflation also tend to have higher correlations in output. Vigfusson *et al.* (2009) examined the exchange rate and inflation[36] pass-through to export prices and found that a 1 per cent change in the NEER (of the exporting countries) leads to 0.26, 0.24, 0.47 and 0.16 per cent changes in export prices for the European Union, Japan, Asian newly industrialising economies (NIEs) and the US, respectively, while a 1 per cent change in the producer price index leads to 0.75, 0.35, 1.01 and 0.72 per cent changes in export prices for the European Union, Japan, Asian NIEs and the US, respectively.

5 Conclusions

Both foreign and domestic factors influence the inflationary processes in Saudi Arabia and Kuwait. External factors play a dominant role given the dependence of the Saudi and Kuwaiti economies on imports and foreign labour to meet domestic demand for tradables and nontradables. In the long run, the main driving force for inflation in Saudi Arabia and Kuwait is trading partners' inflation. Recent inflationary pressures have been largely driven by rising trading partners' inflation. The experience of the last two decades suggests that this will be a temporary deviation, reflecting supply constraints in food and other commodities. The slide of the US dollar and the rapidly rising domestic demand in Saudi Arabia and Kuwait since 2003, and to a lesser extent the expansionary monetary stance imported from the US through the dollar peg have also contributed to the recent inflationary pressures.

Given the authorities' lack of control over trading partners' inflation, the limited pass-through effect, and projected global oil prices, containing inflationary pressures under the peg regime would have to be based on containing domestic demand and addressing nontradable supply bottlenecks, especially in the real estate sector. Containing inflation through expanding the subsidy system has to be balanced with the fiscal and efficiency cost of subsidies. In any case such domestic factors should play only a temporary role. Similarly, the experience of the last four decades indicates that changes in the NEER have centred around zero in the long run (see Figure 12.4).

The similarity between the inflationary processes in Saudi Arabia and Kuwait suggests that the cost associated with the planned monetary union would be limited. The other four GCC countries share with Saudi Arabia and Kuwait the dependence on imports and foreign labour to meet domestic demand and have similar trading partner weights (see Table 12A.3 in Appendix 1). In addition, domestic demand in all GCC countries depends heavily on government spending from oil revenues. Changes in oil prices and revenues and other global or regional shocks are likely to have on average similar impacts on domestic demand given the similarity between these countries, including in the response of government spending to higher revenues. Similarly, the impact on investors' and consumers' confidence is likely to be similar.

Appendix 1 Detailed ECM results

Table 12A.1 Saudi Arabia: vector error correction estimates[1]

Long-run equation:

LCPI(−1)	1
LNEER(−1)	0.193503
	[2.61963]
LP*(−1)	−0.83295
	[−3.46133]
LNOIL(−1)	−0.015192
	[−0.69371]
t	0.02437
C	−2.452129

Adjustment coefficient	−0.590394	−0.29976	−0.146682	−0.352519
	[−5.68420]	[−0.59112]	[−2.81524]	[−0.11693]

Short-run dynamic:	D(LCPI)	D(LNEER)	D(LP*)	D(LNOIL)
D(LCPI(−1))	−0.426935	0.674566	−0.057502	0.047198
	[−2.38712]	[0.77253]	[−0.64092]	[0.00909]
D(LCPI(−2))	−0.046071	−0.400145	−0.121144	0.097514
	[−0.22511]	[−0.40046]	[−1.17998]	[0.01642]
D(LNEER(−1))	−0.076536	0.82224	0.02256	−0.684718
	[−1.12178]	[2.46841]	[0.65915]	[−0.34576]
D(LNEER(−2))	0.052052	−0.708183	−0.026664	−1.242781
	[0.65559]	[−1.82691]	[−0.66946]	[−0.53928]
D(LP*(−1))	2.19899	−7.487908	0.579738	9.679396
	[3.94399]	[−2.75075]	[2.07279]	[0.59811]
D(LP*(−2))	0.288106	8.000537	0.133669	10.15454
	[0.41400]	[2.35473]	[0.38290]	[0.50272]
D(LNOIL(−1))	−0.006189	0.017723	0.004724	−0.769907
	[−0.49728]	[0.29167]	[0.75672]	[−2.13129]

D(LNOIL(-2))	-0.004191	-0.041379	-0.006129	-0.76952
	[-0.28875]	[-0.58389]	[-0.84170]	[-1.82648]
C	-0.314956	-0.179664	-0.003172	-3.125865
	[-4.49995]	[-0.52577]	[-0.09034]	[-1.53869]
t	0.007442	0.00467	0.000153	0.082024
	[4.22018]	[0.54243]	[0.17247]	[1.60253]
DHP(-1)	0.025416	0.029103	0.011968	0.890744
	[0.66390]	[0.15571]	[0.62322]	[0.80164]
EXCM(-1)	0.010846	0.027831	0.00017	0.262364
	[1.69759]	[0.89226]	[0.05304]	[1.41484]
D(LRGDP(-1))	-0.241897	0.688252	0.022634	0.475622
	[-2.88765]	[1.68282]	[0.53862]	[0.19561]
D(LRGDP(-2))	-0.254532	-0.457277	-0.066389	-2.189804
	[-3.38752]	[-1.24651]	[-1.76136]	[-1.00408]
D(LNM3(-2))	0.093719	0.183189	0.044988	0.182607
	[1.73405]	[0.69425]	[1.65936]	[0.11641]
D(LNM3(-1))	0.153114	-0.346162	0.050919	0.118933
	[1.81560]	[-0.84074]	[1.20363]	[0.04859]
R-squared	0.927232	0.749014	0.961036	0.604763
Adj. R-squared	0.797867	0.302816	0.891767	-0.097879
Sum sq. resids	0.00073	0.017398	0.000184	0.614927
S.E. equation	0.009006	0.043968	0.004518	0.261391
F-statistic	7.167548	1.678657	13.87399	0.860698
Log likelihood	99.35656	58.13069	117.2935	11.78413
Akaike AIC	-6.33512	-3.163899	-7.714882	0.401221
Schwarz SC	-5.512518	-2.341298	-6.892281	1.223822

Note 1: Sample 1980–2007, t-statistics in [ ].

Table 12A.2 Kuwait: vector error correction estimates[1]

Long-run equation:

LCPI(-1)	1
LNEERC(-1)	0.1514
	[2.4188]
LP*(-1)	-0.7843
	[-50.887]
LNOIL(-1)	-0.0546
	[-3.1636]
C	-1.5346

Adjustment coefficient				
	-0.5925	-0.0039	0.2415	-7.5675
	[-5.3101]	[-0.0062]	[2.4367]	[-2.3590]

Short-run dynamic:	D(LCPI)	D(LNEER)	D(LP*)	D(LNOIL)
D(LCPIG(-1))	0.2030	-0.0174	0.0865	7.4426
	[1.0302]	[-0.0154]	[0.4941]	[1.3136]
D(LCPIG(-2))	-0.2038	0.6253	-0.1993	-2.3061
	[-1.5302]	[0.8179]	[-1.6840]	[-0.6021]
D(LNEERC(-1))	-0.0118	0.3404	-0.0355	-1.2551
	[-0.2291]	[1.1540]	[-0.7774]	[-0.8495]
D(LNEERC(-2))	0.0861	-0.3928	-0.1045	2.0855
	[1.5578]	[-1.2378]	[-2.1267]	[1.3120]
D(LPP(-1))	1.1141	-1.1598	0.8474	12.1881
	[4.3398]	[-0.7871]	[3.7154]	[1.6513]
D(LPP(-2))	0.1224	1.9271	-0.1960	-5.3480
	[0.4193]	[1.1503]	[-0.7557]	[-0.6373]
D(LNOIL(-1))	0.0047	0.0534	0.0082	-0.0142
	[0.3553]	[0.7035]	[0.6948]	[-0.0375]
D(LNOIL(-2))	-0.0091	0.0590	0.0000	-0.1580

	[-0.7486]	[0.8481]	[0.0018]	[-0.4537]
C	-0.0336	-0.0566	0.0200	-0.4916
	[-2.7895]	[-0.8191]	[1.8671]	[-1.4191]
DHP(-1)	0.1015	-0.2590	-0.0186	1.1210
	[3.0378]	[-1.3512]	[-0.6259]	[1.1675]
EXCM1(-1)	0.0319	0.0379	-0.0141	0.9140
	[1.7825]	[0.3688]	[-0.8875]	[1.7751]
D(LRGDP(-1))	0.0672	0.0183	-0.0014	1.1999
	[2.8536]	[0.1355]	[-0.0653]	[1.7728]
D(LRGDP(-2))	0.0046	0.0300	-0.0182	-0.0024
	[0.2530]	[0.2891]	[-1.1358]	[-0.0045]
WAR	0.0552	0.0022	0.0030	-0.7473
	[3.6797]	[0.0254]	[0.2245]	[-1.7322]
R-squared	0.9622	0.4962	0.9409	0.4491
Adj. R-squared	0.9215	-0.0464	0.8772	-0.1442
Sum sq. resids	0.0011	0.0348	0.0008	0.8734
S.E. equation	0.0090	0.0517	0.0080	0.2592
F-statistic	23.6320	0.9145	14.7703	0.7569
Log likelihood	102.8564	53.9317	106.1703	8.8149
Akaike AIC	-6.2755	-2.7808	-6.5122	0.4418
Schwarz SC	-5.5618	-2.0672	-5.7985	1.1555
Mean dependent	0.0314	0.0130	0.0432	0.0297
S.D. dependent	0.0322	0.0506	0.0229	0.2423

Note 1 Sample 1979–2007, t-statistics in [ ].

Table 12A.3 GCC Selected trading partner trade weights, excluding commodities (%)

	Saudi Arabia	Kuwait	Qatar	UAE	Bahrain	Oman
United States	20.2	14.4	15.3	11.8	23.3	13.7
Japan	12.8	14.4	11.8	8.4	8.8	14.6
Germany	8.4	10.2	8.9	7.8	8.5	7.1
United Kingdom	7.6	7.2	9.0	9.2	7.2	8.3
China	6.2	5.6	3.9	5.5	4.9	3.2
Italy	5.7	7.3	7.7	5.3	5.5	4.3
Korea	4.7	3.6	5.5	4.7	3.5	3.6
France	4.5	4.9	7.2	6.5	7.6	4.9

Table 12A.4 PPP assumption and residual tests

	Saudi Arabia			Kuwait		
1 PPP assumption (LR test)	*Chi-square statistic*	*P-value*	*Conclusion*	*Chi-square statistic*	*P-value*	*Conclusion*
Null hypothesis: PPP holds	6.93	0.0313	Reject the null	28.21	0.0000	Reject the null
2 Residual serial correlation LM tests	*LM-statistic*	*P-value*	*Conclusion*	*LM-statistic*	*P-value*	*Conclusion*
Null hypothesis: no serial correlation at lag order h						
Lag 1	20.39251	0.2031	Fail to reject the null	26.03687	0.0535	Fail to reject the null
Lag 2	16.21565	0.438	Fail to reject the null	19.45255	0.2459	Fail to reject the null
Lag 3	16.05634	0.449	Fail to reject the null	10.70245	0.8275	Fail to reject the null
3 Normality test joint (Jarque–Bera)[a]	*Chi-square statistic*	*P-value*	*Conclusion*	*Chi-square statistic*	*P-value*	*Conclusion*
Null hypothesis: residuals are multivariate normal	62.65	0.223	Fail to reject the null	55.1877	0.4675	Fail to reject the null

Note
a   The residual normality test is the multivariate extension of the Jarque–Bera normality test, which compares the third and fourth moments of the residuals with those from the normal distribution. We use the method for the test suggested by Urzua (1996).

Appendix 2. The money demand equation and excess money supply

This appendix presents the estimation of the money demand equation and how excess money is constructed. Table 12A.5 shows the cointegration test using the nominal money supply, real GDP, GDP deflator and interest rate. It shows that the null of no cointegration is strongly rejected in favour of at least one cointegration relationship for Kuwait data. The trace test indicates that there might be two integrated relationships while the maximum eigenvalue test indicates that there is only one cointegrating vector. For Saudi Arabia, the trace test rejects the null that there is no cointegration. However, the maximum eigenvalue test indicates that there is no cointegration relationship but the test statistics are really close and can be rejected at 1 per cent significance level. The possibility of more than one cointegrating vector is clearly rejected in both tests.

Table 12A.5 also shows the standardised eigenvectors and adjustment coefficients for both Saudi Arabia and Kuwait. The estimated cointegrating vector for money demand in nominal terms is given in the standardised eigenvectors shown in the table, that is:

Saudi:
$$m = 19.64 - 0.12 * t + 3.814 * gdp + 1.10 * p - 23.221 * r$$
$$[4.55] \qquad [1.92] \quad [-4.70] \qquad \text{(A1)}$$

Kuwait:
$$m = -6.96 + 0.768 * gdp + 1.553 * p - 0.354 * r$$
$$[4.55] \qquad [13.23] \quad [-0.22]$$

Given the money demand equation, the excess money supply can be estimated as $excm = m - \hat{m}$ where $\hat{m}$ is the nominal money supply and is the estimated money demand from equation (A1). Another way to estimate money demand which overcomes the I(2) problem in Kuwait data is to use real money supply (see Juselius, 1994). Using real money results in the following long-run real money demand function:

Saudi:
$$rm = -11.70 - 0.094 \cdot time + 3.20 * gdp - 17.30 * r$$
$$[-3.51] \qquad [7.49] \qquad [-3.51]$$

Kuwait:
$$rm = -3.31 + 0.406 * gdp - 4.66 * r \qquad \text{(A2)}$$
$$[2.00] \qquad [-2.31]$$

where rm is the money supply in real terms. Excess money supply is then equal to real money supply minus the estimated real money demand. The estimated excess money supply based on nominal or real money supply suffers from the noise introduced by the oil GDP. It is likely that the money demand function is more stable with non-oil GDP. However, the unavailability of data precludes this. Hence, the money demand function provides only an approximate measure of the excess money supply.

Table 12A.5 Cointegration test for money demand equation

	Null hypothesis								
	r = 0			r ≤ 1			r ≤ 2		
	Eigenvalue	Trace stat. (95% CV)	Max stat. (95% CV)	Eigenvalue	Trace stat. (95% CV)	Max stat. (95% CV)	Eigenvalue	Trace stat. (95% CV)	Max stat. (95% CV)
Saudi Arabia	0.55	71.83* (63.88)	31.00 (32.12)	0.38	40.84 (42.92)	18.41 (25.82)	0.35	22.43 (25.87)	17.05 (19.39)
Kuwait	0.61	62.73* (47.86)	31.74* (27.58)	0.45	31.00* (29.80)	20.50 (21.13)	0.26	10.50 (15.49)	10.28 (14.26)

Saudi

Standardised eigenvectors

Variable	m	gdp	p	r
	1.000	-3.814	-1.100	23.221
	0.191	1.000	-1.059	3.974
	1.215	-3.050	1.000	-22.944
	0.046	-0.077	0.080	1.000

Standardised adjustment coefficients

Equ.	m	gdp	p	r
m	-0.048	0.059	-0.053	-0.450
gdp	0.024	-0.006	0.032	-0.321
p	-0.054	0.403	0.023	0.021
r	-0.030	-0.010	0.015	-0.032

Kuwait

Standardised eigenvectors

Variable	m	gdp	p	r
	1.000	-0.768	-1.553	0.354
	2.166	1.000	-6.871	0.215
	-0.458	-0.261	1.000	-7.080
	0.130	-0.379	-0.394	1.000

Standardised adjustment coefficients

Equ.	m	gdp	p	r
m	-0.155	0.025	0.000	0.001
gdp	0.198	0.022	0.005	0.029
p	0.132	0.068	-0.003	-0.001
r	0.005	0.006	0.000	-0.009

Notes

1. Sample size 1966–2007 for Saudi Arabia, 1974–2007 for Kuwait.
2. The vector autoregression has two lags on each variable for Saudi Arabia while it has one lag for Kuwait; these are based on SIC criteria. VEC has an intercept for both countries and a trend in case of Saudi Arabia.
3. A war dummy variable is introduced for Kuwait, and a break from 1966–1980 for Saudi Arabia.
4. The null hypothesis is in terms of the cointegration rank r. r = 0 means no cointegration equation between the variables.
5. * indicate rejection of the hypothesis at 95% CV.

Notes

1   This does not mean that the driving forces for inflation in the short term do not influence the regime choice. However, given their short-term nature, policy makers would probably assign lower weights to them in deciding on the exchange rate and monetary regimes.

2   The permanent nature of the changes in the price level makes it essential for importers to pass the impact through to consumers, so that they can preserve profitability over the long run.

3   As defined in the IMF trading partners weights.

4   If petrochemical exports are excluded from Saudi Arabia and Kuwait's exports, the ratio would be even lower.

5   Openness to imported labour has led to a large expatriate work force at all skill levels (constituting more than 80 and 60 per cent of the total labour force in Kuwait and Saudi Arabia, respectively), mostly from South Asia and other Arab countries.

6   However, the large influx of expatriates has occasionally created demand pressures on nontradables, especially in the real estate sector, where the supply response is relatively slow.

7   Mark-up models to analyse inflation empirically are unlikely to be appropriate in the context of GCC countries, given the unavailability of wage data and the flexible labour market.

8   For simplicity, we assume the existence of one cointegrating vector.

9   De Brouwer and Ericsson (1998) used private demand to construct a proxy for the output gap in their estimate of the short-term inflation dynamics in Australia.

10   For the HP filter, $\lambda = 100$.

11   For simplicity, we assume the existence of one cointegrating vector.

12   By including monetary variables in (6), we control for the effect of the monetary stance when we assess the impact of excess demand.

13   Juselius uses wage inflation to assess excess demand in the internal sector while we use simpler measures (see note 7). The treatment of excess money supply is similar between the two models.

14   However, the model allows for the PPP hypothesis to be tested.

15   The data used in the analysis are annual data given the absence of more frequent data for most variables.

16   This decline may have reflected, in part, the revaluation of the Kuwaiti dinar by 4 per cent against the US dollar in 1978.

17   For example, a negative impact for trading partners' inflation and money supply on inflation.

18   We also examined changes in money supply and lagged money supply.

19   Khan and Schimmelpfennig (2006) suggested using credit as a proxy for money supply. The use of the credit to GDP ratio produces weak model selection criteria.

20   Juselius (1992b) and Sekine (2001) used excess money supply in estimating the short-term dynamics of inflation.

21   Cointegration tests for the period 1980–2007 indicate the existence of two cointegrating vectors at the 5 per cent significance level and one at the 1 per cent significance level. These different results could be due to the fact that the eigenvalue and trace statistics tests have a tendency to over-reject the null hypothesis due to small sample bias, i.e. they suggest more cointegrating vectors as the sample size falls, or the number of variables or lags increases (Gregory, 1994).

22   Numbers in [ ] are t-statistics.

23   We also tried including a commodity price index in the analysis but it did not yield significant results. This was motivated by the large increase in commodity prices between 2003 and 2008. Many have blamed inflationary pressures on commodity

prices as outlined in the introduction. While commodity prices might have played a role in the recent inflationary pressures, this was a short-run effect that is hard to capture given the span of the time series examined in the analysis.

24 The speed of adjustment is the number of periods (years) required to reduce one-half of a deviation from the long-run equilibrium. It is calculated as $\log(0.5)/\log(1+\delta_1)$, see Rogoff (1996).

25 The time trend was included to account for the possibility of a trend in the cointegration relationship. As Figure 12.4 shows, inflation appears to be declining slightly faster in Saudi Arabia than in its trading partners. This might capture the impact of improved credibility due to the peg. Table 12.3 shows that including the time trend enhances the results.

26 The results were also robust to shorter sub-samples.

27 The results for the WPI should be interpreted cautiously since the WPI is stationary. However, this could be due to the shortness of the data series.

28 It is hard to explain why trading partners' inflation would have an impact that is higher than one in an open economy with a very low and stable tariff system.

29 Given that real money supply is I(1), changes in real money supply were included in this model to ensure comparability with the model for Saudi Arabia. However, the results are not sensitive to that.

30 This was done by using the inflation rate implied by the WPI index to calculate the CPI index for 1977. The CPI index for 1974–1976 was obtained by using the inflation rate implied by the pre-1978 CPI series.

31 The restriction of equal NEER and trading partners' inflation coefficients ($\alpha_1 = -\alpha_2$) was rejected on the basis of a log likelihood ratio test for the two countries.

32 With the exception of Japan, inflation in trading partners was always positive.

33 Several studies have pointed out that distribution costs make up an important component of the retail price of imported goods (Burstein, Neves, and Rebelo, 2003; Campa and Goldberg, 2005).

34 While subsidising tradable commodities limits the pass-though effect, it has a fiscal cost, can create market distortions, and may encourage wasteful consumption.

35 For example, the Mexican peso depreciated by an average of 31 per cent per year against the dollar between 1977 and 1995, while the Mexican inflation rate averaged about 30 per cent per year higher than the US inflation rate.

36 They used quarterly data from the 1950s to 2004.

37 They used producer price indices.

References

Al-Mutairi, N., (1995), 'Examining the causes of inflation in Kuwait: an application of a vector auto regression model', *OPEC Review*, 19 (2): 137–47.

Al-Raisi, A., and Pattanaik, S. (2003), 'Pass-through of exchange rate changes to domestic prices in Oman', Central Bank of Oman Occasional Paper No. 2005-1.

Bonato, L. (2008), 'Money and inflation in the Islamic Republic of Iran', *Review of Middle East Economics and Finance*, 4(1).

Burstein, A., Neves, J., and Rebelo, S. (2003), 'Distribution costs and real exchange rate dynamics during exchange-rate-based stabilisations', *Journal of Monetary Economics*, 50: 1189–1214.

Burstein, A., Eichenbaum, M., and Rebelo, S. (2007), 'Modelling exchange rate pass-through after large devaluations', *Journal of Monetary Economics*, 54: 346–68.

Campa, J., and Goldberg, L. (2005), 'Exchange rate pass-through into import prices', *Review of Economics and Statistics*, 87: 679–90.

——(2006), 'Distribution margins, imported inputs, and the insensitivity of the CPI to exchange rates', IESE Business School, University of Navarra, working paper no. 625.

Cunningham, A., and Haldane, A. (2000), 'The monetary transmission mechanism in the United Kingdom: pass-through and policy rules', Central Bank of Chile working paper 83.

Darrat, A. (1985), 'The monetary explanation of inflation: the experience of three major OPEC economies', *Journal of Economics and Business*, 37: 209–21.

De Brouwer, G., and Ericsson, N. (1998), 'Modelling inflation in Australia', *Journal of Business and Economic Statistics*, 16: 433–49.

Diouf, A. (2007), 'Modelling inflation for Mali', IMF Working Paper 07/295.

Gagnon, J., and Ihrig, J. (2004), 'Monetary policy and exchange rate passthrough', *International Journal of Finance and Economics*, 9: 315–38.

Gregory, A. (1994), 'Testing for cointegration in linear quadratic models', *Journal of Business and Economic Statistics*, 4: 347–60.

Juselius, K. (1992a), 'On the empirical verification of the purchasing power parity and the uncovered interest rate parity', *Nationaløkonomisk tidskrift*, 130: 57–66.

Juselius, K. (1992b), 'Domestic and foreign effects on prices in an open economy: the case of Denmark', *Journal of Policy Modeling*, 14: 401–28.

Juselius, K. (1994), 'On the duality between long-run relations and common trends in the I (1) versus I (2) model: an application to aggregate money holding', *Econometric Reviews*, 13: 151–78.

Keran, M., and Al-Malik, A. (1979), 'Monetary sources of inflation', in Saudi Arabia', *Federal Reserve Bank of San Francisco Economic Review,* Winter supplement.

Khan, M., and Schimmelpfennig, A. (2006), 'Inflation in Pakistan: Money or wheat?', IMF Working Paper 06/60.

Laflèche, T. (1996/1997), 'The impact of exchange rate movements on consumer prices', *Bank of Canada Review*, Winter 1996/97: 21–32.

Lim, C., and Papi, L. (1997), 'An econometric analysis of the determinants of inflation in Turkey', IMF working paper 97/170.

Mishkin, F. (2008), 'Exchange rate pass-through and monetary policy', NBER working paper 13889.

Rogoff, K. (1996), 'The purchasing power parity puzzle', *Journal of Economic Literature,* 34: 647–68.

Sekine, T. (2001), 'Modeling and forecasting inflation in Japan', IMF working paper 01/82.

Taylor, J. (2000), 'Low inflation, pass-through, and the pricing power of firms', *European Economic Review*, 44: 1389–1408.

Urzua, C. (1996), 'On the correct use of omnibus tests for normality', *Economics Letters*, 53: 247–51.

Vigfusson, R., Sheets, N., and Gagnon, J. (2009), 'Exchange rate passthrough to export prices: assessing some cross-country evidence', *Review of International Economics,* 17 (1), 17–33.

Wang, P., and Wen, Y. (2007), 'Inflation dynamics: A cross-country investigation', *Journal of Monetary Economics*, 54: 2004–31.

Yam, J. (2008), 'Exchange rate pass-through to domestic inflation', *Viewpoint* (April), Hong Kong Monetary Authority.

Index